I0093924

Preserving Democracy

What The Founding Fathers Knew,
What We Have Forgotten, & How It Threatens Democracy

Third Expanded Edition

Elgin L. Hushbeck, Jr.

Energion Publications
Cantonment, Florida
2024

Copyright © 2009, 2024

Elgin L. Hushbeck Jr.

All rights reserved. No part of this book may be reproduced or transmitted in any form or by any means, electronic or mechanical, including photocopying, recording or by an information storage and retrieval system without permission in writing from the Publisher, except for brief quotations in books and critical reviews.

ISBN: 978-1-63199-893-5

eISBN: 978-1-63199-894-2

Library of Congress Control Number: 2024935788

Cover Design by Jason Neufeld

Cover image: Stock Photo Pro (stockphotopro.com) Copyright © Joe Sohm, used by permission

Energion Publications

1241 Conference Rd

Cantonment, FL 32533

energion.com

pubs@energion.com

In Loving Memory
of my sister
Trudy Ann Newman

TABLE OF CONTENTS

ACKNOWLEDGMENTS

This book was the product of many years in both formulation and writing, and many people shaped how it turned out. First, I would like to thank all those with whom I have engaged in discussions over the years for exchanging ideas that resulted in this book.

I would particularly like to thank those who disagreed with me for four reasons. First, the at times vigorous back and forth helped me try out my arguments and ideas, exposed weaknesses and flaws, and, with their challenges, helped me to understand these issues better. Second, their challenges encouraged me to learn more and explore new investigation areas. Third, for allowing me to know how to challenge ideas without attacking people. And finally, for being willing to discuss these issues. In particular, I would like to thank Alfi, Bets, Elaine, jlescallette, Dor, JC, Jo Dakotah, Koka, Pheebs, Leith Anne, Mara, Roberta, Tom, Whit, and Woodsey, along with many others.

I would also like to thank my good friends, Larry and Diane Nixon, for their insights and perspectives. Without them, this book would have been, at a minimum, vastly different, and probably I would have never written it. I would also like to thank my students, particularly those in critical thinking. They were a constant source of new ideas and different ways of seeing things.

When working on the third edition of this book, I received wonderful and very helpful feedback from my fellow writers at the Wisconsin Writers Association: Thekla Fagerlie-Madsen, Naomi Yaeger, Joan Downs, Jeffery Lewis, Rosie Klepper, Rose Bingham, and Laurie A. Scheer.

Special thanks go to Jonathan William, who read a draft of the third edition. He often disagreed, yet he gave me extremely valuable feedback and suggestions. Many of these caused me to add additional comments to address weaknesses in the earlier draft. It is how disagreement should work and it made this book better.

Key to all of this has been my editor, Henry Neufeld, who not only had the faith to take on the work but also worked diligently in the editing process with corrections and suggestions to make the book better. And, of course, none of this would have been possible without my wife Hanna's loving support and encouragement. Thank you for putting up with me. Lastly, I want to thank my mother and father, who taught me a love for this country and an interest and concern for how government works.

FOREWORDS

From the Publisher

It is perhaps unusual for a publisher to write part of a foreword. But as a small businessman and owner of a small publishing company, I am more involved in individual book projects than you might expect. I look for manuscripts that will communicate across political, religious, social, or intellectual lines. I could make money publishing books to be read by the already convinced, reaffirming their existing beliefs. But I see my business as a service as well, so I want to challenge people's thinking, not just reaffirm their beliefs.

In addition, I hope to reach more than an intellectual elite. Our problems in this country can eventually be traced to "we the people" and the behavior we tolerate in media, government, and academia. Some things can be done, but effective action requires clear understanding. So, whether you call yourself a Democrat, Republican, independent, or member of another party, whether you are liberal, moderate, or conservative, I invite you to use this book to clarify and test your understanding, I don't mind if you leave your reading in serious disagreement with the author; I only hope that you will leave with a better understanding of what you believe and a greater determination to do your part in renewing our political system.

You will notice that our endorsements come from a variety of people—a military veteran, someone in the professions, some in academia. In presenting this second, paperback edition, we present three forewords. These are from people like you, who live and work, and who care about their country. They are remaining anonymous because they are not famous and they represent many others. As publisher, of course, I cannot remain anonymous.

— Henry Neufeld, Florida

From a Liberal

America! What a country!
(With apologies to Yakov Smirnoff).

Countless movies and books contain the theme of the family whose children seem to spend most of their time fighting with each other over just about anything. Occasionally, they band together to accomplish some great project, but basically, their lives seem to be one chaotic brawl after another. Unless, of course, someone else threatens one of the groups. Then they all band together, shoulder to shoulder, and fight off the threat. Ten minutes later, everyone is back to infighting.

That in a nutshell is my view of America. It is a country populated by "Americans," a rough and tumble, often brawling, sometimes cooperating, family of hundreds of millions of individuals. What is the unspoken force that naturally draws Americans together, whether left or right, religious or secular, natural-born or recent immigrant? It seems to be this strange mix of traditions, attitudes, hopes, and commonly-held views that America is a concept worth fighting for. Each of these attributes is a natural offshoot of a country centered on that wonderful instrument entitled the U.S. Constitution. A historical document that we all agree to adhere to, even today.

Only two things can really define the end of America. The first is the refusal of Americans to stand, shoulder-to-shoulder, against all comers. The second would be the removal or diminishment of the Constitution as the underpinning of our daily lives. Under either situation, Americans would simply be a loose gaggle of geographically grouped people without any purpose. Before this begins to sound like yet another description of the

Founding Fathers as demigods who knew everything about everything, I should mention that this is being written by a self-professed, flaming liberal. That's right. I grew up with a picture of Roosevelt on the mantelpiece and was ecstatic at the outcome of the 2008 elections.

This book is not about politics. It is about America, and serves as a reminder of the responsibility each of us has to cast our votes thoughtfully. If we acknowledge this responsibility and act upon it, we can pass our inheritance, America, to the generations that follow. If we refuse to participate in this democracy, or vote exclusively on emotions rather than thoughtful analysis, we threaten the Life, Liberty, and Pursuit of Happiness for our own descendants. Who are we to squander the gifts handed down to us so that later generations cannot share in the wondrous experience of being an American?

I would urge any American, of any political persuasion or demographic group, to read Elgin's thoughtful journey to the foundations of the American psyche, and ponder the issues he presents to us. He only asks us to think through our several opinions, and measure their consequences: "…in order to form a more perfect union."
— Bob, Wisconsin

From a Moderate

Inviting and informative, I wish I could have had *Preserving Democracy* in a political science class in college. It is incredible the way it lays out the essence of the current structure of our laws, taxes, and the analysis of the effects on our democracy and the Constitution in light of past cultures and leaders. Elgin Hushbeck is a modern-day historian providing pertinent information on how and why our Constitution and our United States' way of life is so unique.

I grew up in the Midwest and came from a large family who once owned their own company. We lived in an affluent suburb until we succumbed to the economics of the '60s. To keep food on the table, we transitioned to being a family of a Union working father. In those years, both father and mother taught us the value of voting for the right reasons. My Red, White, and Blue parents voted moderately. Mom always said a change in government was a good thing and we should all vote for the individual who will do the most good, which usually translated into voting incumbents out every election. I, being the youngest, was able to travel with Mom and Dad on weekends and patriotic holidays, and during those times witnessed the earliest speeches of some of our great Senators and Representatives today.

In college I was able to study in Kentucky, right in the heart of coal mining country. Later, when I lived as a young married woman with children in Southern Georgia I came to understand a different kind of political landscape, one of many that make up the richness of the United States. Here I learned about the importance of voting for the same person every election. As one Southerner told me "We vote knowing that we already understand whom we are dealing with; in changing we might not do as well."

I also lived a bit in Virginia, "The center of a Commonwealth," a place where the history of this great land is a constant reminder in places like the Williamsburg Historical Center. Being able to see the reenactment of our early years as a new nation, puts today into perspective. "Preserving Democracy" strengthens that understanding of what our forefathers envisioned. Mr. Hushbeck, a sincere thank you for preserving and explaining so many important details that are so often left out, and for simplifying the complexity of it all.

I urge everyone to take the challenge Mr. Hushbeck sets before us. Read "Preserving Democracy." Bring up at dinner conversation the questions at the end of the book. I am certain you will have many hours of amazing discussion. But most importantly, you will be able to be more informed as to our treasured way of life.
— Di, Wisconsin

From a Conservative

"Preserving Democracy" is one of the most timely books that has been written. Although it has been years in the making it raises the alarm as if it had been compiled from and for current events. It is the very current events that make this work so well-timed and consequently a most important read; and unlike just any instrument for alarm, it can be used as a handbook, a starting point for significant change or better yet preservation.

As the subtitle (*Preserving Democracy - What the Founding Fathers knew, What we have forgotten, and How it Threatens Democracy*) states, it explores what the Founding Fathers knew from their study of history, their knowledge of the greatest thinkers throughout history, and the wisdom they gained from the teachings of God; it discloses what we as a nation have in large part forgotten, repressed, or intentionally altered as to reasons that we are a great and blessed country; and how the dereliction of our times, the inane zeitgeist, is threatening the very existence of what we hold dear and require for life itself. We are losing the ability to exercise and maintain our form of government, a representative democracy.

"We The People" is not just another political slogan or a blurb we bring to the surface when campaigns flair. "We The People" goes to the very soul of who we are and how we conduct our lives from day to day. Like fish, we seem to be totally unaware of the medium in which we exist. We take our way of living for granted. Only when we see it become polluted do we notice something is not right.

Indeed it is the very system of government, the system that is to protect and not trample our God-given rights, is now polluting our lives with its particulates and toxins. Fortunately, unlike fish, it is our system. We have the God-given intelligence to step back and objectively examine our situation, the choice to correct it, and the power to do so.

Preserving Democracy goes directly to the heart of the matter, to wit, the preserving of the most rarified and valued commodity in history — Liberty. With love for this great nation, a well-rounded education, and life experience, coupled with a great sense of humor, Mr. Hushbeck began to put down his thoughts. That began ten years ago, a time when things appeared to be just right for America. No matter one's political viewpoint, it was a fact that America was the one sole superpower left standing in the world; that the dangers represented by its advisories had been mitigated if not entirely eliminated; that the wealth of the world in general had increased, not just for some, but for vast populations throughout the globe. In spite of the good times, Elgin could see, through his unique perspective of theology, history, business, and science, that there were fundamental cracks in the foundation. As the intrepid adventurer, an apt analogy found in the book, are we as a nation on a journey where there may be a point of no return?

If you love liberty and despise equalitarian outcome, then you will love *Preserving Democracy*. You will find it a must-read.
— Larry, California

Preface To The 2010 Paperback Edition

It has been a tumultuous and challenging couple of years. When I started writing *Preserving Democracy* nearly a decade ago, the threats and problems I described, though accurate in the long term, had a theoretical feel about them. Sure, the country had concerns that, if not corrected, could lead to severe difficulties. Still, those problems seemed to be in the distant future.

While serious, the Internet bubble, the events of 911, and the recession that followed were not out of line with the types of problems that the country had faced and survived in the past; and survive the country did. Yet, as I finished the book, it was becoming clear that another bubble, the housing bubble, was popping and that this would send the country into another recession.

It was unusual to have two economic bubbles so close to each other, though at first, it looked to be just another period of economic difficulty like those the country had experienced before. Early indications were that this recession might even be on the mild side.

Yet, as my publisher readied the hardcover edition for publication, it became clear that this was not the case. Something was different this time, and something had changed. The theoretical dangers in the future I had written about seemed suddenly more real and closer.

In the aftermath of the housing bubble came the lockup of the credit markets, TARP, the bailouts, the takeovers, the stimulus plan, and the hitherto unimaginable explosion in government spending and its corresponding budget deficits. When it came time to write a new chapter for the paperback edition, the subject was pretty straightforward: what happened? How did we get here?

In many respects, the issues, dangers, and problems discussed in the first nine chapters are what happened. This new chapter will briefly explain why the bubble grew and how officials mishandled it. The previous chapters will give you a better understanding of the depth of the particular issues and some suggestions on how we can avoid them.

Still, all in all, I remain hopeful and upbeat. America has faced some pretty severe challenges in its history, both internal and external. Each time the American people have rallied to the challenge, there have been many "Greatest Generations." The American people give all indications of doing the same this time.

Elgin Hushbeck
Wausau, WI
May 2010

PREFACE TO THE 3RD EDITION

A lot has changed since the first edition of *Preserving Democracy* in 2009 and the paperback edition in 2010. The Obama administration, which started with a hopeful optimism that the country had finally turned a page on its racist past, ended with the country having higher racial tension than when it began. Then came the division of the Trump years. 2020 was particularly difficult. It started with Impeachment, followed immediately by the COVID pandemic with its lockdowns, the Black Lives Matter protests, many of which ended in violence, and a tumultuous election in 2020. 2021 didn't start any better with the Capitol Riots.

Nor have things returned to normal. 2021 saw the reemergence of inflation and the debacle of Afghanistan. Since then, the world has become increasingly unstable with wars in Ukraine and the Middle East and threats of war over Taiwan and in North Korea.

Nor have things been much better on the domestic front; people struggle to make ends meet with a reemergent inflation while facing increases in crime and homelessness; millions are streaming into the country, straining social services. Everywhere you look, America seems pushed to the breaking point. People openly question whether our democratic system will survive.

The core message of *Preserving Democracy* is more relevant than ever. Yet it was clear that so much had changed, and a new edition was needed. Some issues discussed and left unresolved in earlier editions are now resolved. Some are no longer issues. Some of the more theoretical threats discussed are now major political issues. In some cases, new concerns have arisen. As such, the third edition is both a significant rewrite and an expansion, adding a new chapter in one case.

With all this change, the goal remains to keep a nonpartisan focus that stresses issues rather than people. While I think the situation has worsened since the earlier editions, I remain hopeful it is not too late.

What really needs to happen is for individuals to stop demonizing those who disagree and begin to discuss the issues with them, focusing more on thoughtful listening rather than simply telling them they are wrong. We need engagement, not polarization.

Suppose more and more people on both sides do this. Only then can we start moving toward consensus, which is vital to any healthy democracy. As the number of people doing this grows, the politicians must follow at some point. Democracy cannot be saved from the top down; it can only be saved from the bottom up. It is the people who have the real power, and it is only from them that any real solution to our problems must come.

Elgin Hushbeck
Wausau, WI
January 2024

Introduction

The Last Best Hope

Fellow-citizens, we cannot escape history. We of this Congress and this administration, will be remembered in spite of ourselves. No personal significance, or insignificance, can spare one or another of us. The fiery trial through which we pass, will light us down, in honor or dishonor, to the latest generation. We say we are for the Union. The world will not forget that we say this. We know how to save the Union. The world knows we do know how to save it. We – even we here – hold the power, and bear the responsibility. In giving freedom to the slave, we assure freedom to the free – honorable alike in what we give, and what we preserve. We shall nobly save, or meanly lose, the last best hope of earth.

Abraham Lincoln[1]

America today is at a crossroads. Many are unclear about where we have come from or where we are going. Based on the recent presidential elections, the only clear message is that people are unhappy and want change. Obama even made the slogan "Change" central to his winning campaign. Since the 1970s, the Presidency changed parties with each president, except in 1988. Half of these presidents served a single term. But, with this constant back and forth, what people want to change is unclear.

The challenges facing the country are both numerous and varied. When I wrote the first edition of this book in 2009, radical Islam threatened attacks, Russia was reemerging as an adversary,

---

1   Abraham Lincoln, "Message to Congress," December 1, 1862, cited in National Park Service, "Secession Will Destroy Democracy," http://www.nps.gov/liho/historyculture/secdemocrary.htm (accessed April 3, 2009).

and a few people saw the looming threat of China. An unstable government in North Korea had nuclear weapons, while Iran sought to acquire them, with the real danger that, if acquired, they would use them.

We still have most of these problems. Russia has invaded Ukraine. The threat of China has only grown, though now many in both parties recognize the problem. Still, the fact that China could invade Taiwan is a growing concern. North Korea and Iran remain problems, though they have receded a bit.

Then there are all the domestic problems. At the time of the first edition, there were the bailouts, the housing crisis, the economy, unemployment, health care costs, energy policy, and the environment, to name just a few. Some of these, like the housing crisis, are no longer significant concerns or have at least changed. Thus, the housing crisis, driven in part by people who could not pay back their loans, has changed into a problem of finding a house in the first place. Others are newer problems or problems that have worsened: inflation, the border, crime, declining cities, homelessness, and the growing number of deaths resulting from fentanyl.

While such ongoing concerns often consume our attention, some problems threaten democracy itself. These problems don't always get the coverage of the more immediate issues, but that does not change the fact that they are both real and severe.

Many of these problems come from a fundamental split in the electorate over the country and the Constitution. Is the country centered on the individual and liberty, or the group and equality? While we might all want both, these are fundamentally mutually exclusive, something we will explore in more detail in Chapter 9. The result is division and stalemate. Even over problems deemed severe by both parties, this division results in paralysis, and nothing happens.

For example, both parties have recognized that Social Security has been going bankrupt for decades. Still, there is no agreement on what to do. There is also the problem that there will be some pain whatever the politicians choose, and voters will probably be unhappy. The sooner we do something, the less painful the fix will be. Still, politicians get reelected by making voters happy, so the net result is a stalemate, and they do nothing. Bankruptcy, rather than fifty years away, is now only about ten.

The premise of this book is that the opinion of almost all the prominent thinkers, from Plato and Aristotle forward, is that democracy was an unworkable system of government. As we will see in Chapter 1, they believed it was doomed to fail, dissolving into tyranny. The Founding Fathers understood these criticisms when developing the system of checks and balances that has worked so well.

Since then, we have made repeated changes to the government, some minor, some major. As we make changes, how many of us understand the key weaknesses of democracy? Are the changes we make simply removing deadwood unnecessary in the 21st century? Are we eliminating critical foundational supports, essential checks, and balances? How would we know the difference?

This is the central question of the book. Rather than just an abstract discussion of political philosophy, the book focuses on several important issues like taxes and the different approaches to government. We will examine the Rule of Law, the role of justice, voting, and how we discuss or fail to discuss issues. We will explore the concepts of an informed voter and American values. Finally, we discuss the financial crisis in 2007-9.

Many of these issues were more in the realm of potential concerns at the time of the first edition but have since become, like voting, more visible and thus, more political concerns. Each chapter looks at a current trend that, if left unchanged, could cause American democracy to fail, just as all the earlier attempts have failed.

While I have firmly-held views in all these areas, I have tried to avoid being overtly partisan. Moving beyond theory without citing specific examples is impossible, and examples automatically risk partisanship. Still, while using examples, I try to be non-partisan. Some will undoubtedly be critical of my lack of success in this area.

I have at least attempted to remain balanced in my presentation. In some cases, I passed up recent examples because they were too partisan and used others because they were more balanced. In all the examples, I kept party affiliation to a minimum. I focused on the policies and problems rather than the people and parties. Some examples are not as recent as they could have been because older examples are easier to treat more dispassionately and objectively. The 'heat of battle' has subsided a bit. I did, however, include some recent examples simply so the book would not be dated.

Finally, the main focus of this book is on the problems that face our democracy. I firmly believe not only that these problems are solvable, but in many cases, ignorance of the problem is more dangerous than the problem itself. For many, if we had a consensus on the nature of the problem, the solution would follow naturally. For others, if we had a better understanding of the reasoning behind these solutions, at least the people could decide on the country's direction.

Because of this, I have focused on the problems rather than on possible solutions. While each chapter ends with a *What Can be Done* section, I have not put much detail into that discussion. In fact, at one time, I was not even going to include any potential solutions. Still, I decided that discussing the problems without mentioning possible solutions could leave the reader with a sense that we are doomed. While I believe these problems are severe, I don't believe we are doomed.

The brief nature of the solutions' sections opens them up to the criticism of superficiality. I only ask you to remember that I offer these as a first step toward solving these problems, not the final word. Ultimately, we must solve these problems through the democratic process. As we will see in the first chapter, attempts to fix these problems by imposing solutions are doomed to fail. Once the person or body imposing the solutions relinquishes power, the imposed solutions will be abandoned.

The only proper solution must be a democratic one, where people debate the problems, suggest solutions, and consider the pros and cons and their ramifications. Then, the people must decide how we as a country will proceed.

An important obstacle will be the prevailing attitude that democracy is about winning elections. While a common view, it is both false and dangerous. When viewed as winning elections, democracy, likewise, becomes defeating the opposition. It becomes focused on depriving the opposition of having a say in the democratic process.

Granted, there will be winners and losers in any vote, so it is easy to see how such an attitude can become dominant. Still, if that is the attitude, eventually, democracy will fail. The alternative view prevailed at the Constitutional Convention and during the ratification process. It is a view of democracy that seeks consensus.

Building consensus is hard work. It sees everyone as part of the process, with a voice to consider. Those who disagree are not people to demonize; they are people with perspectives one must consider in any solution. It focuses on working together rather than defeating.

Building consensus was the attitude that founded the country. The Constitution was a compromise document on virtually every point. Nobody got everything they wanted. Everybody gave up something. Even during the ratification process, supporters made compromises, resulting in the Bill of Rights. In a healthy democracy, the goal is to seek the most significant majority possible. It requires a good understanding of the issues and the various points of view.

Our system currently focuses on fifty percent plus one, or whatever is required to win. Such a focus can only lead to division and polarization, which is where we find ourselves. It breeds instability since no decision is final. They only last until the current group loses power.

The only way to ensure policies remain in effect is to keep the other side from winning. The issues become secondary. You don't need a good understanding of the issues or why the other side disagrees. You only need to know they are the enemy and must be defeated. The only way to ensure this long-term is some sort of tyranny, which is why democracies fail.

This book will focus on understanding the core issues. You may disagree with some of the analysis or the proposed solutions. That is fine. These are present, not as the final word, but the beginning of a course correction. The hope is that this will be a starting point, not for mandating this or that policy solution, but to begin the discussion toward reaching the broadest possible consensus. Anything short of this would be self-defeating.

NOTHING LASTS FOREVER

Those who cannot learn from history are doomed to repeat it.
George Santayana

It was a huge party. The one thousand guests, a veritable Who's-Who of society, enjoyed the best foods served on golden plates and the best wines in golden goblets. Perhaps some enjoyed the wine a little too much.

It seemed a strange time to celebrate, for the city was under attack. But the guests at the party were unconcerned. A wide moat and high walls protected them. While almost certainly an exaggeration, the ancient Greek historian Herodotus' claim that they were over 80 feet thick and 300 feet tall conveys the sense of safety the walls provided. No attacker had gotten past the defenses in over a thousand years. They had stored up plenty of food, and a river ran under the walls, providing plenty of water should the attacking army try to starve them out. So, the party went on safely behind the walls.

The safety was only an illusion. Not only would the city fall, but it would fall that night. Knowing they could not breach the walls and not wanting to wait the years it might take to starve the city's inhabitants into surrender, they did something the guests had not even considered.

They diverted the Euphrates River to no longer flow under the city walls. Instead of a river providing water, there was now an empty river bed, allowing Cyrus's army to march directly into the city under the wall. With virtually all its leaders and top officials drunk at the party, Babylon fell in a single night. It was over before the guests even knew what was happening.

There is often a fine line between ignorance and arrogance. So fine that it is often challenging to distinguish if someone is arrogant or does not know any better. Of course, the worst case results from a mixture of the two: arrogance based on ignorance.

This was the case with the rulers of Babylon and their arrogance in throwing such a party while the city was under siege and their ignorance of the grave danger. They took it for granted that they were safe, unaware of the danger around them.

There are some similarities with 21st-century America. Many take for granted much of what is good and even great about this country. It is just how things are, how they should be, and how they will always be. Most are unaware of the weaknesses and dangers in the system that enemies could exploit, resulting in its downfall.

Instead, we have slogans. Democracy is good, and the more democracy, the better. Count every vote. For some, it does not matter whether the voter is a citizen or if they are here legally.1 They are persons, and in a democracy, shouldn't everyone have their say? Aren't we all just citizens of the world?

And, of course, anything the people want and vote for is automatically good. The people voted for it democratically, and democracy is good; therefore, anything they vote for must likewise be good.

Conversely, anything that stands in the way of voting, and therefore democracy, is terrible. Voter registration must be simple and easy, with minimal hassles, lest any inconvenience becomes a

---

1   Jessie Mangaliman, "San Francisco considers school board voting rights for non-citizens", *San Jose Mercury News* June 21, 2004

barrier to voting. The epitome is the ability to register when you vote.

Voter fraud is merely an abstract concept, a red herring used by those wishing to limit democracy. Asking potential voters to demonstrate their identity to ensure only those with a legal right to vote do so or that they vote only once raises too many barriers. It hinders democracy.

Voting itself must be easy. The old-fashioned ideas of 'election day' and 'going to the polls' are too restrictive and limit people's ability to vote. So, now we have early and absentee voting, not just for those who need it but for anyone who wants it. Now, many vote weeks in advance before the candidates can debate, or in the case of primaries, drop out.

Voting is simultaneously a sacrosanct right and a troublesome nuisance. We must do everything we can to ensure that people can cast a vote and that we count the votes. Whether or not fraud or illegal voting ultimately negated one's vote is irrelevant. That a vote was cast and counted is what is essential.

Anything the people want is automatically good simply because it is an expression of their will. Thus, the problems we face can only result from the people's will being thwarted or blocked in some way by that most evil of all groups, the special interest.

As a result, politicians then fall into two groups. Not Republicans or Democrats, though they use those names. No, the meaningful categories are those fighting for the people and those representing the dreaded special interests. Of course, the problem is that most politicians say they fight for the people and that their opponent represents the dreaded special interests. A few babble on about some policy details, but they are dull.

One message that does seem to resonate with the voters is change. The direction is irrelevant, and change to what is likewise irrelevant. What resonates is change for change's sake. Thus, every so often, the office of the president changes the party in power. However, this type of change is restricted mainly to the president, as, for the most part, that is the only politician people can name. Voters typically spare Senators and Representatives from this regular change unless things are really bad. After all, if you don't know who they are or how long they have been there, how do you know if it is time for a change?

The other central theme that resonates is what they (the politicians) give us (the voters). Yet, here, a conflict exists. There are those receiving from the government and those paying the bill. Voters must then go to the trouble of deciding whether to vote for more benefits or more tax cuts, though even here, the politicians have become accommodating enough to promise both frequently.

The net effect is that the size and cost of government have exploded over the last century. But not to worry because that is what the people want, and what the people want must be good.

A Looming Danger?

Most Americans would probably be surprised to learn that the Founding Fathers were suspicious of democracy, seeing it as dangerous, something to be controlled and limited. Going back at least as far as the ancient Greek philosophers Socrates, Plato, and Aristotle, many serious thinkers saw democracy as a dangerous and unworkable form of government. It could last only a short time and would end badly. Alexander Hamilton summed up the view of many in a speech at the New York Ratifying Convention,

> It has been observed by an honorable gentleman, that a pure democracy, if it were practicable, would be the most perfect government. Experience has proved, that no position in politics is more false than this. The ancient democracies, in which the people themselves deliberated, never possessed one feature of good government. Their very character was tyranny.[2]

---

2   A. Hamilton, "New York Ratifying Convention. First Speech of June 21 (Francis Childs's Version), [21 June 1788]," 21 6 1787. [Online]. Available: https://founders.archives.gov/documents/Hamilton/01-05-02-0012-0011. [Accessed 6 10 2020]

Nor were such views merely the musings of ancient philosophers. As Hamilton noted, this view had been borne out time and time again in history. Wherever tried, democracy failed. Ancient Athens tried democracy, and Democratic Athens led the Greek city-states to defeat the Persians. However, internal wars among the city-states weakened democratic rule. Eventually, it succumbed to another democratic government, the Roman Republic.

The Roman Republic also weakened and collapsed, but no other democracy waited at the gate to take over. So, it collapsed into the dictatorship of the Caesars. The Republic built Rome, but then it was ruled by the Empire. More minor attempts at democracy likewise collapsed and failed. Perhaps the most notable was the Renaissance city of Florence, led by Savonarola and Machiavelli. Thus, wherever tried, democracy failed. That is until the United States.

The genius of the Founding Fathers is in their understanding of these earlier democracies. The success of the United States is not despite these earlier failures but because of them. They drew deeply on their knowledge of these earlier attempts along with the work of political philosophers from Socrates, Plato, and Aristotle to more recent ones, such as John Locke and Montesquieu, constructing a government based on a written Constitution. The goal was to avoid the inherent dangers and pitfalls of democracy that had caused the failure of the earlier attempts. The government they established has lasted for over 200 years.

So, did the Founding Fathers avoid all the problems? They certainly did much better than Renaissance Florence, which lasted only 17 years. They also avoided the catastrophe that befell the near-contemporaneous French Revolution. It ended so badly in the Reign of Terror that today, when people think of the French Revolution, the Guillotine comes more readily to mind than democracy. But we still have not reached the benchmark set by Rome that was still going strong at comparable points in their history.

A Cause for Concern?

But not to worry, the Founding Fathers were geniuses. The government they constructed considered all these dangers by setting up a system of checks and balances. These will protect us. So, we have nothing to worry about. Or do we?

Suppose we assume the Founding Fathers were geniuses and the government they established did provide checks and balances for all the dangers. One possible cause for concern is that we amended the Constitution and, thus, no longer have the government they created. This is not necessarily bad.

One of the first things the new Congress did after being established by the Constitution was to change it by adding the Bill of Rights. They also quickly passed two more amendments to fix some problems that had arisen. Since then, we have formally changed the Constitution another fifteen times, the last in 1992. More importantly, the courts have informally changed, or at least reinterpreted, the Constitution numerous times. They continue to do so virtually every year.

Thus, we are changing our government all the time. These changes are needed to keep up with societal changes, technology, etc. Still, today, when we make a change, are we just allowing the government to be more responsive and effective? Are we just fixing problems unforeseen by the Founding Fathers? Or are we changing something more fundamental? Are we changing critical supports that keep the whole system functioning, an essential check or balance that keeps the system from collapsing?

In 1913, we ratified the 17th amendment, changing how we chose Senators. Before that, state legislatures chose them. Now, the people directly elect them, making the process more democratic. Yet, why didn't the founders have them directly elected from the beginning? They did this for members of the House of Representatives. What were their reasons for the original method? Was this a good change? What is the effect on the checks and balances? Should we go back to the old system? Maybe we should;

perhaps we shouldn't. How would we know the difference if we do not understand the reasoning?

One of the things I learned from teaching Critical Thinking in college was that most students knew little about the Founding Fathers beyond their names, except perhaps George Washington. The recent musical *Hamilton* introduced many to Alexander Hamilton. As for the problems of democracy and the reason for the system of checks and balances, most don't even realize they exist.

But not to worry, we can change the Constitution if we make a mistake. Once we realize the problem, we can fix it and continue. We did this with the 21st amendment in 1933, which repeals the 19th and, thus, prohibition. The following analogy demonstrates the problem with such thinking.

A Stroll in the Desert

Imagine an intrepid but somewhat naive adventurer staying at a beautiful resort on the edge of a vast desert. In the distance, he sees a hill and wonders what is on the other side. So, our adventurer decides to hike to the hill and see for himself.

After hiking for some time, he finally reaches the top. The view is gorgeous and well worth the hike. In the distance, our adventurer sees another hill and instantly has the same question: What is beyond it? He feels pretty good, but he didn't think to bring any food or water; after all, he is not only intrepid but naïve. Still, he tells himself he can always return to the resort's safety if needed. So, he decides to press on.

From the moment our intrepid adventurer set out on his journey, the maximum distance he could travel before he died was limited and unknown. It was limited because the human body has limits on how far it can go without food or water. Since our intrepid adventurer wanders through a desert, water will be the primary issue.

The only water in our mythical desert is at our mythical resort, so the distance our adventurer can travel is also limited. Eventually, his body will give out, and he will die.

Exactly how far he can go is unknown for several reasons. How fast he loses water will be determined by the heat and whether he runs, walks briskly, or slowly. But while unknown, there remains a limit to how far he can go. So, with each step our intrepid adventurer takes, he comes closer to death.

Early on, this is hardly even worth considering. He is close to the resort and can easily make it back. Still, the farther he travels from the resort, the smaller the safety margin. Assuming that our adventurer always walks in a straight line, the point of no return is half the maximum distance he can travel. The resort will be too far to reach if he goes beyond the halfway point, and he will die before getting back.

The real problem, however, is that body functions do not decline in a linear or straight-line fashion. The halfway point of our perceived energy differs from the halfway point of the distance we can travel. In short, our adventurer can cover ground much faster when he starts his trek across the desert than at the end when he has only the strength left to crawl.

As a result, our explorer does not even realize it when he reaches the point of no return, beyond which the resort is too far away to make it back. He does not understand the danger. Sure, he may feel tired and thirsty, but it is not all that bad, and he feels he can go a little more before returning to the resort.

And so he continues, not realizing that he is a dead man from the moment he crosses the halfway point. When he finally decides he has a problem and should go back, it is already too late. His body begins to run down quickly, and each step becomes harder until he can only crawl, and then he can't even do that. And so he dies.

This story illustrates the problems of democracies. They likewise do not proceed in a straight-line fashion. Changes that will threaten a democratic system may not show any issues and may even seem beneficial until it is too late. A farmer who eats all of their crop, including the part they should set aside as seed for next year, will seem better at first. They will have more to eat. Yet, when the next year comes, there is no seed to plant and, thus, no crop. Yet, it is too late; They have already eaten the seeds for next year's crop.

So, in theory, we can always undo any change in a democracy and repeal any bad law. While true in theory, the reality is vastly different. For one, there is a natural resistance to change. In a democratic system, getting a majority to approve a change is difficult. Even when all recognize the problem, getting a majority to agree on a particular solution can be difficult.

For example, today, virtually everyone agrees that Social Security has problems. While there is some disagreement concerning the exact date, there is general agreement that the Social Security system will run out of money at some point in the near future. There is also agreement that the sooner we address this issue, the easier it will be to fix. Still, while there is a general agreement on the problems, there is no agreement on how to fix Social Security. It is working at the moment, and proposing a change is risky. So, the politicians do nothing, and the system continues its stroll into the desert.

There is a further problem. The root cause may only be recognized by a few or perhaps not at all. The apparent problem may be a severe economic slowdown, with the voters demanding more government intervention to fix it. Yet, suppose government intervention caused the problem in the first place. In that case, more government intervention will only exacerbate the situation, leading to more demands for more intervention. They cross the point of no return before anyone realizes it.

While, as in Florence, things can spin out of control quickly, collapse does not always happen this fast. A democracy can pass the point of no return and still function as a democracy for decades before the system collapses. Such was the case with the Roman Republic.

The Roman Republic

When most people think of the fall of Rome, they think of the end of the Roman Empire some 400 years after the birth of Christ. For many, Rome was always ruled by Caesars, without much thought about the situation in Rome before the first Caesar, Julius, came to power.

In its earliest days, kings ruled Rome[3]. At that time, Rome was just another city on the Italian peninsula competing with many others. But the Romans quickly tired of the rule of kings. They wanted liberty, so in 509 B.C., they overthrew the monarchy, setting up a Republic.

They still needed someone to be in charge. Yet, a single ruler, able to rule year after year, could quickly become a new king. So, instead of a king, two consuls led the new Republic, sharing power and could veto the acts of the other. They were also limited to a single year in office. While they could run again, they usually had to wait ten years before seeking another term. The Romans kept the king's body of counselors, or Senate, to counterbalance the consuls.

It was not a perfect democracy by any means. Class played a considerable role in Rome, as did class struggles. At the top were the patricians, the ruling class from which the consuls and most of the Senate came. Next were the equites, often businessmen, their distinguishing feature being, at least initially, that they were rich enough to afford a horse. It is from the equites that we get the word equestrian. These two groups were called the good and were

3   The history of Rome that follows in taken primarily from the following sources:
Will and Ariel Durant, *The Story of Civilization III: Caesar and Christ.* (New York: Simon and Schuster, 1944).
Tom Holland, Rubicon: The Last Years of the Roman Republic (New York: Doubleday: 2003).

the people of Rome, at least at first. Next in line were the plebs, which included all the rest except those in the lowest category: the slaves.

The plebs did have the vote, at least in theory, but key leaders often instructed them for whom they should vote. Still, they did have some political power. Periods of unrest that resulted in expanded political power for the plebs marked the early history of Rome. These new powers took the form of new offices, written laws, and eventually, the opening of existing offices to the plebs. Ultimately, these even included the consul, though again, this was often more in theory than practice.

One of the most significant changes was also the earliest. Following a revolt in 494 B.C., the office of Tribune, to represent the plebs, was created. Like consuls, there were two, and their term was limited to a single year. Over time, the office of Tribune grew in power to rival even that of consul, as a Tribune could veto any bill.

For nearly 400 years, through many changes, Rome maintained a delicate balance of power, preserving the Republic. Rome divided power between Consuls, Tribunes, the Senate, and the Assembly. They maintained this balance with the force of tradition and the fact that Consuls and Tribunes only ruled for a year. While in office, they were immune from prosecution. Still, once their term ended, they could be brought before the courts to answer for any illegal actions.

Yet, problems were growing. As Rome expanded and new areas opened up, Italian farmers began finding it increasingly difficult to compete with crops grown in conquered lands by slave labor. Not only was slave labor in the new regions a problem, but many of those captured were sent back to Rome as slaves.

The largest farms, farms that could afford many slaves, began using them for work, putting further pressure on the small farmers. With no work in the countryside, the plebs came to Rome.

Yet, there, they struggled for what little work they could find as the use of slaves grew there as well.

At the same time, attitudes were changing subtly yet very significantly. Rome's conquests brought great wealth and an influx of new ideas. Not the least of which were ideas from Greece. These ideas weakened the concept of 'Rome' as a shared collective idea. In its place was a new one: the importance of the individual.

One side effect of this change was that people began to look more to individuals, instead of institutions such as the Senate, to deal with problems. This shift gave individuals a more significant opportunity to gain political power. They likewise began to think more of themselves than the state. While Rome had conquered the world, in many ways, it would be a series of individuals who ended the Republic. The old saying,[4] the road to hell is paved with good intentions, pretty much sums up the early period of the Roman Republic's downfall.

Decline of the Roman Republic

Tiberius Gracchus was elected one of the two Tribunes in 133 B.C. Tiberius combined his ambition with what appears to be a genuine concern for the problems he saw. Still, while Gracchus saw the developing problems, he was blind to their root cause: slavery.

Slavery was so ingrained into the Roman culture of the period that dealing with it would have been literally unthinkable. It is just the way things were. Only with the fall of the Roman Empire 500 years later and Christianity's subsequent rise did a new set of values dominate the culture, one that questioned slavery.[5]

---

4   This saying is often attributed to the 18th-century literary figure Dr. Samuel Johnson. However, Dr. Johnson said, "Hell is paved with good intentions," and his biographer Boswell notes that this was a proverbial saying.– Boswell, The Life of Samuel Johnson, April 15, 1775, pg 550.

5   Slavery did largely disappear in Europe following the rise of Christianity. It only reappeared following the Renaissance as the Church's hold on the culture weakened, and European explorers started sailing down the coast of

Instead of the root cause, Tiberius focused on the results; large farms displacing smaller ones forced smaller farmers off their land and into the city without jobs. To counter this, he wanted legislation limiting the size of a farm. He also wanted to buy back land previously sold by the state at the original selling price so it could be divided into smaller lots and given to the poor. Tiberius argued eloquently for his bill, appealing to the plebs,

> You fight and die to give wealth and luxury to others. You are called masters of the world, but there is not a foot of ground that you can call your own.[6]

Not surprisingly, Tiberius's plan faced significant opposition, particularly from the large landowners. Their property had appreciated, either from their improvements or inflation. Opposition was especially firm from those who had purchased their land from a prior owner at a higher cost than the government was now willing to pay. Thus, many in the Senate denounced the proposed law. When the Assembly passed it, Senators convinced or persuaded the other Tribune, Octavius, to exercise his veto.

While Tiberius' proposed law caused a significant uproar, it did not in and of itself threaten the Roman Republic. However, his reaction to the veto was the first step in its subsequent downfall. While Tiberius could have waited until Octavius' term was up at the end of the year, his term would have been over as well. He would no longer be in a position to push his reforms.

So, he concocted a scheme to remove Octavius. He had the Assembly pass a law permitting them to immediately remove from office any Tribune who acted contrary to the wishes of the plebs. As soon as the Assembly passed this new measure, Tiberius had his people forcibly remove Octavius, which effectively negated the Tribunal veto.

While it achieved his purpose, many saw Tiberius' actions for what they were: a subversion of hundreds of years of Roman

---

Africa. There they encountered and then became a part of the slave trade.
6   Will and Ariel Durant, *The Story of Civilization III: Caesar and Christ.* (New York: Simon and Schuster, 1944), 114.

law. His enemies could not touch him while he remained Tribune, but they made it well known that as soon as his term ended, they would bring charges against him.

Tiberius faced an almost certain conviction. He had already circumvented Roman law, so he decided the only way out was to retain the immunity granted him as Tribune. Thus, Tiberius ran for an unprecedented second term, an act that cost him what little support he had left in the Senate. With nowhere else to turn for help, he appealed to the plebs, promising a whole new series of laws to buy enough votes to win reelection.

The flouting of law and tradition and the uproar over all the new promises caused tensions to grow even higher. Critics charged that Tiberius was trying to set himself up as king. Tempers flared, resulting in violence in the Forum on election day, during which someone killed Tiberius.

Though Tiberius was gone, the plebs saw him as their hero and a martyr, and tensions remained high. The Senate put many of Tiberius' laws into effect to end the unrest. Still, the plebs remained restless. Anyone perceived as betraying Tiberius' memory could turn up dead, as happened to Scipio Aemilianus, Tiberius' brother-in-law. He had intervened before the newly created land board on behalf of some landowners.

Tiberius' brother, Gaius, was determined to complete his brother's work. While also a brilliant orator, though not idealistic like his brother, he was a much more practical and skilled politician. In 124 B.C., he became Tribune. He built a large following through a series of laws tailored to build support among specific groups.

The most significant were the Corn Laws, laws saying the state would now sell grain to the poor at what amounted to half the market price. These shattered the Roman notion of self-reliance, replacing it instead with dependence on the state, a dependency later politicians were to exploit.

Having amassed an enormous power base, Gaius busted the crack his brother had made wide open. He not only ran for but won a second term. Yet, before long, Gaius also overreached. The Senate still opposed and constantly fought against his reforms. Gaius sought to remedy the situation by doubling the Senate's size. This change would allow him to put his supporters into the newly created Senate seats and give him a majority.

Gaius' greatest mistake, however, was his attempt to expand the vote to varying degrees throughout Italy. The masses in Rome were in no mood to dilute their own political power. His opponents seized on this mistake by submitting a series of laws aimed at enticing political support away from Gaius with their own set of giveaways.

It worked, and when Gaius tried for a third term, he was defeated. Once out of power, his opponents began repealing his laws. Again, tension flared, and his opponents forced Gaius to flee Rome. But they overtook and killed him.

Tiberius and Gaius set in motion the chain of events that eventually led to the collapse of the Roman Republic. To be sure, they did not cause the problems that were plaguing Rome. Still, their overreaching to solve those problems had three key results, which, when combined, had lasting and detrimental effects.

First was an increase in the political power of the plebs. Appeals to the plebs of Rome were behind Tiberius' and Gaius' rise to power. In the end, appeals to the plebs brought Gaius down. These appeals were not in and of themselves a bad thing until combined with the second factor.

The second factor was an increased dependency on the state. The Gracchi brothers and their opponents appealed to the plebs through giveaways like Gaius' Corn Laws. Many of these giveaways made the plebs dependent in one way or another on the state.

The third factor was that the Gracchi's actions had raised the specter of tyranny, such that many saw any further attempt at significant reform as an attempt to destroy the Republic.

The result was a government where people gained political power by appealing to the plebs with giveaways: the bread and circuses for which the Roman Empire became known. These giveaways made the plebs increasingly dependent on the state, a state where no real significant change was permitted. Rome had reached its point of no return. Though it did not know it, the Republic was doomed.

The paralysis made it increasingly difficult to get anything done. Action required power, and power required political support, yet political power depended on who could sway the masses. As a result, political power began to center around personalities that could attract many followers.

While this was going on, Rome still faced threats on many fronts. Defeating these threats and making Rome 'safe' combined with the wealth such victories brought was the surest way to gain the support of the plebs. A general with the military skills to win battles and political skills to appeal to the masses could rise quickly.

Within twenty years of the death of Gaius, a new figure arose, this time a general named Marius. Following a series of military victories, rather than causing controversy by seeking a second term, Marius was reelected consul not only for a second but for five consecutive terms, later adding a sixth and even a seventh. What had caused controversy was now an accepted norm.

The giveaways continued. Leaders reduced food prices even further. To please the people, leaders gave away more and more. In 105 B.C., the state began to sponsor gladiatorial games, adding entertainment to the growing list of dependencies.

Frustrated at seeing all these benefits going to Rome, the rest of Italy revolted in 91 B.C. When it became clear that Rome could not win, it ended the war by granting the rest of Italy complete

Roman citizenship. However, some procedural maneuvering undercut this citizenship such that little actually changed, and the paralysis continued.

Still, political paralysis in the face of significant problems breeds instability, which produces a desire to get something done. Political battles became more pronounced, and the courts increasingly became little more than a tool politicians could use against opponents.

A further problem was Rome did not have a written constitution; its government depended mainly on tradition and norms. Each break from these made the next easier. As the years passed, few even remembered them. They grew up in an era of political leaders pushing boundaries and breaking norms. They were restrained only by what they could get away with, and those who were successful became the new models to emulate.

Increasingly, political contests ended in bloodshed, both with individuals and, given the political importance of generals, in some cases, armies from the opposing factions. In 82 B.C., an army supporting the Senate led by Sulla, who had once been a general under Marius, defeated an army supported by the Assembly and led by Marius' son.

Following the victory, Sulla demanded that the Senate make him a dictator. The Senate agreed so he could restore order and get something done. Sulla further expanded the vote to include his supporters, restored the power of the Senate, and re-instituted the one-term limit on consuls.

His rule was brutal. He created lists of enemies to be arrested and killed. He also allowed some supporters to add names to these lists. This opportunity was something a person we will meet shortly, Crassus, took advantage of to eliminate his rivals and gain their property. Sulla also greatly limited the office of Tribune of the Plebs, an office that had, in his eyes, caused so much trouble.

Confident that he had restored Rome to its former glory and that most of his enemies were dead, he stepped down as dictator after only two years. Still, the examples set by Sulla and Marius proved more lasting than Sulla's reforms, needing only another crisis to reemerge. The next crisis came just seven years later. Looking at it in more detail will highlight some of the factors troubling Rome at the time.

Revolt

It started at a gladiatorial training compound in Campania that trained slaves for the games. During a mass escape attempt, seventy-eight gladiators made it out. Led by Spartacus, they began raiding nearby villages for food.

At the time, Pompey was Rome's best general. He was already famous and very popular, yet he was away fighting in Spain. Still, it was only a small group of gladiators, less than 80, so Rome sent an army of 3,000 men to deal quickly with them before the situation got out of hand.

Unlike the Spartacus of the movie, the real Spartacus was not born into slavery. Instead, he had been a mercenary who had served in the Roman army. As a result, Spartacus not only knew how to fight as a gladiator, he knew how the Roman armies fought and, thus, how to fight them.

When the Romans believed they had trapped the gladiators on a mountainside, they relaxed and waited to starve them out. At some point, the gladiators would get desperate and storm the front of the camp. When they did, the 3,000 troops could readily handle them.

Yet, instead of attacking the army directly, the gladiators used vines to climb down the cliffs and sneak around behind them. They struck the rear, not the front as the Romans had expected, and thus, where the Romans had not prepared. It was over quickly, but not as the Romans had hoped.

The gladiator's defeat of a Roman army of 3,000 sent shock waves across the countryside. Spartacus issued a call for all slaves to revolt and join him. And come they did. The small group of gladiators who escaped became a band of raiders. Then, it became a disciplined army of 70,000 men, defeating several more Roman armies along the way.

The considerable mass of slaves moved north to the Alps and freedom, looting whatever they needed from the towns they passed along the way. In response, Rome sent an even larger army, headed this time by the two consuls. One consul found a tiny splinter group and defeated it. The other consul found Spartacus' main force. However, this consul, Gellius Publicola, was known more for his ridicule of Athenian philosophers than his generalship. Spartacus defeated Publicola's army.

The way to the Alps and freedom was now open, but the slaves, having their freedom, instead sought to be like their former masters. Having defeated all that Rome had thrown at them and looted the towns they passed had given them the confidence that they were invincible. The rest of Italy would be theirs for the taking.

The former slaves became masters. They even took some of the prisoners from Gellius' army and made them fight in their own gladiatorial games. Then they turned and headed south. Their numbers continued to grow, and the army of 70,000 became 120,000. It could have grown even larger, yet Spartacus, fearing the problems of maintaining an even larger force, began turning recruits away.

Rome panicked and recalled Pompey from Spain, but that would take time. An ambitious and wealthy man, Marcus Licinius Crassus, seized the opportunity and stepped forward. He demanded complete authority, as he did not want to share the glory that would come as the savior of Rome or the power that would surely follow from it.

While an accomplished general, he was also the wealthiest man in Rome. Some wealth came from his skill as a businessman, some from the property of rivals he had added to Sulla's lists. Some came from his fire department. Crassus had the only fire department in Rome. Unlike modern departments, they would show up at a fire but not do anything until Crassus gave the go-ahead. As the property burned, Crassus offered to buy it at a very low rate. The longer the person held out, the lower the price would get.

Having such wealth, some questioned whether he had what it took to defeat Spartacus. His opportunity to remove all doubts occurred when two legions, disobeying his orders, attacked Spartacus before Crassus was ready and were defeated.

Crassus had the legions decimated as a punishment. Decimation was an ancient but rarely used punishment. He had the legions line up, and then every tenth man was selected and killed. It was a brutal punishment that convinced Rome that Crassus would do whatever it took to win.

As Spartacus headed south, Crassus and his army pursued. Spartacus, realizing the new danger, sought to escape to Sicily. When the pirates he had hired betrayed him, he was trapped in the toe of Italy. Crassus built a barricade across the entire peninsula to lock them in. After two failed attempts to get away, time was running out for Spartacus and the former slaves.

Still, Crassus faced time pressures as well. Pompey was coming and, as the senior general, would take charge when he arrived. If that happened, Pompey, not Crassus, would get any glory from the victory. Knowing this, Spartacus sought a negotiated settlement. Yet, such a settlement would not serve Crassus' need. He wanted all or nothing.

When a third attempt to break the barricade succeeded, a mad dash across Italy ensued. Spartacus and his forces attempted to reach Brundisium, hoping to get passage out of Italy. Crassus' forces were in pursuit, and Pompey's forces were getting closer.

Finally, Crassus could force the main body of Spartacus' army into battle. Crassus' victory was complete. Contrary to the movie, Spartacus died in the battle. Crassus had six thousand of the captured slaves crucified along the Appian Way.

Yet, while he achieved total victory, Crassus did not get the full glory that he had sought or that his success had earned. Pompey arrived on the scene just in time to clean up some stragglers.

Militarily, Pompey's contribution was negligible. Politically, Pompey, being already popular with the people, claimed and received half the glory of 'saving Rome.' Always seeking the best in any situation, Crassus allied with Pompey. The two commanders marched their armies back to Rome and wanted to be consuls together.

Collapse

This move violated a whole new series of traditions. But by this time, what was Roman law had ceased to matter. The only thing that mattered was what one could get away with, at least as long as your side controlled the courts. If they didn't, the law still didn't matter all that much. Still, the idea of the Republic remained important or at least helpful. So, Rome maintained the facade of elections. Pompey and Crassus sought or bribed the support they needed and were elected.

Pompey's base of power was in the plebs, and true to his base, he favored the Assembly over the Senate. Crassus, always the pragmatist, rode the wave of popularity and went along, though hedging a bit with the Senate should the tide of fortune change. Once in office, they set about undoing Sulla's reforms, including restoring power to the office that had previously caused such problems, the Tribune of the Plebs.

In Rome's stroll into the desert, the Republic was now well past the point of no return. While the facade of democracy remained, it was no more accurate than a Hollywood set and a run-down set at that. In reality, a democratic vote of the people no longer ruled Rome. Instead, powerful men were the real powers behind the scenes. Law and tradition ceased to be necessary. For these men, law and tradition were nothing more than tools they could manipulate in their quest for power.

While the true power was behind the scenes, it was still fractured and divided. By the end of their consulship, Pompey and Crassus were at odds with each other. Neither had amassed enough power to do without the other, nor were they the only power players in Rome.

When their consulship ended, both went their separate ways. Pompey's power was grounded in his military successes. So, after taking on and disposing of the pirates troubling shipping, he set off to the East. There, he quelled some trouble and conquered more territory, including the conquest and sack of the city of Jerusalem.

Crassus, on the other hand, had his true base of power in his wealth, which was prodigious. Thus, Crassus sought out and supported many promising young men, helping them in times of financial trouble. The most notable being a promising young nephew of Marius, Julius Caesar.

Some, like Crassus, sought power for the wealth and security it brought. Some, like Pompey, were just so talented they seemed to drift into power as boats floating in the current. With such men, a facade of democracy is undoubtedly no hindrance and can be beneficial. So, the democratic facade was allowed to continue.

But it was only a facade, and it would just be a matter of time until some new crisis or ambitious person came along to whom the facade was a hindrance. When that happened, they would tear it down completely.

The first attempt occurred a few years later in 62 B.C., when another of Crassus' promising investments, Catiline, becoming impatient with the pace of things, planned to seize power. His attempt failed, ending in Catiline's death along with many of his supporters, including five senators. However, two of his known associates escaped legal implication, if not suspicion: Crassus and the young Julius Caesar.

In 60 B.C., Caesar, now a political force in his own right, convinced Crassus and Pompey to settle their differences, forming an alliance of mutual support, the First Triumvirate. Caesar lacked only one thing to make his power base complete: an Army.

Unlike Catiline, Caesar was very patient and used his power to secure the command of an army in Gaul, modern-day France. Over the next ten years, while keeping a close eye on Rome, he led his army to victory in Gaul with even a brief excursion into Britain, earning himself the solid loyalty of his troops in the process.

By the time Caesar's military service in Gaul was over, the alliance of three had become two, Crassus having died. Pompey, with no real ambition, was not seen as a threat. But Caesar's ambition was strong, and he planned to return and run for consul. Caesar was a force to be reckoned with before, and he was now a military force.

His opponents feared he would be unstoppable. But there was one way to stop him. While serving as Governor in Gaul or as consul in Rome, Caesar was immune from prosecution. The problem for Caesar was that there would be a gap of several months from when his Governorship ended until the consul elections. Typically, this would not have been a problem. There were several ways to manipulate events to maintain his immunity. But two could play at this game, and his opponents blocked his every move.

In all this political maneuvering, his opponents had two key advantages; first, they were in Rome. Caesar's power base was in the masses but out of sight, out of mind. Second, by this time, his opponents had managed to turn Pompey against Caesar.

In the end, there was no way for Caesar to keep his immunity. Nor was it likely that he could win in court, which had ceased to be a source of justice. Now, it was little more than just another tool to be used to attack political opponents or to protect political allies, depending on who was in power at the moment.

Then again, there was the problem that Caesar had played a little fast and loose with the law. Like so many others of the time, for Caesar, the law was simply another tool to be manipulated, when possible, for one's political purposes. If Caesar left his command and returned to Rome, he faced a certain conviction and the end of his career, if not his life. Yet, his career was still over if he did not return to Rome, the center of all political power.

When his opponents got the Senate to declare him an enemy of the state, for Caesar to continue his power, just one way remained open. So, in 49 B.C., Caesar crossed the Rubicon, the river in northern Italy that at the time marked the end of Gaul and the beginning of Italy, and came to Rome. But he did not come alone. He came with his army, bringing down for the last time the remaining facade of a democracy that had lasted for 460 years.

Parallelomania?

There are two significant dangers whenever we try to learn from past events. The first would be to focus on the similarities and see too many parallels. When early scholars of religion began to compare the different religions of the world, they started to see parallels between them. Out of this came several theories on the interrelationship of beliefs, which they began to pursue.

They found that the more they looked, the more parallels they found. For several decades, they believed they had discovered something truly significant and continued to search even deeper. When they did, they started seeing similarities everywhere, even between things without connection.

The noted Jewish scholar Samuel Sandmel began to set things straight in the early 1960s in an article entitled *Parallelomania.*[7] The main flaw in parallels is that they are selective and superficial. They are selective in taking only those things that match and ignoring differences. This tendency makes them superficial in that the mere appearance of a parallel becomes significant. The net result is that you can find meaning and significance where it does not exist. For example, consider all the similarities noted between

7   Samuel Sandmel, "Parallelomania", *Journal of Biblical Literature,* 81, (1962) 1-13, http://www.biblicalstudies.org.uk/pdf/parallelomania_sandmel. pdf (accessed April 3, 2009).

the assassinations of Presidents Lincoln and Kennedy.[8] They are interesting but ultimately meaningless.

So, the easiest way to go wrong would be to claim that American democracy will fail, 'just like Rome.' One could undoubtedly find parallels between Rome and America. For example, one can find similarities between Gaius Gracchus and Franklin D. Roosevelt. Both, when frustrated with their political aims, tried to increase the size of the institution blocking them. That way, they could stack it with their people.

Gaius Gracchus tried to increase the size of the Senate and FDR the Supreme Court. Both would also go on to break the tradition that limited their terms. But while perhaps interesting, this ultimately has little significance in and of itself. In contrast, one can always find such parallels but also lots of differences—history rarely, if ever, repeats itself in that way.

The other equally flawed claim is that American democracy is so different from the Roman Republic or any of the other earlier attempts that we have nothing to learn. American democracy will always exist. It is true that the parallels, in and of themselves, are irrelevant, as are the differences. They tell us little about what will happen to American democracy.

But there are some important and valuable lessons to learn here. There is truth in the saying that history does not repeat itself, but it does rhyme.[9] A more reasoned approach looks past the superficial parallels and differences to find the underlying factors and conditions that led to the demise of the Roman Republic. While events and situations change, people, in large part, remain the same.

---

8   *FreakyPhenomena.com*, "Lincoln-Kennedy Coincidences," http://freaky-phenomena.com/2008/12/19/lincoln-kennedy-coincidences/ (accessed April 3, 2009).

9   This quote is often attributed to Mark Twain. The website Quote Investigator says this attribution is incorrect, and the closest earliest occurrence is attributed to psychoanalyst Theodor Reik in 1965. https://quoteinvestigator.com/2014/01/12/history-rhymes/

There may be little similarity between the threats Rome faced during the time of Marius and Sulla and the dangers faced by America in the 21st century. Still, the fundamental factors that drive peoples' actions, ambition, fear, greed, love, etc., have not changed much. These factors will work out differently given the time, culture, and circumstances as people respond to various events and conditions. But they still exist.

While the parallels between Gaius Gracchus and Franklin D. Roosevelt mentioned earlier are not all that significant in and of itself, there is something to worry about at a deeper level. As we saw, one of the things that caused Roman democracy to fail was the breakdown of law and tradition.

A critical difference between a democracy and a dictatorship is that in a democracy, there are strict rules that govern what those in power can and cannot do. While the superficial parallels tell us little, the more profound disregard for the rules and traditions that such actions reveal is troubling. Once rulers break the norms, they become difficult to re-establish. In Rome, actions that were a source of great controversy when they happened the first time quickly became the new norm everyone followed. The system moved closer to the point of no return.

This idea is not new or revolutionary. The Founding Fathers knew very well the story of Rome. They knew of the other democracies and their failure and the philosophical writing on the strengths and weaknesses of democracy. The resulting system they created included checks and balances.

In the following chapters, I will look at some of these deeper issues and show there are troubling trends. American democracy is well into its own stroll into the desert. I don't think we have yet reached the point of no return, but as we will see, there is at least some cause for concern.

TAXES AND THE
WELFARE STATE

There is no part of the administration of government that requires extensive information and a thorough knowledge of the principles of political economy so much as the business of taxation.
Alexander Hamilton[1]

IT ALL SEEMED SO SIMPLE and straightforward. The war had lasted seven years and was, in fact, the most expensive the country had ever waged to that point in its history. Over the course of the war, the national debt had more than doubled. At least partly, they fought the war to defend a remote area governed by the country. In addition, it had been started by those living there.

Compounding the problem was that those who lived in that area, while prosperous, paid only one-fiftieth of the taxes compared to the average citizen in the rest of the country. Making matters even worse, the government lost significant amounts of tax money from this area due to tax evasion. What better way to pay off the debt incurred during the war than by raising taxes on the people who most benefited from it? This was particularly true given that they were not, in any event, paying their fair share.

---

1   Hamilton, Federalist No. 35 http://www.constitution.org/fed/federa35. htm (accessed April 3, 2009).

But it wasn't quite so simple. Taxes never are, especially to those who have to pay them. Abstract concepts like fairness do not have as much weight as the more concrete reality that suddenly, one has to do with less because they have to pay more than before.

The issue divided even those who did not have to pay the new taxes. Dr. Samuel Johnson, one of the leading thinkers of the period, defended the new taxes, saying taxation was "the supreme power of every community" and that it was, in fact, "considered, by all mankind, as comprising the primary and essential condition of all political society."[2] Yet, his close friend and biographer, James Boswell, disagreed with the government's action, believing that the newly taxed were "well warranted to resist."[3]

Resist they did, which only brought on a more determined effort to collect the taxes on the part of the government. Before long, what had been a resistance to paying increased taxes became a resistance to the government in general and then a desire for independence from that government. Finally came another war, a war for independence. So, what had started as a means for Great Britain to pay off its debt from the Seven Years' War[4] (1756-63) ended in the American War of Independence.[5]

---

2   Samuel Johnson, "*Taxation No Tyranny*", *1775*, in *The Works of Samuel Johnson,* (New York: Pafraets & Company, Troy, 1913); volume 14, 93-144. also http://www.samueljohnson.com/tnt.html (accessed April 3, 2009).

3   James Boswell, *The Life of Samuel Johnson,* (New York: Everyman's Library, Alfred A. Knopf, 1791), 522.

4   Also called the French and Indian War.

5   Paul Johnson, *A History of the American People,* (New York: Harper-Collins, 1997) During the course of the Seven Years' War, Britain's national debt went from £60 million to £133 million. (p. 132). The war had started as a result of the action of a young George Washington in an encounter with the French that left ten French soldiers dead, including their commander (p. 124). At the time, the average Englishman paid 25 shillings per year in taxes while a colonist only paid sixpence, and it is estimated that up to £500,000 was lost each year to evasion of duties (p. 132).

A Strange Paradox

It is a strange paradox that taxes are the lifeblood of government while simultaneously being one of its greatest dangers. During the Middle Ages, government, if it could be called that, was financed by the ruler's wealth.

Yet, as the State evolved and the need for a standing army and more consistent government services grew, the King had to seek additional sources of revenues. Taxes became the primary funding source, and this was a necessary and essential precursor to the establishment of democracy. After all, if the King pays for the government, how can you get rid of the King? Taxes are not only necessary; democracy requires them.

Yet, while they are required, taxes present one of the greatest single dangers for a democracy, particularly a democracy that seeks to better the lives of its citizens. The more a democracy tries to do, the more it costs. The more it tries to meet those costs, the more it is in danger. This paradox is the reason for Alexander Fraser Tytler's famous quote,

> A democracy cannot exist as a permanent form of government. It can only exist until the voters discover that they can vote themselves largesse from the public treasury. From that moment on, the majority always votes for the candidates promising the most benefits from the public treasury with the result that a democracy always collapses over loose fiscal policy followed by a dictatorship.[6]

Serious students of government have long recognized the reason for this paradox. Plato describes this process as resulting from the leaders' desire to please. In order to please the people, the leader needs money to pay for programs that will benefit them. To get the funds, one must go to those with it, the rich. Thus, the ruler

---

6   Alexander Fraser Tytler, *The Decline and Fall of the Athenian Republic, 1776* cited at: http://www.conservativeforum.org/authquot.asp?ID=723 (accessed April 3, 2009).

will "deprive the rich of their estates and distribute them among the people."[7]

Naturally, the rich will not appreciate a ruler who takes their wealth, so they will resist those taxes. Soon, the citizens of the government are split into two groups: the rich, i.e., those who have the money that the government wants, and the people, those who desire whatever the money will buy.

If the rich resist too much, the ruler will "charge them with plotting against the people." To defend themselves, the people always get

> some champion whom they set over them and nurse into greatness… This and no other is the root from which a tyrant springs; when he first appears above ground he is a protector… How then does a protector begin to change into a tyrant? Clearly when he does what the man is said to do in the tale of the Arcadian temple of Lycaean Zeus.[8]

Plato's view does not translate directly into the 21st century. Few know what the man did in the tale of the Arcadian temple of Lycaean Zeus.[9] Still, while the details and specifics deal with Ancient Greece, not modern America, the underlying principles have not changed.

Plato was concerned with the origin and rise of tyranny, what we would now call a dictatorship or totalitarian government. The tyrant starts as one protecting the people, or at least as one who rises to power on that claim. But the bottom line for Plato is that tyranny "has a democratic origin."[10]

---

7   Plato, *Republic, Part IX §8, 565a-d*

8   Plato, *Republic, Part IX §8, 565a-d*
http://classics.mit.edu/Plato/republic.9.viii.html (accessed April 3, 2009).

9   Plato does in fact go on to explain the story and to describe how it parallels the protector's transformation into a tyrant. With the power of the people behind him, he is unrestrained in his pursuit of those who disagree to the point that he is either killed by his enemies or becomes a tyrant.

10   Plato, *Republic, Part IX §8, 565a-d*
http://classics.mit.edu/Plato/republic.9.viii.html (accessed April 3, 2009).

The Core Problem

At its core, the problem that threatens democracy is the same one that most families face with their home budgets – there always seems to be more month than money. Except for the very rich, and perhaps even for them, there is never enough money to do everything one would like.

Even the rich are limited to some extent. While they can afford a lot, they can't afford everything, at least if they wish to remain rich, as many formerly wealthy have found out.

For most, this is not just a problem of luxuries; there are medical bills to pay, braces for the kids, educational costs, not to mention food, clothes, the roof over your head, utility bills, and even the cost of transportation to and from work, or the cost of an internet connection to work from home so that you can make the money needed to pay all the bills.

This struggle goes under the general heading of *The Rat Race*. In short, there never seems to be enough money. Most families have to live within a budget, either a structured and planned budget or an unstructured one where you spend until you run out of money and then wait for the next paycheck.

Democracies face many of these same problems. This problem is particularly acute for the modern welfare state that seeks to better the lives of its citizens through a whole range of government programs beyond the traditional functions of government, like defense and courts.

The modern welfare state adds to this list a range of other activities. These include things like building roads, education, health care, the arts, broadcasting, and scientific research, to name just a few. Like the family budget, there never seems to be enough money to do everything that people, or at least their politicians, want.

When a family faces a money crunch, there are limited options for additional money. They can borrow or change their employment situation by getting a raise, a better-paying job, or a second or perhaps even a third job.

Some families try to get around the shortage by borrowing the money they need. Borrowing can make sense for a significant purchase, such as a house or car used for a long time. But if they use credit to add to their monthly income, while it will work in the short term, it will only be a temporary fix. Credit is not a good long-term option.

Temporarily, one can artificially increase their disposable income with credit. Need an extra $200 per month to make ends meet? Transfer $200 per month of spending onto credit cards, and you solve the problem for a while.

Yet, as balances go up, so do your minimum payments. Before long, that extra $200 per month is consumed by $200 in monthly payments. In short, when you use credit, you create new bills you must pay. In the long term, these new payments only add additional burdens to the monthly budget. Borrowing is not a good option for monthly expenses. Thus, the only real long-term solution for individuals is extra money through a raise, a better-paying job, or another job.

Governments can also borrow money, yet this has a similar effect. Again, for major long-term projects, this can make sense. It can also make sense when dealing with short-term problems with long-term implications, such as wars or recessions.

The government also has the additional rationale that when it borrows money for long-term projects like a highway, the funds will be paid back by those using the road over its lifetime. Some of those using a highway in twenty years may not even be alive today.

An additional option that governments have that families don't, at least not legally, is to print the money. However, this is not a very good option. Simply increasing the number of dollars only makes each dollar worth less. In short, you have inflation, and while you have more money, everything now costs more.

When it comes to additional money, governments have to raise taxes. Raising taxes is somewhat like an individual asking for a raise. Yet, whereas an employee can ask, the government demands under penalty of law.

Therein is the danger, for taxes act as a burden on the economy. If this is clear, you can skip the next section and go directly to Taxes in Action. However, if it is unclear or you question this, then continue reading.

Foundations

The foundation of our entire economic system is providing goods and services for a fee. Businesses either succeed or fail based on whether they provide goods or services that people want at a price they are willing to pay.[11] The companies that do this well tend to make a lot of money; those that don't do not stay in business very long.

When someone gets a job, they are like a business providing a service.[12] Their 'customer' is their employer. They get a job if they can provide a service for which an employer is willing to pay. Now, just as some businesses can charge more for their goods and services, some jobs pay more.

Discussion of the specific price difference involves going into the theory of supply and demand and is beyond this discussion's scope. Still, for a better-paying job or successful business, a person must find a need that no one is meeting or meeting well and address it better than the competition. (We will look more in-depth at competition in the next chapter.)

This issue boils down to a question of simple value. If a business can deliver more value per dollar, it will get more business.

---

11   Willingness to pay includes both the desire to pay and the ability to pay. Someone may desire to purchase a product, and would be willing to pay if they had the money, but if they don't have it, they can't spend it.

12   This is not completely true as there are numerous labor laws effecting employer/employee relationships. Then there are limiting factors such as unions, which actively seek to limit competition and Thus, drive up wages. On the other hand, there is the growing trend of contract work, where employees sell their services to employers as independent business units.

If not, people will go elsewhere if they can. This is what makes monopolies so harmful; there is no real choice for consumers. Monopolies attack the foundations of our economic system.

An employee's service is valuable to the employer because it helps the business meet its customers' needs more effectively. In addition, as the employee has more disposable income, they can purchase more goods and services.

The companies people purchase from generate more revenue and, thus, can buy more goods and services, hire additional employees, or distribute the extra funds to their owner(s), who then can purchase more goods and services. In short, it is a classic win-win situation where everyone does better, and the economy grows.

The problem with the government is that it does not provide goods and services this way. Many people can think of stores or businesses they like. But who wants to deal with the government?

When was the last time you heard somebody say they wanted to go to the DMV or the IRS when not forced by the government? While the government does provide goods and services, they do not compete in the marketplace for business. Instead, they require people to be their "customers."

A business charges for its services based on people's willingness to pay, which is how it gets its money. From these monies, the business must pay for its costs, such as raw materials, labor, taxes, etc. What is left over, if anything, is profit for the owner(s).[13]

Again, if there is a lot of profit, the owner(s) will probably want to invest back into the business so that it grows. If there is not enough profit, it fails. Most do.

As a result, companies have a strong incentive to provide services that people want at a price they are willing to pay. Even when doing so successfully, they must be on guard for others who may come along and do it better.

---

13   This is somewhat of a generalization. For a discussion of some of the nuances here see: Ludwig von Mises, *Human Action, 3rd Edition* (New York: Regnery, 1966), and the section on Entrepreneurial Profit and Loss, 289-294.

No such incentive exists for the government. Most people deal with the government only when required, avoiding it as much as possible. When people do deal with the government, the service is often not good.[14] This difference is not because the people who work for the government are not as smart or talented but because they operate in a different system with different incentives and objectives.

If the government depended on a willingness to pay for revenues, many departments would cease functioning quickly. People would pay in a few areas, like National Parks, but the vast majority would 'go out of business' fast.

After all, how many people want to go to the DMV and pay to have their car registered because they like the services and how they provide them? As such, government services must be mandated and paid for through taxes or required fees.

A classic example of how this leads to different approaches occurs in transportation, where government and private choices exist. When privately run modes of transportation, such as the airlines, don't have enough money, they often try to attract more customers by providing better service or cutting fares. Lower fares mean more riders and more riders result in increased revenues.[15]

When government transportation, such as local bus systems or subways, encounters similar problems, their typical response is

14   During one of my last encounters with government, after waiting to get "served" we finally got to the window and presented all of our documentation, only to be told by the clerk "slow down, we have all the time in the world." It was then I realized that I was more concerned about the people behind me in line than he was.

15   This approach is impacted by government and as airlines have become more regulated, they have also become less focused on providing good service at a low price and more focused on pleasing government. For example, they will at times pull away from that gate, knowing they cannot take off, even though it means passengers will be forced to sit in their seats until they get into the air because that allows them to maintain a good record with the government for on-time departures, even though this comes at the expense of passenger comfort. The more regulated a business is, the more likely it will put pleasing the government ahead of pleasing its customers.

to raise rates. The reason for this difference is that they have different incentives, and therefore they have different reactions.

Both business and government offices focus on satisfying those providing the money that pays the bills. For a private business, that is the customer, and unhappy customers will take their business and their money elsewhere.

With a government office, one might see the person entering the office as a customer. Yet, they do not provide the money to pay the bills, except in the general sense that they are taxpayers. Even as individual taxpayers, they have very little say in how the government spends tax dollars.

In addition, most of the time, they cannot take their business elsewhere. They are there because they are required to be there. For a government office, the ones who provide the money to pay the bills are the politicians who appropriate the funds. They are the ones that employees must keep happy.

Ultimately, the problem with taxes is that they burden the economy. As we saw earlier, a business or an employee can increase revenue by providing additional value for a lower cost, and the net effect grows the economy. Taxes have the opposite effect; they reduce people's spending ability while not providing any additional direct value or a value lower than the increased cost. If your taxes increase, this reduces your ability to spend.

This is not to say that nothing the government does has value; it does and is an issue of value in relation to cost. Given the competition in the marketplace, a primary business concern must be providing the best value for the lowest price, lest customers go elsewhere. There is no competition for the government, so the government tends to be wasteful.

Thus, the government has little incentive to keep costs down. Instead, incentives are frequently reversed. A business that works hard to reduce costs and save money is rewarded with the extra money it did not spend. A government agency or department that works hard to reduce costs and save money will often be 'rewarded' by having its budget cut. They did not use it, so they must not have needed it. In contrast, those who waste money will often have their budgets increased.

This is why so much government spending occurs at the end of the fiscal year, as departments spend large amounts of money to demonstrate that it is really "needed."[16] Furthermore, the government budgeting process often has built-in automatic yearly increases, further insulating departments from any pressure to cut costs.

Thus, the government does not "price" their services based on the willingness of consumers to pay in the marketplace but instead on how much money they think they will need. Because of these different incentives and ways of thinking, government services will often come at a higher cost, usually a much higher one than private businesses.[17]

While getting a better job has a net positive effect on the economy, taxes act as a burden that will often slow economic growth because of the inefficiencies.

Taxes in Action

Tax increases have demonstrated this effect on the economy time and time again when they failed to bring in the expected amount of revenues. While many examples could be given, one good instance occurred in California during the early 1990s. California of the 1990s is also a good case study for, while a solidly democratic state today, in the early 1990s, the control of Gov-

---

16   For example, one study found that while the fourth quarter represents 25% of the year, it accounted for 31% of the spending on contractors, something for which there is some discretion, as opposed to fixed monthly bills. https://globalservicesinc.com/2021/07/30/4th-quarter-q4-spending-statistics-in-government-contracting/ (Accessed 4/8/2023)

17   Along these lines private businesses often find government contracts the most lucrative of all, which sets up additional problems of lobbying for such contracts and businesses that seek them often end up mirroring many of the same inefficient practices.

ernment was split between the parties; therefore, this example is bi-partisan.

Like many states, California spent freely during the good times of the 1980s. During the decade, economic growth was strong. As a result, revenues to the state increased at a very healthy eight percent per year. With all that money flowing in, politicians spent freely, so freely that, as is often the case, the spending increases outstripped the revenue.

While revenues increased at an average rate of eight percent yearly, spending increased at about eleven percent. As a result, the state budget grew from $32.8 billion in 1980 to $72.6 billion by 1989, an increase of 121 percent.

While the economy was strong, California could get away with such increases. There was always more money next year. Still, the problem was that such economic growth couldn't last forever. When the economy eventually did begin to slow, so did revenues. California ended up with a huge budget deficit of $8 billion, the country's most significant state budget deficit at that time.[18]

In response to the deficit, California did what governments tend to do when there is a shortage of money; they 'asked'[19] the taxpayers to give them more. While in this case, they did make some 'cuts' in the state budget, new taxes made up the majority of the shortfall. Thus, California passed a combination of sales tax and income tax increases on 'the rich,' i.e., on those in the upper tax brackets. These tax increases were supposed to produce $7 billion of the $8 billion needed to close the deficit.

While it may have looked good on paper, the politicians failed to consider taxes' adverse economic effects. Rather than bringing in the expected $7 billion in new revenues and closing the budget deficit, the increased taxes caused the economy to slow even more. It slowed so much that not only did the state fail to increase rev-

18   Stephen Moore, "*State Spending Splurge: The Real Story Behind the Fiscal Crisis in State Government*", *Cato Policy Analysis No. 152 May 23, 1991* http://www.cato.org/pubs/pas/pa-152.html (accessed April 3, 2009).

19   Many of the terms in single quotes are discussed in Chapter 7 on Language.

enue by the expected $7 billion, but revenues went down by $1 billion per year over the subsequent two years.[20]

To make matters even worse, while the rest of the nation was recovering from the recession that had initiated the problem, the burden from the 1991 tax increase slowed California's recovery such that real per capita personal income fell 5.6 percent over the next three years.[21] In short, increasing taxes, rather than bringing in more money, cost the state money and reduced people's incomes.

It would seem that California politicians learned little from this experience. After getting out of this hole, just before the first edition was published, politicians again went on a spending spree. When the economy turned down, as it always does, budget deficits soared. Once again, they were the largest in the country. Yet, rather than the $8 billion deficit they faced last time, the shortfall exceeded $40 billion this time.[22]

Lessening The Burden

If increasing taxes depress the economy, resulting in fewer tax revenues than expected, should not cutting taxes conversely stimulate the economy? If stimulated, won't the economy generate more tax revenues for the government than expected such that the tax cuts will not "cost" the government as much as predicted?[23]

20   Alan Reynolds, *"Fixing California"*, *Cato Institute, September 2, 2003*, http://www.cato.org/research/articles/reynolds-030824.html (accessed April 3, 2009).

21   Alan Reynolds, *"Fixing California"*, *Cato Institute, September 2, 2003*, http://www.cato.org/research/articles/reynolds-030824.html (accessed April 3, 2009).

22   *Schwarzenegger: $42 billion deficit weighing down California, USA Today,* 1/15/2009 http://www.usatoday.com/news/nation/2009-01-15-schwarzenegger-california-deficit_N.htm

23   This is sometimes distorted as "cutting tax = more money." While this certainly can and sometimes does happen, it is by no mean automatic. In reality the claim is simply that cutting taxes will have some stimulative effect on the economy that will result in higher *than expected* revenue. Thus, a $10 billion tax cut might not result in the loss of $10 billion in tax revenues, for some of the $10 billion will be regained in taxes resulting from increased economic growth

The answer is yes, and this also has many historical examples going back at least as far as the Presidency of Calvin Coolidge. Following the significant increase in spending and taxes during World War I, Coolidge sought to reduce both from their wartime highs. As he described his plan in a speech before a meeting of the Business Organization of the Government in 1925,

> We have met this evening to take counsel together for the purpose of securing greater efficiency in government by the application of the principles of constructive economy, in order that there may be a reduction of the burden of taxation now borne by the American people. The object sought is not merely a cutting down of public expenditures. That is only the means. Tax reduction is the end.[24]

For Coolidge, tax reduction was an essential function of government, as it freed the people to have more money, leading to better lives and more freedom.

> We are seeking to let those who earn money keep more of it for themselves and give less of it to the Government. This means better business, more of the comforts of life, general economic improvement, larger opportunity for education, and a greater freedom for all the people. It is in essence restoring our country to the people of our country. It reendows them not only with increased material but with increased spiritual values.
>
> It can not be too often emphasized that the property of this country belongs to the people of this country. The Government can not touch a cent of it save for a public purpose. Government extravagance is not only contrary to the whole teaching of our Constitution, but violates the fundamental conceptions and the very genius of American institutions. It is the high privilege of the people of this country to spend their own money.[25]

because of the reduced burden on the economy.

24   Calvin Coolidge, *Address at a Meeting of the Business Organization of the Government, June 22, 1925*
https://www.presidency.ucsb.edu/documents/address-meeting-the-business-organization-the-government (accessed on 3/17/2003)
25   Calvin Coolidge, *Address at a Meeting of the Business Organization of the Government, June 22, 1925*

As the tax cuts took effect, the resulting revenues were higher than expected, making it possible to do even more in subsequent years.

> As a result of Coolidge's budget and tax policies, it unleashed a period of economic growth and expansion. It also resulted in low unemployment and an increase in the standard of living for the middle-class.[26]

Tax cuts in the 1960s, 1980s, and more recently, 2003 also saw this effect. Following the 2003 tax cuts, for example, by mid-2005, revenues were 14 percent higher, while the budget deficit dropped by nearly $100 billion more than projections.[27]

While it is not always the case, some tax cuts result in more revenues than predicted and an increase over the pre-tax cut projection—part of the 2003 tax cuts involved cutting the capital gains tax from 20 to 15 percent.

At the time, the Congressional Budget Office (CBO) predicted this cut in the capital gains tax would correspondingly reduce the money the government would receive. Before the tax cut, the CBO estimated that the government would receive $186 billion in revenues from capital gains taxes over three years.[28] But when Congress passed the tax cut, the CBO reduced this to $147 billion, a reduction of $39 billion resulting from the lower rates.[29]

---

https://www.presidency.ucsb.edu/documents/address-meeting-the-business-organization-the-government (accessed on 3/17/2003)

26   John Hendrickson, *Budget and Tax Lessons from President Calvin Coolidge, Calvin Coolidge Presidential Foundation, Dec 10, 2014,* https://coolidgefoundation.org/blog/budget-and-tax-lessons-from-president-calvin-coolidge/#_edn1 (accessed 3/17/2003)

27   Review & Outlook, "Windfall for Washington", *Wall Street Journal, July 15, 2005, pg A10* http://www.opinionjournal.com/editorial/feature.html?id=110006973 (accessed April 3, 2009).

28   *Congressional Budget Office, "Budget and Economic Outlook : Fiscal Years 2004-2013, January 2003", Table 3.5 pg 82* http://www.cbo.gov/ftpdocs/40xx/doc4032/EntireReport_WithErrata.pdf (accessed April 3, 2009).

29   *Congressional Budget Office, "Budget and Economic Outlook : Fiscal Years 2004-2013, January 2003", Table 3.5 pg 82* http://www.cbo.gov/ftpdocs/40xx/doc4032/EntireReport_WithErrata.pdf (accessed April 3, 2009).

When the tax cuts took effect, the results were somewhat different. Rather than the reduction in revenues that the CBO had expected, revenues increased, exceeding not only the predicted $147 billion but the original pre-tax cut prediction of $186 billion.

When the CBO analysts finished, they noted that the actual revenues received from capital gains taxes over the three years following the tax cuts were $216 billion. This result was $30 billion more than expected before the tax cuts and $69 billion more than anticipated after them.[30] In this case, cutting taxes resulted in more money, not less.

Theoretical Limits

Now, there is, at least in theory, a limit on a democratic government's ability to raise taxes, and that is the people's willingness to pay. If taxes increase too much, people will complain, politicians will get worried, and see the new programs the taxes were to support as unnecessary. At least, this is the theory.

The Founding Fathers understood this well. Taxes were one of the main issues sparking the Revolution. Taxation was a significant concern for writers of the Constitution. Federalist Papers 30-36 were devoted to this subject. Taxation deserved this much treatment, for as Hamilton observed early in Federalist #30,

> Money is, with property, considered as the vital principle of the body politic; as that which sustains its life and motion and enables it to perform its most essential functions.[31]

Not only did they recognize it as a necessity, they also recognized its dangers. Madison noted,

---

30   *Congressional Budget Office, "Budget and Economic Outlook : Fiscal Years 2005-2014, January 2004", Table 4.4 pg 112. www.cbo.gov/ftpdocs/49xx/ doc4985/01-26-BudgetOutlook-EntireReport.pdf* (accessed April 3, 2009)
31   Hamilton, Federalist No. 30 http://www.constitution.org/fed/federa30. htm (accessed April 3, 2009).

the apportionment of taxes on the various descriptions of property is an act which seems to require the most exact impartiality; yet there is, perhaps, no legislative act in which greater opportunity and temptation are given to a predominant party to trample on the rules of justice.[32]

Hamilton wrote on this subject that,

The ability of a country to pay taxes must always be proportioned in a great degree to the quantity of money in circulation and to the celerity with which it circulates.[33]

Then, in a later Federalist, #35, Hamilton added,

There is no part of the administration of government that requires extensive information and a thorough knowledge of the principles of the political economy so much as the business of taxation. The man who understands those principles best will be least likely to resort to oppressive expedients, or to sacrifice any particular class of citizens to the procurement of revenue. It might be demonstrated that the most productive system of finance will always be the least burdensome.[34]

The concern was not just that taxation would become too burdensome on the economy but that the burden would not be fairly distributed. "Every shilling with which they overburden the inferior number is a shilling saved to their own pockets."[35] The tax the Founding Fathers designed was an attempt to strike a balance between the needs of the government for revenue and the dangers inherent in taxation.

A significant change to this balance occurred during the early 20th century with the passage of the 16th amendment to the U.S. Constitution, allowing for the progressive income tax system. The issue was further complicated when the collection of taxes was

---

32   Madison, Federalist No. 10 http://www.constitution.org/fed/federa10. htm (accessed April 3, 2009).

33   Hamilton, Federalist No. 12 http://www.constitution.org/fed/federa12. htm (accessed April 3, 2009).

34   Hamilton, Federalist No. 35 http://www.constitution.org/fed/federa35. htm (accessed April 3, 2009).

35   Madison, Federalist No. 10 http://www.constitution.org/fed/federa10. htm (accessed April 3, 2009).

made much easier in 1943 with the establishment of the current income tax withholding system. These two changes have allowed the government to tax at ever-growing rates while significantly reducing the opposition of those paying the taxes. The effect on the government's ability to tax has been dramatic.

How Much Do We Even Pay?

The Federal Government's budgeted spending for the fiscal year 2008 was $2.9 trillion. In 2022, it was $6.3 trillion, and this was after most of the extra expenditures resulting from COVID-19 had expired. These amounts are so large that they are utterly incomprehensible for most people. They are just numbers with no real meaning other than that they are really, really big. When combined with increases due to inflation and growth in the population, it is hard to comprehend just how much the government has grown. Often the attitude is, 'Yes, the budget has grown, but then so has the country'.

The current tax code is highly complex, and this complicates matters further. The government taxes so many things in so many ways, with so many exceptions, deductions, and credits, that it is extremely difficult for anyone to know how much they pay in taxes, even to the federal government, much less state, county, and city.

Then there are the hidden taxes; taxes passed on to you in the cost of the goods and services you purchase. In short, it is virtually impossible to determine what you precisely pay in taxes even if you want to.

Because of all this complexity and confusion, a fundamental disconnect would exist between government spending and taxes, even with a balanced budget. But the budget is not balanced and has not been for a long time. Since 1960, the federal government has been in the red every year, except for 1999 and 2000. These deficits further disconnect spending from taxes.

Suppose the 2008 budget had been $2.8 or $3.0 trillion. Would you know what impact that would have had on your taxes? Given the deficits, would it have any at all? And yet that is a difference of $100 billion from the $2.9 trillion projected.

To try and get some sort of handle on this, every year for the last 40 years, an organization called the Tax Foundation has waded through federal, state, and local government economic reports to come up with a summary of government spending. They seek to answer how much it costs us. To put all this confusion into some perspective, they have devised a way of measuring this, which they call Tax Freedom Day.

The Tax Foundation calculates Tax Freedom Day by taking government figures on income and taxes. They then determine the percentage of income, on average, the government takes to pay for all the programs it funds. This calculation gives them a single overall "effective tax rate." They then use this to determine "Tax Freedom Day," the day you theoretically have earned enough money to pay all your taxes for that year.

Tax Freedom Day is when you can start working for yourself instead of the government. Given the vast complexities of the tax system, this is not a good measure of any single person's taxes, as some will pay more, others less. Still, it gives a good idea of the relationship between the taxes people pay and government spending.

More importantly, because it is fundamentally a percentage for individuals, it eliminates issues such as inflation and the size of the country. As such, it shows the trend in taxes from year to year and decade to decade; the overall direction is evident and problematic. For the early part of the nation's history, as the Tax Foundation Report notes,

> The United States has traditionally been a low tax nation. From the founding of the country until the early part of the twentieth century, the United States was in part defined by

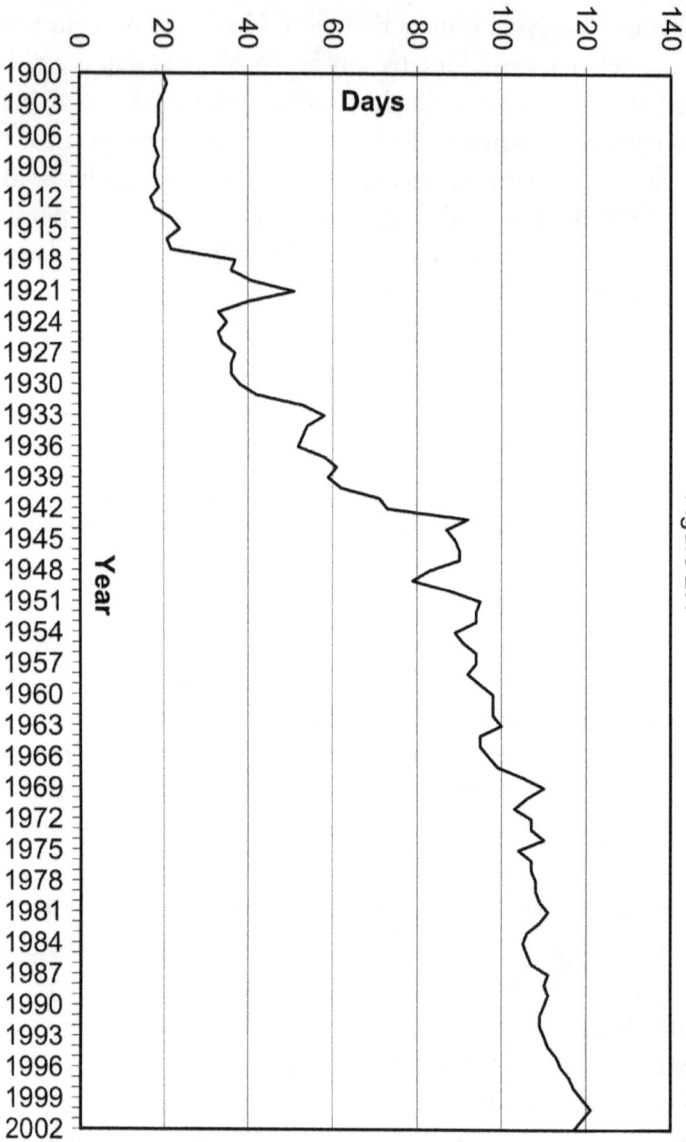

Days Worked to Pay Taxes
Figure 2.1

its mistrust of government power and its correspondingly low taxes.[36]

As such, it would appear that the checks and balances the Founding Fathers put in place to control the dangers of taxation worked pretty effectively.

At the beginning of the 20th century, Tax Freedom Day was January 22nd, meaning you had to work the first 22 days of the year to pay your taxes. After that, you could spend everything you earned in the other 343 days on your expenses, housing, food, vacations, or whatever you wanted. This level of spending meant an overall effective tax rate of 5.9 percent between federal, state, and local taxes.

As shown in Figure 2.1, Tax Freedom Day declined slightly until 1918, when it jumped sharply, coinciding with our entrance into World War I. Given the increased government expenses during a war, this is not too surprising.

After the war, while Tax Freedom Day dropped from a high of 53 days, it only dropped to 35 days in 1923 and again in 1925. This new "low" was about 60 percent higher than the pre-war level. Following this post-war low, it started a steady increase.

The next big jump occurred during the 1930s with the Great Depression when Tax Freedom Day exceeded its World War I highs, jumping to the 50s and then even to the low 60s, reaching a new high of 66 days in 1940.

In this light, the reason for the depression lasting so long becomes much more apparent. When the economy was struggling, the government significantly increased the tax burden, making it impossible for the economy to recover. Thus, the worst part of the Depression was in 1937, five years into the New Deal's attempts to reverse it.

Then came the start of World War II. At this point, the levels of taxation were already at historic highs, three times their pre-

36 *Tax Foundation, Special Report, April 2008, No. 160* http://www.taxfoundation.org/files/sr160.pdf (accessed April 3, 2009

World War I levels, but the demands of the war meant it had no place to go but up. By 1943, Tax Freedom Day set a new high, occurring on April 4, 94 days into the year. This new high meant an effective tax rate of 25.7 percent, which marked a whopping 327 percent increase over the tax burden at the century's start.

Given the demands of World War II, again, this is understandable. But following the war, while there was some drop, it was not very much. By 1949, Tax Freedom Day came down to only 81 days, over double its pre-depression value and four times the lows of the early part of the century. By the following year, it was back into the 90s, where it spent the rest of the decade usually exceeding even its World War II highs. In 1960, Tax Freedom Day exceeded 100 days for the first time in American history.

Following Kennedy's tax cuts, it dropped down, hitting a "low" of 98 days in 1965, a low that still exceeded the highs reached during World War II. Following this new "low," it started up once again, heading for new highs. In 1966, it passed 100 for the last time, topping out at 114 in 1981. Following Regan's tax cuts, it dropped to a new "low" of 107 by 1984. But then, once again, it started climbing ever higher and higher.

At the beginning of the 21st century, Tax Freedom Day set a new record, occurring on May 3, 123 days into the year, with an effective tax rate of 33.6 percent. It dropped back to a "low" of 106 days following tax cuts in 2003. Still, as many times before, it rose again, climbing to 113 days in 2008.[37] Since the first edition, it has grown slightly until further tax cuts brought it back to 105 days in 2019.

This increase represented an astounding 459 percent growth in taxes over the century. More importantly, this new high in 2000 occurred during peace and economic growth. The country was not at war; even the Cold War had been over for a decade, giving the

---

37   Not all of these increases reflect actual tax increases. Some of the increases are the result of people moving into higher tax brackets as a result of economic growth.

country a "Peace Dividend." There were no other unusual events to require extra spending by the government.

While the economy was slowing and heading for a recession, this was still in the future and was not yet a factor in spending. This spending was the new "normal." When we did slide into a recession and then went to war following the attacks on 9/11, the need for government spending once again shot up from this new low.

Looking over the entire century, a few things become clear. Before World War I, the tax burden on the American people remained relatively low and declined slightly. The significant increases in the tax burden between 1917 and 1945 occurred during times of major problems facing the government: World War I, The Great Depression, and World War II.

Another clear trend, however, is that once these problems passed, while there was some movement toward the earlier and lower tax burden, it was mainly marginal and temporary. So, while clear concerns justified the new taxes, although the higher taxes probably lengthened, not shortened, the depression, once the justification disappeared, the taxes mostly remained.

Since World War II, there has, on the whole, been a fairly steady increase in the overall burden. While partly due to the Cold War and conflicts such as Korea and Vietnam, these do not explain the steady increases. Nor do they account for the rise during the 1990s. The Cold War ended in 1989, and the country had peace and prosperity.

Another thing the graph shows is that while we have had "major tax cuts," the effect of these has been relatively minor and, on the whole, temporary. Even after the tax cuts, the total tax burden increased by 459 percent over the century.

This increase is before we consider that the first decade was a period of decline. The effective tax rate went from 5.9 percent in 1900 to a low of 4.9 percent in 1909, while 1906 and 1907 had 5.1 percent rates. The rate for 1910 was 5.0 percent, and this was

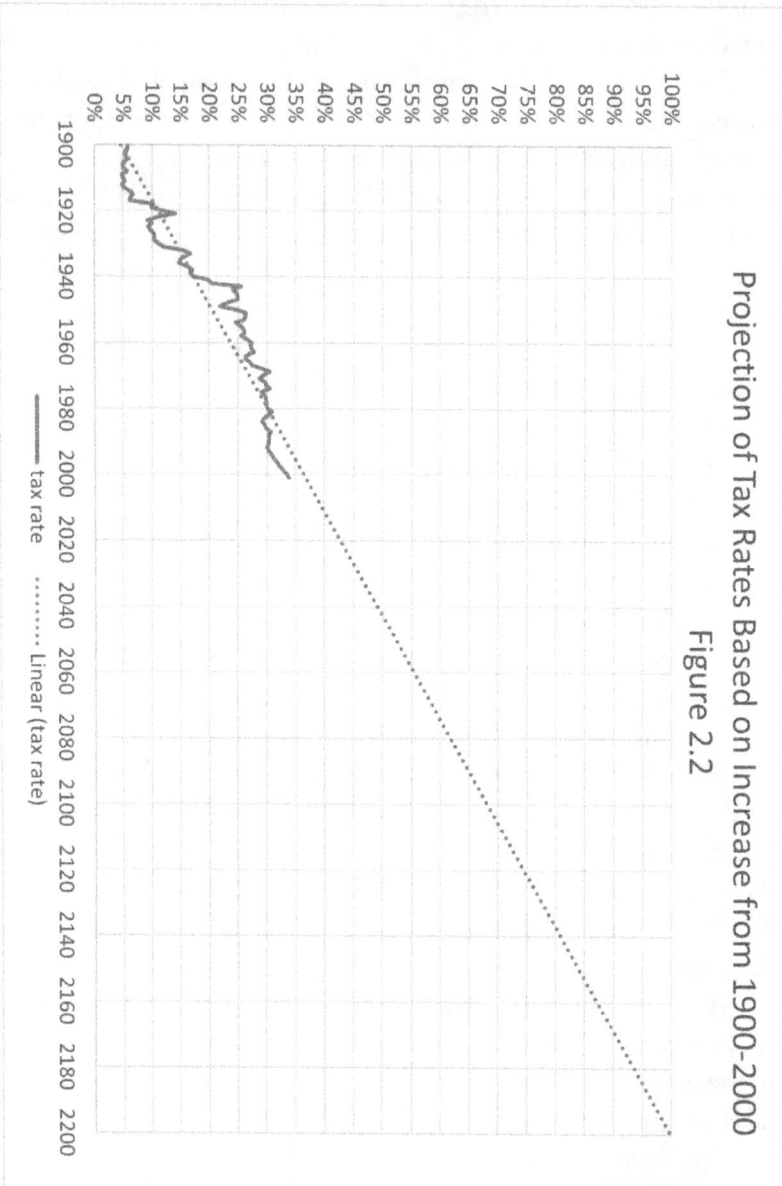

Projection of Tax Rates Based on Increase from 1900-2000
Figure 2.2

nearly a 17 percent decrease. If we calculate the increase using the low for the century instead of the rate in 1900, it would be an astounding 585 percent!

Looking Ahead

The country cannot maintain such a phenomenal rate of increase. If taxes go up only 300 percent during this century, it will be at a 100 percent effective tax rate by the end of the century. At such a rate, you would spend all your time working to pay your taxes with nothing left to pay for your living expenses. This is impossible.

A more reasonable projection would be to take the rate of increase in taxes over the last 100 years and project this into the future. I have done this in Figure 2.2, showing that if the current trend continues, we will reach a 100 percent tax rate around 2200.

But again, this is impossible, as a 100 percent effective tax rate is impossible.[38] The point is not to show that we will reach a 100 percent effective tax rate in any particular year. Any number of assumptions could have a tremendous effect on this projection.

Instead, it is to show that the trends that have existed over the last 100 years cannot be maintained. At some point, long before we reach a 100 percent effective tax rate, the burden on the economy will become too great, and the system will collapse.

Unfortunately, no one knows where this collapse will take place. We are on a 'stroll into the desert,' and the point of no return is approaching. But we don't know if it is close or still some distance away, and we only know we cannot continue in this fashion forever.

We certainly will not be able to maintain this rate of increase in taxes for another 100 years. And yet, as we look to the future, the need of the government for more money to fund programs such as Medicare and Social Security is vastly larger than even

---

38 Note that only a 100 percent overall effective tax rate is impossible. It is entirely possible to have 100 percent tax rate, or even greater, on a narrow section of the economy, i.e., if you make over a certain amount of money, the government will take it all the money over that limit, and possibly even penalize you for doing so.

today's record highs. Yet, politicians still push for expansions of existing and new programs.

A significant problem is that a primary driver for growth in the tax burden is that the government has become increasingly involved in daily life, providing more services that people depend on. The real danger is that once the tax burden reaches the point where the economy can no longer support it, it will decline.

At that point, the only thing the government can do to revive the economy is to reduce the burden causing it. However, with the decline, the demand for government services will likely increase when they need to cut.

Given the history of the last century, in all likelihood, the burden will increase, further hastening the economic system's collapse. As the Great Depression showed, increased taxes during financial problems only slowed recovery. In short, if the trend continues, we are headed for precisely the type of failure predicted by Alexander Fraser Tytler's quote at the beginning of this chapter,

> with the result that a democracy always collapses over loose fiscal policy followed by a dictatorship.[39]

The Problem With Theory

Of course, this analysis depends on the assumption that these trends continue. Some will argue that we are doing okay and there is no need to worry. Yet, as you look at the trend over the last 100 years, when will this change? If taxes are not too high yet, when will they be too high? As we go deeper into the desert, where is that point of no return?

As was pointed out earlier, in theory, in a democracy, if the tax burden becomes too high, the people can always demand that the government reduce their taxes. But herein lie three other prob-

---

39   Alexander Fraser Tytler, *The Decline and Fall of the Athenian Republic, 1776 cited at:* http://www.conservativeforum.org/authquot.asp?ID=723 (accessed April 3, 2009).

lematic trends. While the tax burden has increased over the last century, the tax code has become more complex and challenging to understand. It is also becoming increasingly more progressive. Finally, the federal government has increasingly looked to borrowing rather than taxes to fund increased spending.

A tax code that is complex and difficult to understand is a problem, for how can we know if our taxes are too high if we do not know what we are paying? This problem is further compounded by withholding, as many people overlook their gross pay or how much the government takes. They focus on how much they get to take home, particularly if they have direct deposit: out of sight, out of mind.

The quickest way to start a tax revolt would be to end withholding and have people write a check to pay taxes. Just to be clear, I am not suggesting that we do this. Still, forcing people to write a check would remind people how much they pay, at least in income taxes. Many people have told me they don't pay income taxes; they get a yearly refund. As we will see shortly, this is very possible. Still, I suspect many of these people did not realize that the refund was just how much they overpaid, not how much they paid.

Then, there is the issue of hidden taxes. Companies see the taxes they pay as just another cost of doing business, and thus, something they build into their price, like labor and materials. Therefore, in a very real sense, they do not pay taxes; their customers do.

One somewhat visible example of this is gas prices. When you look at the cost of gas around the country, there is a slight difference due to location resulting from transportation costs, but it is relatively minor. Most of the difference is due to the different taxes from state to state.

As I write this, AAA reports for two states leading in oil production, Texas, had a price of $3.248 per gallon. In contrast, California's price was $4.880, $1.632 higher because of taxes. Given that oil companies must pay for the cost of finding, drilling, producing, refining, and transportation, Governments make far more on a gallon of gas than the oil companies. Still, people rarely blamed taxes for the high cost of gas, which is fine by the government. We return to gas prices in Chapter 8.

The second problem is that taxes have become more progressive. On the one hand, some progressivity is good, as those who make more pay more. Those with the most money carry the most significant share; those who can least afford taxes pay the least. But like much in life, if you have too much of a good thing, it becomes a problem. Table 2.1 shows data from the IRS provided by the Joint Economic Committee showing the distribution of taxes for the year 2000.[40]

This table shows that the bottom 50 percent of people filing returns paid only 3.91 percent of the taxes. This percentage is down from 6.46 percent in 1986, or a 39 percent reduction. The top 25 percent increased their share from 76.02 percent to 84.01 percent in the same period. Thus, the overall tax burden grew and shifted onto an ever smaller percentage of the population.

Percentiles Ranked by AGI*	Adjusted Gross Income Threshold on Percentiles	Adjusted Gross Income Share Percentiles	Percentage of Federal Personal Income Tax Paid
Top 1%	$313,469	20.81%	37.42%
Top 5 %	$128,336	35.30%	56.47%
Top 10%	$92,144	46.01%	67.33%
Top 25%	$55,225	67.15%	84.01%
Top 50%	$27,682	87.01%	96.09%
Bottom 50%	<$27,682	12.99%	3.91%

*Adjusted Gross Income

Percent of Income and taxes for 2000 by Income.

Table 2.1

---

40   Joint Economic Committee, Press Release, Oct 24, 2002 http://www.house.gov/jec/press/2002/10-24-02.htm (accessed April 3, 2009).

While generally a good concept, the problem is that it creates a dangerous imbalance and threatens one of the primary checks in the system.

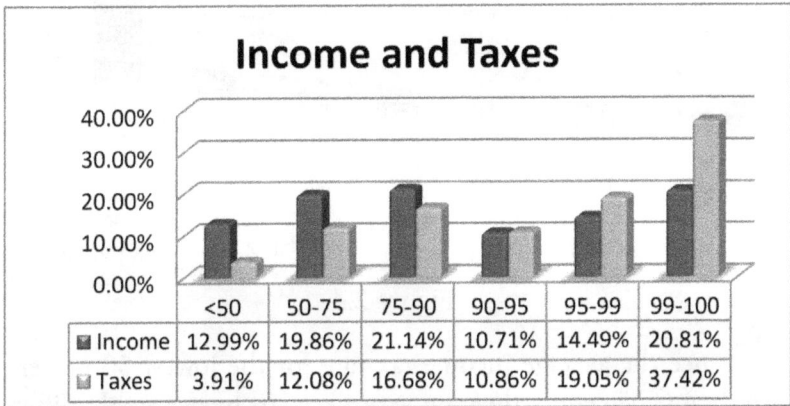

Income and Taxes

	<50	50-75	75-90	90-95	95-99	99-100
Income	12.99%	19.86%	21.14%	10.71%	14.49%	20.81%
Taxes	3.91%	12.08%	16.68%	10.86%	19.05%	37.42%

Figure 2.3

Figure 2.3, Income and Taxes, shows this imbalance in the share of income earned compared to the percentage of income taxes paid. As this figure shows, the first 90 percent of those filing income tax returns pay a smaller share of income taxes than their share of income. The top 5 percent pay a higher percentage of income taxes than their share of income.

We can see this imbalance better by looking at the share of taxes paid minus the percentage of income earned, as is done in Figure 2.4. As this figure shows, the first 90 percent of income earners pay less of a share of income taxes than the share of income they earn, while those above 95 percent pay more.

As mentioned earlier, if taxes get too high, people can vote to lower them. But what does this mean when most people pay only 3.91 percent of all income taxes? These percentages are only personal income taxes and do not consider the monies paid by corporations or other hidden taxes that individuals do not pay directly or see.

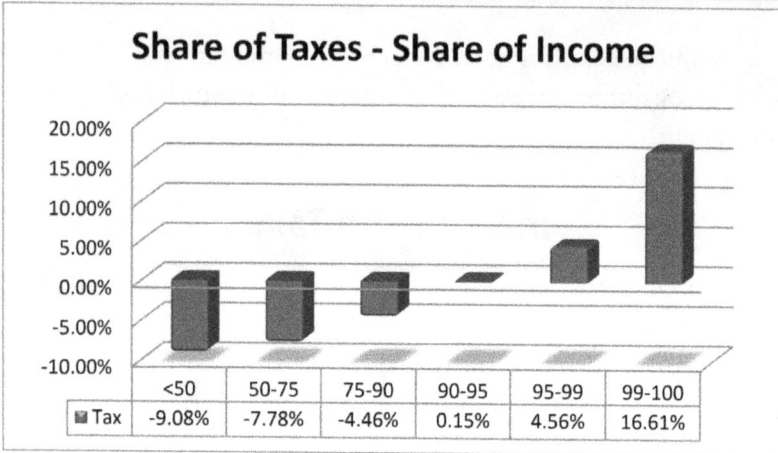

Share of Taxes - Share of Income

	<50	50-75	75-90	90-95	95-99	99-100
Tax	-9.08%	-7.78%	-4.46%	0.15%	4.56%	16.61%

Figure 2.4

Since the average income tax rate for the lowest 50 percent is only 4.6 percent,[41] they are very likely to have a vastly different view on whether taxes are too high than those in the top 25 percent, whose average rate is 19.09 percent or those in the top 1 percent whose average rate is 27.45 percent.[42] Again, this is only federal income tax.

Some would argue that we should look at other types of taxes. While this is undoubtedly legitimate, other taxes have different rationales. For example, payroll taxes pay for specific programs such as Social Security and Medicare. As such, the Social Security tax is more a retirement system payment than a general tax to fund the government. In addition, according to the U.S. Treasury Department, as of April 30, 2023, individual income tax revenues make up 52 percent of all federal revenues.[43] Social Security and Medi-

---

41   Joint Economic Committee, Press Release, Oct 24, 2002 http://www. house.gov/jec/press/2002/10-24-02.htm (accessed April 3, 2009).

42   Joint Economic Committee, Press Release, Oct 24, 2002 http://www. house.gov/jec/press/2002/10-24-02.htm (accessed April 3, 2009).

43   U.S. Treasury Dept, *How much revenue has the U.S. government collected this year?* Government Revenue | U.S. Treasury Fiscal Data, (Accessed, May, 31, 2023)

care make up another 34 percent. So, when talking about the taxes to pay for government, income taxes make up the vast majority.

The next most significant source of revenue comes from Corporate Income Taxes at 8 percent.[44] Should these be counted as a separate source of revenue or a hidden tax that people must pay in the end, passed on by Corporations as a cost of doing business? However you look at this, while the numbers may shift a bit, the core problems remain.

Thus, why shouldn't the majority of people continue to demand and vote for more and more government services and programs when they pay only a fraction of the bill if anything at all? There is little incentive to cut taxes, and considerable incentive to increase them.

Finally, there is the problem of the growing deficit. Like a family using credit cards to fund monthly expenses, the government has increasingly sought to increase spending while not increasing taxes. Initially, this was done with increased borrowing. In recent years, this has increasingly come from expanding the money supply, the modern-day equivalent of printing money.

While there was little difference between Tax Freedom Day based on taxes and debt, this has changed. Recently, the Tax Foundation started reporting a Tax Freedom date that includes deficit spending. For pre-COVID 2019, Tax Freedom Day was April 19, yet if you factor in the deficits, it was May 8, 19 days later.

Again, this could be justified if this were for long-term spending or short-term problems with long-term consequences. Yet, it has become the norm even for the good times. It is like a family using credit cards to meet monthly expenses. The interest payments by the government are growing and already represent 8% of the federal budget.[45]

---

44   U.S. Treasury Dept, *How much revenue has the U.S. government collected this year?* Government Revenue | U.S. Treasury Fiscal Data, (Accessed, May, 31, 2023)

45   How much has the U.S. government spent this year? Fiscal Data, U.S. Treasury. Federal Spending | U.S. Treasury Fiscal Data (Accessed, April, 9,

If these trends continue, that is, a problematic and confusing tax code, a steadily increasing tax burden, an increasingly progressive tax burden, and growing deficit spending, disaster is inevitable.

On the positive side, there are periodic calls for tax cuts and some pass. Yet, as we have seen, these only temporarily slow the tax growth. Once the burden comes down, the economy begins to grow. In a growing economy, the burden of taxes becomes less critical. In addition, as the economy grows, revenues to the government increase, and this is money politicians of both parties are all too eager to spend.

Tax Cuts For The Rich?

As a result, even with periodic tax cuts, the overall trend of the tax burden is to increase. Yet, to get these cuts passed, those proposing the reductions try to mitigate the charge that inevitably comes from opponents: that the tax cuts are "for the rich."

To avoid these charges, the tax cuts typically result in an even more progressive tax system. With the tax cuts in 2003, "the highest percentage tax cuts go to the lowest income Americans."[46] Such cuts temporarily ease the tax burden and, thus, improve the short-term situation.

Yet, they do so at the cost of further unbalancing the system by shifting taxes onto an ever smaller percentage of taxpayers, making further cuts even harder. After all, how can you have meaningful tax cuts that are not "for the rich" when the rich pay the vast majority of the taxes?

Some dispute this shifting of the burden, but a 2004 CBO study on the effects of these tax cuts demonstrated it. The CBO projected that if these tax cuts had not occurred, the top 20 percent of those filing income tax returns would have paid 78.4 per-

---

2023)
46   George W. Bush, *The President's Agenda for Tax Relief,* http://www.
ustreas.gov/press/releases/reports/report30652.pdf (accessed April 3, 2009).

cent of the total income tax burden in 2004. Yet, due to the tax cuts, this increased nearly 4 percentage points to an even higher 82.1 percent. On the other hand, those in the lowest 40 percent saw their share of income taxes drop from -0.1 to -2.8 percent.[47] Yes, those last numbers were negative.

How can you have a negative percentage of taxes paid? Easy; it means that because of the various credits given to low-income earners, the government, on average, sent more money to the people in this group than was received in taxes. Thus, on average, for the lowest 40 percent of those filing returns, the income tax was a source of additional income rather than something they had to pay.[48]

So, while cutting overall taxes, these tax cuts further increased the imbalance by shifting the burden of taxes away from the majority and onto an ever-smaller minority. Someone for whom income tax is a source of income is likely to have a significantly different view of whether taxes are too high than someone who has to pay.

Supporters of the tax cut did this to avoid the charge of "tax cuts for the rich." Yet, this charge is effective because of the progressive nature of the income tax system. If the rich pay the most taxes, any effective tax cut will be for the rich. Thus, opponents attack any such tax cut with complaints about how it could fund various government programs and how the rich are not paying their 'fair share.'

There are numerous problems with such claims. For one, just who 'the rich' are is rarely specified. This is because it is much more effective to leave this term vague. For example, if the rich are the top 25 percent of income earners, then as we saw in Table 2.1,

---

47   *Congressional Budget Office, "Effective Federal Tax Rates Under Current Law, 2001 to2014", August 2004, Table 2 and Table 3, http://www.cbo.gov/ showdoc.cfm?index=5746&sequence=0* (accessed April 3, 2009).

48   This represents over all figures for this group. It does not mean that this is true for everyone in this group as again, because of the complexities of the tax system, taxes can vary greatly from person to person.

in 2000, 'rich' started at $55,225. I would guess that few, if any, making this income level think of themselves as rich. Even if we limit this charge to those with the highest incomes, there are still some problems.

For example, one IRS study reported on the top 400 income tax returns for the years 1992-2000. One of the interesting findings was that most of the people were not on this list very long. Of the 400 people in any given year, only about half could expect to be on the list the following year. Only 21 people were on the list for all nine years, while 1,679 people fell into this category only once. Thus, the IRS treats people who do well one year as if they have been rich and will remain so for the rest of their lives.

This study highlights another problem with the concept of 'rich' regarding income taxes. When we think of the rich, we usually think of people with lots of money. But having money and earning money are not quite the same things. After all, consider someone who works very hard one year and, with salary, overtime, and bonuses, earned $100,000. Would we see them the same way as someone who does not work but has millions of dollars invested, such that they make $100,000 from these investments? Probably not, but to the IRS, they are both equally 'rich.'

In fact, from the IRS's point of view, the person who works hard to earn $100,000 may be 'richer' than the person who has millions of dollars. This is because what is essential to the IRS is not just income but taxable income. A multi-millionaire might have most of their money invested in tax-free bonds. While they may have considerable income, they may have little or no taxable income and, thus, may pay little in taxes.

There is a mismatch here. When we talk about the rich, we are talking about wealth. Yet, when we talk about income taxes, we are talking about income, and income and wealth are different.

In any event, the real problem is that this tax-the-rich rhetoric feeds into precisely the problem with democracy stated by Plato earlier in this chapter. Again, Plato said that the leader, to gain favor, would "deprive the rich of their estates and distribute them among the people."[49] This problem also goes to the heart of Tytler's statement that,

> the majority always votes for the candidates promising the most benefits from the public treasury with the result that a democracy always collapses over loose fiscal policy followed by a dictatorship.[50]

We are heading for disaster based on the long-term trend that has existed for the last 100 years. The ever-increasing taxes will continue to burden the economy until it can no longer maintain economic growth. At that point, we will enter into an economic decline.

Once this happens, the only way to correct the problem would be to reduce the tax burden. Still, given the increasingly progressive nature of the tax system and the growing dependence on government programs, this will be extremely difficult, if not impossible. As the economy declines, the need for these same services will increase. As such, the system will collapse into chaos.

The European Example

One only has to look at Europe to understand the government's problems. Most European countries have extensive welfare states and correspondingly high taxes to support them. The burden on the economies in many countries of Europe is so high that they are increasingly falling behind.

Jean-Philippe Cotis, the chief economist at the Organization for European Cooperation and Development, based in Paris, warned in early 2006 that,

---

49   Plato, *Republic, Part IX §8, 565a-d* http://classics.mit.edu/Plato/republic.9.viii.html (accessed April 3, 2009).

50   Alexander Fraser Tytler, *The Decline and Fall of the Athenian Republic, 1776 cited at:* http://www.conservativeforum.org/authquot.asp?ID=723 (accessed April 3, 2009).

At current trends, with demographics the way they are, the average U.S. citizen will be twice as rich as a Frenchman or a German in 20 years.[51]

When politicians have attempted even modest reforms to address the growing stagnation, the results have frequently been thousands taking to the streets in protests and, in some cases, riots.

For example, in March 2006, the French Government tried to address the growing unemployment problem among younger workers that had reached a rate of 24 percent. The problem was the high cost of benefits and the difficulty in firing problem workers under French law. Given this, employers were reluctant to hire younger workers with little or no track record.[52]

The government's solution was to allow employers to fire younger workers without cause during their first two years. This change would reduce the risk of hiring a younger worker, thereby reducing the high unemployment rate for that age group. As one news story described the result in their opening paragraph,

> PARIS – French students and unions insisted Sunday they will go ahead with a one-day national strike and more street protests unless the government withdraws a youth labor law that has sparked violent demonstrations and shut down universities.[53]

In other European countries, attempts at any economic reform to reduce the burden stifling their economies met with strong resistance. In 2004, an estimated 495,000 people turned out in Berlin, Cologne, and Stuttgart to oppose economic reforms proposed by German Chancellor Gerhard Schröder.[54]

---

51   *The European Disease, Wall Street Journal, Feb 8, 2006, pg A16.*
52   Robert J. Samuelson, "The French in Denial",
Washington Post, March 28, 2006; Page A23 www.washingtonpost.com/wp-dyn/content/article/2006/03/27/AR2006032701301.html (accessed April 3, 2009).
53   Jean-Marie Godard, "French Unions Vow to Hold Major Strike",
The Associated Press, March 26, 2006 http://www.accessmylibrary.com/coms2/summary_0286-14036668_ITM (accessed April 3, 2009).
54   Deutsche Welle, "Mass Protests Show Public Distrust of Reform Programs" April 4, 2004 www.dw-world.de/dw/article/0,,1161417,00.html (accessed April 3, 2009).

The German protests were part of a much larger series across Europe as people resisted their governments' attempts to reduce the burdens stifling their economies.[55] When the changes are most needed, public pressure by those depending on the services and protection makes the necessary modifications extremely difficult, if not impossible. Europe might have already passed the point of no return.

What Can Be Done

How can this be avoided? The best way to fix the system is to restore the checks and balances, a key feature of which would be tax simplification. As we have seen, the current system is so complicated that it is challenging for people to know what they actually pay and impossible to understand how their taxes relate to government spending.

For most people, taxes are one of their most significant, if not the largest, expense. Yet, unlike their other expenses, few know how much they pay in taxes. Frankly, many people, and probably most, do not even know how much they pay in income tax. They only know how much their refund was. But their refund is only a measure of how much they *overpaid* during the year, not how much they paid. Thus, many see tax time as when they get money, not when they must pay.

There are many different possible solutions. One is to simplify the tax system greatly in some fashion. Another is replacing the current progressive income tax system with a flat tax, where everyone pays the same rate after personal deductions. This change would retain some of the progressive nature of the tax code so those who earned more still pay more. The key, however, would be that everyone would pay the same rate.

To simplify the math, say there was a 15 percent flat tax rate with a personal deduction of $10,000. A person who made

55   BBC News, "Europe's pensioners hit streets", April 3, 2004
http://news.bbc.co.uk/2/hi/europe/3596351.stm (accessed April 3, 2009).

$35,000 would first subtract the personal deduction of $10,000, leaving $25,000 in taxable income. At a 15 percent rate, this would result in a tax of $3,750.

On the other hand, if a family of three made the same income, they would have a personal deduction of 3 x $10,000 or $30,000. This would leave a taxable income of $5,000, with a resulting tax of $750. If a single person made $100,000, they would do the same and subtract their deduction of $10,000, leaving $90,000 in taxable income for which the tax would be $13,500. So, even with a flat tax, you would maintain the principle that those who make more pay more.

Yet, as the rate is the same, any increase would affect all or at least everyone with incomes above the amount allowed for personal deductions. The government could still increase the progressive nature of the tax system by increasing the personal deduction.

Still, even here, all would have the same deduction. In the current system, not only do the rates go up as you make more, but you also lose deductions, resulting in more taxable income and, thus, higher effective tax rates.

Another benefit of such a simplified system would be a closer link between the tax rate people pay and the government's spending. In the current complex system, with its many different rates and the vast number of deductions, it is unclear how spending increases affect taxes. But with a flat tax, estimating how much a spending increase would affect the tax rate would be possible.

Again, to simplify the math, let's say a 15 percent tax rate covered the 2008 budget of $2.9 trillion. If everything else remained the same, increasing the federal budget to $3.0 trillion would mean increasing the tax rate to 15.52 percent to keep up. On the other hand, cutting federal spending to $2.8 trillion could decrease the tax rate to 14.48 percent.

It would not be quite this simple. As we saw above, changes in taxes affect the economy. Still, the critical point is that it would at least be possible to talk somewhat intelligently about the relationship between government spending and taxes.

The current system almost completely disconnects government spending from taxes. Even when politicians talk about how they will pay for a new program, this rarely translates into terms the average citizen could understand concerning the difference they will pay.

Yet, with this system, if spending went from $2.9 trillion to $3.0 trillion, the family of three mentioned above paying $750 would see their taxes go up $25.86 to $775.86. On the other hand, the single person making $100,000 would see their taxes go up $466 to $13,966.

This ability to connect spending to taxes would be a vast improvement over the current system, where it is virtually impossible to tell the effect of such an increase. As a result, there is seemingly little, if any, link at all. This lack of a clear link is particularly true given how much the government now borrows each year.

Another Way

Another proposal is called "The Fair Tax."[56] It scraps the income tax altogether, replacing it with a national "consumption" or sales tax. Under the Fair Tax, there is an equivalent of the personal deduction seen in the flat tax, but here, it takes the form of a 'rebate' for a portion of the tax paid in advance each month.

At the beginning of each month, everyone would receive a check from the government, reimbursing them for a portion of the sales taxes they would pay that month. The government would determine the rebate based on the poverty level such that those close to it would not pay tax. Those above the poverty level would effectively be paying taxes only on money they spent beyond the poverty level or whatever level the government sets.

Again, the Fair Tax would still be somewhat progressive because the rich would pay more simply because they consume

---

56   The Fair Tax, www.fairtax.org (accessed April 3, 2009).

more. More importantly, like the Flat tax, the rate and the rebate (deduction) would be the same for everyone.

As such, this would have the same benefits of simplicity and linking taxes to spending as did the Flat Tax. There are additional economic benefits to the Fair Tax, such as encouraging savings, outside the scope of this discussion[57].

Many of the drawbacks to the Fair Tax stem from something that plagues most significant reforms. There are always two parts to any proposed change: the new system and the transition to that system. While often treated as the same, they are quite different.

The Fair Tax, as a system, has a lot of merits. Still, switching to such a tax has a lot of problems to address. For example, with the Fair Tax, taxes only occur when you spend money on something. Great, that encourages people to save rather than spend.

Still, what about the people who save money under the old system? Many had already paid taxes on that money when they earned it. Yet, when they spend it now, they will be taxed again. How are we going to deal with this issue of double taxation?

The critical aspect of these approaches or any other solution is a more explicit link between taxes and spending. Also, these approaches treat everyone the same. If politicians need more money to pay for additional government programs, the rates will increase for everyone.

The majority of people would not be able to impose higher taxes on a minority to pay for government programs they want but do not wish to pay for themselves. Thus, either of these proposals would restore one of the key checks and balances needed to preserve democracy.

With the increasing visibility of taxes and the more explicit link between taxes and spending, we could bring the steady growth in taxes seen over the last century under control. If we don't get it under control, we are just going deeper into the desert.

---

57   In short these benefits stem from the fact that whatever you tax you tend to get less of. As such, an income tax tends to suppress the earning of income, while a consumption tax would tend to suppress consumption. Thus, a movement to a consumption tax would tend to stimulate growth in income, and in savings.

PLANNING VS COMPETITION

The failure of European bureaucracy was certainly not due to the incapacities of the personnel. It was an outcome of the unavoidable weakness of any administration of public affairs.

Ludwig von Mises[1]

THE PEACEFULNESS OF the early San Francisco morning broke suddenly and without warning. Officer Jesse Cook was making his rounds. He had stopped to talk to a vegetable seller busily preparing for the coming day's business.

Then, just off the coast of Mussel Rock, deep under the Pacific Ocean, the tectonic plates that had been locked together suddenly broke free and began slipping roughly against each other. The resulting shock waves radiated from the epicenter at 7,000 miles per hour.

Officer Cook's first warning of the impending destruction was "a deep and terrible rumbling."[2] Standing near the Embarcadero and looking west down Washington Street, he saw the street ripple wave-like as if made of water. The streets began to split open, and,

---

1   Ludwig von Mises, *Bureaucracy,* (Libertarian Press, Grove City, PA, 1983) 61.
2   Simon Winchester, *A Crack In The Edge Of The World* (HarperCollins Publishers, 2005) pg. 244.

as Officer Cook later described it, the buildings started to "tumble and fall and kept me pretty busy for a while dodging bricks."[3]

The San Francisco earthquake began at 5:11:58 AM. The noted scientist George Davison, 81 years old at the time and living in San Francisco, timed the length of the quake at about one and a half minutes.

Amongst all the destruction caused by the earthquake, numerous small fires broke out. These grew and spread and began to link up. Soon, they were large and hot enough to create their own winds, feeding them further. By noon, a wall of fire stretched a mile and a half long, smoke extending two miles into the sky.

To make matters worse, the earthquake broke most of the water mains feeding the fire hydrants. The fire burned for three days, dying out only after the fire breaks, created in the city with dynamite, deprived it of any more fuel.

The devastation was enormous. The earthquakes and fire killed over 3,000 people, destroying over 28,000 buildings. Around half of the pre-earthquake population of 400,000 were left homeless.[4]

Despite this devastation and the vast numbers left homeless in the wake of the earthquake and subsequent fire, economist Thomas Sowell observed that,

> When the *San Francisco Chronicle* resumed publication a month after the earthquake, its first issue contained 64 advertisements of apartments or homes for rent, compared to only 5 ads from people seeking apartments to live in.[5]

Approximately 75,000 left following the earthquake, while 30,000 lived in temporary shelters. This still meant that in the chaos following the earthquake, the city absorbed nearly a quar-

---

3   Simon Winchester, *A Crack In The Edge Of The World* (HarperCollins Publishers, 2005) pg. 245.

4   Simon Winchester, *A Crack In The Edge Of The World* (HarperCollins Publishers, 2005) pg. 301-2.

5   Thomas Sowell, *Basic Economics: A Citizen's Guide to the Economy* New York: Basic Books, 2004), 30

ter of its pre-quake population, such that 30 days later, when the paper resumed publishing, people were advertising to find renters.

Compare this to the experience of Sweden following World War II. Rather than leaving things to chance, Sweden took a more planned approach, one aspect of which was to control the price of housing. In 1950, there was such a housing shortage that it took, on average, nine months to get a house. This waiting time grew steadily such that by 1958, the average time it took to get an apartment had grown to 40 months.[6]

This shortage was not due to the number of apartments suddenly decreasing. In fact, during this period, the number increased even faster than the population.[7] Yet, while the number of apartments per 100 people increased, those waiting to get an apartment grew from 2,400 in 1948 to 24,000 in 1960.[8]

The cause of the housing shortage in Sweden was not fewer housing units but rather the Swedish government's attempt to have a plan that included price controls on housing.

Such price controls have three effects. First, they will often limit supply by limiting the production of new homes. The Swedish government attempted to deal with this issue by increasing production. Second, they also limit supply through people holding on to homes longer. They might do this simply because the price is low or the supply of alternative housing is limited. For example, someone holds onto an otherwise too-large home rather than moving to something smaller.

Price controls also increase the demand. An artificially low price will mean that people who otherwise could not afford a home, at least by themselves, will now try to get one. Others might decide they can afford a second home. One can easily argue

6   Thomas Sowell, *Basic Economics: A Citizen's Guide to the Economy* New York: Basic Books, 2004), 24

7   Thomas Sowell, *Basic Economics: A Citizen's Guide to the Economy* New York: Basic Books, 2004), 23

8   Thomas Sowell, *Basic Economics: A Citizen's Guide to the Economy* New York: Basic Books, 2004), 24

that not needing a roommate to share expenses is more desirable. Still, two people seeking homes are twice the demand compared with two people seeking to share a home.

For Sweden, the net effect of their planned approach kept housing prices so artificially low that the gap between the numbers of people seeking houses and those available constantly grew, even with new housing units growing faster than the population. Contrast this with the uncontrolled "chaos" following the San Francisco earthquake. Here, there was a huge decrease in supply and a corresponding increase in those needing houses. Yet, there were houses and apartments for rent thirty days later.

Another Paradox

In this contrast lies another paradox that poses a grave danger for democracies. In the last chapter, we examined the paradox of how taxes, which are the very lifeblood of government, pose one of the greatest threats.

Yet, taxes are simply a means to an end. While politicians may seek to raise taxes on the few to gain the votes of the many, merely raising taxes does very little. The whole purpose of increasing taxes is to fund programs to improve people's lives.

A vital aspect of any democratic government is freedom. As Thomas Jefferson stated, "It is to secure our rights that we resort to government at all."[9] He also said, "The equal rights of man and the happiness of every individual are now acknowledged to be the only legitimate objects of government."[10] Yet, the more democracies try to improve their citizens' lives, the less freedom they will have.

The most straightforward and apparent reason for this loss of freedom is that, for the government to do anything, it must

---

9   Thomas Jefferson to M. D'Ivernois, 1795. http://etext.virginia.edu/jefferson/quotations/jeff0150.htm (accessed April 3, 2009).
10   Thomas Jefferson to A. Coray, 1823. http://etext.virginia.edu/jefferson/quotations/jeff2.htm (accessed April 3, 2009).

restrict or control behavior to one degree or another. Granted, this is not absolutely true. The government could, for example, build a park, which one might easily see as expanding freedom or at least the quality of life.

Similar arguments apply to government projects such as interstate highways and water projects.[11] Still, while possibly large undertakings, these are a relatively small part of government action. For most activities, particularly those involving planning, the government must remove from people the freedom to act in specific ways.

Some of these restrictions on freedom are necessary and good. We do not, for example, want people to be free to murder, so the government passes laws against murder. For safety reasons, we remove from people the freedom to decide which side of the road to drive and limit how fast they can go. A whole range of governmental restrictions are necessary and reasonable. Still, the critical point is that for the government to act, some freedom must be given up.

Then, there is the relationship between need and revenue. One aspect of this is straightforward: the greater the need, the more revenue required to address it. Yet, the founders, notably Alexander Hamilton, writing in Federalist 30, saw the reverse as also true. There, he stated,

> I believe it may be regarded as a position, warranted by the history of mankind, that *in the usual progress of things, the necessities of a nation in every stage of its existence will be found at least equal to its resources.*[12] (emphasis in original)

11 Even in these areas, there is some loss of freedom. If nothing else, there is the loss of freedom to spend the money taxed to pay for these projects, but this is often insignificant compared to the benefit such projects provide, even after considering the waste inherently involved in government projects. In addition, these benefits are often societal, rather than individual. For example, the interstate highway project greatly improves the movement of goods and improves the overall economy, benefiting even those who never use the system.

12 Hamilton, Federalist No. 35 https://founders.archives.gov/documents/Hamilton/01-04-02-0187 (accessed July 11, 2023).

Hamilton's point was that as the nation became more prosperous, its needs would likewise grow. Thus, there would be enough money for the government to tax. Yet, this is a two-edged sword. What about money and power taken by the government for a short-term need? Once the need passes, the government will find some other justification or some new requirement to retain the power and money. Thus, the need will continually expand to match the money. The government's ability to find justification will always match the money it has.

The Double Nickel

The abovementioned issues are generally simple and straight-forward but are not without problems. An excellent example is the life and death of the federal 55 mph speed limit.

During the 1970s Arab Oil embargo, President Nixon, to reduce oil consumption, proposed lowering the speed limit, and Congress passed the federal 55 mph speed limit in 1973.[13] As with everything the government does, this came at the cost of freedom. In this case, we lost the freedom to drive faster than 55 mph without the threat of a fine. But this was not the only freedom lost. State governments also lost the freedom to control their highways' maximum speed. In exchange for this loss of liberty, we reduced our dependence on foreign oil. While the embargo lasted, most people accepted this exchange and slowed down to save oil.

The oil embargo came and went, and yet like so many laws, even when the reason for the restriction of freedom was gone, the federal government was very reluctant to give up its control and return this issue to the states. With the oil embargo gone, supporters began substituting other reasons to justify the continued loss of freedom and why the Federal government needed this control.

Since saving fuel was no longer a significant concern, they justified the 55 mph speed limit by claiming it saved lives. This

13   Clocking the 55 mph Debate, *Washington Times,* June 7 1995, http://www.ibiblio.org/rdu/a-clok55.html (accessed April 3, 2009).

reasoning was a catch-all that could justify anything. Such issues are always trade-offs. If saving lives were the only concern, why not make the maximum speed limit 45, 35, or even 25? That, too, would save lives.

The issue also exposed what is, in the Western States, a well-known problem, yet one often ignored in the Northeast, where most of the population lives. Different states have different circumstances.

Compared to the West, the Northeastern states are crowded. If you live in New York City, you are about half a day's drive from several other major cities. You can travel from Washington, D.C., to Boston in a day, passing Philadelphia and New York City on the way. The trip would take you through six states, with several others within easy reach. Traffic congestion will be a significant concern.

The West is sparsely populated by comparison, and traffic congestion is virtually non-existent, even in the cities. New York and Philadelphia each have populations larger than many Western states, while Washington, D.C., and Boston have populations comparable to many Western states. In the West, it can take several hours to drive to the closest city, one that is a small fraction of the size of those in the East.

If you want to go from the capital of Montana to the capital of the neighboring state of Wyoming, that will take you about 30% longer than the trip from Washington, D.C., to Boston, with no other major cities in between. Today, the trip will take you approximately 10.5 hours without counting stops.

As a result of the much larger distances and lower populations, the answer to the question: "Why do you need to go faster," is likely to have a vastly different answer in the West than in the East. Traveling only 70 rather than 55 cuts drive time by about 20 percent. In the East, the time saved is usually less than an hour; in the West, it is often several hours. Given the distances involved and the need for rest, it could be a day. Just going to the store could be an all-day affair in many places.

As a result, for the next 20 years, many, particularly in the larger western states, lobbied to have the federal speed limit repealed, yet to no avail. Then, Congress changed hands. After two decades of struggle and with a lawsuit looming in the federal courts, the new Congress repealed the national 55 mph speed limit in 1995, returning the issue to the states.

Today, speed limits vary by state. A few Northeastern states have a maximum speed limit of 65, and most others have 70. Seven states have 80, and in a few parts of Texas, it is 85. This variability is what the founders intended.

Most issues are best solved locally by the people involved. The life experience of a New Yorker, who might not even own a car and with access to subways and other public transportation, will be significantly different than someone living in a rural part of a Western state with an hour or more drive to the nearest store. Each will have little understanding or possibly even comprehension of the situation faced by the other.

An interesting side note to this debate was that rather than the higher death rates predicted by those wanting to keep the 55 mph limit, deaths, injuries, and injuries/100 million vehicle miles actually fell following the law's repeal.[14]

Government Increase

The Founding Fathers understood these issues. Too little power and the government cannot act effectively. Too much, and it suppresses liberty. Under The Articles of Confederation, the federal government had too little power and was ineffective. Many, like Hamilton, wanted a new system that would better balance the ability of the Federal Government to rule without threatening

---

14   Stephen Moore, "Speed doesn't Kill", *Cato Policy Analysis No 346,* May 31, 1999. http://www.cato.org/pubs/pas/pa-346es.html (accessed April 3, 2009).

liberty. This effort resulted in the Constitution's increased power, with dual sovereignty split between the state and federal governments and controlled by a series of checks and balances.

The federal government maintained a reasonably limited role from the time of the Constitution until the Progressive era. Progressives rejected the founders' view of checks and balances in favor of an active and more powerful Federal Government that could get things done. This change began during the presidency of Theodore Roosevelt, continued with Woodrow Wilson and WWI, but increased dramatically with the presidency of Franklin Roosevelt.[15]

Not only did FDR break tradition by seeking and winning a third and then even a fourth term, but more importantly, he fundamentally changed the federal government's role. Roosevelt needed a much larger and more powerful federal government to do what he wanted, so he sought one.

At first, the Supreme Court blocked some of his efforts by ruling many of his programs unconstitutional. In response, he attempted to change the court's composition to get a court permitting him to do what he wanted. While his efforts to pack the court failed, he finally did get a court more willing to side with him. The result has been an ever-growing federal government.

The stated goal of this larger federal government was a government that could do more for the people. The more it sought to do, the more it grew. We can see this in the steady tax growth required to fund the government discussed in the last chapter.

Freedom Decrease

Not only does the increase in taxes threaten democracy, but the sheer size of the government itself also does. As the government grows, our freedom to make choices must decrease. Not

---

15   See, Elgin Hushbeck, *The United States Constitution: A History,* Gonzalez FL: Energion Publications, 2022), 49-69

only does a larger government directly limit freedom through laws and regulations, but there are more subtle and indirect limitations.

For one, we no longer have the freedom to make choices we would otherwise have made, simply because after we pay so much of our income to the various levels of government in the form of taxes, we no longer have enough money left. Perhaps we would have chosen to go out to dinner, make a significant purchase, or take a vacation. But we no longer have those options because we no longer have the money after taxes.

As we saw in the last chapter, the effective tax rate went from 5.9 percent to 33.6 percent by the end of the century. This difference represents a loss of freedom to control 27.6 percent of your income.[16] Thus, the government, not you, will now determine how to spend 27.6 percent of your money.

In addition, the more the government does for people, the more the people will be dependent on the government. People dependent on something, whether on the government or something else, are not as free as those who are not.

Social Security is an excellent example of this. Many people now depend on Social Security, and thus, the government, for a significant portion of their retirement income. As a result, there is no real choice about whether or not to have a Social Security system. Representatives made that decision during the 1930s, and now too many people depend on it. We could not get rid of it even if we wanted to.[17]

Not only is the option of getting rid of Social Security gone, but even the options for modifying it are minimal. For example, as mentioned before, many people across the political spectrum agree that Social Security will face severe problems in the future, one that is ever nearer. Yet, all efforts to address these problems

---

16   This is income before tax, not take-home pay. Measured in terms of take-home pay, the percentage would be an even higher 37%

17   These comments should not be taken as an argument to eliminate Social Security. Rather it is simply pointing out that once the government takes on such commitment it is very hard, if not impossible, to go back.

have failed because so many people depend on it. Since they rely on it, they are very resistant to any changes.

The critical danger here is that, in its effort to improve people's lives, the government will make so many commitments that people depend on, it cannot keep all of them. It is very easy for a politician to commit to solving a problem, especially when the resulting government programs are phased in slowly, with the actual cost postponed for many years.

Promises, Promises

Experience has shown that the government often vastly underestimates future costs. While the current program might fit into today's budget, particularly if they borrow the money, the costs often escalate far beyond the projections as the government implements the complete program.

Say you wanted to have a house built. You get some land, find a contractor, and develop plans that combine what you want with what you can afford. Once you finish the plans and the cost estimates, you begin construction.

Before long, you discover that the estimates were off. Digging the foundation was a lot more expensive; material costs were higher. At every turn, things cost more than the estimates. In addition, you discover that you did not account for many things in the plans and, thus, the estimates. You will need a retaining wall and landscaping, which you did not include. Then, of course, you will need new furniture for some rooms. At every turn, prices are higher than expected.

For this to happen the first time you build a home is not all that uncommon. But what if you build houses for a living, and these unexpected cost overruns were both the norm and very large? This is the government's experience. In 1970, Medicare cost $7.7 billion;[18] by 2000, it cost $224 billion. Nor has the government gotten much better at predicting future costs.

18   *Answers.com, s.vv. "Medicare Act (1965)"* http://www.answers.com/top-

An expansion of Medicare added a prescription drug benefit that went into effect in 2006. Supporters initially estimated the cost at $400 billion over ten years. Once passed into law, yet before the law took effect, those costs jumped to $395 billion in just five years.[19] In fact, the costs rose so quickly that some were concerned that the program's cost through 2010, just the first four years, could exceed projections by as much as $750 billion.[20]

In short, the risk is that the government could promise more than it can afford. This danger is not just a theoretical possibility. Some would argue that our government has already made many more promises than it can ever afford. According to a study by Jagadeesh Gokhale and Kent Smetters on the long-term cost of programs the government has already committed to:

> ...the Fiscal imbalance associated with today's U.S. federal fiscal policy is very large. Taking present values as of fiscal-year-end 2002 and interpreting the policies in the federal budget for fiscal year 2004 as "current policies," the federal government's total Fiscal Imbalance is equal to $44.2 trillion. ...Our estimate of federal Fiscal Imbalance is more than 10 times as large as today's debt held by the public.[21]

To get some idea of how enormous $44.2 trillion is, consider that the entire 2008 federal budget was only about $3 trillion. And yet, rather than attempting to cut back, politicians continue to pass even more laws, expanding old programs and creating new ones.

So, what will happen when people depend on these government programs, but the government cannot meet the commit-

ic/medicare-act-1965 (accessed April 3, 2009).
19   Peter Baker, "President Sends '06 Budget to Congress"
Washington Post, Feb 8, 2005, pg A01 http://www.washingtonpost.com/ac2/wp-dyn/A4563-2005Feb7 (accessed April 3, 2009).
20   Spyros Andreopoulos, "Medicare Part D threatens program budget"
SFGate, Feb 27, 2008, http://www.sfgate.com/cgi-bin/article.cgi?f=/c/a/2008/02/27/EDBJV8O9K.DTL (accessed April 3, 2009).
21   Spyros Andreopoulos, "Medicare Part D threatens program budget"
SFGate, Feb 27, 2008, http://www.sfgate.com/cgi-bin/article.cgi?f=/c/a/2008/02/27/EDBJV8O9K.DTL (accessed April 3, 2009).

ments that it made decades earlier? What will the government do when it has reached a limit on how much it can tax and still does not have enough money to meet the promises made by politicians? In many respects, this is driving the steady increase in taxes and borrowing seen in the last chapter, which will bring the country to disaster if not stopped.

A Controlling Interest

But as if these problems were not enough, there is a deeper philosophical issue at work here that only fully came to light in the 19th and 20th centuries and was highlighted in the example at the beginning of this chapter. The issue is not about whether there should be control but how to achieve it.

There is no doubt that for society to remain orderly and operate effectively, there must be some control over the actions of individuals. Freedom must be limited to some degree. Be it control over crimes such as murder or safety issues such as which side of the road to drive on, there must be some control.

Historically, societies achieved control through community standards, religion, and the law. Community standards generally served as the first means of control, whether in the form of village customs or social morals. These standards describe acceptable actions and what brings disapproval. Society enforces these with peer pressure and stigma.

Religion provides both a moral framework and a second means of control, providing supernatural support for moral actions. We will have more to say on this in chapter nine.

Still, for some actions, community standards and religion are insufficient as a means of control. Even though there is a community standard or a religious injunction against a particular activity, if one is willing to suffer the consequences of being looked down upon by the community or rejects religion as false, one is still free to act in that manner.[22] Society looks down on liars, but that does not stop all people from lying.

So, while community standards and religion may be satisfactory for controlling actions such as lying, some activities, such as murder, are so unacceptable that societies will not tolerate even limited violations of the standard. As a result, they require a more powerful means of enforcement. At this point, they bring the power and force of the government into play as a means of enforcement, which requires laws.

The law plays a significant role in how society defines itself; what will be allowed and forbidden. As society has become more complex and the economy more important, controlling the economy has increasingly become a significant issue.

Capitalism

Over several hundred years, in terms of the economy, another means of control began to take shape in the writings of philosophers like Locke and Hume. These ideas came to full force in the writings of Adam Smith, in particular his *Inquiry into the Nature and Causes of the Wealth of Nations,* published interestingly enough in 1776. Smith saw this new means of control as enlightened self-interest governed by competition.

According to Smith, we should not measure a nation's wealth by the amount of gold or silver owned by the government. Rather than being found in government treasuries, we see the true wealth of a nation in its people, along with the goods and services they produce. By using people's self-interest to accumulate more, the wealth of a country can increase. As Smith saw it,

> According to the system of natural liberty, the sovereign has only three duties to attend to; three duties of great importance, indeed, but plain and intelligible to common under-

---

22   An exception to this would be when the religion is the government or is able to enlist government to enforce its rules. However, in these cases religion is functioning as a government and its religious teachings are effectively laws.

standings: first, the duty of protecting the society from violence and invasion of other independent societies; secondly, the duty of protecting, as far as possible, every member of the society from the injustice or oppression of every other member of it, or the duty of establishing an exact administration of justice; and, thirdly, the duty of erecting and maintaining certain public works and certain public institutions which it can never be for the interest of any individual, or small number of individuals, to erect and maintain; because the profit could never repay the expense to any individual or small number of individuals, though it may frequently do much more than repay it to a great society.[23]

As Will and Ariel Durant characterized this in their *The Story of Civilization,* "Here was the formula of Jeffersonian government, and the outline of a state that would enable the new capitalism to grow and flourish exceedingly well."[24] And flourish the United States did.

Today, we can clearly see capitalism's benefits in the prosperity it created and the resulting increase in living standards. No other economic system has lifted so many people out of poverty and continues to do so as it continues to spread.

Still, in another example of the difference between a system and the transition to that system, the transition to capitalism was not easy. For the average worker, it was downright painful. As described by the Durants,

> Both employer and employee had to change their habits, skills, and relations. The employer, dealing with ever more men, and in a faster turnover lost intimacy with them, and had to think of them not as acquaintances engaged in a common task, but as particles in a process that would be judged by profits alone... We must not idealize the condition of the common man before the Industrial Revolution; nevertheless we may say that the hardships to which he was subjected were such as had tradition, habituation, and in many cases the open air to

23   Adam Smith, *The Wealth of Nations (1776), Book II.* http://www.bibliomania.com/2/1/65/112/frameset.html (accessed April 3, 2009).
24   Will and Ariel Durant, *The Story of Civilization X: Rousseau and Revolution.* (New York: Simon and Schuster, 1967), 771.

soften them. As industrialization advanced, the hardships of the employee were mitigated by shorter hours, higher wages, and wider access to increasing flow of goods from the machines. But the half century of transition from craft and home to factory, after 1760, was for the laborers of England one of inhuman subjection sometimes worse than slavery.[25]

For many, competition, with its winners and losers, is harsh and seems chaotic and inefficient. These problems were aggravated further by the unbridled competition that led to exploitation and monopolies that marked the early phases of capitalism.

A common misperception is that capitalism is an anything-goes system. Nothing can be further from the truth. For capitalism to work effectively, there must be real competition and choice. Capitalism aims to construct a system where the best interest of individuals, in general, will also lead to the best interest of society as a whole.

Capitalism requires a carefully drawn framework of laws and regulations. Too much or too little regulation and competition and choice suffer. Most, if not all, of the problems of Capitalism occur when the system allows the individual's self-interest to overwhelm the best interests of society as a whole.

For example, effective competition and consumer choice are the heart of capitalism. The more you limit either of these, the less capitalism you have. Still, for the business owner, competing is difficult. It is in the self-interest of the business owner to eliminate competition and create a monopoly. Yet, monopolies destroy competition and, as a result, choice. Rather than an expression of capitalism, they are an enemy of it. It is the role of the government to prevent them. If they exist, the government has failed in its function.

---

25 Will and Ariel Durant, *The Story of Civilization X: Rousseau and Revolution.* (New York: Simon and Schuster, 1967), 677.

A 'Scientific' Alternative

As a result of the problems that plagued early capitalism during the 19th century, an alternative began to gain ground: Socialism. Socialism is a very broad term, encompassing many subgroups from its more extreme forms found in Communism and Fascism[26] to the more benign forms of Democratic Socialism currently found in much of Europe.

But they all have a crucial component that sets them apart from Capitalism. Controlling the economy utilizing centralized planning is a significant component of Socialism. Instead of the chaos of uncontrolled competition found at the core of Capitalism, Socialism emphasizes planning. As F. A. Hayek notes,

> Socialism means the abolition of private enterprise, of private ownership of the means of production, and the creation of a system of 'planned economy' in which the entrepreneur working for profit is replaced by a central planning body.[27]

Hayek discusses pure political theory, and there is ultimately no such thing as a pure Socialist or Capitalist government. Rather than two binary choices, economics is a spectrum with actual governments falling somewhere between and mixing these approaches. Still, the difference between Capitalism and Socialism is not trivial.

Competition leaves choices to the marketplace. Individual consumers decide what they wish to purchase and how much they

---

26   Fascism and Communism are often viewed as political philosophies on opposite ends of the political spectrum. While significant differences exist between them, and they were strong rivals, they also have a lot in common. Both are forms of socialism, and it was very common for adherents to move between them. Along these lines, it is interesting to point out that Hitler's party was actually called the *National Socialist German Worker's Party* or *National Socialism*. The word Nazi is actually a popular contraction of Nationalsozialismus or National Socialism. For a more in-depth discussion on the relationship between Fascism and Communism, and why they are incorrectly seen as opposites, see my book, *Seeking Truth*, Energion Publications, 2022.

27   F. A. Hayek, *The Road to Serfdom, 50th Anniversary edition* (University of Chicago Press, 1944) 37.

are willing to pay for it. Businesses then compete to provide goods and services they think consumers will want at a price they are willing to pay. Those businesses that best meet consumer demand at a price they are willing to pay will succeed. Those businesses that don't will either reform themselves or they will fail. The result is that consumers get what they want at the best price.

Socialists see this as wasteful. When a company produces a product consumers do not want, they waste money and effort. When a business fails, the capital and effort that went into that business is lost. To avoid this waste, they look to planning.

In a planned economy, the government, not the consumer, makes the ultimate economic decisions. Different types of socialism have different levels of planning and control. Communism and Fascism make almost all of the decisions; the main difference being that Communism holds that state ownership is a prerequisite for the plan, whereas Fascism allows private ownership just as long as there is still strict state control to follow the plan. Democratic Socialism makes only some of the more critical decisions. But the core of socialism is that, ultimately, it is the government, not the consumer, which controls the economy. You can do what you want within the confines of the plan.

As mentioned above, a key factor driving the move to planning was the suffering caused by the transition to Capitalism. No one had ever done this before, and people were literally working out how this new system worked as they went along. In addition, the government also was learning how much control was too much or too little. All the while, the economy was undergoing fundamental changes. As such, it was not until the end of the 19th century and the beginning of the 20th that people realized the need for Anti-Trust laws.

A crucial second factor in the move from the chaos of competition to organized central planning was the growing desire of some to bring the principles of science to the problems of society. After all, the 19th-century view was that science allowed people to control and manage the physical world, tame nature's chaos, and provide a more comfortable life.

Why not apply the same scientific principles to the economy as well? Why not use science to manage the economy better and achieve a more equitable allocation of resources, making a better society? This was the goal of socialism. As Hayek put it,

> The task of creating a suitable framework for the beneficial working of competition had, however, not yet been carried very far when states [governments] everywhere turned from it to that of supplanting competition by a different and irreconcilable principle... It is important to be quite clear about this: the modern movement for planning is a movement against competition.[28]

This idea of a scientific plan versus the chaos of the market is one of the main attractions of socialism and, at the same time, is at the heart of its problem.

Planning To Fail

At first blush, planning seems to have a lot going for it. Wouldn't planning at least be better than leaving things to the dog-eat-dog world of competition where nobody is in control? The goal of a planned economy for Socialists is to improve the standard of living by controlling the allocation of resources. Yet, while this sounds good, there are, in fact, serious problems with planning when it comes to the economy, and these problems are fatal for democracy.

One significant problem is that controlling something as large as a national economy is such a tremendously difficult task that it is virtually impossible. The planner must consider too many variables. Anyone who has started a business and seen it grow can appreciate the problem, at least on a miniature scale.

---

28   F. A. Hayek, *The Road to Serfdom, 50ᵗʰ Anniversary edition* (University of Chicago Press, 1944), 45.

When a new business starts, it often is just the owner or the owner and a few employees. At this stage, the owner can know almost every aspect of the business in great detail. Thus, the owner can reasonably plan and run the business. As the business grows, so does everything else. There will be more customers, more employees, more suppliers, and even more locations. At some point, just controlling the business becomes a significant issue.

If the growth continues, eventually, it becomes too large for one person to manage. Many businesses run into problems at this point, for the owner still thinks of it as their business. As their business, they are very reluctant to let go of control.

When this happens, the business stagnates. Often, the business will even begin to shrink because of the inability of the owner to control it. In short, the owner effectively strangles their business because they refuse to let go.

To continue growing, the owner must delegate some of their control to others, such as Vice Presidents, Division or Department managers, etc. When they do this, these new leaders can understand their part of the business and, therefore, make business decisions in a timelier manner. The company is freed and can grow to the next level. Still, at each new stage of growth, new problems of management and control are encountered. When you reach the size of a large corporation, it is challenging for management to control.

These problems stem from conflicting trends. On the one hand, those running the company divide the business into more and more individual units, with more and more layers. They do this to organize the business into manageable parts. On the other hand, this structure eventually gets so large it becomes unwieldy and unmanageable in and of itself.

Large businesses can operate effectively only by delegating power to smaller, more manageable business units. A more decentralized approach replaces centralized planning, at least to some extent. Upper management delegates authority to lower levels of the business, and with that delegation comes responsibility. Business units that are not running effectively can learn from others that are. Those that cannot compete are closed or sold off. Competition, not planning, is still the driving force for large businesses. If they do not compete, they do not survive. If nothing else, they must, in the end, compete in the marketplace.

Planning and Control

The fatal problem with central planning is that the national economy is, by definition, far more extensive than even the largest corporations. In reality, it is so large as to be completely unmanageable. It also lacks many of the options a business might use. For example, if a region of the country is not performing well, it cannot simply be sold off or closed down.

Most importantly, since a planned economy doesn't rely on competition, it does not have the critical self-correcting mechanism that large businesses use. Thus, even before we consider the implications of planning for democracy, it is clear that planning at the level of a national economy demands a level of economic control with serious problems.

Perhaps someday, we can use Artificial Intelligence to control the economy. We are not there yet, and serious questions exist about whether we want to do this. Turning control of the economy over to AI would still leave problems for democracy.

For democracy, the most dangerous problem with planning is that planning, by its very nature, requires government control in a much different fashion than in a Capitalist system. With both methods, there is a significant role for the government to play. For Capitalism, the government's role is to encourage competition and choice by stopping things like monopolies. For socialism, the government seeks to limit competition and choice and encourages monopolies as long as the government runs them. Thus, in the United States, restaurants operate in a Capitalist model with significant choice and competition. Public schools, on the other hand, follow a largely socialist model, with government-run schools having little, if any, choice. Recently, some states have allowed more choice and competition.

Without the power to impose control, there would be no way for planners to implement any plan. Just creating a plan would be a meaningless exercise. Planners must implement their plans, and people must follow them; they must mandate what the plan calls for while forbidding what the plan restricts.

The more extensive the plan, the greater the degree of control required to implement it. In short, the more you plan the economy, the more the ability to make economic choices is removed from the people and given to the government. You are not free to choose if the government has already made that choice for you.

For the sake of argument, let us assume that a government tries to avoid these problems by making the plan as limited as possible so that it will be the least intrusive to freedom. The problem with such a plan is that the economy is so large; such a limited plan must fail.

People will react in their own best interests, not in the best interest of the plan. They will seek ways around the plan wherever it is in their own best interests to do so. The more limited the plan, the easier it will be to find ways around it. In short, a limited plan is doomed to fail because it is limited. Before looking at the ramifications of this failure, we first will examine a more fundamental difference between Capitalism and Socialism or how people react in their own best interests.

Human Nature?

It is no mere coincidence that before Adam Smith wrote *The Wealth of Nations,* he was a professor of moral philosophy at the University of Glasgow, and his previous work was *Theory of Moral Sentiment.*

His theories on economics detailed in *The Wealth of Nations* were deeply rooted in his research into human nature, motivations, and actions, and this is one of the reasons his theories have worked out in practice as well as they have. Socialism, however, often requires that people act contrary to their nature.

In short, Smith premised his theories on the belief that people can generally be counted upon to act in what they see as their own best interests. This characterization is a generalization; there are many caveats and qualifications[29], such as short-term vs. long-term interests. Still, as a generalization, it works.

When a conflict exists, Socialism depends on people sacrificing their self-interests for the good of the plan. The hope is that they will benefit from a better society in the future if it succeeds.

Even if the planners could ensure the ultimate success of a plan and, thus, guarantee a better society, it would still be a very dubious proposition to get people to sacrifice immediate self-interest for such an abstract long-term benefit. But given the problems and difficulties involved, the success of any plan is in grave doubt. Therefore, government programs frequently ask people to act contrary to their self-interest for a goal that most likely will never come about.

Any plan faces two significant hurdles before it can be successful. First, the planners must design it well enough to achieve the long-term goals when put into action. Second, it must convince the people to act contrary to their self-interest in the hope of some future benefit. Neither of these are very realistic prospects.

Failure Begets Failure

Returning to the plan's failure, we saw that a limited plan is doomed to fail from the beginning. It is possible, of course, that the plan was bad. Still, even an otherwise good but limited plan

---

29 This is not a completely black-and-white issue. For example, behaviorists question the strict cost-benefit analysis implied by capitalism. Overall human behavior is far more complex and people's "analysis" is also often flawed and very risk-adverse. Still, history has shown that people will resist any plan they perceive as not in their own best interest or one that puts them at undue risk.

can fail from one of two hurdles. Either the plan was too narrow, leaving too many factors outside its scope, or too many people acted in contrary ways, undermining it. Most likely, it will be a combination of both.

The remedy for both of these problems is the same: greater control. The government needs more control over the economy and people's choices. Yet, as the government attempts to gain greater control, it faces the same problems of control and management businesses face as they grow: the inability to control such a large entity, just on a much larger scale.

However extensive the plan, factors will always remain beyond the planner's control. As the planner attempts to control these factors, the ability to regulate itself becomes a major limiting factor. More importantly, for democracy, control, by its very definition, restricts freedom.

Hayek pointed out that if planning is to work, "the responsible authorities must be freed from the fetters of democratic procedure."[30] If left unchecked, the result of attempting to plan a national economy is a totalitarian state. Thus, the paradox for the democratic socialist is,

> Socialism can be put into practice only by methods which most socialists disapprove…The old socialist parties were inhibited by their democratic ideals; they did not possess the ruthlessness required for the performance of their chosen task.[31]

In light of this characteristic of socialism, it should be no surprise that the two primary forms of totalitarianism that dominated the 20th century resulted from attempts to implement a planned economy: Communism and Fascism.[32]

---

30   F. A. Hayek, *The Road to Serfdom, 50th Anniversary edition* (University of Chicago Press, 1944), p 75

31   F. A. Hayek, *The Road to Serfdom, 50th Anniversary edition* (University of Chicago Press, 1944), p 151

32   These two political theories, while often at odds with each other, are actually very similar. The main difference between them is over the question of ownership of property. In Communism the government owns the means of

A Middle Way?

Given these problems, some countries have attempted a "middle way" between Socialism and Capitalism, a sort of Socialism lite, which attempts to strike a balance between a planned economy and democratic principles. But these halfway measures still suffer from the same problems and, thus, have had great difficulties. Such halfway measures only strangle their economies more slowly. The result will still be either the failure of the plan or more government control to get it to work; it will just take longer.

Supporters of a middle way often cite Sweden as an example of a successful implementation of Socialism. Still, recently, the problems of such an approach have also become apparent. As we saw at the beginning of this chapter, Sweden's attempt to plan housing costs failed, and they abandoned it. More recently, Mauricio Rojas, Associate Professor at Lund University, wrote that Sweden, under the control of the Swedish Social Democratic Party, produced

> the most pervasive and costly welfare state ever known, a welfare state with an impressive capacity to tax and regulate society that in its heyday could present itself, or be presented by enthusiastic visitors, as a model for the rest of mankind, a successful 'middle way' between totalitarian communism and egoistic capitalism.[33]

But as he goes on to point out,

> This 'Swedish model' is today a society in deep crisis, shocked by mass unemployment and its own incapacity to hold the generous promises made in better times.[34]

We can see this problem in the statistics on job growth in the 1990s for Europe in general, as most of its countries have chosen

production. In Fascism, private ownership is permitted, but while the means of production are privately owned, control is still through the state.

33   Mauricio Rojas, *The Historical Roots of the Swedish Socialist Experiment*, (1996).

34   Mauricio Rojas, *The Historical Roots of the Swedish Socialist Experiment*, (1996).

this "middle way" to one degree or another. As reported in *Investors Business Daily*, 1990-1999 was a decade of strong economic growth. During this period, the United States economy generated 19 million new jobs. As a result, the unemployment rate dropped to a 29-year low. Yet, during the same period, Europe, with its more socialist-oriented approach to planned economies, had no net increase in jobs.[35]

Swedish economists Fredrik Bergstrom and Robert Gidehag found similar results in 2004 in a study entitled *The EU vs. USA*. Comparing Gross National Product per capita showed that European countries were well below the U.S. average except for Luxembourg, with the U.S. average 32 percent higher than the European average.[36] This difference amounted to roughly an additional $9,700 per person Americans could spend on things they wanted (TVs, cars, vacations, retirement savings, etc.) than their European counterparts. Why such a significant difference? As Bergstrom and Gidehag pointed out,

> The expansion of the public sector into overripe welfare states in large parts of Europe is and remains the best guess as to why our continent cannot measure up to our neighbor in the west.[37]

While, as we saw in the last chapter, effective tax rates in the U.S. are about 30 percent, European governments consume over 40 percent of their GDP and sometimes exceed 50 percent.[38]

---

35   Editorial, "The Great American Job Machine," *Investor's Business Daily*, January 19, 1999.

36   Review & Outlook, "Europe vs. America," *Wall Street Journal*, June 18, 2004, A10 http://online.wsj.com/article/0,,SB108751426815241018,00.html?mod=opinion%5Fmain%5Freview%5Fand%5Foutlooks (accessed April 3, 2009).

37   Review & Outlook, "Europe vs. America", *Wall Street Journal*, June 18, 2004, A10 http://online.wsj.com/article/0,,SB108751426815241018,00.html?mod=opinion%5Fmain%5Freview%5Fand%5Foutlooks (accessed April 3, 2009).

38   Review & Outlook, "Europe vs. America", *Wall Street Journal*, June 18, 2004, A10 http://online.wsj.com/article/0,,SB108751426815241018,00.

This difference occurs because of the inefficiencies inherent in any plan, such that the burdens imposed on the economy by planning are more significant than the benefits provided. As a result, Socialism, over the long term, can only offer benefits if it can tap resources generated from another source.

Socialism cannot survive as an independent economic system. This is one of the reasons that the U.S. economy is often referred to as the engine that drives the world economy. Capitalism's emphasis on competition reduces inefficiencies and, thus, generates wealth. Some of this wealth is then used to purchase goods from more socialist nations, allowing those nations to fund their planning.

A Matter of Math

If this were not enough, there is still another factor to planning that threatens democracy. It is simply a matter of mathematics that the fewer people in any democratic process, the more input each individual will have in any decision. For example, if you were on an island alone, you would have 100 percent influence over any decision. If ten people were on the island making decisions democratically, your impact in the process is 1 in 10. If there were 1,000 people, it drops to 1 in 1,000. The more people you have, the less of a say you will have.

The Founding Fathers were well aware of this. They attempted to construct a system of government, keeping governmental decisions close to the people. They supported dual sovereignty with a system of local, state, and national governments.

They left most decisions to state and local governments. The federal government only dealt with those issues that were national in scope. The lower levels of government could effectively deal with regional and local problems. This view of government even entered into the common language with the idiom, 'Don't make a

---

html?mod=opinion%5Fmain%5Freview%5Fand%5Foutlooks (accessed April 3, 2009).

federal issue out of it.' That this saying has dropped from common usage is telling.

This decentralized approach to government resulted in the wide variety of laws that states and localities enacted. People in different states were free to govern themselves as they saw fit. This freedom meant that some things were legal in some states yet not in others. Many saw such differences as democracy in action. People were free to choose, so they did not all make the same choice. But increasingly, others were disturbed by such "chaos" and began to seek a more unified planned approach.

In addition, such freedom contradicts the type of control needed to plan. You cannot plan if everyone is free to make their own choice. As a result, those who push for a more planned approach have, by necessity, also wanted a more prominent and centralized role for the federal government.

As the control has moved from local and state governments to the federal, the ability of individuals to have a say in the laws that govern their lives has proportionately decreased. Again, this is just math; the greater population of the nation compared to local and state governments means less of a say. For an issue handled at the city level where an individual voter had one vote in a few thousand, the same voter will only have one vote in millions when moved to the federal level.

Thus, through planning, democracy is attacked in two ways. It is attacked directly due to the control needed to implement any plan and indirectly as people's input into the process decreases as decisions are moved to the national level to achieve the centralization that planning requires.

Education Planning

One place where the effects of planning are apparent is in public education. The United States has a long history of commitment to the education of the general public. Historically, education was very decentralized and initially was not run by the government. When governments began to take over the responsibility of education, it was local government through local school boards in control.

But as is often the case with such a decentralized system, some were uncomfortable with the difference that such freedom permits. In particular, people pointed to the differences in education that resulted from different economic conditions from one area to the next.

As a result, there has been a move to a more centralized, planned approach to distribute money where it is most needed and institute more uniform standards. Initially, those efforts moved education from a local issue to the state level.

By now it should come as no surprise that the resulting centralization of planning at the state level did not achieve the desired results. This failure predictably resulted in calls for even more centralized planning. Education increasingly became a national issue. Then, in 1980, the Department of Education (DoE) was created. Since its founding, the DoE's budget has grown from $14.0 billion in 1980 to $59.7 billion in 2008 and $81.2 billion in 2019.[39]

What have been the results of this increasing move to centralized control and planning of education? They are just what one would expect based on the problems just discussed in this chapter. Few, if any, would attempt to claim that public education is better than before the attempt to improve it with a more centralized planned approach. Here are just some of the examples of the decline in educational standards from *The Index of Leading Cultural Indicators 2001*[40]:

- Average verbal scores on the SAT decreased by 49 points between 1960 and 2000, while math scores decreased by 7.

---

39 Data.gov, *U.S. Department of Education Budget History,* https://catalog. data.gov/dataset/u-s-department-of-education-budget-history (accessed, 6/8/2023)
40 William J. Bennett, "The Index of Leading Cultural Indicators 2001" Chapter 3. *EMPOWER.org 2001.*

- Average SAT scores were at their highest level (980) in 1963–64. Between 1964 and 1980, when they were at their lowest level, scores dropped 90 points.
- Since 1983, more than ten million Americans have reached the 12th grade without learning to read at a basic level. More than 20 million students in their senior year could not do basic math. Almost 25 million did not know the essentials of U. S. history.
- Four out of five seniors from the top 55 colleges and universities in the United States received a grade of D or F on a recent standardized American history test. Only 34 percent of the students surveyed could identify George Washington as an American general at the Battle of Yorktown, the culminating battle of the American Revolution. Over one-third could not identify the U.S. Constitution as establishing the division of power in the American government. Less than one quarter (23 percent) correctly identified James Madison as the "father of the Constitution." On the other hand, 99 percent know who the cartoon characters Beavis and Butthead are, and 98 percent can identify the rap singer Snoop Doggy Dogg.[41]

The situation has remained basically the same in recent years, with the scores going a little up or down each year. So, what is the response to such declines? Predictably, those supporting centralized planning call for even more centralization. While the National Education Association states, "America's public schools have always been under local control. This is as it should be,"[42] it still argues for a more significant federal role. In particular, they claim,

> Only the federal government can articulate the vision that every child should have an equal and full opportunity to excel in school with the leadership needed to bring it closer to reality. Only the federal government can make it America's national mission to strengthen public education and ensure that every public school is a quality public school.[43]

---

41   National Center for Education Statistics, The National Report Card, 2022, https://nces.ed.gov/nationsreportcard/ (Accessed, 6.8,2023)
42   *NEA, "The Opportunity to Excel - NEA's Plan for Excellence in Education"*
43   *NEA, "The Opportunity to Excel - NEA's Plan for Excellence in Education"*

They also call for more federal spending to implement this vision. And with increased federal spending will come even more federal control.

While the wording is somewhat different, this is still classic centralized planning. To claim "only the federal government can articulate the vision" (i.e., plan) and that only the federal government has "leadership" (i.e., control) "needed to bring it closer to reality" is effectively saying there should be one centralized plan for education and that the plan must be under federal control.

Even when there are short-term gains, the nature of planning and government inefficiencies means they come at a tremendous cost and waste. In short, throwing enough money at a problem can result in some positive results, at least sometimes.

One of the main positive results in recent years has come from charter schools. Charter schools move away from a centralized planned approach and back towards local control, again demonstrating the problems with centralized planning.

The experience with public education is a perfect example of how the move to centralized planning leads to problems and how those problems generate yet further calls for even more centralization and control. Meanwhile, teachers complain they already cannot determine what will happen in their classrooms. There are just too many government mandates (controls) they must follow.

Again, it is essential to remember that it was not until 1980 that we even had a Department of Education. Creating this department has not helped public education. A decline in education has marked the period since the Department of Education's creation. We have significantly increased the DoE's budget, thereby increasing centralized control, but this, if anything, has only made matters worse. In addition, the increase in federal spending this centralized control requires only further drives up the need for increased taxes, as discussed in the last chapter.

What Can Be Done

In light of this analysis, the solution seems clear. Instead of pursuing solutions involving more centralized planning and control, we should look at ways to decentralize control and increase competition. We should return to the vision of government set by the Founding Fathers. In this government, the people handle issues themselves whenever possible.

When the people determine there is a role for government, the lowest possible level should handle it, the level at which individual people have the most input, starting with the local government. When local government is insufficient, it should move to the county level. If the county level is inadequate, then the state. We should look to the federal government only as a last resort and only for issues requiring national control.

In addition, when government intervention is required, governments should, as much as possible, look for solutions that allow freedom and choice governed by competition rather than solutions requiring planning and, thereby, control; control that, by necessity, must restrict individual freedom.

Again, public education is an excellent example of these principles. In response to the problems of public education, some have called for solutions involving even more centralized planning and control. Still, others have proposed a different approach with solutions based on choice and competition.

Unfortunately, many people equate the desire for government control with individual concern. The more government control and the higher the level of government one wants, the more concern one must have for the issue. Thus, those who have attempted to transfer control over education back to the local level get attacked for lack of concern for education.

Similar to this problem is the equation of spending with concern. The more spending one wants on an issue; the more one must care. Conversely, someone who wants to cut spending must not care. Yet, numerous studies have demonstrated the error of such thinking. For example, a study in 2003 showed that the U.S. spends more per student than any other country in the world but is only average when it comes to education.[44]

The same is valid at the state level. States with lower spending often do as well, if not better, teaching children than states where spending is twice as high. For example, while at $4,800 per student, Utah spends about a third of New York's $12,000 per student, students scored about the same on Math and Reading in the *National Assessment of Education Progress,*[45] Utah Students scored about 30 points higher when compared to the District of Columbia even though the District's much higher per student spending allows them to have a pupil to teacher ratio of 13.8, versus Utah's 22.1.[46] In a system governed by centralized planning and control, often more spending only buys you more waste and inefficiencies.

Choice?

Contrary to some critics, a competition-oriented approach does not require abandoning the goal of universal public education, closing public schools, and leaving everyone to their own means to find an education. Nor does a government role necessarily imply centralized planning. One can be for competition and still fully support the belief that government should play an essential and critical role in public education.

In fact, one possible solution has already been in place for many decades when it comes to colleges and universities. Following World War II, many believed it was essential to encourage and enable people to pursue higher education.

44   *U.S. Tops the World in School Spending but not Test Scores, USA Today Sept 16 2003* http://www.usatoday.com/news/education/2003-09-16-education-comparison_x.htm (accessed April 3, 2009).

45   Kavan Peterson, "State of Education: Who Makes the Grade" *Pew Research Center, Jan 26, 2006* http://pewresearch.org/obdeck/?ObDeckID=5 (accessed April 3, 2009).

46   *National Center for Educational Statistics, "State Education Data Profiles"* http://nces.ed.gov/programs/stateprofiles/ (accessed April 3, 2009).

Since many colleges and universities were private, Congress decided the best way to do this was to give grants and loans to individuals instead of schools. The individuals could choose which school was best for them, public or private. As a result, over the same period when public education, with its increasingly centralized control, has seen such a decline in standards, the higher education system, with its choice and competition, has remained among the best in the world.

Thus, rather than trust in an extensive, centrally controlled system, which not only has major theoretical problems but has seen those problems borne out, we could allow parents to make choices in their children's best interests through the use of a system modeled after what is currently working for higher education.

The government could give parents vouchers, which they then take to any accredited school, public or private. Schools that did well would be in demand; schools that did not do a good job would not. If the schools that did a poor job wished to continue to attract students, they could look at what the successful schools were doing and follow their example.

As a result, schools would adopt educational practices that worked while abandoning those that failed. The net effect is that education levels and standards would improve. If governments constructed the system correctly, they could even reduce costs.

While those seeking a solution based on even more centralized planning oppose such an approach, there is little question that such a program would work. Again, we have already seen it work at the higher education levels.

In 2002, the U.S. Supreme Court removed one of the significant roadblocks to vouchers, ruling that a pilot voucher program in Cleveland did not violate the Constitution.[47] In addition, as Krista Kafer reported in a Heritage Foundation Report in 2003, there is

---

47   Terry Frieden, "Supreme Court affirms school voucher program", *CNN. com/LawCenter, June 27, 2002,* http://www.cnn.com/2002/LAW/06/27/scotus.school.vouchers/ (accessed April 3, 2009).

a growing body of evidence that choice often improves the academic performance of at-risk students promotes parental involvement and satisfaction, and fosters accountability in public school systems.[48]

The further expansion of school choice provided additional support. A report in 2008 showed that school choice increased parental satisfaction with "teachers, academic standards, and order and discipline," in addition to academic improvements.[49]

The growing school choice movement gives hope for public education. Yet, the overall trend remains for more federal control over our lives, as the government seeks solutions based more on planning rather than competition.

For example, healthcare remains a prime target as many people see the solution to the current healthcare problems in ever-increasing government planning and control of healthcare resources. One has only to look back to the Clinton health care plan, the expanded role of the government with Obamacare, or the continuing calls to put the federal government in control of a "single payer" approach to see that the calls for centralized planning and control remain.

Yet, it need not be this way. There is an alternative that has repeatedly demonstrated an ability to work. Rather than centralized planning and control, governments at all levels should seek to develop infrastructures that promote competition and individual choice. Such approaches are much more likely to produce tangible benefits but also promote the freedom and liberty vital to a democracy.

---

48   Krista Kafer, "Progress on School Choice in the States", *Heritage Foundation. July 10, 2003,* http://www.heritage.org/Research/Education/bg1639. cfm (accessed April 3, 2009).

49   Dan Lips, "School Choice: Policy Developments and National Participation Estimates in 2007-2008", *Heritage Foundation, Jan 31, 2008* http://www.heritage.org/Research/Education/bg2102.cfm (accessed April 3, 2009).

THE RULE OF LAW

We are in bondage to the law so that we might be free.

Cicero

Liberty is the right to do as the law permits

Montesquieu

IT WAS A VERY TYPICAL story. A local nobleman, one Duke of Istria, had misused and abused his power and position for his selfish advantage rather than ruling in the best interests of his subjects. Not only was he ruling unjustly, but he was also using his power to intimidate the people to increase his wealth. It was not an unusual story at all, but it was an extraordinary time.

While the Duke was unconcerned with the welfare of those he ruled, the king was interested. The king was Charlemagne, who ruled areas of France under various titles from 768 to his death in 814. It was a difficult time. Rome had been gone for 300 years. Earlier in the century, Charlemagne's grandfather, Charles Martel, had stopped an Islamic invasion of Europe at the Battle of Tours in 732.

The greatest of the medieval kings, Charlemagne was a ruler ahead of his time. While he used war to solidify his rule, he preferred administration to war. Charlemagne reformed the laws and education while encouraging commerce and scholarship and standardizing writing. As a result of these and other reforms, historians refer to his reign as the Carolingian Renaissance.

During his rule, Charlemagne worked to better the lives of his subjects. Among his reforms was the *Capitulare missorum,* which established emissaries whose job it was to monitor local officials,

> to review their actions, judgments, and accounts; to check bribery, extortion, nepotism, and exploitation, to receive complaints and remedy wrongs, to protect "the Church, the poor, and wards and widows, and the whole people" from malfeasance or tyranny... the *Capitulare missorum* establishing these emissaries was a Magna Carta for the people, four centuries before England's Magna Carta for the aristocracy.[1]

As a result of the *Capitulare missorum,* the Duke of Istria no longer had a free hand to do as he pleased. When one of Charlemagne's emissaries arrived, he found the Duke guilty of

> divers injustices and extortions, [and] was forced by the King to restore his thieving, compensate every wronged man, publicly confess his crimes, and give security against their repetition.[2]

In short, the Duke of Istria discovered he could no longer do as he pleased. He was no longer above the law but was under it like his subjects.

All societies are defined and controlled by a series of laws. These laws may be written or unwritten, detailed or vague, formal or informal, just or unjust. But these are the rules that define society. These laws determine what actions are to be allowed, what actions are forbidden, and how we should do certain things in many cases.

More Than Law

Perhaps the greatest accomplishment of Western Civilization is something so taken for granted that few even think about it. It

---

1   Will and Ariel Durant, *The Story of Civilization IV: The Age of Faith.* (New York:: Simon and Schuster, 1950), 464.
2   Will and Ariel Durant, *The Story of Civilization IV: The Age of Faith.* (New York:: Simon and Schuster, 1950), 464.

is the Rule of Law. Before discussing the Rule of Law, let us clarify what it is not. The Rule of Law is not law.

Laws have been around since before recorded history. All societies of the past and all societies today have laws. As we pointed out in the last chapter, laws are simply the morals of a community that the ruling powers consider so important they enforce them with the state's power.

Yet, while laws have existed for a long time, the Rule of Law has not. While the Duke of Istria fell victim to the Rule of Law, his experience is sadly much more the exception than the rule when put into the context of all human history. While laws are the rules of conduct of a society that the state backs up by its authority, the Rule of Law is a concept that deals with how law itself is to be understood. More importantly, to whom it applies. In its simplest form, we can sum up the Rule of Law in the statement: No one is above the law, not even the ruler.

In societies that lack a Rule of Law, the law is whatever the current ruler or rulers say, be they a dictator, king, or tribal leader. In short, the ruler rules the society, not the law. The law is simply a tool, one of many, that rulers use to exercise control over their subjects.

An early advance in civilization occurred when people began to write down the laws of society. A written law gives many advantages. If nothing else, a written law lets a person have a better chance of knowing in advance whether their actions will be in accord with the wishes of the ruler. It enables you to see where you stand. After all, how can someone comply with the ruler's wishes if they do not know what those wishes are?

In addition, it provides a means of continuity between rulers. While new rulers could, and often did, change the law, there was at least some continuity. If a new ruler altered the law, the people would have a means of knowing about any changes.

Another benefit a written law provides is at least the potential to defend one's actions. A person could point to what the law says and argue how their actions complied with the law. A defense was only a potential benefit, for a successful defense depended on several factors.

Foremost of these factors would be the ruler. Since the ruler makes the law, nothing prevents them from simply deciding that what you did was illegal. Still, if the ruler is fair and just, a written law gives a person at least the chance of a successful defense.

Finally, and probably most importantly, a written law allowed for the growth of civilization, for a written law makes it much easier for the ruler to delegate their authority to make legal judgments to others, i.e., judges. It not only provided a means for the people to know what to do if they wished to stay out of trouble, but it also provided a basis for a judge appointed by the ruler to determine whether or not an individual's actions conflicted with the ruler's wishes.

The written law's benefits rely on it being clearly written, easily understood, and relatively unchanging compared with a ruler's whims. It allows people to know what they can and cannot do so they can act accordingly. A written law that is vague, hard to understand, or changes frequently defeats much of the purpose of putting it in writing.

While written law is a big step forward for society, nothing is free. With every advance comes new problems. While a written law made it easier to delegate the ruler's authority to others, this delegation also introduced the potential for corruption and error.

Whether you liked the ruling or not, when a decision came from the ruler, you could be sure it was the ruler's decision. As soon as you have a judge making the decisions in place of the ruler, there is always the potential that the decision may differ from the ruler's.

This error could arise from several causes. The judge may have misunderstood what the law says or what the ruler himself would have ruled. Judges may substitute their own beliefs and values instead of the ruler. Or perhaps the judge was simply corrupt and was bribed. Whatever the reason, a judge can make the wrong ruling, and when they do, corruption has entered into the law.

Some might quibble with the last point and argue that some-one could just as well bribe the ruler. While a ruler can be bribed, this raises a question. Would bribing the ruler be a corruption of the law? The surprising answer is no. Since the law is whatever the ruler says it is, and since the ruler is free to change it for whatever reason they wish, bribing a judge would be corrupt, but bribing a ruler would not.

This distinction applies equally to ancient civilizations and some relatively modern ones. During the 18th century, for example, you could still see leading figures, such as Samuel Johnson, arguing,

> The King is the head, he is supreme: he is above every thing, and there is no power by which he can be tried. Therefore, it is, Sir, that we hold the King can do no wrong;[3]

In more recent history, one only has to look at the Holocaust in Nazi Germany or the more extensive mass murders committed by Stalin and Mao, which were legal. They were undoubtedly im-moral and, in fact, evil, but they were *legal.*

Why? Because Hitler, Stalin, and Mao ultimately determined what was legal and illegal in their societies.[4] In short, the real prob-lem was that the Rule of Law did not govern these societies; their rulers governed them. Whenever there was a question between the wishes of the ruler and what the law said, the wishes of the ruler were more important. The ruler controlled the law; the law did not control the ruler.

---

3   James Boswell, *The Life of Samuel Johnson,* (New York: Everyman's Li-brary, Alfred A. Knopf, 1791), 267.
4   Some argue that these evils were, in fact, illegal because the rulers in-volved did not come to power legally, or usurped their power by illegal means. While true, once they were in power, legally or illegally, they were the rulers, and what they wanted was the law.

Above or Below

A critical aspect of the Rule of Law is that nobody is above the law, not even the ruler. Thomas Sowell wrote,

> There is a fundamental difference between a society where a ruler can seize the wealth or the wife of any subject and one in which the poorest citizen can refuse to allow the highest officials of the land inside his home. There is a fundamental difference between a time when the great English jurist Coke cringed as King James threatened to beat him physically with his own hands – resistance being treason, punishable by death – and a world in which the Supreme Court of the United States could order President Nixon to turn over evidence to a special prosecutor. No clever trivializing can erase these differences. Centuries of struggle, sacrifice, and bloodshed went into creating the ideal of a government of laws superior to any ruler or political organ.[5]

The Rule of Law is not only the result of a hard-fought struggle; it is a vital part of any proper democratic government. A genuinely democratic government depends on a whole series of laws for its maintenance.

For example, to have meaningful elections, laws must exist concerning when and how to hold them. Leaders above the law are free to change these at will. When this happens, democracy effectively ceases to exist.

A leader would need only to decide to stop any more elections. More likely, the leader could keep holding elections for the sake of appearance but change the election laws to guarantee their winning. Thus, you find that most modern dictatorships, from Napoleon forward, hold elections in which the people re-elected them with 90 percent or more of the vote.

In October 2002, the Iraqi dictator Saddam Hussein gave a perfect example of this when he won reelection with 100 percent of the 11,445,638 votes cast. Apparently, in a country of 22 million people, no one could be found who would vote against

5   Thomas Sowell, *The Vision of the Anointed*, (New York: Basic Books, 1995), 219.

Hussein! Iraq conducted the vote using paper ballots that asked if Saddam Hussein should rule for another seven years. Yes and no were the only options. They allowed no other potential candidates on the ballot.

While some raised questions, such as how officials could count 11 million paper ballots from all across the country overnight, Izzat Ibrahim, Vice Chairman of Iraq's Revolutionary Command Council, dismissed these questions concerning the vote, claiming that "We don't have opposition in Iraq."[6] Given the numerous mass graves that continued to be discovered for years following Saddam's removal,[7] this was probably not a real surprise.

Thus, while it may seem esoteric and abstract, which to some extent it is, the Rule of Law is vitally important to maintaining a democratic form of government. Lose the Rule of Law, and unless restored, it will only be a matter of time before democracy fails.

Abstract but Vital

One of the real dangers here is that since the Rule of Law is somewhat abstract, it exists more in people's subconscious perceptions of the law rather than as a conscious thought. As a result, weakening the Rule of Law often goes unnoticed.

For example, in any court ruling, there are several components. There is the broader issue, for example, murder. There is the immediate issue that comes before the court: Did a particular person commit a specific crime? There is the court's ruling on that issue. Is the accused guilty or not? Finally, there is the legal reasoning behind the verdict.

The broad and immediate issue and the ruling get the vast majority of the news coverage and, thus, the focus of attention.

6   *Associated Press, "Saddam Wins Presidential Referendum – as Expected."*
Oct 16, 2002 http://www.foxnews.com/story/0,2933,65656,00.html (accessed April 3, 2009)
7   U.S. State Dept, Mass Graves of Iraq: Uncovering Atrocities.
December 19,2003, https://2001-2009.state.gov/g/drl/rls/27000.htm (accessed August, 1 2023)

People then tend to judge the correctness of the verdict based on their beliefs about the issue.

Yet, the legal reasoning behind the ruling most impacts the Rule of Law. Since legal reasoning usually gets little coverage outside legal circles, it can undermine the Rule of Law before the public realizes it.

This threat is not just theoretical. It is always present to some extent among one group or another. Yet, the attacks have been growing in recent decades. While many factors weakened the Rule of Law, the United States Supreme Court's rulings on the Constitution are the most critical area where this happened.

In the United States, the Constitution is the supreme law of the land, at least in theory. British Prime Minister W. E. Gladstone said,

> The American Constitution is, so far as I can see, the most wonderful work ever struck off at a given time by the brain and purpose of man.[8]

When put into effect in 1789, it "was the first important written constitution and a model for a vast number of subsequent constitutional documents."[9] It epitomized the Rule of Law.

The Constitution divided the United States Government into three branches and divided the power to rule between these areas. Since it was a written constitution, it had the same advantages as the first written law. It clarified the supreme law of the land and gave a solid basis on which judges could rule. Yet,

> a written constitution, without a commitment to its principles and civil justice, has often proved to be a temporary or rapidly reversed gesture... Adolf Hitler never formally abolished the constitution of the Weimar Republic, and the protections of

---

8   The Charters of Freedom, Constitution of the United States, Questions and Answers, *National Archives.* http://www.archives.gov/exhibits/charters/constitution_q_and_a.html (*accessed April 3, 2009*).

9   *The Columbia Encyclopedia Sixth Edition, s.vv. "Constitution, principles of government", 2001,* http://www.bartleby.com/65/co/constitu.html (*accessed April 3, 2009*).

personal liberties contained in the Soviet constitution of 1936 proved to be empty promises.[10]

As with the earliest examples of written law, unless enforced and adhered to, unless there is the Rule of Law, a written constitution is of little value.

A New Threat

In the past, the most significant danger to the Rule of Law came from rulers who did not want to be bound. Today, the threat comes from a different source. At least in the United States, the most significant danger facing the Rule of Law comes from judges and a new view concerning how they should judge a case.

Historically, good judges set aside their beliefs and ruled based solely on what the law said. Sure, there have always been judges who allowed their opinions, desires, and values to influence their rulings. It probably is impossible for a judge to be completely objective. But complete objectivity and strict adherence to the law were at least seen as the goals a judge would strive for. The more objective a judge was, the more they adhered to what the law said, the better judge they were.

There is also the issue of interpretation. Laws are not an exact science. If they were, there would never be a dispute. Some laws are ambiguous, vague, or just poorly written. Some laws conflict with other laws. In such cases, a judge must interpret the law to understand how it applies to the particular case.

Even with the traditional view of a good judge, there is a great deal of judgment and discretion for a judge when applying the law to individual cases. Life is messy; many cases are not clear-cut. The judge must often consider several factors when making a ruling. Yet, there are some limits to this judgment. If pushed too far, eventually, a judge is no longer applying the law and begins to

---

10 *The Columbia Encyclopedia Sixth Edition, s.vv. "Constitution, principles of government"*, 2001, http://www.bartleby.com/65/co/constitu.html (*accessed April 3, 2009*).

change it. At that point, the judge is no longer under the law but above it.

In the 20th century, increasing numbers called for judges to reject the old basis for making decisions and include other factors besides the law in their rulings. These new theories do not see the Constitution as a fixed standard upon which judges base their decisions. Instead, they see the Constitution as a "Living Document," a Living Constitution that can grow and change to meet the needs of an ever-changing society.

The Living Constitution view traces back to the Progressive movement in the early Twentieth century. Progressives believe that while the Constitution may have worked at the beginning of the nineteenth century, times had changed. Frank Goodnow, an early progressive intellectual, wrote,

> The political philosophy of the eighteenth century was formulated before the announcement and acceptance of the theory of evolutionary development. The natural rights doctrine presupposed almost that society was static or stationary rather than dynamic or progressive in character.[11]

Goodnow rejected that the role of the government was to protect rights. He believed,

> We no longer believe as we once believed that a good social organization can be secured merely through stressing our rights... But we have come to the conclusion that man under modern conditions is primarily a member of society and that only as he recognizes his duties as a member of society can he secure the greatest opportunities as an individual. While we do not regard society as an end in itself we do consider it as one of the most important means through which man may come into his own.[12]

---

11   F. Goodnow, "The American Conception of Liberty," 1916. [Online]. Available: http://www.nlnrac.org/critics/american-progressivism/primary-source-documents/american-conception-of-liberty. [Accessed 6 10 2020]
12   F. Goodnow, "The American Conception of Liberty," 1916. [Online]. Available: http://www.nlnrac.org/critics/american-progressivism/primary-source-documents/american-conception-of-liberty. [Accessed 6 10 2020]

Woodrow Wilson was critical of the Constitutional system, which he saw as too rigid and inflexible. The government needed to grow, but the founders created a system of checks and balances, limiting government action. Wilson objected to the notion of checks and balances because the government was more like a living thing than a machine,

> No living thing can have its organs offset against each other, as checks, and live. On the contrary, its life is dependent upon their quick cooperation, their ready response to the commands of instinct or intelligence, their amicable community of purpose. Government is not a body of blind forces; it is a body of men... Their cooperation is indispensable, their warfare fatal. There can be no successful government without the intimate, instinctive coordination of the organs of life and action. [13]

As for the constitutional system of government created by the founders, Wilson said,

> And they constructed a government as they would have constructed an orrery,–to display the laws of nature. Politics in their thought was a variety of mechanics. The Constitution was founded on the law of gravitation. The government was to exist and move by virtue of the efficacy of "checks and balances." The trouble with the theory is that government is not a machine, but a living thing. It falls, not under the theory of the universe, but under the theory of organic life. It is accountable to Darwin, not to Newton. [14]

For Progressives, the government was a living thing. Checks and balances should not constrain it as it needs to grow and develop. These views continued to develop and eventually became

---

13   W. Wilson, "What is Progress," 1912. [Online]. Available: https://constitutingamerica.org/what-is-progress-by-woodrow-wilson-1856-1924-reprinted-from-the-u-s-constitution-a-reader-published-by-hillsdale-college/. [Accessed 6 10 2020].

14   W. Wilson, "What is Progress," 1912. [Online]. Available: https://constitutingamerica.org/what-is-progress-by-woodrow-wilson-1856-1924-reprinted-from-the-u-s-constitution-a-reader-published-by-hillsdale-college/. [Accessed 6 10 2020].

the Living Constitution view in which it is not only the job of the Judge to interpret and apply the law to individual cases but also to understand and adapt the law in light of changing times.

The Yale constitutional law professor John Hart Ely wrote that judges shouldn't be bound simply to what the Constitution says. For Ely, the constitution was incomplete and "needs filling in."[15] Another Yale law professor, Alexander Bickel, argued that there should be

> a function which might (indeed, must) involve the making of policy, yet which differs for the legislative and executive functions; which is peculiarly suited to the capabilities of the courts; which will not likely be performed elsewhere if the courts do not assume it.[16]

In short, Bickel argued that judges need to write the law in some cases because if they do not do it, no one else will. Laurence H. Tribe, professor of constitutional law at Harvard Law School, is a leader in this movement. He rejects a fixed Constitution; it is more like constellations, something the mind imposes on the text.

> The Constitution is like the night sky. You look at the constellations. You see the stars. The light from the stars comes to you from different eras maybe millions of years apart. And the constellations that you superimpose upon those stars are constructs of the human mind.

Tribe goes on to describe the Constitution,

> The Constitution by which we govern ourselves is neither the dead parchment of September 17, holy though it may be, in a secular sense, downstairs here in this building nor the equally inert September 18 print on which the ratifiers physically gazed before they voted for it in the years leading to 1789. Rather, the real Constitution, I would submit, is the living law as ratified, amended, interpreted over time and thereby

---

15   cited in Robert Bork, *The Tempting of America*, (New York: Free Press, 1990), 194.
16   cited in Robert Bork, *The Tempting of America*, (New York: Free Press, 1990), 1898-9

absorbed into an ongoing organic tradition that forms and frames our political order.[17]

This view is significantly different from the founders'. Chief Justice Marshall wrote in one of the most important early Supreme Court cases, Marbury v. Madison,

> The powers of the legislature are defined and limited; and that those limits may not be mistaken or forgotten, the constitution is written. To what purpose are powers limited, and to what purpose is that limitation committed to writing; if these limits may, at any time, be passed by those intended to be restrained? The distinction between a government with limited and unlimited powers is abolished, if those limits do not confine the persons on whom they are imposed, and if acts prohibited and acts allowed are of equal obligation. It is a proposition too plain to be contested, that the constitution controls any legislative act repugnant to it; or, that the legislature may alter the constitution by an ordinary act.
> Between these alternatives there is no middle ground. The constitution is either a superior, paramount law, unchangeable by ordinary means, or it is on a level with ordinary legislative acts, and like other acts, is alterable when the legislature shall please to alter.

Robert Bork, an opponent of the Living Constitution view, described Tribe's position as,

> The Constitution is what we want it to be… and that what we should want it to be is the charter of a radically equalitarian[18] society.[19]

The theorists of the Living Constitution attempt to define guidelines for how judges should do this "filling in" without altogether leaving it up to the judges' own bias. But since they have

---

17   Laurence Tribe, *The Invisible Contituion, September 17, 2008, The National Archives*
https://www.archives.gov/files/nae/news/featured-programs/080917tribetranscript.pdf (accessed September 27, 2023)
18   I will have more to say on the change from liberty to equality this last statement embodies in Chapter Ten.
19   cited in Robert Bork, *The Tempting of America*, (New York: Free Press, 1990), 200.

effectively cut themselves off from any objective standard in favor of more subjective views, not too surprisingly, all come up with somewhat different answers.

A simple fact remains: If judges do not base their ruling on the Constitution and the law, they are free to pick whatever standards they want. Their choice from among these many other standards will be strongly affected by their values of what is essential.

Ultimately, the standards proposed by the theorists reflect the theorist's views on what is important or ought to be. This view directly or indirectly undermines the Rule of Law, for it puts the judge in control of the law, not the law in control of the judge. In short, it makes the judge more of a ruler than a judge.

Numerous court rulings in recent years demonstrate this breakdown in the Rule of Law. Again, these are difficult to discuss, for there is no way to discuss them without referencing the issues before the court. One's view on these issues often gets in the way of understanding the ruling's impact on the Rule of Law.

Concerning the Rule of Law, we will examine the Supreme Court's ruling in Everson v. Board of Education (1947). It is an excellent example because the ruling seems, at first glance, to be at odds with its reasoning, as many now understand that reasoning. It also significantly changed how the court understood the First Amendment. To understand this change, we must first understand how the court and the country viewed religion before Everson.

The Role of Religion

Religion played a key and crucial role in the history of America. Many of the early settlers came to this land for religious reasons. They came both to set up religious communities reflecting their own beliefs and to escape the religious persecution that was so prevalent in Europe.

The historian Paul Johnson notes that the Great Awakening, a prominent religious revival in the early 18th century, "had been the original dynamic of the continental movement for independence."[20] The Declaration of Independence is solidly grounded in religion. It speaks of an "equal station to which the laws of nature and of Nature's God entitle them" and goes on to proclaim as the premise for Independence,

> We hold these truths to be self-evident, that all men are created equal, that they are endowed by their Creator with certain unalienable rights, that among these are life, liberty, and the pursuit of happiness.

The founders grounded the revolution on the claim that we have rights, and the claim that we have rights depended, at least for them, on the belief in God. Remove God, and you undermine the whole foundation.[21]

The main body of the Constitution omits any mention of God while forbidding any religious tests for office. Yet, religion remained important for the founders. We can see this importance in the fact that the first clause of the First Amendment protects religion. Madison described "the belief in God All Powerful wise and good" as "essential to the moral order of the World and to the happiness of man."[22]

In 1796, George Washington wrote in his Farewell Address, "Of all the dispositions and habits which lead to political prosperity, religion and morality are indispensable supports."[23] He went on to say,

---

20   Paul Johnson, *A History of the American People*, (New York: Harper-Collins, 1997), 204.

21   While the original foundation, many now reject the notion that rights are God-given. Yet, while there have been many attempts to find some alternative, to date, no other suitable foundation for rights has been found. As a result of this lack of foundation, the whole field of Human Rights has been thrown into great turmoil.

22   John Eidsmoe, *Christianity and the Constitution*, (Grand Rapids, Michigan: Baker Books House, 1987), 136.

23   eorge Washingtion, *Farewell Address 1796*, http://www.yale.edu/lawweb/avalon/washing.htm (*accessed April 3, 2009*).

Where is the security for property, for reputation, for life, if the sense of religious obligation deserts the oaths which are the instruments of investigation in courts of justice? And let us with caution indulge the supposition that morality can be maintained without religion. Whatever may be conceded to the influence of refined education on minds of peculiar structure, reason and experience both forbid us to expect that national morality can prevail in exclusion of religious principle. It is substantially true that virtue or morality is a necessary spring of popular government. The rule, indeed, extends with more or less force to every species of free government. Who that is a sincere friend to it can look with indifference upon attempts to shake the foundation of the fabric.[24]

This view of the importance of religion existed for most of the country's history. Samuel P. Huntington, the Albert J. Weatherhead II University Professor at Harvard, summarized the role of religion in general and Christianity in particular as,

Along with their general religiosity, the Christianity of Americans has impressed foreign observers and been affirmed by Americans. "We are a Christian people," the Supreme Court declared in 1811. In the midst of the Civil War, Lincoln also described Americans as "a Christian people." In 1892 the Supreme Court again declared, "This is a Christian nation." In 1917 Congress passed legislation declaring a day of prayer in support of the war effort and invoking America's status as a Christian nation. In 1931 the Supreme Court reaffirmed its earlier view: "We are a Christian people, according to one another the equal right of religious freedom, and acknowledging with reverence the duty of obedience to the will of God."[25]

The Founding Fathers saw religion as a vital part of society's fabric and essential for maintaining a free society. But as important as religion was, the Founding Fathers knew that religion posed some severe dangers. Based on the historical experience of Europe,

---

24   George Washingtion, *Farewell Address 1796,* http://www.yale.edu/law-web/avalon/washing.htm (*accessed April 3, 2009*).

25   Samuel P Huntington, "Under God", *Wall Street Journal, June 16, 2004* http://opinionjournal.com/editorial/feature.html?id=110005223 (*accessed April 3, 2009*).

the fear was that leaders might declare one religion the official religion and then use its favored position to limit and suppress the religious practices of others. Madison, in Federalist No. 51, wrote,

> In a free government the security for civil rights must be the same as that for religious rights. It consists in the one case in the multiplicity of interests, and in the other the multiplicity of sects.[26]

Madison cites that as a danger, "[t]he stronger faction can readily unite and oppress the weaker."[27] When it came to religion, this was a real fear. Most European countries had official state churches, which historically used their power to oppress other sects.

So, the Founding Fathers sought a way to ensure the importance of religion without actually making it a part of government. On June 7, 1789, Madison proposed the following First Amendment to the Constitution.

> The Civil Rights of none shall be abridged on account of religious belief or worship, nor shall any national religion be established, nor shall the full and equal rights of conscience be in any manner, or on any pretext infringed.[28]

After debate, the wording of the religious clause eventually read,

> Congress shall pass no law respecting the establishment of religion, or prohibiting the free exercise thereof.

As historian Paul Johnson summarizes this amendment,

> In effect, the First Amendment forbade Congress to favor one Church, or religious sect, over another. It certainly did not inhibit Congress from identifying itself with the religious impulse as such or from authorizing religious practices where all could agree on their desirability. The House of Represen-

---

26   Madison, Federalist No. 51 http://www.constitution.org/fed/federa51. htm (*accessed April 3, 2009*).

27   Madison, Federalist No. 51 http://www.constitution.org/fed/federa51. htm (*accessed April 3, 2009*).

28   John Eidsmoe, *Christianity and the Constitution,* (Grand Rapids, Michigan: Baker Books House, 1987), 109.

tatives passed the First Amendment on September 24, 1789. The next day it passed, by a two-to-one majority, a resolution calling for a day of national prayer and thanksgiving.[29]

The representatives who passed the First Amendment the next day also passed a resolution calling for a national day of prayer and thanksgiving, demonstrating that they did not see the First Amendment as saying that the government must avoid any religious expression altogether.

Frederick Mark Gedicks, professor of Law at Brigham Young University, writing in the *Oxford Companion to the Supreme Court of the United States,* describes this view of the First Amendment as a "de facto Establishment." Gedricks states,

> Nineteenth-century Americans understood the Constitution to require separation of church and state only at the institutional level. This meant that constitutionally prohibited establishments of religion were created when the government coerced funding of or participation in a particular denomination or sect. However, it did not require that government be secular.[30]

Interpreting or Rewriting?

This de facto establishment understanding of the First Amendment lasted throughout the first 160 years of the country. But starting in 1947 with Everson v. Board of Education of Ewing Township, the Supreme Court began to change this. They, in effect, began to rewrite the Constitution.

At issue in Everson was a New Jersey law that reimbursed parents of school children for the cost of bus fare to and from school. Arch Everson, a resident of Ewing Township, opposed this because the law also reimbursed parents whose children went to

---

29   Paul Johnson, *A History of the American People,* (New York: Harper-Collins, 1997) 209.
30   Kermit L. Hall, ed. *The Oxford Companion to the Supreme Court of the United States,* (1992), s.v. "Religion" 718.

Catholic parochial schools. Everson claimed this violated the First Amendment.

The judges reviewed the comments of the Founding Fathers on the dangers of state support for religion. Yet, this did not lead them to conclude that the New Jersey law was unconstitutional. In fact,

> The net result was the opposite. We must not, he [Hugo Black] said, strike down New Jersey's statute because it reaches the verge of its power or deprives its citizens of benefits because of their religion. The First Amendment requires the state to be neutral in its relation with groups of religious and nonbelievers, it does not require the state to be their adversary. The State power is no more to be used to handicap than to favor religions.[31]

Thus, the court ruled that the New Jersey law was constitutional. Yet, while the ruling itself was in accord with the understanding of the First Amendment of the Founding Fathers, the country, and the courts for the first 160 years, the judges included in their reasoning some principles that effectively rewrote the First Amendment. As Gedricks points out,

> With *Everson,* the Supreme Court clearly signaled that de facto establishment would be abandoned as a guide to church-state relations.[32]

In its place, the Court would use a new standard, quoting a now-famous phrase not from the Constitution but from a letter written by Thomas Jefferson. In 1802, Thomas Jefferson wrote to a Baptist group in Danbury, Connecticut. These Baptists had supported Jefferson in a dispute with some mutual political opponents during the presidential election in which Jefferson was a candidate. He responded to them by writing:

---

31   Kermit L. Hall, ed. *The Oxford Companion to the Supreme Court of the United States, (1992), s.v. "Everson v. Board of Education of Ewing Township",* 263.
32   Kermit L. Hall, ed. *The Oxford Companion to the Supreme Court of the United States, (1992), s.v. "Religion",* 719.

I contemplate with solemn reverence that act of the whole American people which declared that their legislature should "make no law respecting an establishment of religion, or prohibiting the free exercise thereof," thus, building a wall of separation between Church and State.[33]

This letter, not the Constitution, is where we get the phrase "separation of church and state." Jefferson stated that the institutions of the State, his opponents in Connecticut, could not persecute the institutions of the church, his supporters, the Danbury Baptists, because the First Amendment provided a wall that protected them. He was supporting the Baptists.

As John Wilson and Donald Drakeman wrote in their book *Church and State in American History,*

...the letter is a wholly conventional response, and might question whether it provides a likely foundation for the "wall of separation" it allegedly supports.[34]

The effect of the Supreme Court's ruling was to make Jefferson's statement more significant to interpreting the Constitution than what it actually said. It effectively tossed out the old establishment clause, replacing it with Jefferson's statement, which is now, for all practical purposes, the new religious clause of the First Amendment.

Nothing reflects this change more than when most people now want to refer to what the First Amendment says about religion; they usually do not quote what the First Amendment says. Instead, they unknowingly cite the court ruling that quoted Thomas Jefferson's statement on a "separation of church and State."

Many are surprised that the words "separation of church and State" are not in the Constitution. In short, the First Amendment,

---

33   Thomas Jefferson, *To Messrs. Nehemiah Dodge and Others, a Committee of the Danbury Baptist Association of the State of Connecticut, 1802,* http://www.lonang.com/exlibris/misc/danbury.htm *(accessed April 3, 2009).*
34   John Wilson and Donald Drakeman ed, *Church and State in American History,* (Boston, MA: Beacon Press 1987), 78.

as written, does not say what most people now believe the First Amendment means. So, they quote the new meaning provided by the court in 1947 rather than the old words adopted in 1789.

Again, the issue here is how this change happened. Perhaps you think this was a good change; Perhaps not. Still, the people working through the democratic process did not decide to make this change in the country's foundation. It was a change made by unelected judges and then imposed on the country.

From or For

Not only is this a change to what the Constitution says, but it is also a significant change to the underlying purposes of the First Amendment. The Founding Fathers believed religion to be so important that it needed protection from the corrupting power of government that would seek to restrict it. As Huntington points out,

> At the end of the 18th century, religious establishments existed throughout Europe and in several American states. Control of the church was a key element of state power, and the established church, in turn, provided legitimacy to the state. The framers of the Constitution prohibited an established national church in order to limit the power of government and to protect and strengthen religion. The purpose of "separation of church and state," as William McLoughlin has said, was not to establish freedom from religion but to establish freedom for religion.[35]

However, by the middle of the twentieth century, many no longer accepted this view within the intellectual elite. On the contrary, there was a growing belief in secularism.

> The 1930s also saw elaboration of the "secularization hypothesis" by intellectuals in both the United States and Europe. Under this hypothesis, progressive secularization of society was seen as an inevitable and positive long-term trend that would

35   Samuel Huntington, *Atheists ARE Outsiders in America,* Wall Street Journal, June 16, 2004, https://historynewsnetwork.org/article/samuel-huntington-atheists-are-outsiders-in-americ (Accessed March 26, 2024)

eventually end in the elimination of religion as a public influence... In *The Crisis of Democratic Theory* (1972), intellectual historian Edward Purcell, Jr. describes how in the Twentieth century, religion "emerged as the preeminent symbol of everything that was bad in human society" ... Religion had come to be seen as a reactionary obstacle to secular progress.[36]

This latter view was clearly not the view or intention of those who wrote the Constitution, the First Amendment, or those who ratified it. Nor was it the view of the country or the courts for the first century and a half of its existence. So, the question for the intellectual elites was how to get this new view into law.

Supporters of this new view faced a considerable obstacle in the fact that in the 1940s, the vast majority of the American people would still have agreed with the opinion of the Founding Fathers; they would reject promoting secularism. Thus, had an amendment to the constitution been proposed, changing the First Amendment to "separation of church and state," such an amendment would undoubtedly fail.

The Supreme Court got around these problems by reinterpreting the First Amendment to accord with this new view of religion. I am not saying there was some sort of conscious conspiracy to change the First Amendment. Such a conspiracy would be implausible and completely unnecessary. Instead, this view grew naturally from the judges' worldview and, more importantly, the new theory that judges should set policy rather than rule on the law.

The new view of secularism, widespread among the intellectual elites, instead of seeing religion as so necessary that it needed protection, now saw religion as so dangerous society needed protection from it. The Court simply reinterpreted the First Amendment in accord with this new view. That is how they saw their role. To be clear, this was not a political decision but one based on their different views of the Constitution.

---

36   Kermit L. Hall, ed. *The Oxford Companion to the Supreme Court of the United States, (1992), s.v. "Religion."*

The result of this reinterpretation or change is that the First Amendment, passed to ensure the freedom of religion, has been turned into the primary tool of those opposed to religion to suppress it. It has, in effect, been turned entirely on its head.

I have focused on religion in this discussion, but the same thing has happened in many other areas. For example, the founders intended the Free Speech Clause to protect political speech. Not only has it significantly been extended to include things like pornography, but now this has been turned on its head to the point that political speech is the only speech the government can control and limit.

Many laws regulating campaigns effectively control speech in one fashion or another. Potential candidates have to play coy games about whether or not they will run for a particular office, for once they announce, a whole series of laws and regulations kick in. These are often very complex; novice candidates and grassroots movements often inadvertently run afoul of them. Today, speech codes and cancel culture place severe limits on dissenting views.

Before the Kelo vs. New London ruling, the government could only take your land for public use, such as building a road. Now, if someone wants to buy your land but you don't want to sell it, the government can take it from you and sell it to them. In short, they can take your land for any reason they want. In area after area, there was what the Constitution says and was understood to say for most of the country's history, and then there is what the court now tells us it means.

Judges or Kings

The critical issue here for the Rule of Law is not so much that there was a change in the understanding of the First Amendment or any of these other areas but rather how the court brought about this change. The critical point for the Rule of Law is that rulers are under the law instead of the law under the rulers.

If the new secularization hypothesis is accurate, and the original understanding of the First Amendment is outdated or needs to be changed, the founders provided an amendment provision within the Constitution to allow this. Supporters of the change could write an amendment that would have changed the First Amendment from "Congress shall make no law respecting an establishment of religion or prohibiting the free exercise thereof" to "there shall be a separation of church and state" or to whatever new wording was deemed necessary.

If the people did not support such a change, they could have argued why it is needed. Sure, this would take time. It could fail. But that is the democratic process. That is the rule of law.

Yet, rather than wait for a constitutional amendment, the court took it upon itself to make what they believed were the needed changes. By making this change, the Supreme Court put itself above the Constitution and the law. In the words of Chief Justice Charles Evans Hughes, "The Constitution is what the judges say it is."[37]

Over the decades since, the Court has taken further steps, reinterpreting old rights by giving them new meanings and even creating new rights, thereby adding to the Constitution. The court then used some of these new interpretations in later rulings to justify even further changes.

As a result, these decisions sometimes contradicted each other, causing confusion and uncertainty and clearly demonstrating that the justices were imposing their own views on the Constitution rather than basing their rulings on it.

Those with this new Living Constitution View defend this confusion, claiming that it is the legitimate role of the courts to interpret the law, and as such, rulings are not making new laws but rather that these rulings are a legitimate function of courts. The courts interpret the law, so it is whatever the courts say.

---

37   cited in Robert Bork, *The Tempting of America,* (New York: Free Press, 1990), 176.

This view is, in effect, the same argument as 'the King can do no wrong' that we looked at earlier in the chapter. The King makes the law, so anything the King does is proper. The only real difference is that we have judges instead of a king. With this line of thinking, it is the court's job to interpret, so any interpretation they give is proper; the court can do no wrong.

When is a Change a Change?

Despite claims to the contrary, the ability to reinterpret the law, giving it new meaning, is effectively the same as making a new law. For those affected by the change, there is no practical difference between, for example, Congress passing a law forbidding students at high school graduation from saying a voluntary prayer and the Supreme Court issuing a ruling based on their new understanding of the First Amendment that such prayers are unconstitutional. In both cases, the students cannot pray.

Before the new 1947 interpretation, such a law passed by Congress would violate the First Amendment clause, saying Congress shall pass no law "prohibiting the free exercise" of religion. Yet, despite this, in 1992, the Supreme Court, using the new understanding of the First Amendment, banned such voluntary prayer in Lee v. Weismann.

The wide swing in the court's rulings based on this new view occurred during the presidency of Franklin Roosevelt. Early in his term, the Court was balanced 4-4, with Justice Owen Roberts, a Hoover appointee, being the swing vote. While Roberts sometimes sided with the progressives, the court still struck down much of the New Deal Legislation. These rejections prompted FDR to propose changing the court's composition so he could appoint judges more favorable to him. People saw this proposal as trying to pack the court. It was rejected even by many within the Democratic party.

While Roosevelt's court-packing scheme failed, he did get a more progressive court because of retirements. Running for an unprecedented third and then a fourth term, he replaced all the justices with progressives by the end of his presidency. Using a living document understanding of the Constitution, these judges greatly expanded the federal government's scope far beyond what enumerated powers had formerly understood through a series of rulings.

Unfortunately, this meant that many increasingly saw the Court's rulings as political. While ideology, not politics, drove their decisions, they made decisions that earlier courts had left to the legislative body. At a minimum, they were making decisions that, until then, had been political and, thus, seemed political.

Those opposed to this new Living Constitution view began to crystallize around the term Originalism, and they started the effort to get Originalist justices on the court. At first, the Living Constitution Justices had such a majority there was not much concern. As the number of Originalist justices grew, so did the political battles over the court.

Nothing shows the increasing polarization between these two views more than the politicization of judicial appointments, particularly to the Supreme Court. Even into the 1980s, the appointments to the Supreme Court were minor stories. Antonin Scalia, appointed by Ronald Reagan to the Supreme Court in 1986, faced no real opposition during his senate hearing and was approved 98-0.

The first real fight occurred the following year when Ronald Reagan appointed Robert Bork. His appointment sparked the first in what would become a series of hotly contested nomination fights. Bork was defeated, and Anthony Kennedy went on the Supreme Court instead.

The reason for the battle was simple; these two views of the Constitution produced starkly different rulings. Under the Living Constitution view, the Founding Fathers' view of the courts as the weakest and least important branch[38] was no longer valid. Judges

38   Hamilton, Federalist No. 78 https://founders.archives.gov/documents/Hamilton/01-04-02-0241 (*accessed July 15, 2023*).

were to take on a more prominent role in determining public policy. If that is true, then the judge matters greatly.

Once Kennedy joined the court, Originalists and Living Constitutionalists were divided equally for the next few decades, with one or more justices being swing votes. In 2018, Anthony Kennedy, then the swing vote, retired, resulting in one of the most significant fights. Ultimately, the Senate confirmed Brett Kavanaugh, giving Originalists a 5-4 majority. However, there was some question that Chief Justice Robert was becoming the new swing vote. Two years later, the Originalist majority expanded to 6-3 upon Ruth Bader Ginsburg's death and Amy Coney Barrett's appointment to replace her. Kavanaugh and Barrett's appointments gave the Originalists their first majority on the Supreme Court in 90 years.

Today, the battle over the Living Constitution versus Originalism as a method for judicial interpretation continues. The main difference is that with the change to a slim Originalist majority, which side is complaining about the current court and which side is supporting their ruling has switched.

The re-emergence of Originalism saw several rulings grounded in the Living Constitution view overturned. Just as some accused the court of acting politically in earlier rulings, others made the same charge about the current court. Only the sides have changed. Still, both are incorrect. These rulings result from different judicial philosophies, not different political views.

Democracy hangs in the balance. If the Constitution is a living document, it would no longer mean what it says but only what a current majority of justices on the Supreme Court tells us. That meaning would be subject to change/reinterpretation with each new court ruling. It would cease to be the United States's controlling document and become a tool for the current court to reshape the country as they saw fit.

This view is especially troubling for democracy because such court action, by its very nature, is anti-democratic. When a court rules a law unconstitutional, it removes the right to democratically pass such laws. It is saying, in this case, the democratically expressed will of the people cannot be allowed. The more the courts make such rulings, the less say the people have in the country.

This issue ultimately comes down to who will define the society in which we live. Will people, through the democratic process, determine the type of society we live in, or will it be chosen by a few unelected judges, who then impose their view of society on the people?

One of the reasons this can be such a problematic issue is that those who like a court's rulings will tend to support the court. In discussions on this issue, I have seen the court's actions defended with the argument that the groups supporting them 'just don't have the political power to legislate.' Thus, the courts were the only way to get them into law.

Other chapters end with a "What can be done" section. In this case, before discussing what can be done, we need to look at one more issue recently coming to the forefront of the discussion. As the Originalist court overturned earlier rulings that depended on the Living Constitution view, some critics have charged that this threatens the Rule of Law. There is at least the potential for merit in this charge, and we will take up the issue of *stare decisis* in the next chapter.

THE RULE OF LAW
PART II: *STARE DECISIS*

The power of the lawyer is in the uncertainty of the law.
Jeremy Bentham
If we desire respect for the law, we must first make the law respectable.
Louis D. Brandeis

S cott was born when the new government under the Constitution was only ten years old. The nation's second president, John Adams, would soon be replaced by its third, Thomas Jefferson, following one of the most contentious elections in American history. The peaceful transfer of power following a very controversial election demonstrated the new system could work. Nevertheless, the new government, founded on liberty, failed a significant segment of the population, including Scott, as he was born into slavery.

During his early life, the Blow family that owned Scott moved several times from Virginia to Alabama to Missouri, where his owner, Peter Blow, died. The family sold Scott and another slave to an Army doctor, John Emerson. Scott disliked Dr. Emerson and tried to escape but was captured and returned.

As an Army doctor, Emerson frequently moved to new posts, one of which was Fort Snelling, situated on Mendota Heights overlooking the confluence of the Minnesota and Mississippi Rivers. At the time, this was the Wisconsin territory; now, it is the state of Minnesota, near Minneapolis.

While at Fort Snelling, Scott met Harriet Robison, another slave. Harriet's owner was a Justice of the Peace, and even though not legally recognized, he married the couple and transferred ownership of Harriet to Dr. Emerson so they could be together.

The Army transferred Dr. Emerson to Louisiana. He initially left the couple at Fort Snelling, sending for them later. The Army then reassigned Dr. Emerson back to Fort Snelling the following year. In 1840, Dr. Emerson returned to Missouri, where he left the Army two years later. When he died in 1843, his widow, Irene Emerson, began leasing the Scotts to nearby farms.

By then, the Scotts had several children and feared that Mrs. Emerson might sell their daughters. While a slave, he could earn some money, and when he had saved enough, he attempted to buy freedom for his family and himself. But Emerson's widow refused.

With few options left, Harriet's pastor, a well-known abolitionist, connected the Scotts with a lawyer, and they filed suit to win their freedom in St Louis Circuit Court. At first, things went well; the law and precedent were on their side.

The lower Court ruled that since they lived for two years in Wisconsin Territory, which did not permit slavery, the couple had become free, and "once free, always free." But later, this ruling was reversed by the Missouri Supreme Court in Scott v. Emerson, overturning 28 years of Missouri precedent, which provoked a sharp dissent from Justice Gamble.

Irene Emerson had moved to Massachusetts, a free state. Not wanting to deal with the issue any longer but unwilling to sell the Scotts their freedom, she transferred ownership to her brother, John Sanford, a citizen of New York. This transfer gave Scott a new recourse.

Since Scott, if free, was a citizen of Missouri, and his new owner was in New York, this made it an interstate issue where Federal courts had jurisdiction. Scott filed suit again, this time in Federal court. He initially lost and appealed to the Supreme Court. Due to a clerical error, this case, perhaps the most infamous in the Court's history, came down as Dred Scott v. Sandford.

In the ruling, made in 1856, Chief Justice Roger B. Taney wrote that,

> A free negro of the African race, whose ancestors were brought to this country and sold as slaves, is not a "citizen" within the meaning of the Constitution of the United States.[1]

Taney justified this conclusion on the notion that while the Declaration of Independence stated that "all men are created equal,"

> it is too clear for dispute, that the enslaved African race were not intended to be included, and formed no part of the people who framed and adopted this declaration;[2]

In another part of the Court's decision, Taney tried to justify his decision with some of the most despicable words found in a Supreme Court decision. He wrote that Blacks were,

> regarded as beings of an inferior order, and altogether unfit to associate with the white race, either in social or political relations; and so far inferior, that they had no rights which the white man was bound to respect; and that the negro might justly and lawfully be reduced to slavery for his benefit.[3]

That many people at the time agreed with Taney is indisputable, but so is the fact that many didn't. Certainly, Justices McLean and Curtis didn't; both wrote lengthy dissents. Justice McLean wrote

> free colored persons born within some of the States are citizens of those States, such persons are also citizens of the United States... I dissent, therefore, from that part of the opinion

---

1   Dred Scott v. John F. A. Sandford, https://tile.loc.gov/storage-services/service/ll/usrep/usrep060/usrep060393a/usrep060393a.pdf (Accessed, 6/23/2023)
2   Dred Scott v. John F. A. Sandford, https://tile.loc.gov/storage-services/service/ll/usrep/usrep060/usrep060393a/usrep060393a.pdf (Accessed, 6/23/2023)
3   Dred Scott v. John F. A. Sandford, https://tile.loc.gov/storage-services/service/ll/usrep/usrep060/usrep060393a/usrep060393a.pdf (Accessed, 6/23/2023)

of the majority of the Court, in which it is held that a person of African descent cannot be a citizen of the United States.[4]

Mclean also argued that when in the free territory of Wisconsin, Dr. Emerson and Scott were subject to the territory's laws duly enacted by Congress. As such, the Scotts were "free, as the law was then settled, and continued for fourteen years afterward." The fourteen years afterward refers to when the Missouri Supreme Court overturned it. Yet, as a state, Missouri did not have a basis for overruling the laws passed by Congress for the Wisconsin territory.

Justice Curtis rejected, among other things, the claim that "the Constitution was made exclusively by and for the white race." As he wrote in his dissent,

> It has already been shown that in five of the thirteen original States, colored persons then possessed the elective franchise, and were among those by whom the Constitution was ordained and established. If so, it is not true, in point of fact, that the Constitution was made exclusively by the white race. And that it was made exclusively for the white race is, in my opinion, not only an assumption not warranted by anything in the Constitution, but contradicted by its opening Declaration, that it was ordained and established by the people of the United States, for themselves and their posterity. And as free colored persons were then citizens of at least five States, and so in every sense part of the people of the United States, they were among those for whom and whose posterity the Constitution was ordained and established.[5]

In addition to rejecting Scott's claim, the Court's majority also ruled that Congress could not prohibit slavery in the territory and overturned the Missouri Compromise, only the second time the Court overturned a federal law.

---

4   Dred Scott v. John F. A. Sandford, https://tile.loc.gov/storage-services/service/ll/usrep/usrep060/usrep060393a/usrep060393a.pdf (Accessed, 6/23/2023)

5   Dred Scott v. John F. A. Sandford, https://tile.loc.gov/storage-services/service/ll/usrep/usrep060/usrep060393a/usrep060393a.pdf (Accessed, 6/23/2023)

In the Dred Scott decision, Taney not only ruled that Scott had remained a slave even in areas where slavery was illegal, but he reinterpreted slavery from something that was allowed to something the federal government could not limit. Like some of the decision discussed in the last chapter, he effectively created a new right, this time a right to own slaves. As legal scholar Robert Bork summarized it,

> when he was done he had denied the power of the federal government to prevent slavery in any state or territory and the power of the federal government to permit any state or territory to bar slavery within its territory.[6]

His ruling was not only an attempt to guarantee the rights of southern slaveholders but, if allowed to remain in effect, would have erased the distinction between free and slave states. By 're-interpreting' the Constitution, all states would have become slave states, for no state could have banned slavery.

Taney and the other justices in the majority may have hoped to settle the issue of slavery once and for all, which had plagued the country even in the Constitutional Convention. Yet, their ruling had the opposite effect. A little over a year later, Lincoln repeatedly referred to this ruling in the Lincoln – Douglas Debates. During the fifth debate at Galesburg, Illinois, he challenged Taney's claim that the Declarations statement that "all men are created equal" referred only to white men, a view Judge Douglas accepted.

> I believe the entire records of the world, from the date of the Declaration of Independence up to within three years ago, may be searched in vain for one single affirmation, from one single man, that the negro was not included in the Declaration of Independence; I think I may defy Judge Douglas to show that he ever said so, that Washington ever said so, that any President ever said so, that any member of Congress ever said so, or that any living man upon the whole earth ever said so, until the necessities of the present policy of the Democratic party, in regard to slavery, had to invent that affirmation. And

6   Robert Bork, *The Tempting of America*, (New York: The Free Press, 1990), 30

I will remind Judge Douglas and this audience, that while Mr. Jefferson was the owner of slaves, as undoubtedly he was, in speaking upon this very subject, he used the strong language that "he trembled for his country when he remembered that God was just;" and I will offer the highest premium in my power to Judge Douglas if he will show that he, in all his life, ever uttered a sentiment at all akin to that of Jefferson. [7]

We can see a strong justification for Lincoln's claim that this was a new idea less than three years old at the time of the debate in the person of John C. Calhoun. Calhoun was a significant figure in the discussion over slavery until his death in 1850. He was also an ardent racist who saw slavery not as a necessary evil but as a positive good.

Calhoun rejected the Declaration of Independence, for he recognized the transformational quality of its claim,

> that all men are created equal, that they are endowed by their Creator with certain unalienable Rights, that among these are Life, Liberty and the pursuit of Happiness.

The problem was he did not like the transformation he was seeing. During the summer of 1848, the Senate debated a bill establishing a government for the Oregon territory. This territory was much larger than the current state, covering the northwest coast eastward into parts of present-day Montana and Wyoming. Whether a new territory or a new state, the issue of slavery always came up. Would this area be slave or free?

In his speech on the bill, Calhoun rejected the "erroneous" claim all men are created equal found in the Declaration. He argued the error had germinated and was now producing fruit, such as, limits on slavery.

> We now begin to experience the danger of admitting so great an error to have a place in the Declaration of our independence. For a long time it lay dormant; but in the process of time it began to germinate, and produce its poisonous fruits. It had strong hold on the mind of Mr. Jefferson, the author

---

7   Lincoln, Abraham, Lincoln-Douglas Debate, Fifth Debate, Oct 7, 1858
https://www.nps.gov/liho/learn/historyculture/debate5.htm

of that document, which caused him to take an utterly false view of the subordinate relation of the black to the white race in the South; and to hold, in consequence, that the latter, though utterly unqualified to possess liberty, were as fully entitled to both liberty and equality as the former; and that to deprive them of it was unjust and immoral.[8]

Within eight years after the speech, some, like Taney, would attempt to reconcile the Declaration's claim with the existence of slavery by claiming the men in this statement only included white men.

Yet, it seems clear that Calhoun never heard of this or at least did not consider it a serious option. If he had, he certainly would have adopted it. Calhoun believed the Declaration's claim did include all men, which, being a racist, is why he considered it "so great an error to have a place in the Declaration of our Independence."

Rather than settle the issue, the Dred Scott decision inflamed the sides. While hardly the only factor, it contributed to the growing division within the country that resulted in the Civil War four years later. As President, Lincoln worked hard and was instrumental in passing the 13th Amendment to overturn Dred Scott v. Sandford. Following his assassination, the required number of states ratified it.

Stare Decisis

As stated in the last chapter, a critical component of the Rule of Law is the ability of people to know and understand what the law is. A law that depends on the will of a ruler precludes the Rule of Law. A ruler can change their mind at a moment's notice or even after the fact. You can never have confidence in the law when the laws are subject to such change.

---

8   John C. Calhoun, *Speech on the Oregon Bill,* In *The U.S. Constitution: A Reader.* (Hillsdale College Press. Kindle Edition, 2012) 425

This presents a critical problem for judges. Judges are people. Even the best judges can and do make mistakes; some are better than others. So, how should a judge rule when they think an earlier judge made a mistake? The law would have no certainty if current courts constantly changed the rulings of earlier courts.

The legal doctrine of *stare decisis* helps protect from that. *Stare decisis* is a Latin phrase that means to stand by a decided matter. It recognizes the importance of consistency in the Law. It argues that current judges should not overturn earlier rulings unless there is a compelling reason to do so.

Yet, like so many valuable principles, it is not absolute. Some rulings are so problematic they need to be overturned. So, the real question is when. When should a prior ruling be overturned, and when should it be upheld? This question is subtle and complex, and controversy often accompanies these cases.

In any legal case, there are multiple concerns. Parties are involved in some conflict before the court, and then there is the law. Ruling based on the law is often confused with taking sides in a dispute; this is especially true when a case involves an issue concerning *stare decisis*.

To see this, consider a case before the Court. One side likes the earlier decision. They argue that it was correct and that *stare decisis* means it should stand. The other claims the earlier decision was incorrect and the court should overturn the prior ruling. Suppose you are the judge, and the latter's arguments concerning the law convince you the earlier ruling was incorrect, but what about *stare decisis*?

While most today would agree that the Court should not have overturned the precedent in Scott v. Emerson, would it have been equally wrong for a judge to overturn Dred Scott v. Sandford? An equal number would probably say no; Dred Scott v. Sandford was so wrong it could not stand. Nor was the Dred Scott decision the last major mistake made by the court, and thus, the issue of *stare decisis* plays a role in many recent decisions.

Plessy v. Ferguson

The reconstruction era following the Civil War saw a significant expansion in freedom for Blacks. In addition to the 13th amendment, the 14th and 15th amendments were passed to try and secure the civil liberties of Blacks in the Constitution. Under the leadership of Ulysses S. Grant, these were largely successful. Tragically, they did not last.

The election of 1876 ended in confusion with no clear winner and disputed electors. It was finally settled four months later with the compromise of 1877. In the Compromise, Hayes would become President by one electoral vote. In exchange, he would withdraw Federal troops from the South, ending reconstruction.

With reconstruction over and the troops gone, Southern Democrats quickly expanded their efforts to restrict the freedom of Blacks through Jim Crow laws, named after a character in a Black minstrel show. In 1880, Louisiana passed a law requiring separate but equal rail cars for Blacks and Whites. While separate in practice, typically, they were equal only in theory.

Homer Plessy was arrested for sitting in the wrong car and found guilty by Judge John Ferguson. In Plessy v. Ferguson (1896), the Supreme Court upheld Plessy's conviction, enshrining separate but equal into the Constitution for the next 60 years. In the lone dissent, Justice John Marshall Harlan, who also dissented from the Civil Rights Cases (1883), wrote,

> But in view of the constitution, in the eye of the law, there is in this country no superior, dominant, ruling class of citizens. There is no caste here. Our constitution is color-blind, and neither knows nor tolerates classes among citizens. In respect of civil rights, all citizens are equal before the law. The humblest is the peer of the most powerful. The law regards man as man, and takes no account of his surroundings or of his color when his civil rights as guaranteed by the supreme law of the land are involved.[9]

9   Plessy v. Ferguson, 163 U.S. 537 (1896) https://supreme.justia.com/cases/federal/us/163/537/ (Accessed, 4/3/2024)

Justice Harlan predicted, "In my opinion, the judgment this day rendered will, in time, prove to be quite as pernicious as the decision made by this tribunal in the Dred Scott Case." He was proved correct. While the other cases are still considered "good law," both Dred Scott and Plessy v. Ferguson are considered anti-canon by virtually all modern legal scholars, mistakes by the Court.

The court's doctrine of separate but equal lasted for sixty years until the issue of segregation came up again over schools. While highly controversial at the time, today, few question the correctness of the ruling in Brown v. Board of Education (1954) or the lesser known but simultaneous ruling, Bolling v. Sharpe (1954). It is a prime example where the court should reject *stare decisis* and overturn a previous ruling.

The Court Giveth, The Court Taketh Away

Even for those who like how the court is ruling, if it moves away from either the law or from *stare decisis* without a good reason, this is, at best, a short-term solution. The problem with getting the court to impose a particular view on society instead of working through the democratic process is that if the court is free to determine such values, it is just as free to do pretty much whatever they want. The court's rulings will not be determined by what the law says but by the values of the current judges. Without the law as a foundation, rulings will only be as good as the values of the current majority of judges.

Even if a group can get a majority of judges on the court that agree with them, there is no guarantee that this majority will last. If history is any guide, believing that any particular group can maintain a majority on the court indefinitely is unreasonable.

As we saw in the last chapter, FDR established a favorable majority that lasted until recently, but now there is an Originalist majority. A court that gives rights is free to take them away or cancel them out with other new "rights" in the future. If you ignore *stare decisis* when your group dominates the Court, then trying to claim it when you lose control will likely be unpersuasive.

It should be no surprise the Supreme Court building has become the site of significant political gatherings and protests over the last several decades. The more judges place themselves over the law, the more they take on a legislative role rather than just a judicial role; the more they will become subject to political debates. People instinctively know when judges are making laws. Thus, they regularly lobby the court in the same fashion as they would lobby the President or Congress.

Most of the court's work has little, if any, policy implications. It is not affected by these differing philosophies, so most court rulings have no consistent ideological alignment. The alignment became more significant during the twentieth century. It became increasingly controversial in the last quarter of the century, as while few in number, the policies they set were visible to the public at large and a source of controversy.

We can see this new political role in the appointment of judges. At one time, the appointment of judges, even Supreme Court judges, caused little stir or controversy. And why should it? People believed that judges could only rule on the law; they couldn't make it. So, as long as the judge was knowledgeable concerning the law and had shown the judicial temperament to make rulings objectively, that was all that was important.

Judges who ruled based on what they thought the law should be always existed. We can see this in Justice Tawney's ruling in Dred Scott. Still, as we saw in the last chapter, a new view began forming with the Progressive era, which held that a judge should rule in this fashion. Such rulings were not an aberration but a desired outcome.

As judges started to take an increasingly legislative role, the appointment of judges became the source of major political battles. How could they not? Under the Living Constitution view, the judge's personal views play a more prominent role in rulings.

Political conflicts became inevitable as competing groups jockeyed to get their judges on the court or keep other judges off.

These battles are important since federal judges have lifetime appointments. Losing such a battle does not mean 2 to 6 years until you can replace someone you opposed, as in the case of a politician. In the case of judges, they can be there for decades, rewriting laws long after those who appointed them are gone.

Judges, particularly on the Supreme Court, influence the court's makeup when they adjust their retirement so that a president or governor with favorable political views will choose their replacement. The greater the legislative role judges play, the higher the stakes for particular nominations. Thus, the prominent political battles. As we saw in the last chapter, such conflicts were non-existent until the mid-eighties and have grown since.

Battles over judicial nominations weaken the Rule of Law as those on both sides of an issue increasingly define a 'good' judge as one who will rule on matters the way they want rather than on what the law and Constitution say. Even worse, as the trend to legislate from the bench continues, those judges who restrict their rulings solely to the law and Constitution are considered a significant threat.

This threat stems from the fact that a judge ruling based solely on the law and Constitution would tend to overturn the new reinterpretations of the law made by earlier activist judges. They might restore the law to its original meaning. The only check would be *stare decisis*, but as we have seen, that is not an absolute rule.

Some supporters of a Living Constitution see judges who would rule based solely on the law and Constitution as activists. The whole judicial system becomes distorted to the point where the issues are more important than the law and the Constitution. At that point, the Rule of Law is dead.

The more the courts become politicized, the more the Rule of Law is threatened. The more legislative decisions the courts make, the less democratic the society becomes. When judges impose their will on the people, the people can no longer express their will in the democratic process. The Court ultimately sets policy, not the people. The President and Congress administer the court's decrees under strict guidance.

Theoretically, the solution to this problem is easy: We insist that all judges restrict their ruling to the law and the Constitution. Suppose the law is flawed, or the Constitution is out of date. In that case, it should be addressed not in the courts but through the democratic process, either in the legislative body or, in the case of the Constitution, through the amendment process.

While straightforward in theory, in practice, this is difficult. Such a view would result in the reversal of many previous court rulings, and these rulings have significant political support that will resist any such change. In short, the very politicization that so threatens the Rule of Law and, thus, democracy also resists any attempt to correct the problem. Many people don't mind a king if the king is doing what they like.

For those who support the Rule of Law, there is also the issue of *stare decisis*. A bad decision weakens the Rule of Law. Reversing a prior decision because you think it is wrong also weakens the Rule of Law. There is an unavoidable conflict in these views.

When should a judge uphold a prior ruling because of *stare decisis*? When should a judge overturn it? Again, if you like the policy instituted by an earlier judge, there will be a strong temptation to argue *stare decisis*. But some earlier decisions should not be allowed to remain. We saw this with both Dred Scott and Plessy v. Ferguson.

To better understand *stare decisis*, we will examine some recent decisions to highlight these complexities. With the change in the court's majority, supporters of the earlier decisions argue the court should still uphold them because of *stare decisis*. The first is Roe v. Wade, recently overturned by Dobbs v. Jackson Women's Health Organization. The second is Obergefell v. Hodges, which instituted same-sex marriage. Following the overturning of Roe, some raised concerns that the court might also overturn Oberge-fell. That is unlikely. Again, the focus here is not on the issues themselves but on how the Court made the initial ruling; why it overturned Roe but probably will not overturn Obergefell.

Roe v. Wade

Contrary to the common notion, technically, Roe did not make abortion legal. Before Roe, abortion was a state issue; states were free to do what the people wanted. From the country's found-ing till 1967, abortion was largely illegal across the country.

Initially, this was based on common law, which restricted abortion after quickening, the time when the mother begins to feel the baby move. During the nineteenth century, many states passed specific laws limiting abortion. Before 1967, abortion was illegal across the country. Between 1967 and the Court's ruling, about a third of the states enacted laws to legalize abortion in at least some cases.

What Roe did was rule laws against abortion unconstitution-al. It removed from states, and thus, the people in those states most of the ability to regulate abortion. Roe set up a trimester system, allowing abortion in the first trimester, permitting limited regulation in the second, and allowing states to ban it in the third.

This system proved difficult and problematic, and the court effectively overruled it in 1992. As a matter of law, Planned Par-enthood v. Casey (1992) became the controlling case on abortion before Dobbs. Still, Roe remained the symbol for both sides.

Roe is an excellent example because, as we will see shortly, the Court's decision is right in line with the Living Constitution view and, in fact, requires it. It is also a perfect example of the Court taking on a legislative role from the Originalists' perspective.

The Founding Fathers certainly could have included a right to abortion if they had wanted. After all, abortion is not a new technology like TV or computers, which would have been unfamiliar. Abortion existed long before the Constitution, but it does not mention it.

Because of dual sovereignty with the states, since it is not mentioned, from an Originalist point of view, the Court would have to rule this is not an issue for the federal courts. It was an issue of customary law and, like laws with murder or contracts, left to the people to decide through their state governments.

The Court based its ruling in Roe on an earlier ruling in Griswold v. Connecticut (1965), which similarly found another new right, in this case, the right to privacy. Griswold is a good example of the differences between the issue under consideration, and legal reasoning used in the decision. The issue under consideration was whether the State of Connecticut could pass a law banning birth control for married couples.

Few, if any, today would support such a law. Most would probably think such a law was extremely unwise or even silly. Yet, there is no Constitutional ban on unwise or silly laws. Virtually, everyone can point to laws they think are unwise or silly. The problem is there is no consensus on which laws fall into that category. If there was, then they would repeal these laws.

The question before the court was not whether the Connecticut law was wise, rather could the people of Connecticut working through the democratic process pass such a law; not should they but could they.

These are separate questions, and it is entirely possible that one could say they could but shouldn't. I happen to believe there should be law banning prostitution. Yet, while I believe states should not pass laws legalizing prostitution, I also believe that this is something they could do. It is a matter left to the people to decide and there are a few places in the country where prostitution is legal.

Still, while I oppose it, I do not believe there should be a federal law banning prostitution, as under dual sovereignty this is not a federal concern. On the other hand, with growing calls to legalize prostitution, it is not hard to envision a lawsuit going to the Supreme Court claiming this was right. A Living Constitution judge may or may not agree with them. It would depend on the judge not the Constitution.

A society that legalizes prostitution will be different than one that does not. I think banning prostitution has been an advancement. Still, I trust the democratic process more than the legal system for making these judgments.

In the ruling on Griswold, the court ruled that the people of Connecticut did not have the ability to pass such a law. That leaves the question of the legal justification for the ruling. Justice Douglas, writing for the majority, based his decision on the right to privacy inherent in the marriage relationship which he saw as special and unique.

Yet, there was a problem. The Constitution does not mention a right to privacy. He had to find one. He found this new right coming from the rights that are specified. In his words, he found them in "penumbras, formed by emanations from those guarantees that help give them life and substance."

If this talk of penumbras and emanations sounds vague, it is. Penumbras come from the Latin words meaning 'almost' and 'shadow.' It refers, for example, to the area of partial shadow visible between the sun's corona and the black disk of an eclipse.

Douglas argued the rights specified in the Constitution give off "emanations." These emanations create shadows where he and the other judges in the majority discovered some rights not specified by the Constitution's framers. For Justice Douglas, the marriage relationship was so special and unique, there must be a right to privacy for married couples.

While creating a new right, a right to privacy, what does that even mean? How far does this privacy extent? Is it only limited to the marriage relationship? Thus, Griswold resolved the question in a way virtually all would now agree with, yet did so by creating a new right, one that was vague and ill defined. It would be left to later courts to clarify what this new law meant and how far it extended, and these future rulings would have nowhere near the broad acceptance.

A significant problem is that, once the Court discovered new rights, they became precedents for future judges to use in future rulings. Originalists argue that a judge could use such legal reasoning to justify pretty much anything they would like to find. It turns the Constitution into a legal Rorschach test where judges are pretty much free to see what they want to see. Is a client engaging a prostitute something done in private and thus covered by the right to privacy? What is covered? What is excluded? How are we to know?

It would seem, however, that penumbras and emanations are insufficient, as some more recent Supreme Court Judges have sought additional justifications for their ruling, such as appeals to foreign law. Of course, given the large number of countries and the vast arrays of laws worldwide, a judge could find justification for virtually anything.

A judge only needs to pick the right countries with laws they seek to impose on U.S. citizens, and they have their justification.[10] Of course, this is all dressed up and justified with the appropriate legalese and phrases like 'judicial temperament.' But in the end, there are only two logical options here. Either the judge must derive a ruling from the Constitution or impose one on it. When they resort to emanations, penumbras, foreign law, or other external justifications, they are not basing their ruling on what the Constitution says.

When Roe came before the court, as the Constitution did not address abortion, the Court could not base its ruling on what it

---

10   As an indication of where we have come, a friend who used to create fantasy worlds for role playing games told me that he once created a place where any law anywhere would have to be accepted by the courts as a valid precedent as long as it could be documented. He was criticized at the time as being too unrealistic even for a fantasy world as 'nobody would ever do something that stupid.'

said. Still, the Court, using Griswold's reasoning, discovered the right to abortion. This reasoning is perfectly valid from a Living Constitutional view. From an Originalist view, Roe is something imposed on the Constitution, not derived from it. Thus, polarization.

What-is vs. Should-be

What makes the issue of the court's ideology so tricky is that much of the battle takes place over the results rather than the reasoning. In this case, the issue of abortion itself, rather than what is the Constitutional view of abortion. If, as you have read this, you agreed with Roe or disagreed with Roe because of your views on abortion, you have fallen victim to the very problem of the ruling versus the reasoning.

There is also a problem in that the differing views use different types of reasoning, what-is, and should-be. What-is reasoning focuses on the very narrow question of what the law says on a given topic. Using what-is reasoning, one can look at the statutes to determine the speed limit on a given road at a given time. Thus, it is perfectly possible to determine that the law said the speed limit was 25, yet believe it should be different. This is because what-is reasoning only concerns itself with what the law says on a given issue.

Should-be reasoning is, in many respects, the opposite. Rather than focusing on what the law says, should-be reasoning attempts to determine what the law should be. This type of reasoning leads to a much broader range of concerns. For a speed limit on a given road, you might look at issues like traffic, the neighborhood, visibility, and the number of curves.

Regarding Originalist vs. Living Constitutional views, Originalists confine themselves to what-is reasoning, or at least that is the goal. The key difference with the Living Constitution is that should-be concerns play a role to some degree. If it is the role of the Judge to interpret the Constitution in light of the ever-changing society, the fundamental question changes from what the Constitution says to what our understanding of the Constitution should be.

These two different views of the Constitution have served as the backdrop for the abortion debates for the last 50 years. Each side made arguments that resulted in more conflict than anything else because these arguments were working in different frameworks.

For Pro-Life supporters to say the Constitution does not mention abortion is a what-is argument. For Pro-Choice supporters to say that women need access to abortion is a should-be argument. Both sides were making legitimate arguments from within their perspective.

In contrast, the other side's arguments were, at least to some degree, irrelevant. From a Living Constitution point of view, the fact that the Constitution does not mention abortion is not all that important, given the evolving standards of the time. From an Originalist point of view, should-be arguments are for the legislature, not the courts. Both sides were talking past each other, so the controversy continued.

Dobbs v. Jackson Women's Health Organization

With a new originalist majority on the Supreme Court, it was not long before an abortion case came before the Court, which happened in 2021 with Dobbs v. Jackson Women's Health Organization. At issue was a Mississippi law that prohibited abortion after the fifteenth week, except in cases of "medical emergency or the case of severe fetal abnormality." The issue before the court was whether Mississippi was allowed to pass and enforce such a law.

While not a complete abortion ban, this law directly conflicted with the standards in Roe and subsequent Casey decisions. Both sides agreed that allowing the law would overrule these decisions either formally or informally, as Brown v. Board of Education had effectively overruled Plessy v. Ferguson without actually doing so.

The majority decision by Justice Alito was a solid originalist decision. As he wrote, Roe was an "abuse of judicial authority," valid from an originalist point of view. He described the reasoning in Roe as "remarkably loose in its treatment of the constitutional text." Speaking about the historical analysis upon which Justice Douglas based Roe, Alito argues the analysis,

> ranged from the constitutionally irrelevant (e.g., its discussion of abortion in antiquity) to the plainly incorrect (e.g., its assertion that abortion was probably never a crime under the common law). After cataloging a wealth of other information having no bearing on the meaning of the Constitution, the opinion concluded with a numbered set of rules much like those that might be found in a statute enacted by a legislature.[11]

It should be easy to see the originalist foundation upon which Alito based his arguments. He goes on to argue,

> *Roe* was egregiously wrong from the start. Its reasoning was exceptionally weak, and the decision had damaging consequences. And far from bringing about a national settlement of the abortion issue, *Roe* and *Casey* have enflamed debate and deepened division. [12]

Alito's decision lays out the reason and justifications for his claim. We should note that some legal scholars who are Pro-Choice expressed similar critical views of Roe in the past. Alito cites several of these scholars in his decision. Yet, from a Living Constitutional perspective, these arguments, while possibly valid,

---

11   Dobbs, State Health Officer Of The Mississippi Department Of Health, Et Al. v. Jackson Women's Health Organization Et Al., 19-1392, 19-1392 Dobbs v. Jackson Women's Health Organization (06/24/2022) (supremecourt. gov)

12   Dobbs, State Health Officer Of The Mississippi Department Of Health, Et Al. v. Jackson Women's Health Organization Et Al., 19-1392, 19-1392 Dobbs v. Jackson Women's Health Organization (06/24/2022) (supremecourt. gov)

are not all that important. For them, Abortion should be a right; thus, Roe and Casey were good decisions.

Alito then comes to *stare decisis,* the final argument supporters used to defend Roe and Casey. They argued that Roe and Casey were settled laws for years and that the Court should not overturn them. This argument was not wholly true, at least in the case of Roe, as Casey overruled many provisions in Roe, which is why it was the controlling decision. In addition, given the near-continuous turmoil over abortion in society and the courts, it is hard to consider this settled law. As for the length of time, Plessy was in force longer than Roe and Casey combined.

The question was not, could Dobbs overturn Roe and Casey, but should it? Alito spends considerable time reviewing the court's history and reasoning on *stare decisis.* He summed this up as follows:

> five factors weigh strongly in favor of overruling *Roe* and *Casey:* the nature of their error, the quality of their reasoning, the "workability" of the rules they imposed on the country, their disruptive effect on other areas of the law, and the absence of concrete reliance. [13]

The last reason, concrete reliance, refers to how much overturning Roe and Casey would disturb those things that require advanced planning. Alito spends many pages laying out his arguments for these five reasons. In the end, the court ruled,

> We end this opinion where we began. Abortion presents a profound moral question. The Constitution does not prohibit the citizens of each State from regulating or prohibiting abortion. Roe and Casey arrogated that authority. We now overrule those decisions and return that authority to the people and their elected representatives. [14]

---

13   Dobbs, State Health Officer Of The Mississippi Department Of Health, Et Al. v. Jackson Women's Health Organization Et Al., 19-1392, 19-1392 Dobbs v. Jackson Women's Health Organization (06/24/2022) (supremecourt. gov)
14   Dobbs, State Health Officer Of The Mississippi Department Of Health, Et Al. v. Jackson Women's Health Organization Et Al., 19-1392, 19-1392

A Political Decision?

Many were upset by this decision, and many claimed it was political. As I argued in Chapter Four, decisions based on Living Constitutional views were not political, and neither was this. Dobbs is a carefully reasoned and legitimate decision from the originalist perspective. It is not a Pro-Life decision.

A Pro-Life decision would have looked at the historical record that abortion was generally illegal until the latter part of the twentieth century after the quickening, the first moment when one could be sure there was a living fetus. Given the advancement in medical knowledge and technology that now allows us to see babies in the womb, a Pro-Life decision would conclude that a fetus is a person deserving the protection of the law afforded to all other persons. In short, they would have ruled abortion illegal in some or all cases.

Yet, the Dobbs decision does not do that. Instead, it says abortion is not a Constitutional issue, thereby "returning that authority to the people and their elected representatives." States with large Pro-Choice majorities will see little, if any, change. States with large Pro-Life majorities will see strong limits on abortion. States with populations in between will see some limitations, but not bans, reflecting the views of their population.

Those who want a total abortion ban will dislike that some states still permit it. Those who want no restrictions on abortion will not like that some states have restrictions. Neither side will get everything they want, and laws will vary from state to state, as they do on various other issues. As Winston Churchill famously said,

> Many forms of Government have been tried, and will be tried in this world of sin and woe. No one pretends that democracy is perfect or all-wise. Indeed it has been said that democracy is the worst form of Government except for all those other forms that have been tried from time to time.[15]

Dobbs v. Jackson Women's Health Organization (06/24/2022) (supremecourt. gov)

15   *The Quote Garden, "Quotations about Government,"* http://www.quote-

Marriage

Another clear example of the difference between Living Constitution and Originalist decisions concerns the understanding of marriage. Again, the point of this section is not the marriage laws themselves but how the courts were part of forcing a change.

For a very long time, societies have viewed marriage as a critical foundational pillar of community. As Scott Yenor pointed out in an article, *The True Origin of Society: The Founders on the Family*[16],

> The Founders' occasional statements and their actions generally show that they held marriage and family life to be, in James Wilson's words, "the true origin of society" or the first and most vital foundation on which civil society rests.

They saw its protection in law as necessary. It was a lifelong commitment, till death do us part, that men and women entered into, with not only benefits but also serious obligations and responsibilities. These benefits did not only extend to the individuals but to society, for the family unit was the foundation of communities, and communities the foundation for Society.

As a crucial lifelong commitment, the government encouraged and protected marriage. The promises made in the marriage vows were legally enforceable and protected by law. Married couples received special status and legal privileges to promote such commitments. Divorce was the breaking of legal responsibility, like the breaking of an obligation to repay a loan. Like bankruptcy, it was permitted, but only with sufficient reason.

Since the 1960s, however, marriage has undergone significant changes. Rather than an essential and central pillar of society, it

---

garden.com/government.html (accessed April 3, 2009).
16   Yenor, Scott, *The True Origin of Society: The Founders on the Family*, *The Heritage Foundation*, Oct, 16, 2013, https://www.heritage.org/political-process/report/the-true-origin-society-the-founders-the-family, (Accessed 7/8/2023)

increasingly became a choice some people made. States began relaxing their laws, particularly regarding divorce.

In 1970, California passed the no-fault divorce law. Whatever the reasons for this change at the time, a significant effect was that it effectively abolished the traditional view of marriage as a lifelong commitment. Sure, a couple could still commit "until death do us part," and most did. Yet, in the eyes of the government, such obligations were no longer legally enforceable. They were, in the terms of the law, meaningless.

Over the next several decades, states began to remove many of the legal protections and benefits of marriage. Increasingly, in terms of the law, marriage was just another legal agreement people entered into. Rather than being preferred and protected above other agreements, it became lower and less important; in some cases, it became optional and unimportant.

The devaluation of marriage occurred not only in law but in popular culture; for example, on TV, single-parent families began to replace the two-parent norm for families found in the 1960s. Many two-parent families that did appear were hardly idealized but tended to be dysfunctional. As with all such changes, some disagreed these changes were a net positive, particularly as marriage rates declined and divorce and out-of-wed-lock birth rates increased.

A Speech

In 1992, then Vice President Dan Quayle gave a speech at the Commonwealth Club in California. The address came right after the Los Angeles riots following the verdict in the trial of the officers accused of excessive force in the beating of Rodney King.

In many ways, this was just an everyday campaign speech. 1992 was an election year, so there were plenty of references to the current issues before the country and how the Bush-Quayle Administration were addressing them. But the speech would spark a significant firestorm and still be discussed and debated 20 years later. So, Quayle's speech is a good view of the controversy at that point in time. In his speech[17], Quayle said,

> When I have been asked during these last weeks who caused the riots and the killing in LA., my answer has been direct and simple: Who is to blame for the riots? The rioters are to blame. Who is to blame for the killings? The killers are to blame.

Quayle went on to say,

> But after condemning the riots, we do need to try to understand the underlying situation. In a nutshell: I believe the lawless social anarchy which we saw is directly related to the breakdown of family structure, personal responsibility and social order in too many areas of our society.

Quayle then proceeded to discuss the country's "terrible problem with race and racism" and the "evil of slavery." He also condemned the development of "a culture of poverty - some call it an underclass - that is far more violent and harder to escape than it was a generation ago." To support his claims, he cited the following statistics,

- in 1967 68% of black families were headed by married couples. In 1991, only 48% of black families were headed by both a husband and wife.
- In 1965 the illegitimacy rate among black families was 28%. In 1989, 65% - two thirds - of all black children were born to never married mothers.
- In 1951 9.2% of black youth between 16-19 were unemployed. In 1965, it was 23%. In 1980 it was 35%. By 1989, the number had declined slightly, but was still 32%.
- The leading cause of death of young black males today is homicide.

---

17   Quayle, Dan, Address to the Commonwealth Club of California – On Family Values, May 19, 1992, http://www.vicepresidentdanquayle.com/speeches_StandingFirm_CCC_1.html (Accessed, 7/8/2023)

He laid the blame for much of this on his generation, the
Baby boomers,

> When we were young, it was fashionable to declare war against
> traditional values. Indulgence and self-gratification seemed to
> have no consequences. Many of our generation glamorized casu-
> al sex and drug use, evaded responsibility and trashed authority.

Quayle saw,

> The intergenerational poverty that troubles us so much today
> is predominantly a poverty of values. Our inner cities are filled
> with children having children; with people who have not been
> able to take advantage of educational opportunities; with peo-
> ple who are dependent on drugs or the narcotic of welfare.

After spending some time on how the administration planned
to address these problems, Quayle returned to the importance of
marriage.

> For those concerned about children growing up in poverty, we
> should know this: marriage is probably the best anti-poverty
> program of all. Among families headed by married couples to-
> day, there is a poverty rate of 5.7 percent. But 33.4 percent of
> families headed by a single mother are in poverty today.
> Nature abhors a vacuum. Where there are no mature, responsi-
> ble men around to teach boys how to be good men, gangs serve
> in their place. In fact; gangs have become a surrogate family for
> much of a generation of inner-city boys. I recently visited with
> some former gang members in Albuquerque, New Mexico. In
> a private meeting, they told me why they had joined gangs.
> These teenage boys said that gangs gave them a sense of securi-
> ty. They made them feel wanted, and useful. They got support
> from their friends. And, they said, "It was like having a family."
> "Like family" - unfortunately, that says it all.

After saying this, Quayle then made the comment that would
get all the attention.

> Ultimately however, marriage is a moral issue that requires
> cultural consensus, and the use of social sanctions. Bearing
> babies irresponsibly is, simply, wrong. Failing to support
> children one has fathered is wrong. We must be unequivocal
> about this.

It doesn't help matters when prime time TV has Murphy Brown - a character who supposedly epitomizes today's intelligent, highly paid, professional woman - mocking the importance of fathers, by bearing a child alone, and calling it just another "lifestyle choice."

In what turned out to be a massive understatement, Quayle added,

I know it is not fashionable to talk about moral values, but we need to do it. Even though our cultural leaders in Hollywood; network TV, the national newspapers routinely jeer at them, I think that most of us in this room know that some things are good, and other things are wrong. Now it's time to make the discussion public.

He closed, "So, let the national debate roar on." And roar it did. The New York Daily News summarized Quayle's speech with the headline, "QUAYLE TO MURPHY BROWN: YOU TRAMP!"[18] The New York Times talked about "Dan Quayle's Fictitious World."[19] The speech, or at least the comments on Murphy Brown, which attracted all the attention, was widely condemned. The Bush-Quayle ticket went on to lose to Clinton-Gore.

The Speech Lives On

Yet, the public consciousness lingered on what seemed destined to become a footnote in the 1992 presidential campaign. It would pop up from time to time. Despite being widely criticized in the mainstream media, Quayle's broader statements gained support from a growing body of research beyond the Murphy Brown comments. The problems he described continued to grow.

In the mid-nineties, Maggie Gallagher wrote a book on these changes called *The Abolition of Marriage.* She wrote,

---

18   *Dan Quayle vs. Murphy Brown, Time, Jun 01,1992,* https://content.time.com/time/subscriber/article/0,33009,975627,00.html (Accessed, 7/8/2023)
19   *Dan Quayle's Fictitious World, New York Times, May 22, 1992 (Accessed, 7/8/2023)*

As the twenty-first century looms, concern about family break-down has moved to the very center of American Life. A large and growing body of social science research has confirmed that, as Barbara Dafoe Whitehead put it in her now famous 1993 *Atlantic* article, "Dan Quayle Was Right," "The dissolution of intact two-parent families is harmful to large numbers of children." The overthrow of the marriage culture and its replacement by a postmarital culture is the driving force behind almost all of the gravest problems facing America – crime, poverty, welfare dependence, homelessness, educational stagnation, even child abuse. Above all, the decline of marriage is behind the precarious sense of economic instability haunting so many Americans in this time of statistical economic abundance, low unemployment and inflation, and rising GNP and personal income. Even in sheer economic terms, the greatest threat to the American dream comes not from the productivity of the Japanese but from the instability of our marriages.[20]

Today, Japanese productivity is no longer a concern, but the social problems Quayle discussed remain and have only gotten worse. As a result, articles periodically appeared with some form of the headline, "Dan Quayle was Right." In one such article written twenty years after Quayle's speech, Isabel V. Sawhill, Senior Fellow – Economic Studies at the Center for Economic Security and Opportunity, wrote,

Twenty years later, Quayle's words seem less controversial than prophetic. The number of single parents in America has increased dramatically: The proportion of children born outside marriage has risen from roughly 30 percent in 1992 to 41 percent in 2009. For women under age 30, more than half of babies are born out of wedlock. A lifestyle once associated with poverty has become mainstream. The only group of parents for whom marriage continues to be the norm is the college-educated.[21]

---

20   Gallagher, Maggie, *The Abolition of Marriage,* Regnery Publishing, 1996, 3-4

21   Sawhill, Isabel, *Twenty Years Later, It Turns Out Dan Quayle Was Right About Murphy Brown and Unmarried Moms, Brookings, May 25, 2012,* https://www.brookings.edu/articles/twenty-years-later-it-turns-out-dan-quayle-was-right-about-murphy-brown-and-unmarried-moms/ (Accessed, 7/11/2023)

The research Sawhill conducted with her colleague, Ron Hasking, showed that cohabitating couples split up at twice the rate of married couples before their fifth year, leaving the mother with the children but no support. Children who live with biological parents do better in school and earn more as adults. They are less likely to get pregnant, get arrested, drop out of school, and have lower suicide rates. For obvious reasons, couples do better, on average economically, than single parents. As a result,

> if individuals do just three things—finish high school, work full time and marry before they have children—their chances of being poor drop from 15 percent to 2 percent. [22]

Marriage and the Courts

The change in marriage was huge and had significant effects on society. The courts played a major role in this transformation. Much of this change did not occur through the democratic process, with people discussing the need for a change democratically; much came in the courts, redefining marriage based on a new understanding of the law. Maggie Gallagher described this legal transformation in her book written in the mid-nineties,

> Over the past thirty years, quietly, and largely unremarked outside a narrow group of specialists, American family law has been rewritten to dilute both the rights and the obligations of marriage, while at the same time placing other relationships from adulterous liaisons to homosexual partnerships, on a legal par with marriage in some respects. To put it another way, by expanding the definition of marriage to the point of meaninglessness, courts are gradually redefining marriage out of existence. [23]

Supporters justified this transformation as required to expand individual rights and equality. Yet, such arguments ignored the

---

22 Sawhill, Isabel, *Twenty Years Later, It Turns Out Dan Quayle Was Right About Murphy Brown and Unmarried Moms, Brookings, May 25, 2012*, https:// www.brookings.edu/articles/twenty-years-later-it-turns-out-dan-quayle-was-right-about-murphy-brown-and-unmarried-moms/ (Accessed, 7/11/2023)
23 Gallagher, Maggie, *The Abolition of Marriage*, Regnery Publishing, 1996, 131

reasons marriage had a special status in the first place. Marriage's special status existed to encourage marriage and protect family members. As Gallagher pointed out,

> As these responsibilities blur—as they must when marriage is made indistinguishable from relationships in which parties have few, if any, responsibilities to each other—and the rights are parceled out to the unmarried, marriage itself begins to dissolve. The more other relationships begin to acquire the rights of marriage, and the more the law declines to enforce the special responsibilities of marriage, the more ghostly and insubstantial the marriage commitment becomes.[24]

Gallagher summarized this change,

> Legally and philosophically, the law has been deconstructing marriage into its component parts—a Chinese menu of love in which one takes one's pleasure from Column A.[25]

We can see this legal transformation in two Supreme Court rulings only seven years apart. In the 1965 Griswold decision discussed earlier, the court saw the marriage relationship as so unique that when looking at the "privacy surrounding the marriage relationship,"

> We deal with a right of privacy older than the Bill of Rights— older than our political parties, older than our school system. Marriage is a coming together for better or for worse, hopefully enduring and intimate to the degree of being sacred. It is an association that promotes a way of life, not causes; a harmony in living, not political faiths; a bilateral loyalty, not commercial or social projects. Yet, it is an association for as noble a purpose as any involved in our prior decisions.[26]

Thus, in Griswold, the court used the special and unique status of marriage "to the degree of being sacred" to create the new right of privacy. Once established, however, marriage was no longer needed. Seven years later, the Court ruled that the right

---

24 Gallagher, Maggie, *The Abolition of Marriage,* Regnery Publishing, 1996, 131-2

25 Gallagher, Maggie, *The Abolition of Marriage,* Regnery Publishing, 1996, 132

26 Griswold v. Connecticut (1965) 381 U.S. 479 (1965)

to privacy it created in Griswold actually had nothing to do with marriage. Marriage was not that special or unique. In Eisenstadt versus Baird, the court ruled,

> It is true that, in Griswold, the right of privacy in question inhered in the marital relationship. Yet, the marital couple is not an independent entity, with a mind and heart of its own, but an association of two individuals, each with a separate intellectual and emotional makeup. If the right of privacy means anything, it is the right of the individual, married or single.[27]

Again, we are looking at the effect of the court's rulings on marriage, not the decision's impact on privacy. One can easily agree with the court about privacy and the individual but question their reasoning on marriage.

In a law review article about the court's effects on marriage, John Noonan, later an Appellate Judge for the Ninth Circuit, divided the history of the court's view of marriage into three phases. At first, the court was a defender of marriage. During Phase Two, it created "partial marriage." In Phase Three, "the Court became the upholder of no marriage."[28] As Noonan summarized the problem,

> Lawful marriage in the society's hierarchy of values recognized by *Boddie v. Connecticut* and in the host of laws yet unchallenged-the tax law, the common law of property, the law of evidence-is a constellation of these immunities and privileges. To say that legal immunities and legal benefits may not depend upon marriage is to deny the vital right. To say that Equal Protection requires the equal treatment of the married and the unmarried in all respects is to deny the hierarchy of values of our society.[29]

---

27   Eisenstadt v. Baird, 405 U.S. 438 (1972)

28   John T. Noonan Jr., The Family and the Supreme Court, 23 Cath. U. L. Rev. 255 (1974). Available at: https://scholarship.law.edu/lawreview/vol23/iss2/3

29   John T. Noonan Jr., The Family and the Supreme Court, 23 Cath. U. L. Rev. 255 (1974).
Available at: https://scholarship.law.edu/lawreview/vol23/iss2/3

Competing Concern

Eventually, the legal devaluation of marriage and the growing social problems raised the visibility of marriage as a political issue. This growing concern eventually coincided with the increasing acceptance of same-sex relationships. Initially, these were unrelated movements, with worries over devaluing marriage starting years before any serious discussion of same-sex marriage. Still, eventually, these issues began to overlap with increasing calls to legalize same-sex marriage.

When same-sex marriage came to the forefront of public discussion, it generated a wide range of reactions. Some supported it. Some opposed it as part of a broader rejection of homosexuality. Many, however, opposed it as yet another weakening of marriage, as something that can mean anything ultimately means nothing. Still, others opposed it for more libertarian reasons. They had no objections to same-sex marriage; they objected to the government's decision to make marriage laws in the first place. For them, the government should get out of the marriage business altogether. Of course, the media is terrible regarding nuance and complex arguments. For them, the debate was between the bigots and the people fighting for their rights.

The first significant clash occurred in the mid-nineties. While some argued for same-sex marriage earlier, such as Andrew Sullivan's 1989 article in *The New Republic*[30], these were few and far between. Most action was still in the courts, which caused some concern among supporters of traditional marriage. In 1990, three same-sex couples filed suit in Hawaii, challenging the state's marriage laws. The concern was,

> if Hawaii (or some other State) recognizes same-sex "marriages," other States that do not permit homosexuals to marry would be confronted with the complicated issue of whether

---

30   Andrew Sullivan, *Here Comes The Groom, The New Republic, August 27, 1989* https://newrepublic.com/article/79054/here-comes-the-groom (Accessed September 9, 2023)

they are nonetheless obligated under the Full Faith and Credit Clause of the United States Constitution to give binding legal effect to such unions.[31]

Under Article IV of the Constitution, "Full Faith and Credit shall be given in each State to the public Acts, Records, and judicial Proceedings of every other State." As a result, marriages enacted in one state might be legally recognized in all states.

In response, supporters of traditional marriage proposed the Defense of Marriage Act (DOMA). The law defined marriage as "a legal union between one man and one woman as husband and wife." DOMA's opponents claimed the bill was unnecessary, and the Full Faith and Credit clause would not mandate same-sex marriage, should the Hawaiian court mandate it.[32]

The response to DOMA shows the state of the political debate in the mid-1990s. Congress passed the Defense of Marriage Act 342 – 67, with solid majorities in both parties supporting the bill. Bill Clinton signed it into law. Before signing the law, Clinton, in an interview with the LGBT magazine *The Advocate,* said, "I remain opposed to same-sex marriage. I believe marriage is an institution for the union of a man and a woman. This has been my long-standing position, and it is not being reviewed or considered."[33] That, however, did not end the issue.

In 2003, a majority of judges on the Massachusetts Supreme Court decided that the marriage laws in Massachusetts should be

---

31   House of Representatives, Report 104-664, *Defense of Marriage Act Report* https://www.govinfo.gov/content/pkg/CRPT-104hrpt664/pdf/CRPT-104hrpt664.pdf

32   House of Representatives, Report 104-664, *Defense of Marriage Act Report*
https://www.govinfo.gov/content/pkg/CRPT-104hrpt664/pdf/CRPT-104hrpt664.pdf

33   Aliyah Frumin, *Timeline: Bill Clinton's evolution on gay rights, MSNBC, March 8, 2013*
https://www.msnbc.com/hardball/timeline-bill-clintons-evolution-gay-rig-ms-na19626 (accessed September 25, 2025)

changed to allow for same-sex marriages and ordered the Governor and Legislature to carry out their wishes.[34]

Then, in 2008, the California Supreme Court tried the same thing, even though in 2000, the people of California reaffirmed the traditional view of marriage by a direct vote of the people. Unlike Massachusetts, however, California has a process whereby the people of California can directly modify the state constitution, which they did with Proposition 8 at their first opportunity six months later, overturning the ruling of the California Supreme Court and restoring the traditional view of marriage.

Supporters of same-sex marriage tried to overturn the vote of the people. First, they challenged the law in the California courts. The California Supreme Court later ruled against them and upheld Proposition 8. They then challenged it in Federal Court.

While a lower court initially ruled the State Constitutional amendment unconstitutional under the Federal Constitution, the U.S. Supreme Court eventually vacated this ruling for lack of standing, meaning they reversed the District Court's ruling because those who challenged Prop 8 were not in a legal position to do so. This ruling upheld the vote of the people to retain the traditional view of marriage, but without taking a stand on the issue itself.

Obergefell v. Hodges

Meanwhile, several other cases were filed in numerous states, arguing the traditional view of marriage was unconstitutional. These cases were eventually combined into Obergefell v. Hodges. In 2015, the Supreme Court ruled,

> The fundamental liberties protected by the Fourteenth Amendment's Due Process Clause extend to certain personal

---

34   Rose Arce, *Massachusetts court upholds same-sex marriage,*
CNN, February 6, 2004 http://www.cnn.com/2004/LAW/02/04/gay.marriage/index.html (accessed April 3, 2009)

choices central to individual dignity and autonomy, including intimate choices defining personal identity and beliefs. [35]

They then declared, "The reasons marriage is fundamental under the Constitution apply with equal force to same-sex couples."[36] This ruling ended the matter in terms of the Constitution.

One thing to notice in all this is the lack of the Rule of Law or Democracy. Concerning the Rule of Law, the mere fact that we cannot read the laws and determine what marriage is but must wait for the court to rule, uncertain as to what they will do, shows that they, not the Constitution, not even the people, are the ultimate authority in the land. In many ways, we have returned to the time when we must wait for the King to speak before knowing what to do.

As for democracy, the outcome did not depend on what the law said or what people wanted, as expressed in the democratic process. In fact, the more people were involved democratically, the more they rejected this new definition of marriage, as with the passage of the Defense of Marriage Act or Proposition 8 in California, overturning an earlier Court's attempt to legalize same-sex marriage. In many ways, this was the court trying to force a change and the people working through the democratic process trying to stop them. Ultimately, the people and democracy failed.

Nor was it a victory for the Rule of Law. With four justices following the tradition of the Living Constitution and four Originalism, the Obergefell decision came down to how Justice Kennedy viewed the matter, not what the law or Constitution said.

With a solid Originalist majority on the Court and following the Dobbs decision, some now fear that Obergefell is also at risk. Supporters of same-sex marriage now argue that the court should uphold Obergefell because of *stare decisis*. This argument is some-

---

35   Obergefell et al. v. Hodges, Director, Ohio Department of Health. 14–556, https://www.supremecourt.gov/opinions/boundvolumes/576BV.pdf, 644
36   Obergefell et al. v. Hodges, Director, Ohio Department of Health. 14–556 https://www.supremecourt.gov/opinions/boundvolumes/576BV.pdf, 644

what ironic. Obergefell could overturn thousands of years of law, but we should keep Obergefell because it is less than ten years old.

Still, given the Rule of Law and the Originalist makeup of the current court, it is unlikely that they would overturn Obergefell for three reasons: the Rule of Law, Originalism, and *stare decisis*. The first is the Rule of Law. Court rulings, once decided, have the force of Law. Thus, even if one argues that in Obergefell, the court was wrong, their ruling is now the law. Second, the court is Originalist, not right-wing or conservative, except that Originalism tends to be found on the Right and among Conservatives. As a result, this court will focus more on what the law is, not what they think it should be.

Finally, and most importantly for this chapter, there is the issue of *stare decisis*. As we have seen, this is not a blanket rule but a rule. The court should overturn some rulings, like Plessey v. Ferguson; others, it should not overturn. So, the question becomes, if this court overturned Roe and Casey, why would they not also overturn Obergefell?

Here, Alito's reasoning in Dobbs[37] discussed above is helpful. He gave five reasons for overturning Roe and Casey,

1. the nature of their error
2. the quality of their reasoning
3. the "workability" of the rules they imposed on the country
4. their disruptive effect on other areas of the law
5. the absence of concrete reliance

In terms of practicality, there is also a sixth, which is acceptance of the opinion among the people. Legal scholars will differ on the first two. Those following a Living Constitutional view will tend to see Roe, Casey, and Obergefell as correctly decided, while

---

37   Dobbs, State Health Officer Of The Mississippi Department Of Health, Et Al. v. Jackson Women's Health Organization Et Al., 19-1392, 19-1392 Dobbs v. Jackson Women's Health Organization (06/24/2022) (supremecourt.gov)

Originalists will not. Still, even for Originalists, this is not enough to overturn *stare decisis,* which leaves the other three.

Whatever its merits, Obergefell does not cause the same sorts of legal issues as Roe and Casey did, as it is a far more clear-cut decision. Before Obergefell, same-sex couples could not marry in a legal sense; now, they can. The Roe and Casey decisions were far more problematic, with cases continually coming before the court trying to work out the details. As the Dobbs decision pointed out,

> The experience of the Courts of Appeals provides further evidence that Casey's "line between" permissible and unconstitutional restrictions "has proved to be impossible to draw with precision." Janus, 585 U. S., at ___. Casey has generated a long list of Circuit conflicts. Continued adherence to Casey's unworkable "undue burden" test would undermine, not advance, the "evenhanded, predictable, and consistent development of legal principles." Payne, 501 U. S., at 827. Pp. 56–62.[38]

Regarding point four and the disruption of the law, as pointed out in the ruling, "Roe and Casey have led to the distortion of many important but unrelated legal doctrines."[39]

For the fifth point, concrete reliance, there will be more reliance on something that can last a lifetime, marriage, than something that lasts nine months, pregnancy. Thus, even an originalist who sees Roe, Casey, and Obergefell as equally flawed legal decisions might still reach different conclusions for the other three factors than the Dobbs decision.

Finally, while not strictly a legal consideration, there is another practical one. The courts can only rule on cases brought before them. From Roe to Dobbs, there were yearly and growing protests over Roe and a constant political effort to overturn the decision, both in the Law and getting originalists appointed to the bench.

---

38   Dobbs, State Health Officer Of The Mississippi Department Of Health, Et Al. v. Jackson Women's Health Organization Et Al., 19-1392, 19-1392 Dobbs v. Jackson Women's Health Organization (06/24/2022) (supremecourt.gov)
39   Dobbs, State Health Officer Of The Mississippi Department Of Health, Et Al. v. Jackson Women's Health Organization Et Al., 19-1392, 19-1392 Dobbs v. Jackson Women's Health Organization (06/24/2022) (supremecourt.gov)

Since Obergefell, no similar reaction has appeared. While people still discuss what they think are problems with the ruling, no states have seriously tried to challenge the decision; no laws have passed to create new cases that would come before the court.

A large part of this lack of reaction is that much of the opposition was grounded, not in opposition to same-sex relationships, but rather in defense of traditional marriage, and its defenders had already lost much of that battle long before same-sex marriage became a national issue. We can see this by comparing those who resisted expanding the definition of marriage to the relatively small number that opposed domestic partnership.

Thus, rather than starting a political debate, as Roe did, Obergefell, for all practical purposes, ended one. People were anxious to put the controversy behind them. In many respects, the real victors, rightly or wrongly, were those who argued that the government should get out of the marriage business and just let people do what they want.

So, if the court remains originalist, the chances of overturning Obergefell are minimal. First, you would need a case brought before the court; it isn't easy to imagine that happening. Then, you would need a majority of the justices who saw sufficient reason to overturn that earlier ruling.

In some respects, the courts have forced us into a vast experiment. For thousands of years of human history in virtually all cultures, the standard view was the family was foundational to society. Yet, since the 1960s, the courts have removed any special status for a married couple.

Whether it is related, this at least coincided with a rise in the types of social problems predicted as a result. This change was primarily, though not totally undemocratic, often without people's awareness and at times in direct opposition to their expressed will. Instead, judges forced this change for primarily ideological reasons. As the social pathologies continue to grow, whether society can find an alternative foundation to the family remains to be seen.

What Can Be Done

The courts are an area where progress has been made since the first edition. The current court has an Originalist majority that focuses more on what the law and the Constitution say than what it should mean or should be. However, advocates for the Living Constitution remain strong. In response, there have even been efforts to try and pack the Court as FDR attempted in the thirties. In addition, many people, if not most, continue to judge court rulings based on whether it is the result they wanted, not the reasoning for the ruling.

The solution is to insist that judges make rulings based strictly on the law and the Constitution. This solution remains difficult because many find it much easier to have courts impose the policies they like rather than deal with the ambiguities of the democratic process. So, one of the first steps will be to have a majority realize what is at stake and the antidemocratic nature of the court rulings based on what the judge thinks the law should be rather than what it is.

Earlier rulings moving the government into areas not enumerated by the Constitution also compounded this problem. In the future, tension will continue between following the Constitution and *stare decisis*, which will be challenging to navigate. Finally, there will be the temptation to overcorrect, for conservative judges to make rulings based on their understanding of what should be, as Living Constitution judges did.

A significant problem will be returning the court to its constitutional role. The Founding Fathers saw the courts as the weakest of the three branches. Hamilton wrote in Federalist #81 that,

> It may in the last place be observed that the supposed danger of judiciary encroachments on the legislative authority... is in reality a phantom... This may be inferred with certainty,

from the general nature of the judicial power, from the objects to which it relates, from the manner in which it is exercised, from its comparative weakness, and from its total incapacity to support its usurpations by force.[40]

But despite Hamilton's beliefs, Living Constitutional judges have made the court the most powerful of the three branches in many respects. Where the Founding Fathers believed that the courts were weak because the other branches could ignore them, the convention now says that when they speak, the other branches must obey lest the public sees them as flouting the law. Today, the courts can check and balance the other two branches, but what is the check on judges?

One check would be to realize that judges who place themselves above the Constitution violate their oath of office and deserve impeachment. While many see this as a shocking overreach of power, this was one of the reasons the Founding Fathers believed there was little to fear from "judiciary encroachments on the legislative authority." As Hamilton went on to say in Federalist #81,

> the inference is greatly fortified by the consideration of the important constitutional check which the power of instituting impeachments in one part of the legislative body, and of determining upon them in the other, would give to that body upon the members of the judicial department. This is alone a complete security. There never can be danger that the judges, by a series of deliberate usurpations on the authority of the legislature, would hazard the united resentment of the body intrusted with it, while this body was possessed of the means of punishing their presumption, by degrading them from their stations. While this ought to remove all apprehensions on the subject, it affords, at the same time, a cogent argument for constituting the Senate a court for the trial of impeachments.[41]

---

40   Hamilton, Federalist No. 81
http://www.constitution.org/fed/federa81.htm (accessed April 3, 2009).
41   Hamilton, Federalist No. 81
http://www.constitution.org/fed/federa81.htm (accessed April 3, 2009).

One of the dangers in this is that early rulings have so damaged the Rule of Law that such impeachment trials would become political, where the judges would be impeached, not for placing themselves above the Rule of Law, but for "ruling the wrong way."

Ultimately, the solution to this will be the re-emergence of the importance of the Rule of Law among the people. If the majority begin to value the Rule of Law more than they value their individual positions on issues, and more importantly, if they insist that elected officials and especially judges do the same, then we can restore the Rule of Law.

If we need to change the law, legislative bodies should do it, not the courts. The courts should rule laws enacted in the democratic process unconstitutional only if they conflict with what the Constitution actually says. If we need new rights in the Constitution, we should add them through the amendment process instead of imposed by the courts. In short, we need to strive for the principle that is so vital to democracy: that no one is above the law, not even the judges who rule on it.

LAW AND JUSTICE

Justice is conscience, not a personal conscience but the conscience of the whole of humanity.

Alexander Solzhenitsyn

If you have ten thousand regulations you destroy all respect for the law.

Winston Churchill

PAUL TULLIUS SERVED and defended his country in two wars as an Air Force pilot. After retiring from the Air Force, Tullius, who collected old cars, looked for a place to store them. In 1988, he purchased a warehouse in Chico, California. Later, he leased the building to a homeless shelter.

In 2003, Tullius found himself involved in a lawsuit over the building brought by the California State Attorney General's Office. As a result of the suit, he faced $75,000 to $100,000 in legal fees if he ultimately won in the long, drawn-out legal process. If he lost, the cost would be much higher. Tullius was worried that his children would end up financially ruined as well.[1]

After a career of serving his country, what did Tullius do that would cause the State of California to bring such a potentially ruinous suit against him? Surprising as it may seem, the answer

---

1   Gary Delsohn, "State is suing ex-dry cleaners,". *The Sacramento Bee,* April 28, 2003

     also Katharine Mieszkowski, "Take To the Cleaners," *Legal Affairs,* March/April 2004 http://www.legalaffairs.org/issues/March-April-2004/scene_mieszkowski_marapr04.msp (accessed April 3, 2009).

to that question is in the paragraphs above. Tullius' transgression that put him in such costly legal jeopardy was that he purchased the building. That's it.

As it turned out, 16 years before Tullius purchased the building, it had housed a dry cleaner. Tullius did not know that the building had once housed a dry cleaner; even if he had known, it would not have concerned him. He did not realize the alleged actions of others 16 years ago could put him in such legal jeopardy.

Tullius's experience is just one aspect of another problem with the law that can threaten democracy. That is the growing disconnect between the law and justice. The law is supposed to be the rules of society. Follow the rules, and you will be all right; disobey the rules, and the government could punish you. Increasingly, however, the legal system is becoming a lottery. Issues of negligence or intent are no longer of much significance. There is little one can do to reap significant benefits or have one's life ruined, as the law is increasingly a matter of arbitrary chance.

Law or Chance?

It is simply a matter of the odds. Find yourself on one side of a suit, and you could get a lot of money; find yourself on the other and face financial ruin. The odds of either happening are small, but so are the odds of winning at any casino. Put a dollar in a slot machine, and you will likely lose the dollar. Still, there is a tiny chance you will hit the jackpot.

It is the same as the legal system but with two significant differences. First, the legal system works both ways. Not only can you win big, but you could also lose everything. Put a dollar in a slot machine; the most you can lose is that dollar until you put in the next one. Your potential losses are limited by how much you choose to put at risk. In the legal system, you can lose everything.

The second difference is that, unlike a casino, you do not have any choice of whether or not to play. No matter how careful you are, like Tullius, you can find yourself in a lawsuit for reasons beyond your control and, as a result, face financial ruin, even if you win.

Even for the original "culprits" in the lawsuit, there are serious problems. In this case, Bob and Inez Heidinger operated the dry cleaner once in the building, which Tullius later purchased. They opened their business in 1954 and operated it until 1974. They had long since retired.

The State of California claims the Heidingers pumped the chemical PCE down the drain, but they say they didn't. Heidinger says that his machines were self-contained and that he followed the standard practice of the period for waste disposal. But how can this be proved one way or another 30 years later? In addition, the state did not even enact the law the state was using until 1980, 6 years after they had retired.[2]

There is something seriously wrong with a system where people can have their lives turned upside down by a lawsuit for actions that 30 years earlier were the standard practice, or, in the case of Tullius, over which he had absolutely no control and nothing to do with.

Law without Justice

In the last two chapters, we looked at the damage to the Rule of Law caused by judges who place themselves above the law instead of under it. Cases like the one above also ultimately undermine the law as well. They remove the concept of justice from the law.

How can it in any way be considered justice to penalize someone for something they did not do and had no control over? How can it be considered justice to punish someone for something they

---

2   Gary Delsohn, "State is suing ex-dry cleaners,". *The Sacramento Bee,* April 28, 2003
also Katharine Mieszkowski, "Take To the Cleaners," *Legal Affairs,* March/April, 2004 http://www.legalaffairs.org/issues/March-April-2004/scene_mieszkowski_marapr04.msp (accessed April 3, 2009).

did 30 years ago, which, at the time, was considered a perfectly acceptable practice? That the state had a legitimate reason for wanting the site cleaned is fine. But if it was in the public interest to clean it up, the public should have paid for it. Why punish Tullius?

Consider all the various things you do every day, which are standard practice and taken for granted. It is just how you do things. Can you identify which of these in 30 years might be considered grounds for a lawsuit that could ruin your life?

These are not isolated cases. In 2003, the Nebraska Supreme Court heard arguments on whether Ford Motor Co. and Bridgestone/Firestone, Inc. should be held liable for a woman's death. Was she killed in a crash? No, she had a flat tire. A man picked her up and later murdered her.

The lawsuit alleged that the flat tire put the woman "at great risk and left her in a situation where she was ultimately abducted, terrorized, raped, and murdered."[3] While her murder was both a tragedy and a crime of great evil, is this the fault of Ford Motor Co. or Bridgestone/Firestone, Inc.?

On February 20, 2003, fireworks caused a horrible nightclub fire that killed 100 people. As expected, lawsuits soon appeared. Somewhat less expected was the inclusion of Shell Oil Company as one of the defendants.

Did they make the chemicals used in the Fireworks? No. Perhaps they made the insulation or building materials used in the building? No. That was American Foam Corp – also included in the suit as if they somehow could predict that someone would use fireworks indoors. It turns out that Shell Oil Company's reason for culpability was the nightclub owners also owned a Shell gas station from which they gave away free tickets to the nightclub.[4]

---

3   *Fremont Tribune, "Murder Victim's parents say flat set off tragic events,".*
June 3, 2003 http://www.fremontneb.com/articles/2003/06/03/news/news4.
txt (accessed April 3, 2009).

4   *Convenience Store News,* "Shell Named in R.I. Nightclub Fire
Lawsuit," May 29, 2003 http://www.allbusiness.com/retail-trade/food-
stores/4478945-1.html (accessed April 3, 2009).

The list could go on and on. The main thing these lawsuits all have in common is that people or companies are being included in the suits, not because of any negligence or wrongdoing on their part. In these cases, they had little or nothing to do with the events that generated the lawsuit. What they do have is money. In short, their inclusion has little to do with justice. Instead, someone wants money, and they have it.

One might say that these are big companies and they can afford it. While it may be true for Shell Oil or Ford Motor Company, is it true for Tullius? At the time of the article, Bob Heidinger, the retired owner of the dry cleaning business, was an 87-year-old retiree with Alzheimer's and blind in one eye. His wife was 83 and had bone marrow cancer.[5] Can they afford it? In any event, even if included because they can afford it, that only demonstrates that justice is not the reason.

Nor is the risk only with Lawsuits. Whether or not you are faced with a criminal prosecution is, at times, more dependent on whether a prosecutor wants to get you than any decision on your part to break the law. Harvey Silberglate, in his book *Three Felonies a Day*, gives example after example of people who ended up charged with a felony without realizing they were doing anything illegal or even wrong.

Silverglate argues that the power and reach of the federal government have become so great and extended into so many areas that the unsuspecting citizen commits, as his title describes, three felonies a day. As Silverglate describes the situation,

> federal criminal laws have become dangerously disconnected from the English common law tradition and its insistence on fair notice, so prosecutors can find some arguable federal crime to apply to just about any one of us, even for the most

---

5   Gary Delsohn, "State is suing ex-dry cleaners," *The Sacramento Bee*, April 28, 2003

     also Katharine Mieszkowski, "Take To the Cleaners," *Legal Affairs*, March/April, 2004 http://www.legalaffairs.org/issues/March-April-2004/scene_mieszkowski_marapr04.msp (accessed April 3, 2009)

seemingly innocuous conduct (and since the mid-1980s have done so increasingly). [6]

Silverglate cites a speech by Attorney General Robert H. Jackson in 1940 in which Jackson warned about the dangers of over-zealous prosecutors seeking to target an individual. As Silverglate says,

> But Jackson also understood the proper limits of power and the dangerous human impulse to exert power over others. The federal law books, explained Jackson, are "filled with a great assortment of crimes," and a prosecutor "stands a fair chance of finding at least a technical violation of some act on the part of almost anyone." Prosecutors can easily succumb to the temptation of first "picking the man and then searching the law books, or putting investigators to work, to pin some offense on him."[7]

Yet, Jackson's warning has sadly, in many cases, gone unheeded. As with lawsuits, the chances of getting prosecuted are minimal. Still, the threat is genuine. If a prosecutor wants to target you, they can probably find something. You can face a choice of admitting your guilt in a plea deal or facing financial ruin with the chance a jury might acquit you.

Given such a choice, many take the deal despite believing they are innocent. Rather than innocent until proven guilty, we are moving closer to a saying by Lavrentiy Beria, Stalin's chief of his secret police, who allegedly said, "Show me the man, and I will show you the crime."[8] Silverglate sums up the current situation,

> The battle to restore proper balance between the power of federal prosecutors and civil society cannot be fought along lines separating liberals from conservatives, law-and-order advocates from libertarians, populists from industry leaders, reporters from moguls, or any of the other categories into

6   Harvey A. Silverglate, *Three Felonies a Day: How the Feds Target the Innocent,* Encounter Books. Kindle Edition, 2009

7   Harvey A. Silverglate, *Three Felonies a Day: How the Feds Target the Innocent,* Encounter Books. Kindle Edition, 2009

8   There are several variations of this saying, and it is at time attributed to Andry Vyshinshy. There is also a long history of similar sayings.

which our increasingly fractious society sorts us. In this arena, the divide between self-interest and the interest of others disappears. When the feds appear on the scene, claiming to represent the public interest by going after some citizen who had no reasonable way of knowing that his or her conduct could be deemed a felony, do not ask for whom the bell tolls. It tolls for all. [9]

Class Action

While larger companies might be able to "afford" individual lawsuits, even they have trouble with class action suits. In theory, a class action lawsuit is where many people combine their suits into one. The idea is that rather than have effectively the same case tried repeatedly, there is only one trial and one result that all must accept.

While it makes sense in theory, the rewards for a lawyer winning such a suit are so great that the entire system gets distorted as there is a huge incentive to bring people into the case as allegedly being wronged. The result is that the lawyer bringing the suit wins big, while the supposedly wronged plaintiffs often get very little.

We see an example of the problem in a class action lawsuit against DVD rental company Netflix. At the time, Netflix's basic plan allowed customers to have 2-4 DVDs out at a time. When a customer mailed them back, Netflix sent another one. Instead of the cost being per DVD, Netflix charges a flat monthly fee. The suit accused Netflix of misleading consumers with claims of "unlimited movie rentals" and a one-day turnaround on rentals.

A consumer complained that the one-day turnaround could take up to six days because of the mail, thus limiting the number of movies they could get in a month. The suit became a class-action suit, including many customers who were very happy with the service.

---

9   Harvey A. Silverglate, *Three Felonies a Day: How the Feds Target the Innocent*, Encounter Books. Kindle Edition, 2009

Eventually, Netflix settled without admitting any wrongdoing. Netflix agreed to upgrade customers by one DVD for one month. A customer with three DVDs out at a time could now have four, but only for one month. Customers were underwhelmed.

The lawyers for the plaintiffs were pleased. According to news reports, one of the attorneys suing Netflix said of the lawsuit, "It accomplished everything we set out to do."[10] One reason for his optimism might be that while customers will get an extra DVD for a month, the attorneys split $2.5 million.[11]

Again, these are not isolated events. Jim Copland, Director of the Manhattan Institute's Center for Legal Policy, reported that "between 1997 and 2000, American corporations reported a 300 percent increase in federal class actions and a 1,000 percent increase spike in state class actions filed against them."[12]

Such cases alleged some wrong, some act or omission leading to harm or injury. The technical legal term for these is torts, and that part of the legal system is called the tort system and is costly. A study in 2007 concluded that

> applying the best available scholarly research, we believe America's tort system imposes a total cost on the U.S. economy of $865 billion per year. This constitutes an annual "tort tax" of $9,827 on a family of four. It is equivalent to the total annual output of all six New England states, or the yearly sales of the entire U.S. restaurant industry.[13]

---

10   Ellen Lee, "Netflix Upgrades settlement," *San Francisco Chronicle, March 15, 2006* http://www.sfgate.com/cgi-bin/article.cgi?file=/chronicle/archive/2006/03/15/BUG6LHO48I1.DTL&type=business (accessed April 3, 2009).
11   Ellen Lee, "Netflix Upgrades settlement," *San Francisco Chronicle, March 15, 2006* http://www.sfgate.com/cgi-bin/article.cgi?file=/chronicle/archive/2006/03/15/BUG6LHO48I1.DTL&type=business (accessed April 3, 2009).
12   Jim Copland, "The Tort Tax," *Wall Street Journal. June 11, 2003, A16* http://www.manhattan-institute.org/html/_wsj-the_tort_tax.htm (accessed April 3, 2009).
13   Lawrence J. McQuillan and Hovannes Abramyan, "The Tort Tax," *Wall Street Journal., March 27, 2007* http://online.wsj.com/article/

More ominous, these costs grew four times faster than the gross national product.[14]

Tort Tax

In chapter two, we looked at the danger of taxes and their stifling effect on the economy. The impacts of lawsuits are just as damaging and amount to a "Tort Tax." The only difference is that the courts impose it instead of the legislature. But the reason in both cases is often the same. These people or companies have money, and someone else wants it.

The effects of a Tort Tax, however, are much more devastating than just the dollars drained out of the economy. With a tax imposed by the legislature, you at least have some idea of what you will have to pay and when. With the Tort Tax, you often have no idea what action may trigger a lawsuit, and at times, they are entirely out of one's control.

In addition, whereas taxes usually have some relationship to your ability to pay, legal judgments can quite literally ruin a person or a business financially. According to an article by Karen Kerrigan on the devastating effect of the numerous asbestos lawsuits, "The avalanche of asbestos litigation has forced more than 60 companies into bankruptcy… they simply cannot withstand the crushing financial burden."[15]

This result is no surprise given that a Rand Institute study estimated that by 2002, companies had already spent $54 billion on asbestos lawsuits. The same study put the total potential cost

SB117496524456750056.html (accessed April 3, 2009).

14   Jim Copland, *America's Capital Markets: Maintaining Our Lead in the 21st Century, Testimony before Congress, April 26, 2006*
http://www.manhattan-institute.org/html/testimony_copland_4-26-06.htm (accessed April 3, 2009).

15   Karen Kerrigan, "Asbestos Lawsuits threaten future of small companies," *Triangle Business Journal, April 21, 2003* http://www.bizjournals.com/triangle/stories/2003/04/21/smallb3.html (accessed April 3, 2009).

at $260 billion.[16] Marcia Coyle of the *National Law Journal* has pointed out that the number of defendants in asbestos cases has grown from 40 in the 1980s to an estimated 8,000.[17] Chief Economist for Citizens for a Sound Economy Wayne Brough points out that many of these companies had "only a tangential link to the original health risks."[18]

Some might argue that this is only just compensation. After all, these people were wronged, and those responsible must pay. While this sounds good in principle, it is often far different in practice.

For example, those now held financially responsible in the asbestos suits sometimes had as little connection to asbestos as Tullius had to dry cleaning or Shell Oil to the Nightclub Fire. When they had a more direct connection, they were often unaware of this potential health risk. Finally, even with all the money paid out, it often does not get to the people who deserve it. Thus, when it comes to asbestos,

> Many recent claims have been filed by workers who were exposed to asbestos and show minor lung damage on X-rays but have no symptoms of illness. Meanwhile, lawyers for plaintiffs who have serious asbestos-related diseases, like mesothelioma, a fatal cancer, say their clients sometimes cannot get their claims paid because companies have exhausted their resources settling claims by plaintiffs who are not sick.[19]

---

16   Alex Berenson, Jonathan Glather, "2 Companies may be close to Resolving Asbestos Suits,". *New York Times, December 12, 2002,* http://www. nytimes.com/2002/12/12/business/2-companies-may-be-close-to-resolving-asbestos-suits.html (accessed April 3, 2009).

17   Marcia Coyle, "Outlook Brightens for Action on Asbestos," *The National Law Journal, March 18, 2003.* http://www.law.com/jsp/article. jsp?id=1046833569783 (accessed April 3, 2009).

18   Wayne T. Bough, "The Limits of Lawsuits," *Citizens for a Sound Economy, March 19, 2003.*

19   Alex Berenson, Jonathan Glather, "2 Companies may be close to Resolving Asbestos Suits,". *New York Times, December 12, 2002,* http://www. nytimes.com/2002/12/12/business/2-companies-may-be-close-to-resolving-asbestos-suits.html (accessed April 3, 2009).

This all assumes that the problem is actually a real problem. As many have found out, the damage claim is sometimes more important than the reality of the damage. Like asbestos, many companies have been sued over silicone gel breast implants, paying billions in settlements. Unlike asbestos, there are serious questions about whether these implants are harmful.

During the 1990s, concerns over silicone gel breast implants turned into a series of lawsuits. Companies pulled the implants from the market, and eventually, these suits grew to the point that the companies involved sought to limit their liability by proposing to pay $7 billion to settle claims. Dow-Corning, one of the manufacturers of the implants, ended up declaring bankruptcy.[20]

Yet, despite these settlements, many studies by reputable organizations such as the Mayo Clinic and the National Cancer Institute found no link to serious health problems. William Adams, Jr. of the University of Texas Southwestern Medical Center at Dallas, said,

> The science around silicone gel is one of most well-researched scientific entities there is. I know of over 20 studies that looked at whether silicone was causing autoimmune illness, and in every one the answer has been no.[21]

The studies were so conclusive that in November 2006, the FDA once again declared them "safe and effective" and permitted their use.[22] Does that mean that the companies wrongfully accused will get their money back? Don't hold your breath.

---

20   Editorial, The Law Disfigured, *Wall Street Journal, June 24, 1999.* http://www.junkscience.com/jun99/disfigur.html (accessed April 3, 2009).

21   Jan Jarvis, "FDA may approve silicone gel implants," *Star-Telegram Aug 11, 2003.*

22   *FDA, "FDA Approves Silicone Gel-Filled Breast Implants After In-Depth Evaluation", November 17, 2006*
http://www.fda.gov/bbs/topics/news/2006/new01512.html (accessed April 3, 2009).

Hypothetical Facts

The point is that in the legal system, demonstrating truth and facts is less important than making claims and alleging victimization. A case against Bushmaster Firearms shows this result. After a sniper terrorized the areas around Washington, DC, in the summer of 2002, the Brady Center to Prevent Gun Violence brought a suit on behalf of the victims. The lawsuit charged Bushmaster with gross negligence that "caused the injuries and deaths that resulted from the sniper shootings."[23]

The gross negligence was that Bull's Eye, a licensed gun dealer selling Bushmaster products, supposedly was the source of the gun used in the crime. Compounding the problem, neither of the two men charged with the crime could have legally purchased a gun. One was under a restraining order, and the other was underage. Therefore, the charge was that Bull's Eye was negligent in handling its inventory. The suit claims that Bull's Eye's

> business practices are so shoddy that, after the shootings, Bull's Eye representatives said they had no record of the sale for the Bushmaster assault rifle used in the sniper shootings and claimed to have no idea how the deadly assault weapon 'disappeared' from the store. [24]

So, how does all this controversy surrounding Bull's Eye get back to Bushmaster? Bushmaster's culpability came from allowing Bull's Eye, a licensed Gun dealer, to purchase their products for resale. Thus, according to the suit, Bushmaster was liable, not for what it did, but for the alleged negligence of a purchaser of its product (Bull's Eye) because they could not produce a sales receipt.

---

23   Review & Outlook, "Bushwacked," *Wall Street Journal,* July 9, 2003, A14
http://online.wsj.com/article/0,,SB105770783122057800,00.html (accessed April 3, 2009).
24   Review & Outlook, "Bushwacked," *Wall Street Journal,* July 9, 2003, A14
http://online.wsj.com/article/0,,SB105770783122057800,00.html (accessed April 3, 2009).

According to a report in the Seattle Times, the alleged sniper told authorities that he stole the gun from Bull's Eye. So, is it any wonder that Bull's Eye cannot produce a sales receipt for a gun they never sold in the first place? In short, Bushmaster was sued for "hypothetical facts." [25]

Lose – Lose

All this makes the legal system closer to a lottery than a justice system. Whether you win is not determined by actual damage; whether you lose is not determined by things like responsibility or negligence or, in some cases, even the facts. It is more determined by chance.

Some argue that this is not a problem, for if companies like Bushmaster did nothing wrong, they would win when they have their day in court. Tell that to Dow-Corning, which went bankrupt, only later to discover that silicone breast implants were not a serious health risk.

The simple fact is that lawyers are so costly and the legal system so slow and time-consuming that even winning your case can be financially devastating for an individual or a company. As a result, many choose to settle out of court as it is often cheaper than "winning."

However, in the long run, while it may be the best decision for those involved in a particular case, for society, it only exacerbates the problem, as it encourages people to file suits with little or no merit with the aim not of winning in court, but at getting a settlement to avoid a costly trial.

While the financial consequences can be devastating, the secondary effects are even worse, particularly for freedom and, thus, for democracy. As a result of all these lawsuits, people and busi-

---

25 Review & Outlook, "Bushwacked," *Wall Street Journal, July 9, 2003,* A14
http://online.wsj.com/article/0,,SB105770783122057800,00.html (accessed April 3, 2009).

nesses become extremely cautious to avoid even the possibility of a potentially devastating lawsuit, and we all have our freedom and choices restricted.

This loss of freedom comes not because of direct governmental restriction but because of the threat of a costly and potentially devastating lawsuit. Companies will not give aspirin for fear of lawsuits; doctors overprescribe and, thus, drive up medical costs to protect themselves from lawsuits; hotel windows can't be opened for fear of lawsuits; businesses have speech codes for fear of lawsuits; people are instructed not to say, "I'm sorry," because it implies liability should there be a lawsuit. Our daily lives are changed and affected in numerous ways, even if we never end up in a lawsuit.[26]

We can see one of these secondary effects in the results of an exercise called TopOff-2. In 2003, the government held a series of exercises on preparing for a terrorist attack. These exercises revealed a lot of strengths and weaknesses, but one that concerns us here was that while plenty of people were willing to volunteer their assistance to help any victims of such an attack, there was also a problem in some areas.

> The problem…is recruitment. Many medical professionals have bitter personal experiences with the tort system and are unwilling to volunteer unless they are protected from lawsuit.[27]

Craig Stevens, a Surgeon General's Office spokesman, said the liability issue was "the biggest problem" in getting volunteers.[28]

---

26   Dennis Prager, *The Legal System is now our enemy June 3, 2003* http://townhall.com/columnists/DennisPrager/2003/06/03/the_legal_system_is_now_our_enemy (accessed April 3, 2009).

27   anie Kirkpatrick, "Al Qaeda and the Plaintiff's Bar," *Wall Street Journal, July 14, 2003*
http://www.ph.ucla.edu/epi/bioter/plaintiffsbar.html (accessed April 3, 2009).

28   anie Kirkpatrick, "Al Qaeda and the Plaintiff's Bar," *Wall Street Journal, July 14, 2003*
http://www.ph.ucla.edu/epi/bioter/plaintiffsbar.html (accessed April 3, 2009).

It is an issue in many aspects of life. An acquaintance volunteers for Ski Patrol. While they are covered under Good Samaritan laws, they still have to document everything they do, including carrying refusal of care documents. An average incident can take about 30 minutes to address and over an hour to complete the paperwork. Do you want to volunteer for hours of paperwork?

Making Policy

Even worse, some are now using lawsuits not to settle disputes or rectify wrongs but to define and shape social policy. Despite the harm caused by the asbestos lawsuits, they originated because of actual health problems with asbestos in some people. Even the lawsuits over silicone gel breast implants developed because of alleged health concerns, even though they were unfounded. On the other hand, an anti-gun group filed the Bushmaster suit, the Brady Center to Prevent Gun Violence, to advance their social policy aims.

Thwarted by the democratic process, advocacy groups have taken to what is a growing trend: the use of lawsuits and the threat of lawsuits to force the social change they desire but have been unable to do democratically. Thus, while advocacy groups may have found that their attempts to get a law passed in the democratic process are unsuccessful, they have found they often can achieve the same or similar results through lawsuits.

We can see one example of this trend in product labeling. Manufacturers must label most food products with fat, sugar, and carbohydrate content, among other things. Yet, when you look at a menu in your local Ice Cream shop, you usually see a list of the flavors. According to news reports, for one lawyer, that is not good enough. He wants ice cream shops to display the fat content and the price.

Now, the democratic process does have a way to deal with this. One could work to have the labeling laws changed to require labels, just like they do on cartons of Ice Cream sold in the grocery store. But this lawyer took a different approach and sent letters to ice cream manufacturers threatening to sue them if they did not start listing the fat content on menu boards in their stores.[29] Even when such efforts fail, they are still costly to the businesses involved.

Up In Smoke

These lawyers pattern such suits on the very successful tobacco suits. The tobacco suits were probably the single most damaging development in the law in decades. Initially, it seemed a worthy goal; a mountain of research demonstrated cigarette smoking was a leading cause of death and illness. Why shouldn't the companies who make cigarettes be held responsible for the harm that their product causes?

The problem with such suits comes from three important factors. The first is that the harmful effects of smoking have been known for a very long time. A hundred years ago, cigarettes were known as coffin nails. For each cigarette you smoked, you put another nail in your coffin.

The second is that one typically smokes for many years before health problems show up, and many studies have shown that if you quit smoking after a few years, your health risks return to normal. The third is that tobacco is a legal product.

These factors do not argue that the tobacco companies are pristine and pure and never did anything wrong, but rather that smoking cigarettes involves personal choice, a choice that society has chosen to permit and for which the risks are well known. Put another way, if the people who smoke are helpless victims of tobacco companies, why do we, as a society, even permit smoking to be legal? Why don't we ban smoking altogether if it is so bad?

---

29   Anna Bakalis, "Ice-cream suits leave folks cold", *The Washington Time*, *July 28, 2003. http://www.washtimes.com/business/20030727-104256-4915r. htm* (accessed April 3, 2009).

At the time, the problem was that a smoking ban would not make it through the democratic process. Too many interests would oppose such a ban. Not just the tobacco companies but the smokers, the farmers who grow tobacco, the stores that sell it, and the government that taxes it.[30]

Unable to get a ban on smoking through the democratic process, some began to take their war on tobacco to the courts. They started filing lawsuits against the tobacco companies on behalf of smokers with illnesses. At first, judges threw out these suits. The smoker, not the tobacco companies, was ultimately responsible. But the lawsuits persisted, and as a result, courts, not legislatures, developed a whole new area of law.

While in the beginning, the lawyers would lose trials, they would win little victories on issues that set precedents for future suits and, thus, future trials. Finally, the lawyers began to win trials as well. Again, the point here is not smoking one way or the other; it is how activists who could not get their way in the democratic process have instead used the courts to circumvent it.

Some think this is okay simply because they do not like cigarettes. However, the legal principles established to sue tobacco companies are general principles not limited to tobacco companies. Lawyers are using the success of tobacco lawsuits to expand into other areas. For example, now we are beginning to see lawsuits by overweight people against fast food establishments. These

---

30 Strangely, government's effort to restrict smoking has actually made it much less likely that it will be banned. As the war on tobacco has "progressed," governments found that tobacco was so disliked by the majority of the public that it was an easy item to tax. This was because they could always claim that the high taxes would reduce tobacco use. Over time government found this to be an easy and lucrative source of income. Now, because of the high taxes involved, government actually makes far more off of a pack of cigarettes than do the tobacco companies. As a result, a total ban on smoking would be opposed because it would amount to a large cut in government revenues. Government is addicted to the money from smoking, as much as the people who smoke are addicted.

principles are also the background for the threat of suits against the ice cream stores discussed above.

Again, the problem is that this short-circuits the normal democratic means for establishing social policy. The constitutionally established process introduces a bill into the legislative body, where representatives debate, discuss, and possibly modify it. They then eventually pass it or vote it down.

If passed, it then goes to the executive to be signed or vetoed, and only if signed (or the veto overridden) does the bill become law. It may be long and messy, but this is the democratic process. Rather than use this process, or having attempted it and failed, these groups seek to have their desired social policy imposed on society by the undemocratic process of the courts. Again, many people like a king that does what they want.

Vigilante Lawsuits

This judicial process is so well-established as a means of affecting social policy that some now write laws to enable and encourage such lawsuits specifically. Lawmakers, knowing they cannot get their policies enacted in the democratic process, write laws making it much easier to impose them by the courts. Nowhere is this as apparent as in the area of environmental law.

Historically, a significant and crucial step in civilizing society is transferring the ability to enforce the legal standards of a community away from the individual and giving it to the governing authority. This transfer eliminates the power of individuals to 'take matters into their own hands.'

If you thought your neighbor had committed a wrong against you, such as stealing some chickens, you are not permitted to go to your neighbor and take some of his chickens in return. Instead, you had to go to the authorities and let them settle the matter. The authorities, not the individual, would decide if the evidence was strong enough to proceed. If it was, then you could go to court for a decision.

This transfer is an important safeguard, checking vengeance and retribution. It not only protected the victim's rights but also provided some protection for the accused. The authorities had to have sufficient evidence that the accused was guilty before they could proceed. People could not make false charges without evidence to harass someone they did not like. Overall, it permitted a more orderly operation of society.

In the last few decades, an increasing number of laws have allowed people to sue, not only for damages done to them but also on behalf of the American people. As a general rule, there has always been access to the courts to sue because of some wrong committed against you.

If someone damaged you somehow, you could sue those responsible to recover the damages. But only the U.S. Government could sue on behalf of the American people. Yet, now, some laws permit "citizen lawsuits" that effectively turn enforcement power over to individuals. As such, these suits remove one of the essential safeguards in the legal system.

Not only can such suits now be filed by those unaffected, but sometimes, the people filing the suits do not even live in the state where the alleged damage occurred. Say a business wants to develop property in Wyoming; someone in New York could file a lawsuit to stop it. Since these suits are often very long and costly to defend against, people use them to intimidate people and companies from taking perfectly legal actions. It is, in effect, a return to vigilante justice where small groups, or even individuals, can threaten and coerce people and businesses through the threat of expensive lawsuits.

As Bruce Fein points out concerning such suits, they result in "a costly and unrestrained growth in litigation against federal agencies," and this shifts "policy making from the legislative and executive branches of government to the unelected and politically unaccountable judicial branch."[31]

31   cited in William Perry Pendly, *War on the West, (Washington DC: Regnery Publishing, Inc 1995), 154.*

It should not be a surprise that there are now counter-citizen lawsuits. Initially, citizen lawsuits were allowed so that environmentalists could take on the enforcement powers of the U.S. Government. They could sue companies for alleged violations of laws like the Endangered Species Act (ESA) even when the federal government did not. A 1997 Supreme Court Ruling permitted suits by farmers and irrigation districts that alleged overly aggressive enforcement of the ESA threatened them.[32]

So, now you have environmental groups suing to enforce the environmental laws and businesses and individuals affected counter-suing. The result is that these public policy decisions are increasingly being determined more by the courts than by the legislature, with all the same problems discussed in the last two chapters.

The Founding Fathers knew that the law was vital to supporting democracy and should be protected and revered. As Hamilton wrote at the close of Federalist No. 25,

> every breach of the fundamental laws, though dictated by necessity, impairs that sacred reverence which ought to be maintained in the breasts of rulers towards the constitution of a country, and forms a precedent for other breaches where the same plea of necessity does not exist at all or is less urgent and palpable.[33]

The Founding Fathers believed that of the three branches of government, the executive, the legislative, and the judiciary, the last was the weakest of the three and, therefore, posed the least risk. As Hamilton pointed out in Federalist No. 78,

> the judiciary, on the contrary, has no influence over either the sword or the purse; no direction either of this strength or the wealth of the society, and can take no active resolution whatever. It may truly be said to have neither FORCE nor WILL but merely judgment; and must ultimately depend

32   Anthony Collings, "Court allows lawsuits to challenge Endangered Species Act," *CNN, March 19, 1997* http://www.cnn.com/EARTH/9703/19/scotus.species/index.html (accessed April 3, 2009).

33   Hamilton, Federalist No. 25 https://founders.archives.gov/documents/Hamilton/01-04-02-0182 (*accessed July 15, 2023*).

upon the aid of the executive arm even for the efficacy of its judgments.[34]

Yet, paradoxically, the weakness of the judiciary stems from the fact that it needs the other two branches to carry out its orders; if the other two branches ignore the court's orders, it is powerless to enforce them.

On the other hand, if the other two branches are automatically bound to carry out any court order, it would become the most powerful body, as it would effectively be the head controlling the other two branches. As we saw in the last chapter, this is what has happened. As Constitutional scholar Robert Bork put it,

> In our domestic affairs and even to some degree in our foreign dealings, the Constitution provides judges with the ultimate coercive power known to our political arrangements. In the hands of judges, words become action: commands are issued by the courts, obeyed by legislatures, and enforced by the executives. The reading of the words becomes freedoms and restrictions for us; the course of the nation is confirmed or altered; the way we live and the way we think and feel are affected.[35]

There are some checks and balances, but,

> perhaps the major check is the judges' and our understanding of the proper limits to that power. Those limits may be pressed back incrementally, case by case, until judges rule areas of life not confided to their authority by any provision of the Constitution or other law.[36]

This threat to the Rule of Law is what we are seeing. In the previous two chapters, this threat came from judges placing themselves above the Constitution and creating new rights or changing old ones by simply reinterpreting the Constitution to fit their de-

---

34   Hamilton, Federalist No. 78 https://founders.archives.gov/documents/Hamilton/01-04-02-0241 (*accessed July 15, 2023*).

35   Robert Bork, *The Tempting of America*, (New York: The Free Press, 1990), *351*.

36   Robert Bork, *The Tempting of America*, (New York: The Free Press, 1990), *351*.

sires. In this chapter, we have seen this through the expanded use of lawsuits and the erosion of the principles of justice.

The net effect of all this is a diminished reverence for the law. With each decision, the Rule of Law weakens, ceasing to be the foundation for our democratic system but instead becoming a tool to be used or gotten around depending on what one wants. Even decisions solidly grounded in the Constitution are denounced as political because they overturn earlier decisions. We are ceasing to be a nation of justice under the law, becoming a nation of law under the increasing sway of lawyers.

The last comment is not a swipe at lawyers, as there is some-what of a chicken-and-egg problem. Are we a litigious society because we have so many lawyers, or do we have so many lawyers because we are a litigious society? Either way, the growing number of lawsuits burdens the economic system and stifles freedom. The ever-increasing ability of citizen lawsuits is a return to the vigilante view of justice that existed before the Rule of Law. It dramatically increases the power of judges to effectively write laws rather than rule on them. In short, it undermines the Constitutional system it is supposed to protect.

What Can Be Done

The solutions here are similar to those for the last two chapters. First and foremost, the primary requirement for any judge should be judicial restraint that will restrict their ruling to what the law says. But even a judge who wants to do this will have trouble if the legislature writes vague laws, leaving it to the judge to make critical decisions. Thus, we must hold all three branches accountable: the judicial, legislative, and executive.

At a minimum, we should eliminate citizen lawsuits that effectively transfer government enforcement powers into individuals' hands. In addition, we need some limits on class action suits that do little to benefit anyone except the lawyers who bring them, and we should link the concepts of accountability to negligence or direct neglect.

No one should have their financial well-being threatened because of actions they had no control over. Yet, this is difficult because many of these are not black-and-white issues where one can draw clear distinctions. Often, this involves tradeoffs. Still, we need a clearer understanding of both sides of the problem, and the current system too often ignores the concepts of justice in its pursuit of money.

Another reform that would help reverse this problem is to have some means of restricting lawsuits that are frivolous and without merit. One option that would do this would be to institute a loser pays system that reimburses winners for their legal expenses. Such a system would quickly halt harassment lawsuits with little or no merit. With little hope of winning, such suits seek to punish the target by requiring them to spend thousands of dollars on legal fees even if they win.

Many people know of a person or a company who settled a lawsuit even though they believed they were right and would have won in court, simply because it was cheaper to pay than going to court and "winning." If given the choice of paying $10,000 to settle a case and be done with it or $20,000 to go to court and "win," which would you choose, especially given that there is no guarantee that you will win? What kind of "justice" system forces such choices?

Finally, we should take steps to streamline the process. Justice delayed is justice denied, and a court system developed centuries ago now seems aimed more at fostering delay, which drives up the costs even further than anything else. For legal professionals, these delays are the norm, and many lawyers get paid by the hour. There is little incentive to change. But this is a burden for the average citizen whose life is in turmoil for years.

As with everything, some of these reforms will have trade-offs and downsides. There is no perfect system. But the heart of the legal system should be the administration of the rules of society so that it can function. It is failing if it is not doing that well and in a timely manner. The soul of the legal system should be justice. These are not only desirable goals to strive for; in a democracy, they are vital.

THE BREAKDOWN OF VOTING

It's not the voting that's democracy; it's the counting.
Tom Stoppard

THE 1988 MEXICAN presidential election looked to be very close. The ruling PRI party had controlled the government for decades since its creation. Corruption was rampant, and the government was indifferent. Among the populace, the desire for change was strong. For once, it looked like the unthinkable would happen: the PRI candidate might lose.

Both candidates campaigned hard. The PRI candidate, Carlos Salinas de Gortari, promised significant reforms of both the economic and political systems. Cuauhtemoc Cardenas, His primary opponent, ran against both Salinas and the PRI party in general, accusing the party of betraying the revolution.

In earlier elections, PRI party candidates won with comfortable margins. The current president won with a very comfortable 74 percent of the vote. While most politicians could only dream of such a victory, it was the lowest ever for the PRI party. So, the PRI party took no chances and spent large amounts of state money to support Salinas. It also prepared a massive effort on election day.

Election Day was July 6, 1988, and, as expected, the PRI was out in force. While standard for the PRI, this was not a typical

democratic get-out-the-vote effort. Fraud was rampant. PRI op-
eratives bused voters to the polling stations and then from poll to
poll to poll so they could vote many times. When this was insufficient, they stuffed the ballot boxes.

The government had recently installed new computer systems
and promised results within 24 hours. The results did not come.
The government claimed "atmospheric conditions"[1] had caused
the system to fail.

After a week of delays in this closely fought election, the government finally announced the winner. Given the rampant fraud
followed by the delay in counting the votes, few were surprised
that the PRI candidate had won again; surprisingly, however, with
only 50.36 percent of the vote.

Democracy & Voting

Nothing is more central to a democratic government than ex-
pressing the public's will through voting. For many, voting and democracy are virtually synonymous. People debate the issues, cast
their votes, and count them to see who wins. While this is simple
in theory,[2] it is a lot more complicated in practice.[3]

------

1   Larry Rohter, "Mexican Ruling Party Candidate Leading in First Official
Returns," *New York Times, July, 12, 1988,*
http://www.nytimes.com/1988/07/12/world/mexican-ruling-party-candi-
date-leading-in-first-official-returns.html (accessed April 3, 2009)
2   *PR Library,* "*Types Of Voting Systems,*" http://www.mtholyoke.edu/acad/
polit/damy/BeginnningReading/types.htm, (accessed April 3, 2009).
3   At each stage of the voting process a whole range of practical issues arise.
For the debate stage how do you have any sort of adequate discussion of the
issues in large groups? Large numbers not only cause problems, but issues such
as time, location, education level, interest level, and language also play roles in
limiting debate. Casting a vote also has problems for large groups. Is there one
voting place or several, how do people know where to vote. What do you do
about those people who cannot make it to the voting place, or those working
during the vote? Even determining the winner is not as straightforward as it
may at first seem. If there are more than two candidates, is the winner the one
with the most votes, or the one with a majority of votes? If the winner requires

The Founding Fathers rejected this type of pure or direct democracy as they saw some problems, and this type of democracy is not in the Constitution. Mention to a group of people that we have a democracy, and often someone will quickly, sometimes forcefully, point out that we do not have a democracy; we have a republic. Yet, they are only half right.

While they are correct that we have a republic, a republic is a form of democracy. When someone says we do not have a democracy, they mean we do not have a direct democracy. Direct democracy is where everyone votes on each issue needing a decision. Given the practical considerations involved in discussing and voting on an issue, direct democracy becomes increasingly difficult the larger the number of people involved.

Many people assume that we have a direct democracy. Nowhere was this clearer than in the U.S. Presidential election in 2000, where the outcome came down to a controversial recount process in a couple of Florida counties and ended up at the steps of the US Supreme Court. Anytime you have an election where the stakes are high and the outcome is close, there are bound to be conflicts and hard feelings on the side that loses. Thus, one can occasionally still see Democrats saying that Bush's presidency was somehow illegitimate because he did not get the most votes in 2000.

Actually, they were only partly correct. While Gore did get more popular votes, Bush won a majority of votes in the Electoral College, and it is the Electoral College that elects the president, not the popular vote. This method is how the Founding Fathers wanted it. Alexander Hamilton, writing in Federalist 68, said of

---

a majority, what are the rules for the runoff? Finally, majority wins is only one of several possible ways that votes can be counted. Majority wins would be a plurality/majority system of voting. There are also proportional representation systems, and semi-proportional systems. In some cases the same votes counted under different systems can result in different outcomes.

the system for electing the President, "if the manner of it be not perfect, it is at least excellent."[4]

Hamilton's assessment stemmed from the framer's attempts to address two competing goals. On the one hand, "it was desirable that the sense of the people should operate in the choice of the person to whom so important a trust was to be confided."[5] On the other,

> it was equally desirable that the immediate election should be made by men most capable of analyzing the qualities adapted to the station and acting under circumstances favorable to deliberation and to a judicious combination of all the reasons and inducements which were proper to govern their choice.[6]

A change in the process of choosing electors later reduced the importance of the second goal. Today, electors are party loyalists who can be counted upon to vote for the candidate who won that state. As such, there is no longer any room for deliberation or analysis.

The Electoral College serves an important function by insulating the candidates from the direct popular vote while forcing them to reach out for votes in all states, not just the states with the most population. It means that presidential candidates must address the issues of the entire nation and not just focus on the concerns of those in large population areas.

The Electoral College grew out of the Founding Fathers' distrust of direct democracy. As Madison put it, with direct democracy, too often, "the passions therefore not the reason, of the public, would sit in judgment."[7]

---

4   Hamilton, Federalist No. 68 https://founders.archives.gov/documents/ Hamilton/01-04-02-0218 (*accessed 7/18/2023*).
5   Hamilton, Federalist No. 68 https://founders.archives.gov/documents/ Hamilton/01-04-02-0218 (*accessed 7/18/2023*).
6   Hamilton, Federalist No. 68 https://founders.archives.gov/documents/ Hamilton/01-04-02-0218 (*accessed 7/18/2023*).
7   Madison, Federalist No. 49 https://founders.archives.gov/documents/ Madison/01-10-02-0270 (*accessed 8/3/2023*).

The closest we currently come to direct democracy is the ballot initiative system found in many states, where voters can directly vote to pass some laws, bypassing the legislator and Governor. Yet, there is no chance for input or modification of an initiative. Often, a few individuals write these; if they qualify, voters must say yes or no.

In a pure direct democracy, there would be the chance to discuss and modify the initiatives so that the resulting measure truly represents the will of the majority. Of course, it's hard to imagine hundreds of thousands of people having meaningful input into the details of anything. Instead, initiatives give voters an all-or-nothing choice. Voters often face a choice of voting for a poorly written law they do not like or voting against an issue they support. We will examine some of these problems in Chapter Nine.

These problems with direct democracy are nothing new. One thing that surprises many people when they begin to read philosophers like Plato and Aristotle on politics is that they held a low opinion of democracy. In Chapter Two, we saw how Plato believed that for tyranny, its "democratic origin is evident."[8] Aristotle's view was similar. In his *Politics,* Aristotle broke down the various forms of government into three main types, each having a good and a bad state.[9]

	Ruled by One	Ruled by a Few	Ruled by Many
Good	Monarchy	Aristocracy	Constitutional Government[10]
Bad	Tyranny	Oligarchy	Democracy

Table 6.1
Aristotle's Classifications of Government.

8   Plato, *Republic, Part IX §8, 562a* http://classics.mit.edu/Plato/republic.9.viii.html (accessed April 3, 2009).

9   Aristotle, *Politics, Book III, Part VII* http://classics.mit.edu/Aristotle/politics.3.three.html *(accessed 8/3/2023).*

10   For Aristotle, a Constitutional Government is where law is democratically determined by the middle class, as opposed to the wealthy few at the top or the masses of poor at the bottom.

At first, this ranking seems very strange to modern readers. They are further confused when they read that among the good governments, Aristotle believed that monarchy was the "first and most divine" form of government.[11]

Before we entirely write off Aristotle as missing the boat, it is essential to realize that Aristotle was talking about political theory. His terminology and categories do not always align with the ordinary meaning of the terms we use today.

For Aristotle, the King in a monarchy is a person of great virtue ruling in the people's best interest. He believed that such a person would not only make the best decisions but that, as a monarch, he would be able to implement them. Thus, Aristotle considered a monarchy the best form of government because it could do the greatest good.

As a political theory, this is all well and good, except the power to do the greatest good also means the ability to do the greatest harm. Aristotle realized this, and while he considered monarchy to be the best, he likewise considered its counterpart, tyranny, to be the worst. He classified the harmful forms of government as

> despotism, which is the worst of governments, is necessarily the farthest removed from a well-constituted form; oligarchy is little better, for it is a long way from aristocracy, and democracy is the most tolerable of the three.[12]

In theory, Monarchy is the best form of government if – and it is a very big if – you could somehow ensure that the king would be an enlightened ruler making decisions that were in the public's best interests. Where Aristotle's theory breaks down is ensuring you will have a good king.

History has very clearly shown that this is pretty much impossible. Even for the rare times in history when rulers generally ruled in their citizens' best interests, there is always the problem

---

11   Aristotle, *Politics, Book IV, Part II.* http://classics.mit.edu/Aristotle/politics.4.four.html (accessed April 3, 2009).
12   Aristotle, *Politics, Book IV, Part II,* http://classics.mit.edu/Aristotle/politics.4.four.html, (accessed April 3, 2009).

of mortality and, thus, succession. Any good that an enlightened and just monarch could do, a tyrant could very quickly undo. The tyrants in history vastly outnumber the excellent monarchs.

Thus, Aristotle's analysis, after the ravages of history, can somewhat be summed up in Winston Churchill's statement,

> Many forms of Government have been tried, and will be tried in this world of sin and woe. No one pretends that democracy is perfect or all-wise. Indeed, it has been said that democracy is the worst form of Government except all those others that have been tried from time to time.[13]

While practical considerations make direct democracy difficult, it is also problematic for other reasons. Again, these go to the heart of some problems with democracy. While majority rule as a general principle is desirable, straight majority rule leaves too little protection for the minority.

The example of four wolves and a sheep voting on what to have for dinner illustrates this problem. In this case, direct democracy works well for the wolves but is hard on the sheep. In the case of wolves and sheep, the problem is easy to see.

The problem is less apparent when discussing four big and one small states. In the current political climate, many ignore this problem when talking about the rich instead of sheep. This problem is why direct democracy was rejected by the Founding Fathers, even in places where practical considerations would allow it, such as in the election of the President of the United States.

It was not by accident the founders set up our system of government as a republic, where we vote, not on issues directly, but for representatives, who then cast votes for us. Yet, representative democracy has its dangers as well. The system breaks down if the representative does not represent the people's will.

This is why the House of Representatives has elections every two years. Since representatives frequently faced a vote of the people, the Founding Fathers believed they would be closest to the

13   *The Quote Garden, "Quotations about Government,"* http://www.quote-garden.com/government.html (accessed April 3, 2009).

people. The Senate, representing states and having six-year terms, was a check and balance to the people's moods. But whether the House of Representatives, the Senate, or the President, even with all the checks and balances, it still ultimately comes down to the will of the people expressed in voting.

At their core, the problems with the presidential election in 2000 were somewhat deeper than simply the majority vote versus the Electoral College. We can see this in that following the election, no serious effort to change the system appeared. The real problem with the presidential election in 2000 stemmed from a much more fundamental disagreement.

Process Versus Outcome

While there were undoubtedly those on both sides with questionable motives who only wanted 'their guy' to win, there were also many on both sides who sincerely thought the other was 'trying to steal the election.' The core difference between Democrats and Republicans appears in each side's main arguments. For the Democrats, it was 'count every vote.' For the Republicans, 'You can't change the rules after the election.'

Both are legitimate goals that virtually everyone would accept as valid. The problem with the 2000 presidential election was that you could not do both. Florida law had specific timetables for counting ballots and rules for determining valid ballots and when to reject one. These are essentially process issues.

The belief that every vote must be counted is an outcome. Given the rules and timetables of Florida law, it was impossible to do all the recounts in the fashion Democrats requested and believed was necessary to 'count every vote' without 'changing the rules after the election.' Conflict was inevitable since the outcome could depend on this question.[14]

---

14   As it turned out, following the election, various organizations did many recounts, including the ones requested by the Democrats at the time. Bush won these. Gore did win some full state-wide recounts, but the Democrats

Which is more critical when we cannot achieve both? Is it more important to follow the process, even if the outcome is not what you desire, or in such cases, is it more important to set aside the process to achieve a result? There are good arguments for both sides. Two factors tilt in favor of process and against results.

First, how will you know you have achieved the proper outcome if you abandon the rules?

To better understand this question, consider the same process versus outcome question in a somewhat different setting: a courtroom. When someone is on trial for a crime such as murder, which is more important, that the rules of the court be followed (process) or justice be done (outcome)?

Again, in a perfect world, we would want both. But this does not always happen. Following the rules of evidence sometimes means letting the guilty go free. Yet, if we say that justice is more important, and therefore, we should break the rules of evidence to achieve justice, how will we know we are getting justice if we discard the rules?

Back to the issue of elections, there is no question that officials should count every legitimate vote. However, it is equally important not to count erroneous votes. Just as not counting a legitimate vote deprives a voter of their say in the process, so does counting an erroneous vote; every erroneous vote negates a legitimate vote.

For example, suppose you had an election where ten people voted for candidate A and ten voted for candidate B. If officials do not count one of the votes for candidate A, that voter has no say in the process. The result would be nine votes for A and ten for B. The election would go to candidate B. In this case, failing to count a vote deprives that voter of their say in the process and changes the election's outcome.

---

had not requested these during the controversy. Thus, it is unlikely that the rulings affected the outcome. Given the inconsistent results of the various recounts, no definitive result exists.

Now, suppose there is an invalid vote for candidate B. An invalid vote has precisely the same effect. If you count an invalid vote for B, the result would be 11 for B, and again, B wins. So, there is really little difference between not counting valid votes and counting invalid ones.

How can election officials tell what is a valid and invalid vote? The rules of the election specify which are which. Not every ballot is a valid vote. Some are spoiled. Sometimes, voters make mistakes or don't follow the rules. The election rules determine which ballots are legitimate and counted and which are erroneous and discarded. If you set aside these rules so that 'every vote must be counted,' how will you determine which votes are legitimate and which are erroneous?

A classic example of this problem occurred in the Senate race in Minnesota in 2008. Following a very close election in which the initial results showed the Republicans ahead, many recounts and court challenges occurred, mostly over what was or was not a legitimate vote. At the end of a lengthy process that involved changing some of the election rules, the Democrat was declared the winner.

The 2000 Presidential election and the 2008 US Senate race in Minnesota reveal an essential distinction; there is at least a possible difference between who the voters voted for and which candidate was declared the winner. In both elections, there was a declared winner. In both elections, many voters on the losing side believed their candidate had won, but the other party stole the election.

The second factor is that rules set and agreed to by both sides before the election are much more likely to be better than those made after the election while counting is in process. This is because there is a greater chance of limiting partisan influences before the election. In the abstract, any rule is as likely to work for your candidate as against them.

Trying to determine these rules in the aftermath of a close election where the outcome may depend on the rules chosen is questionable at best. In such a case, the side whose candidate is behind will have a vested interest in expanding the definition of a valid vote to get more votes. The side whose candidate is already ahead will have a vested interest in limiting the definition lest their side suddenly lose.

This situation strongly tempts both sides to make rules, not in a fair and objective sense, but in a way that will help their candidates. As we have seen, both sides are equally dangerous, as the side trying to expand the definition risks counting erroneous votes, and the side seeking to limit the definition risks not counting valid ballots. In such a process, the losing side will inevitably question the results.

Democracy Versus Voting

Even with all their problems, disputed elections such as the one in Florida or Minnesota are not the most severe problem. Thankfully, they are the exception, though their number has increased recently. The other problems are more dangerous and insidious as they receive far less attention.

While no significant election of any size ever has been, and probably never can be, perfect and completely free of problems, the election system in the U.S. has worked reasonably well. The main exception would be political machines, such as Tammany Hall in New York City, the Pendergast Machine in Missouri, the Daley Machine in Chicago, and others. However, in the last 50 years, several factors have come into play that weaken this vital link between the people and their government.

We know from history that simply having a vote does not mean democracy. As far back as Napoleon, Dictators knew elections could give them an air of legitimacy. They hold them when it is convenient. As Historian Paul Johnson pointed out, Napoleon's various constitutions gave less voting rights to the people than the ancien régime, which produced the Estates General in 1789, and were all based on the anti-democratic principle, "Confidence comes from below, authority from above."[15]

Whereas in effective democratic countries, winning by 60 percent is considered a significant landslide, dictators routinely win their 'elections' by well over 90 percent of the vote.

Here again, Napoleon sets the example. On May 4, 1804, the French Senate passed a resolution proposing that Napoleon be made Emperor. They put it to the French people for a vote. On November 6, 1804, 3,571,329 voted to make Napoleon Emperor. Only 2,570 voted against it. As a result, the measure passed by a whopping 99.9 percent.[16]

We have noted that Mexico was another country plagued by election irregularities during the 1980s. In an article published in 1991, Andrew Reding, the director of the Mexico Project of the World Policy Institute and an observer of some Mexican elections, described what he saw. "I was soon classifying several patterns of irregularities, each suggesting a distinct form of fraud."[17]

Some of the most obvious fraud were precincts where the total number of votes cast exceeded the number of registered voters. "In precinct 3-124 of Monterrey, for example, had 931 ballots for governor with only 872 persons registered voters."[18] Other irregularities included high annulments and precincts in which 100 percent of the votes recorded were for the ruling PRI party.

---

15   Paul Johnson, *The Birth of the Modern* , *(New York, Harper-Collins, 1991), 66.*

16   Paul Johnson, *Napoleon, (New York, Penguin Group, 2002), 47.*

17   Andrew Reding, "The election fraud I saw in Mexico," *Sacramento Bee, Sunday Forum 6 Oct, 1991, pg 1*(accessed April 3, 2009) http://www.worldpolicy.org/projects/globalrights/mexico/1991-1006-bee-electoralfraud.html (accessed April 3, 2009).

18   Andrew Reding, "The election fraud I saw in Mexico," *Sacramento Bee, Sunday Forum 6 Oct, 1991, pg 1*(accessed April 3, 2009) http://www.worldpolicy.org/projects/globalrights/mexico/1991-1006-bee-electoralfraud.html (accessed April 3, 2009).

Holding elections and letting citizens vote is largely irrelevant to whether a government is a functioning democracy. There are other essential factors. The people must be able to express their will meaningfully. They must have a choice that is respected. An election where only one person is on the ballot is not democracy.

Thus, for example, Saddam Hussein held a referendum shortly before he was removed from power by a coalition of countries led by the U.S. and Britain. All of the 11,445,638 votes cast were for him,[19] a slight improvement over his previous showing of 99.96 percent seven years earlier.[20] But what would one expect when Hussein was the only one on the ballot?

Sadly, an increasing number of elections in the United States are little better than those held in the old Soviet Union or, more recently, in Iraq. Many factors contribute to this result. We will look at redistricting, campaign finance reform laws, the power of incumbency, and outright fraud. But whatever the cause, the effect is the same; it weakens the link between the people and their representatives, undermining democracy.

Redistricting

Probably the least understood of these mechanisms is redistricting. Redistricting is the process by which, every ten years, district lines are redrawn. In theory, officials draw these lines to reflect population changes and ensure equal representation.

To see why this is needed, imagine two districts with an equal population, say 10,000 people each. The voters in each district select someone to represent them in the governmental body. Suppose, over time, 5,000 people left District A and moved into District B, so you ended up with 5,000 in District A and 15,000 in District B. If the district lines remained the same, District A's peo-

---

19   BBC News, "Saddam 'wins 100% of vote,'" October 16, 2002
20   Associated Press, "Saddam Wins Presidential Referendum – as Expected.",
Oct 16, 2002, http://www.foxnews.com/story/0,2933,65656,00.html (accessed April 3, 2009).

ple would get three times the representation as those in District B; since they have one-third of the population, one vote in District A has the same effect as three votes in District B. Thus, the district lines need to be redrawn so the districts again have equal numbers of people.

While this is all well and good, the problem arises when politicians draw the lines. If the politicians redraw the lines for their benefit rather than to ensure proper representation, then the result is gerrymandering.

The term gerrymandering goes back to the early 19ᵗʰ century, when a governor of Massachusetts, Elbridge Gerry, redrew the district lines to favor his party. His district lines wandered around, picking up some voters and leaving others out. To some, a map of one of the districts resembled a salamander. The opposition quickly dubbed it a "gerrymander."[21]

While gerrymandering has always been a problem, the politicians' ability to process the necessary voting data to draw the lines accurately limited its effect. Today, large databases combined with GIS (Geographic Information Systems) mapping software have radically changed the landscape. Computers can process voting records and correlate them with a map to redraw the lines, creating as many 'safe seats' as possible.

A safe seat is a district where most voters reliably vote for a particular party. That party's candidate does not have to worry about getting elected, at least in the general election. Since incumbents rarely get a serious primary challenge, they are safe. They will get reelected if they run and don't do something foolish. Safe seats allow politicians to be more concerned with building their power base than representing the people from their district.

---

21   Matt Rosenberg, Gerrymandering, *About.com* http://geography.about.com/library/weekly/aa030199.htm (accessed April 3, 2009).

With careful redistricting, a minority party in terms of votes could even win a majority of seats in a legislative body. This result is not just theory but something that can and does happen. Consider the following example to see how careful redistricting can affect which party controls a legislative body.

Suppose we have an area with a population of 100,000 and two parties, the Silver and the Gold. The voting history shows that the Gold party gets the most votes, typically about 54,000; in contrast, the Silver party receives only about 46,000. There are five seats in the legislative body, and they end up split 3-2 in favor of the majority Gold party.

In the election just before redistricting, perhaps a gold candidate was involved in some scandal, the silvers managed to win a narrow victory, getting three seats. The key is that now the Silver party gets to do the redistricting. If the Silver party carefully draws the lines, they could create districts, as shown in Table 6.2.

Notice that while the split between Gold and Silver votes remains unchanged and the Silver party remains the minority party, they created four safe seats for themselves and one for the Gold. Thus, in the next election, the Silver party expects to win four seats and the Gold only one, even though the Silver party remains the minority party in total votes.

While I grant that this example may seem somewhat extreme, it is not far out of line with what can happen with computers. In reality, the Silver party would probably be more reasonable. They would give themselves three safe seats to ensure their majority and one safe seat to the Gold. The Gold politician in that seat would be happy to get a safe seat. That politician might even support the plan, giving it the veneer of bipartisanship. The final seat would be a marginally competitive district, one where Silver had the advantage but not enough to be called a safe seat to maintain the illusion of competitive elections.

District	Gold voters	Silver voters	Total voters
1	9,000	11,000	20,000
2	9,000	11,000	20,000
3	9,000	11,000	20,000
4	9,000	11,000	20,000
5	18,000	2,000	20,000
Total	54,000	46,000	100,000

Table 6.2
Possible Districts for Silver and Gold

To see how this translated into real-world politics, one only has to consider the example of California and the redistricting that took place following the 2000 census. Out of 53 congressional seats, the politicians in California created 52 safe seats, leaving only one competitive congressional district in the state.

The single competitive seat happened to be the seat of Gary Condit, who was in the middle of a significant scandal following the disappearance and murder of one of his aides. As one political advisor said, "If the average Californian doesn't like his congressman, the only option is to call the moving vans."[22]

We can see the results of redistricting in the average reelection rate of those in Congress. Of those who ran for reelection, 90 percent have won since 1952. In the closely fought election of 2000, where the country split at the presidential level, 98 percent of congress members seeking reelection won.[23] Most were in such safe seats that they did not have a serious opponent. The opposing party realized it was not worth trying to run a candidate against them.

---

22   *The Economist, "How to rig an election," Apr 25*[th] *2002*, http://www.economist.com/world/na/displaystory.cfm?story_id=1099030 (accessed April 3, 2009).

23   *The Economist, "How to rig an election," Apr 25*[th] *2002*, http://www.economist.com/world/na/displaystory.cfm?story_id=1099030 (accessed April 3, 2009).

The Founding Fathers saw the House of Representatives as the house of the people. Madison called the Representatives "the great body of the people of the United States."[24] As such, they gave them two-year terms so that they would be closer to the people. Today, they are the most insulated. The 110th Congress (2007-2009) had members first elected not only in the 1990s but also in the 80s, 70s, 60s, and one first elected in 1954.[25]

Concerning the Senate, Madison said, "The use of the Senate is to consist in its proceeding with more coolness, with more system, & with more wisdom, than the popular branch."[26] The Senate was to be a check on swings of popular opinion and, thus, were more distant from the people, representing the states with six-year terms.

Yet, since the Senate is by states where redistricting does not exist, in recent years, this has reversed. Even with two-year terms, the House is less liable to change hands than the Senate with its six-year terms. From 1955 to 2008, the House of Representatives only changed hands twice, once in 1994 and then again in 2006.[27] Yet, during the same time, the Senate, supposedly the more stable body, changed hands six times.[28]

The net effect of redistricting is that, increasingly, voters are no longer allowed to choose who will represent them. Instead, politicians choose those voters who will most likely return them

---

24   Madison, Federalist No.57 https://founders.archives.gov/documents/Hamilton/01-04-02-0206 (*accessed August 8, 2023*).

25   U.S. House of Representatives, Office of the Clerk, 110th Congress Seniority List, http://clerk.house.gov/member_info/110_seniority.pdf (accessed April 3, 2009).

26   Madison, *The Debates in the Federal Convention of 1787, June 7.* http://www.yale.edu/lawweb/avalon/debates/607.htm (accessed April 3, 2009).

27   U.S. House of Representatives, Office of the Clerk, "Speakers of the House" http://clerk.house.gov/art_history/house_history/speakers.html (accessed April 3, 2009).

28   "Majority and Minority Leaders and Party Whips," *United States Senate,* http://www.senate.gov/artandhistory/history/common/briefing/Majority_Minority_Leaders.htm (accessed April 3, 2009).

to office year after year. Instead of people picking their representatives, it is the representatives picking their people.

Campaign Finance Reform?

Even with a competitive seat, defeating an incumbent is still challenging. Part of this is because of the natural advantage of incumbency. If nothing else, voters already know the incumbent. The prestige of the office makes it easier to attract news coverage and campaign contributions. A less obvious factor is the protective effect of campaign finance reform laws. Efforts to reform campaign finance have made mounting any practical challenge against an incumbent increasingly problematic.

The more damaging phase of campaign finance reform laws started in the post-Watergate era. Supporters touted these laws as limiting the influence of "big money" donors so that the "average voter" could have more say in the process. The idea was that by limiting the amount of money individuals can give to candidates, you can limit the impact of large donors, forcing politicians to give more consideration to "the little guy."

Despite the intentions, the result has been pretty unambiguous. The reforms had little, if any, positive impact on the influence of average voters while having a significant negative one. Much of the impetus for campaign finance reform laws in recent years has been to try to remedy some of the problems caused by the earlier campaign finance reform laws.

As a result of campaign finance reform laws, gone are the days when someone could mount a campaign based solely on volunteers. The campaign laws are now so complex and detailed that any serious candidate must hire costly experts to manage and run their campaigns.

If they don't, they risk hundreds of thousands of dollars in potential fines, fines for which they could be personally liable. These laws are so complex that even the experts often slip up here and there. Even incumbents routinely have to pay these fines. Yet, incumbents can raise the money to pay them.

Rather than lowering the barriers, campaign finance reform laws have made it much harder for average citizens to get involved. The biggest obstacle any potential candidate faces is getting known by enough people to be considered a viable candidate.

Getting known costs money and is one of the reasons for the increasing numbers of millionaires and celebrities running for office. With the current campaign finance reform laws, unless you are a professional politician, you can only effectively compete if you are already a well-known celebrity or rich enough to fund your campaign.

An analysis of the campaign laws among the various states done by the Cato Institute shows the effect of these laws. They found that,

> Even though the playing field may appear leveled by laws constraining all types of donors, parties and the types of candidates that parties back (i.e., challengers) suffer the most from limits. This difference may appear marginal. However, in a state in which very few districts are competitive, this small difference in party control of funds might make a big difference in races that are potentially close.[29]

Campaign finance reform laws had precisely the opposite effect frequently claimed. Instead of leveling the playing field,

> Those limits do not penalize incumbents as harshly as they do challengers, since sitting lawmakers can attract more money from interest groups and individual donors."

That campaign finance reform laws fail in their claimed goals should be no surprise. They are little more than yet another attempt by the government to solve a problem through planning and control. As we saw in Chapter 3, such an approach is doomed from the start. As is often the case, the failure of planning and con-

---

29   Thad Kousser, Ray LaRaja, "The Effect of Campaign Finance Laws on Electoral Competition", *Policy Analysis No. 426, Feb 14,2002.* http://www. cato.org/pubs/pas/pa426.pdf (accessed April 3, 2009) .

trol does not result in a rejection of the policy but an expansion of the effort. These new efforts only result in further problems and a further loss of freedoms.

Given these restrictions always seem to benefit incumbents, it is no wonder that many consider campaign finance reform laws to be more appropriately labeled "Incumbent Protection Acts."

Further Problems

While they remain a formidable barrier to challengers, by the 1990s, incumbents had largely worked around the limitations imposed by the campaign finance reform laws passed following Watergate. In the 15+ years following the passage of the reforms, the incumbents had figured out how to exploit all the loopholes.

More importantly, incumbents realized that the laws had no discernible effect on them. They were able to amass huge war chests of funds. When fined for violations, they paid them with the money raised. The fines were little more than just a cost of doing business and one they could easily afford. This result was especially the case given that even if any fines were assessed, they would come after the election was over and they had already won.

While challengers could, in theory, do the same, they do not start a campaign with a large war chest full of earlier donations. Challengers typically have trouble raising money; what they raise is spent on their campaign. If they win, there is no problem, but challengers usually lose. When they do, they often end the race in debt, a debt for which the candidate is often personally liable.

A fine of tens of thousands of dollars will be insignificant for a victorious incumbent. Even if they are broke following the race, they can raise more funds. Yet, the same fine can be a massive burden to a challenger already in debt with little or no ability to raise funds. After all, who wants to donate to someone who lost? So, while the laws are, at best, a minor annoyance to the incumbents, they are a significant obstacle to challengers.

Over the years, as incumbents continued to push the line, it became apparent that the laws were almost entirely unenforceable for them. Even the few times the violations were so egregious that prosecution followed, the law ultimately had few teeth.

Thus, for example, one fundraiser was convicted on five felony counts resulting from over $100,000 in illegal contributions in what amounted to little more than a money laundering scheme – a deliberate attempt to get around the law. While technically, she faced up to 25 years in prison for this crime, her sentence was 90 days of home detention, three years on probation, and a fine of $5,000.[30]

Given this, is it any wonder that Vice President Gore, when caught up in a fundraising scandal, said, "My counsel advises me, let me repeat, that there is 'no controlling legal authority' that says that any of these activities violated any law."[31] Whatever one's view on the laws, history has shown Gore's statements were correct, at least for incumbents.

Compounding Problems

By the mid-1990s, it was clear that the laws had ceased to be an effective check on incumbents. In addition, they had created some undesirable effects. People who wanted to spend money on politics did not lose their desire to contribute to political issues and go away following the law's enactment. They simply shifted where they sent their money.

As a result, a new political entity appeared: the Political Action Committee or PAC. By the 1990s, PACs were seen as a sig-

30   National News Briefs; "Democratic Fund-Raiser Sentenced to Probation", *New York Times, Feb 8, 2001*
http://query.nytimes.com/gst/fullpage.html?res=9C04EFDE1431F93BA-35751C0A9679C8B63 (accessed April 3, 2009).
31   John F Harris, "Gore: Calls Broke No Law," *Washington Post, March 4, 1997, Page A01*
http://www.washingtonpost.com/wp-srv/politics/special/campfin/stories/cf030497.htm (accessed April 3, 2009).

nificant problem, particularly their ability to raise large sums of money and run commercials against targeted candidates.

Rather than abandoning Campaign Finance Laws as a failure, the push in the late 1990s was to expand them with a new bill sponsored by Senators McCain and Feingold. Proving that the failure of planning and control only produced expanded efforts, McCain-Feingold imposed a whole new layer of controls. It also took the unprecedented step of attempting to limit political speech 90 days before an election. Many politicians voting for the bill believed that such a limit on speech was unconstitutional, and they expected the Supreme Court to reject it.

In late 2003, however, the court surprised many people by upholding McCain-Feingold, including the limits on political speech 90 days before an election.[32] While there was a lot of celebrating among supporters of the bill, it did not last long.

As with previous reforms, rather than limiting the effect of big-money donors, the new law had the opposite effect; it significantly increased their strength and power. Within months of the Supreme Court decision, an essentially new political entity had appeared: the 527, which allows large donors to spend vast amounts of money on political ads. With the political parties and other organizations effectively limited by the law, the result has been to magnify the impact of these large donors, not restrict it.

While redistricting and campaign finance reform laws undermine voting by making it harder for challengers to mount effective campaigns and for voters to have real choices, they are at least still technically playing by the rules. The next threat we will examine, voter fraud, completely ignores the rules.

---

32   Gwen Ifill, "Court Upholds Campaign Reform," Dec 10, 2003, *PBS News Hour,* http://www.pbs.org/newshour/bb/law/july-dec03/cfr_12-10.html (accessed April 3, 2009).

Fraud

Voter fraud is nothing new. Places like Chicago are well known for the number of dead people who voted. Many historians believe that if you were to remove voter fraud from the 1960 Presidential election, Nixon would have won over Kennedy. Both Texas and Illinois were very close. Voter fraud in Chicago and Johnson's machine in Texas probably decided the election.

In Texas, Kennedy won by 46,000 votes. Estimates are that, at a minimum, the Johnson machine in Texas delivered 100,000 fraudulent votes to Kennedy.[33] In Illinois, Kennedy won by only 8,858 votes. While Nixon carried 93 of the 102 counties in the state, he lost in the Chicago area, which was under the control of the Daley political machine and famous for its voter fraud. In the Chicago area, Kennedy received 450,000 more votes than Nixon, enough to wipe out his losses in the rest of the state and give him his narrow victory.

That there was massive fraud in the Chicago area is beyond dispute. Similar to the examples of fraud in Mexico cited earlier in the chapter, at one polling station in Chicago with 4,895 registered voters, 6,138 votes were cast.[34] The ballots above registered voters at this one polling place amounted to 14 percent of Kennedy's narrow margin of victory. As historian Paul Johnson concluded,

> If Nixon, instead of Kennedy, had carried Texas and Illinois, the shift in electoral votes would have given him the presidency, and the evidence of electoral fraud makes it clear that Kennedy's overall 112,803 vote plurality was a myth: Nixon probably won by about 250,000 votes.[35]

While voter fraud has always been a problem, certain factors have made it more of a threat in recent years. As with campaign

---

33 Paul Johnson, *A History of the American People. (Harper-Collins, 1997), 854.*
34 Paul Johnson, *A History of the American People. (Harper-Collins, 1997), 854.*
35 Paul Johnson, *A History of the American People. (Harper-Collins, 1997), 854.*

finance reform laws, attempts to address past wrongs have yielded unintended consequences.

Undoubtedly, many minorities were unfairly kept from voting by provisions, such as poll taxes and literary tests, explicitly aimed at keeping them from voting. The local governments passed rules and requirements that were overly complex and difficult. Election officials could then overlook minor problems as meaningless technicalities for white voters but strictly enforce them for minorities.

To correct these past wrongs, most impediments to voting are now illegal. While they make voting easier and discrimination harder, they also make fraud much easier. Because some states rarely purge their voter rolls, many are registered in several locations. They are registered where they currently live, plus some or all of their previous places.

In some locations, election officials do not check identification; in some states, it is illegal to ask for it. Thus, it would be straightforward for someone to vote in their place.

There are two significant concerns here. The first is the fraud itself. As mentioned above, every fraudulent vote cancels the vote of a legitimate voter, depriving them of their right to vote. This indeed happens in every election to some extent. In a close election, the fraudulent votes can exceed the margin of victory.

While the existence of voter fraud is indisputable, there is a lot of dispute about its extent. Opinions range from it is an insignificant problem to a massive one. Unfortunately, much of the discussion occurs in the aftermath of a close election where the various sides have a vested interest in maximizing or minimizing the extent of the problem.

The Supreme Court addressed this issue in its 2008 ruling in Crawford v. Marion County Election Bd. The case before the court was whether Indiana citizens could be required to show photo identification when voting. In their ruling, the majority wrote concerning impersonating voters,

> the record contains no evidence of any such fraud actually occurring in Indiana at any time in its history. Moreover, pe-

titioners argue that provisions of the Indiana Criminal Code punishing such conduct as a felony provide adequate protection against the risk that such conduct will occur in the future. It remains true, however, that flagrant examples of such fraud in other parts of the country have been documented throughout this Nation's history by respected historians and journalists, that occasional examples have surfaced in recent years, and that Indiana's own experience with fraudulent voting in the 2003 Democratic primary for East Chicago Mayor—though perpetrated using absentee ballots and not in-person fraud—demonstrate that not only is the risk of voter fraud real but that it could affect the outcome of a close election.[36]

Given the well-documented history of political machines in this country, that at times fraud had been a problem is indisputable. The Heritage Foundation's Election Fraud Database shows that it remains a problem. The database contains,

recent proven instances of election fraud from across the country. Each and every one of the cases in this database represents an instance in which a public official, usually a prosecutor, thought it serious enough to act upon it. And each and every one ended in a finding that the individual had engaged in wrongdoing in connection with an election hoping to affect its outcome — or that the results of an election were sufficiently in question and had to be overturned.[37]

As of this writing, the database contained 1,438 examples of proven voter fraud, resulting in 1,240 convictions, 48 civil penalties, 108 diversion programs,[38] 25 Judicial findings, and 17 Official findings.

The second significant concern regarding fraud is that it is often challenging to detect, much less prove. Without identifi-

---

36   Crawford v. Marion County Election Bd., 553 U.S. 181 (2008) https://supreme.justia.com/cases/federal/us/553/181/

37   Heritage Foundation, Election Fraud Database, https://www.heritage.org/voterfraud (Accessed August 9, 2023)

38   A diversion program is a pretrial process that allows courts to remedy behavior without a formal trial and conviction. Defendants are often required to attend, or "diverted into," programs such as counseling instead of being tried and convicted.

cation, when someone goes to a polling place and impersonates another voter who has moved away from the area, how can that be detected? Unless the poll worker happens to be acquainted with the registered voter and knows they have moved away, such fraud would be difficult to detect. Voter impersonation is a problem, yet an even more significant threat making voter fraud more challenging to detect comes from the convergence of three growing trends: easier registration, the expansion of election day, and absentee ballots.

Registration

Easier registration is a problem because there is little or no coordination with other locations. As people move, they can be registered to vote in multiple locations. Thus, according to data from the federal Electoral Assistance Commission, "a minimum of 2.5 million voter registrations are wrongly listed as valid." [39]

Judicial Watch warned that 378 U.S. counties had more voters registered than the total voting-age population. For 19 counties in California, Colorado, North Carolina, Pennsylvania, and Virginia, the problem was particularly severe. It violated the National Voter Registration Act for failing to take reasonable steps to remove ineligible voters.

> Eleven of the 19 counties are located in California, which has had habitual problems updating its voter rolls. Last year, Los Angeles County settled a lawsuit and agreed to clean up its voter rolls after Judicial Watch revealed that it had 1.6 million more voter registrations on file than the eligible voting population in the county. As of last year, the entire state of California had a voter registration rate of 101%. [40]

39   Mark Heminway, *Five States Face Federal Lawsuit Over Inaccurate Voter Registrations*, Real Clear Politics, Jan 07, 2020. https://www.realclearpolitics. com/articles/2020/01/07/five_states_face_federal_lawsuit_over_inaccurate_ voter_registrations__142089.html (Accessed August 9, 2023)

40   Mark Heminway, *Five States Face Federal Lawsuit Over Inaccurate Voter Registrations*, Real Clear Politics, Jan 07, 2020. https://www.realclearpolitics. com/articles/2020/01/07/five_states_face_federal_lawsuit_over_inaccurate_

Given that it is unlikely that every person eligible to register does so, there are a lot of invalid registrations, and every invalid registration is a potential fraudulent vote that would be difficult to detect. This problem is particularly troubling when combined with the other two trends: the expansion of "election day" into a long process lasting weeks and absentee voting.

Election Day?

Voting by mail and early voting distort the election process. Ideally, we have the campaign and then vote on election day. Now, some states allow early voting for as many as 46 days in advance, significantly increasing the cost and complexity of campaigns.

This problem is why, in 2020, the Trump campaign requested moving the debate schedule earlier. The debate scheduled for September 29th occurred after 16 states had already begun early voting. An additional problem is that early voting during the primary effectively disenfranchised many voters because the candidate they voted for dropped out before the election day.

Most people do not follow politics closely. Frankly, this is a good thing as people have busy lives. Political campaigns focus on educating the voting public on their candidate's benefits and their opponent's weaknesses. At the same time, the opposition does the same for their candidate.

An effective campaign requires building a strategy and then executing it. Doing this for a single election day is hard enough. The larger the window for voting, the more difficult and costly this becomes. For incumbents, this is a huge advantage. The more complex and expensive campaigns, the safer incumbents are from challengers.

While both voting by mail and early voting share this problem, at least with early voting, there is the security that your votes will be received and counted if you vote. Voting by mail has additional difficulties in both of these areas.

---

voter_registrations__142089.html (Accessed August 9, 2023)

Absentee Voting

The problem with mailing your ballot is that the process relies on the mail. In short, that you sent your ballot does not mean your ballot will be received or received in time. To test this, CBS News in Philadelphia created 100 simulated ballots and mailed them to a P.O. box from various locations around the city. This simulated people voting by mail. They repeated this with a second group of simulated ballots a few days later.

A week after mailing the first batch of ballots, three were missing. For the second batch, only 79 had arrived, although the P.O. Box did receive other pieces of misdirected mail, such as a birthday card.[41] Even the three percent rate of missing ballots from the first set is larger than the 2016 margin of victory for Trump or Clinton in nine states. These states accounted for 98 electoral votes, nearly three times Trump's margin of victory.

Even if your ballot is delivered, it still can be rejected. In the 2020 spring election in California, officials rejected 70,330 ballots because they arrived too late. Another 13,000 rejections occurred because people forgot to sign the ballot, or the signature did not match the one on record. In total, officials rejected 102,000 ballots,[42] and California is a state that routinely processes large numbers of absentee voting. It is important to remember that these are problems that do not occur with in-person voting, and the problem's size is greater than the margin of victory of many races.

A further issue is that the increased use of voting by mail is also dragging out election night and threatening to turn every election into the chaos of the 2000 or 2020 presidential elections. Six weeks after a 2020 primary election in New York, the results

---

41   Rick Morgan, *USPS Fails Mail-In Ballot Test,* https://pjmedia.com/news-and-politics/rick-moran/2020/07/25/usps-fails-mail-in-ballot-test-n697455 (Accessed August 9, 2023)
42   Michael R. Blood, *California rejected 100,000 mail-in ballots because of mistakes,* https://www.pbs.org/newshour/nation/california-rejected-100000-mail-in-ballots-because-of-mistakes (Accessed August 9, 2023)

remained undecided, and legal disputes raged over 12,500 absentee ballots.[43]

Increasingly, there is the candidate who wins on election night and the candidate who wins after counting all the absentee ballots, sometimes weeks later. These are not always the same person, and such changes undermine confidence in the electoral process. When the election is close, the deciding factor is increasingly the courtroom and lawyers rather than the ballot box and voters.

It is tempting to think such errors are random, affecting both sides equally. Even if the first part is correct, the second is probably not. That is not how randomness works. For example, with a roulette wheel, each number has equal chances. But it is a fallacy to think these numbers will come up equally in the short run.

Over a very long period, the number of times any number wins will be the same as the others. In the short term, one number might come up several times, while another number does not come up at all. Similarly, while possibly equally distributed in the long run, in any given election, there will almost certainly be a preponderance of these errors that favor one candidate or the other.

Making matters worse, the errors won't be completely random. A given mail carrier may be more careless; a given machine may have a problem. Problems such as these will result in rejection rates from some areas that are higher than others.

Voting Security

These problems occur before we consider the potential for fraud, a growing concern. By its very nature, voter fraud is difficult to prove. It often goes unnoticed or is only suspected.

A foreign power could exploit the voter rolls to print large numbers of counterfeit ballots. They could overwhelm the system,

---

43   Karen Matthews, *Judge rules disputed ballots must be counted in NY primary,* Associated Press, August 4, 2020
https://apnews.com/general-news-7ac47be0bc8041cf2969feb115f9e527
(Accessed August 9, 2023)

invalidating the election or selectively add just enough votes to change the outcome. A sophisticated data operation could identify the voters on the list by error and submit counterfeit ballots under their names. If done correctly, it would be virtually impossible to detect.

With the expanded use of mass mailing ballots, unattended drop boxes, and third-party collection and delivery of ballots, this is where the bloated voter rolls come in. I have worked the polls on election day. During those elections, we had to account for every ballot, and at the end of the night, all the numbers needed to match. The number of ballots cast had to equal the number of voters who signed the rolls. The number of ballots returned unused, spoiled, and used for voting had to equal the number we received. We had to account for every ballot.

While such strict controls help ensure the integrity of the vote, they do not exist when election officials mail ballots to all registered voters. Such mass mailing would be problematic even if the voter rolls were accurate. They are very problematic for areas with boated voter rolls. How can there be any certainty that the registered voter was the person who filled out the ballot? The opportunity for fraud is massive.

One opportunity would be simply collecting unused ballots and voting with them. Another would be to collect ballots as a convenience in areas where ballot harvesting is legal or where unmonitored drop boxes exist. Suppose you know the area predominantly supports your candidate; you deliver them. However, if the area is a stronghold for your opponent, those ballots never get returned.

One counter-argument is that once election officials get the ballot, they will check the signature to verify that it matches the signature on record. That would not help if a ballot harvester discarded ballots from areas known to favor an opponent. Still, signature verification only opens up another opportunity for corruption in the system. The official checking the signature can easily have different standards depending on the voter's party affiliation. It can also vary from office to office. Officials in one area might just be more careful than others. Such differences would penalize voters in the strict regions, as those voters see higher rejection rates.

Such differences do occur. Do they show fraud? Therein lies another issue. As we have made voting easier, we have made fraud easier to commit and harder to detect. Expanding the time when voting is allowed also extends the time for fraud to occur. It is far easier to commit significant fraud over two to six weeks than trying to do the same amount in a single day. Pushing out ballots, bloated voter rolls, ballot harvesting, and unmonitored collection sites compound the problem.

With these trends, it is not hard to imagine that a few determined individuals could mail in 20 percent of the total votes in a district, ensuring the election goes their way. Such a scenario is not speculation or part of the distant past; instead, it is what happened in Greene County, Alabama, at least into the mid-1990s.[44]

Normally, absentee votes would run between 3 percent to 4 percent, yet in Greene County, they could be as high as 50 percent. Leewanna Parker, the editor of the Greene County Independent, said, "Races are being stolen here, there's no two ways about it."[45]

Initially, absentee ballots allowed people to vote when they were out of town on election day or could not physically make it to the polls. Recently, some have pushed them as a way to increase voter turnout. Since an absentee ballot does not require someone to go to a polling place, the potential for fraud is enormous.

---

44   Rich Lowry, "Early and Often: Vote Fraud in America", *National Review*, *June 17, 1996, 38.*
http://findarticles.com/p/articles/mi_m1282/is_n11_v48/ai_18399432 (accessed April 3, 2009).
45   Rich Lowry, "Early and Often: Vote Fraud in America", *National Review*, *June 17, 1996, 38.*
http://findarticles.com/p/articles/mi_m1282/is_n11_v48/ai_18399432 (accessed April 3, 2009).

It also threatens the secrecy of the vote and opens up the possibility for influence or even intimidation. No one knows how you vote when you go into the voting booth. When you fill out an absentee ballot, the chance for secrecy is reduced and, in some cases, even eliminated when ballots are filled in the presence or supervision of others.

More importantly, it makes detection and prosecutions difficult, for the ballots are anonymous once submitted. Correction is also virtually impossible. Recounting a mixture of legitimate and illegitimate ballots always gives the same result, as it is impossible to tell which is which. Even when you can demonstrate that ballots are illegitimate, you can't say who those votes were for.

An excellent example occurred in the race between Jane Harman and Susan Brooks for Congress in California's 36th district in 1994. Harman won a narrow victory of 812 votes, the margin of victory coming from absentee ballots. An analysis of the absentee votes showed that in the precincts that strongly supported Harman, at least 1,337 of the absentee ballots were clearly fraudulent. Investigators determined this by checking out the addresses on file with the registrar of voters and discovering that these voters came from abandoned homes, empty apartments, and even vacant lots.

You can say that these are illegitimate ballots, and whoever submitted them voted illegally. The district they came from strongly supported Harman. Still, since you cannot tie an individual voter to a particular ballot, it is impossible to show that these 1,337 fraudulent votes changed the outcome of the 812 vote victory. You cannot prove these illegitimate votes swung the election to Harmon.

Then there is the issue of time. If someone tried to challenge an election like this, such a challenge could easily take up most, if not all, of the entire two-year congressional term. Even if the challenger won, they still might not be able to take office as the term would be over before the legal process concluded. And how could a losing candidate afford to pay for such a challenge?

Nor is this an isolated incident. Similar examples occur around the country in almost every election. Yet, even with all these and many other instances of apparent irregularities in voting and a long history of voter fraud in this country, rather than tightening up the process, the trend has been to make registration and absentee voting, and thus, fraud, even easier and harder to detect.

In 1993, Congress passed the Motor Voter Bill. As columnist Rich Lowry pointed out, this bill "imposes the fraud-friendly rules pioneered in California on the rest of the country."[46] Not only does it mandate that states must provide registration at the DMV, but it also mandates absentee registration, forcing states to register voters by mail. It also limits the ability of the government to purge voters from their roles.

As an example of the problem this bill causes, Lowry cites the example of Mario Aburto Martinez, the Mexican citizen who assassinated Mexican presidential candidate Luis Donaldo Colossio in 1994. Although a Mexican citizen, Martinez had registered to vote in California not just once but twice. Even though he was not a U.S. Citizen, under the provisions of the Motor Voter Bill, officials could not remove Martinez from the rolls until 1996.

In short, the rules for registration have become so loose that a growing concern is that even if you are sure the person casting a ballot is a registered voter, it still does not mean they are legally eligible to vote. Not only are illegal aliens increasingly free to move about and operate in our society, but some are also taking the opportunity to vote.

Ineligible voters are especially concerning when advocacy groups deliberately target non-citizens in attempts to get them to vote. Other advocacy groups oppose any restrictions that would help identify illegal voters as unfair. For example, The Mexican-American Legal Defense and Education Fund (MALDEF)

---

46 Rich Lowry, "Early and Often: Vote Fraud in America", *National Review, June 17, 1996,* 43
http://findarticles.com/p/articles/mi_m1282/is_n11_v48/ai_18399432 (accessed April 3, 2009).

sees asking for identification when registering or voting as a form of discrimination to be opposed.[47]

Again, the concerns here are not just theoretical. In the congressional election in 1996, also in California, Loretta Sanchez won a narrow victory of 984 votes over Robert Dornan. While there were several charges of irregularities, the main one centered around the votes cast by non-citizens who were not legally eligible to vote in congressional elections.

Investigators identified several thousand non-citizen voters, and a later review by the Secretary of State showed that 2,474 non-citizens had actually voted in the election.[48] Yet, the election was allowed to stand. Given the increase in illegal immigration and the further weakening of registration and voting laws, it is likely that this problem has only grown since 1996.

The introduction of computer-based voting machines pushed so heavily following the 2000 presidential election in Florida, raises a whole new series of questions regarding fraud. Sure, they can very accurately count the votes cast, but what about when there are problems? Some of these systems are entirely paperless, with little or no means to check or verify the accuracy of a vote if there is a question. Then there is the whole issue of hackers.

Everyone can understand that if a citizen with a right to vote is prohibited from voting, that is a problem. Yet, every fraudulent vote cast has precisely the same effect on the outcome as preventing a legitimate voter from casting their vote. Whether not counted or canceled out, their vote is nullified.

---

47   Rich Lowry, "Early and Often: Vote Fraud in America", *National Review, June 17, 1996*, 43
http://findarticles.com/p/articles/mi_m1282/is_n11_v48/ai_18399432 (accessed April 3, 2009).
48   "California report cuts number of illegal voters," *Congressional Quarterly Weekly Report, 12/13/97, Vol. 55 Issue 49*, p3074, 1/4p.

What Can Be Done

As the cornerstone of democracy, the right to vote is paramount. It is not enough to make voting easier. To be effective, people must have real choices, their votes must be counted, and they cannot be canceled out by fraud. A breakdown in any of these is a breakdown of the system.

Probably the hardest thing to overcome is the general apathy about the problem. For too many citizens, voting is a bother. Probably the most challenging area to address is redistricting.

In the first edition of this book, I thought the best solution was to take redistricting out of the hands of the politicians and place it into the hands of independent commissions. These would then have a clear set of public guidelines for drawing district lines.

Since then, a few states tried such commissions. The result is that rather than have the gerrymandering done by the party that won a majority in the last election, the party that gained control of the commission did the gerrymandering. So, you still had the gerrymandering, but done by a commission unaccountable to the people. That was hardly an improvement.

The core problem with redistricting is that the people in the best position to draw the lines, the elected representatives who know their districts, are also the people with the strongest vested interest in distorting the outcome.

Perhaps some AI solutions will become available in the future, but problems also exist here. Such a solution might remove short-term partisan interests, but who determines the parameters upon which an AI solution draws lines? One might think a balanced commission from both parties might be best. Still, such a commission could easily draw a line benefiting the two parties but not the people. The best option currently is to let states continue experimenting with various approaches to this problem.

When it comes to campaign finance laws, it is time to realize that they have been stark failures. Rather than increase democracy, they have reduced it. Again, this should not be surprising given the problems faced by any such planning-and-control-based solution. Nor is the answer in a better plan or more control. We should abandon this whole approach in favor of freedom and competition. Let people donate as much as they want to whomever they want as long as there are public records disclosed reasonably quickly.[49]

Finally, with voting, the laws should consider the ease of voting and the safeguards needed to ensure only those legally eligible to vote do so. Unfortunately, this issue has become far more partisan since the first edition of this book.

An important consideration is that any changes must occur before an election. Our system has no actual mechanism for contesting elections after the fact. The only thing a candidate can do is go to court. Yet, the courts are ill-equipped for such time-sensitive matters. I heard one lawyer in a post-election case argue that he would typically spend two years in discovery and preparation for a fraud trial in his practice. Yet, he only had a few weeks.

When it comes to election fraud issues, there simply is no way to allow for the discovery needed to build a case within the time between the election and when the official takes office. Usually, the courts seek some way to dismiss these disputes rather than rule on them. When they do rule, they are charged with partisanship by the candidate who lost.

Politicians in the past realized this. As mentioned above, some historians now believe that except for fraud in Texas and Chicago, Nixon would have won the 1960 presidential election. Many then thought this and tried to prove he lost because of fraud. They also pressed Nixon to contest the election. Nixon, however, decided it would be better for the country not to challenge it. As the historian Paul Johnson noted,

---

49   Often the time frame of 24 hours is suggested; however, an important consideration is the use of volunteers and weekends. If a person gives a volunteer a check for the candidate on a Saturday night, and the volunteer turns it in the first thing Monday morning, should that be a violation of the law since it was not reported within 24 hours from the time the volunteer took the check? Under current reporting laws it can be.

There had never been a recount on a presidential election and the machinery for one did not exist. A study of procedures in six states where fraud was likely showed that every state had different rules for recounts, which could take up to eighteen months. A legal challenge therefore would have been a 'constitutional nightmare' and would have worked heavily against the national interest. Nixon not only accepted the force of this argument but he actually pleaded successfully with the New York Herald Tribune to discontinue a series of twelve articles giving evidence of fraud, when only four had been printed.[50]

It is becoming far more common for losers in both parties to claim fraud and challenge results. President Trump is the most notable example, but hardly the first. Before his victory, Biden's supporters routinely made preemptive claims of fraud. In 2016, Clinton and her supporters thought Trump stole that election with the help of the Russians. They were so convinced it eventually resulted in a three-year investigation by a special council that ultimately found no evidence of Russian collusion. While Romney and McCain accepted their defeats to President Obama, some of Kerry's supporters claimed fraud had caused his loss to Bush in 2004. Then, of course, Gore and many of his supporters thought he had won the election in 2000.

Here, Nixon seems to have had it correct. The winner is the person who wins the vote count. Thus, Bush won in 2000 and 2004, Obama in 2008 and 2010, Trump in 2016, and Biden in 2020. Suppose you think there were problems with any of these elections. In that case, the solution is not a long, drawn-out legal battle that will only divide the country but to work to fix the voting laws to improve voting access while maintaining vote integrity. To be successful, these efforts must be bi-partisan.

---

50   Paul Johnson, *A History of the American People. HarperCollins, 1997, pg 854-5*

The Carter-Baker Commission

Following several close and disputed elections, particularly the presidential elections in 2000 and 2004, there was a bipartisan attempt to develop fair election guidelines. In 2005, former President Jimmy Carter and former Secretary of State James A. Baker, III, agreed to co-chair a bipartisan commission examining how we could reform election laws.

The Commission on Federal Election Reform[51] suggested 87 specific recommendations centered around five pillars.

- A universal voter registration system managed by states rather than localities and connected with other states. Such a system would allow them to maintain accurate and updated lists. This system would enable people to register once, transferring their registration if they move. The commission believed this would "if implemented successfully, eliminate the vast majority of complaints currently leveled against the election system."[52]
- Use a "REAL ID card" or equivalent to ensure the person voting is the registered voter.
- Measures to increase voting participation by making registering and voting easier.
- Automated voting machines with paper backup to encourage voters "that their vote will be counted accurately." [53]

---

51   Building Confidence in U.S. Elections, Report of the Commission on Federal Elections Reform, September 2005, https://web.archive.org/web/20070609115256/http://www.american.edu/ia/cfer/report/full_report.pdf (Accessed August, 10, 2023)

52   Building Confidence in U.S. Elections, Report of the Commission on Federal Elections Reform, September 2005, https://web.archive.org/web/20070609115256/http://www.american.edu/ia/cfer/report/full_report.pdf (Accessed August, 10, 2023) iv

53   Building Confidence in U.S. Elections, Report of the Commission on Federal Elections Reform, September 2005, https://web.archive.org/web/20070609115256/http://www.american.edu/ia/cfer/report/full_report.pdf (Accessed August, 10, 2023) iv

- Strengthening and restructuring the election system, making it more nonpartisan and independent. "We cannot build confidence in elections if secretaries of state responsible for certifying elections are simultaneously chairing political campaigns."[54]

That reform is possible is demonstrated in the aftermath of the 2000 presidential election in Florida. Following that embarrassing election, lawmakers sought to reform their system. The reforms seem to work and work well. During the contentious 2020 election, while many states were struggling to count votes day after day, WPTV political analyst Brian Crowley said,

> When you look at what's going on in some of the other states right now, where there is uncertainty, at least Floridians can put their heads on their pillow and know Florida got it right this time.[55]

While some will question some of the Commission on Federal Election Reform's 87 suggestions, they are at least a bipartisan attempt to achieve both the objectives of increasing participation and strengthening integrity. The latter was made easier with a Supreme Court ruling in 2008 that said states could require voters to produce identification.[56] In addition, safeguards should be placed on absentee balloting, or it should be restricted to those who need it to reduce the potential risk of errors and fraud.

As for voting machines, again, the technical solutions are not that difficult. Automated voting machines should, as some do, print a paper ballot that the voter can check for accuracy before

---

54   Building Confidence in U.S. Elections, Report of the Commission on Federal Elections Reform, September 2005, https://web.archive.org/web/20070609115256/http://www.american.edu/ia/cfer/report/full_report.pdf (Accessed August, 10, 2023) iv

55   Matt Sczesny, *Florida hailed as model after successful election while other states continue to count ballots, WPTV, November 6, 2020*, https://www.wptv.com/news/election-2020/florida-hailed-as-model-after-successful-election-while-other-states-continue-to-count-ballots (Accessed August, 10, 2023)

56   Crawford v. Marion County Election Bd., 553 U.S. 181 (2008) https://supreme.justia.com/cases/federal/us/553/181/

placing it in a ballot box. The voting machine could transmit their tallies electronically, allowing rapid results.

Rapid results would, in and of itself, help ensure the system's integrity. One of the classic tactics of political machines was to delay the results from some precincts. After all the others had reported, they would know how far they were behind and, thus, how many votes they would need to win. The longer it takes to report a result, the more suspicion there will be that fraud is occurring.

The paper ballots would serve as a check on the accuracy or used in case of a malfunction. After each election, officials and poll watchers could randomly select several precincts and physically count the paper ballots to check the machine counts' accuracy.

There is a further reason to do this: voter confidence. Democracy cannot survive when a significant percentage of voters distrust the election process. Why vote if the other side is just going to steal the election? Why not cheat if you think the other side is cheating?

Many people in both parties have thought various elections were stolen in recent years. For presidential elections, losing candidates and their supporters raised significant charges of irregularities in 2000, 2004, 2016, and 2020. These charges came from both parties when their candidate lost.

An essential part of the election process is the post-election analysis of why you lost. Why didn't people vote for you? This analysis can lead to valuable insights and corrections that keep the candidates and parties in line with the public. It does not happen when fraud is suspected. Blaming fraud is much easier than looking at your side's failings and weaknesses. The needed correction does not occur.

Thus, it is essential that people trust the outcome of elections. When they lose, they need to look at why voters rejected them. Yet, stolen elections and problems with voting are not the only reason this critical self-reflection does not happen. Before the election, there must be a debate, which is the subject of the next chapter.

THE DISTORTION OF LANGUAGE

The great enemy of clear language is insincerity. When there is a gap between one's real and one's declared aims, one turns as if it were instinctively to long words and exhausted idioms, like a cuttlefish squirting out ink.

George Orwell

A good catchword can obscure analysis for fifty years.
Wendell L. Willkie

By today's standards, it was almost unimaginable. A critical public issue being debated intelligently and at length in the leading newspapers of the day. Starting on Friday, Oct 5, 1787, the first in a series of articles written by Samuel Bryan, under the pseudonym of Centinel, appeared in the *Philadelphia Independent Gazetteer* and the *Philadelphia Freeman's Journal.*

Bryan argued that the people should reject the new constitution approved by the Constitutional Convention the previous week and submitted to the states. Over the next three weeks, at least three authors writing under pseudonyms, Federal Farmer,[1]

---

1   Thought to be either Richard Henry Lee, Melanchthon Smith, or simply unknown. Scholars once generally believed Lee was the author, but recently they have questioned his authorship. Some scholars support the view that it was Smith based on computer analysis of their writing compared with Federal Farmer.

Robert Yates, writing as Brutus, and someone who wrote under the pseudonym of John DeWitt, a 17ᵗʰ-century Dutch patriot, joined Bryan in calling for rejection.

The response started three weeks later, on October 27. Written by James Madison using the pseudonym of Publius, a famous Roman lawgiver, it appeared in *The Independent Journal,* a newspaper in New York City. John Jay and Alexander Hamilton joined Madison, arguing for adopting the new constitution with all three writing under the pseudonym of Publius.

Soon, these articles were picked up by other papers in Philadelphia, New York, and throughout the country. The debate continued and ultimately consisted of 85 articles on each side. The articles of the supporters of the Constitution are known as The Federalist Papers, with those opposed becoming The Anti-Federalist Papers.

What distinguished the debate was the serious way both the Federalists and Anti-Federalists conducted the discussion. Unlike so many sound bites and 30-second commercials that currently pass for political debate, both sides wrote thoughtful and in-depth analyses of the various issues for and against the proposed Constitution. In his Introduction to The Federalist Papers, Clinton Rossiter called them

> the most important work in political science that has ever been written, or is likely to be written, in the United States. It is indeed the one product of the American mind that is rightly counted among the classics of political history.[2]

While the Anti-Federalists lost the debate and, as a result, did not receive the same amount of attention as *The Federalist Papers,* it was not a complete defeat. As Ralph Ketcham, a professor of History and Political Science at Syracuse University, pointed out,

> anti-federalist ideas have ... surfaced again and again in various guises among later generations of Americans. Those ideas, as well as the enticing prospects held out by Publius, are a vital

---

2   Clinton Rossiter, Introduction, *The Federalist Papers,* (New York: New American Library, 1961) vii.

element in the American political tradition and are properly viewed as part of the philosophy of the Constitution.[3]

This is not to say that all the debate on the Constitution was like this. The discussion on the Constitution also had its share of "promises, threats, bargains, and face-to-face debates"[4] that are much more typical of politics. In the short run, these latter methods, combined with some crafty maneuvering, led to the final passage of the Constitution. But neither were the writings of Publius, Centinel, and other Anti-Federalists inconsequential.

Published in the newspapers of the day, many read these essays. As such, they became somewhat of the 'talking points' of the day and became the basis for some of the more popular forms of political discourse. In this way, they influenced the overall debate and the country's subsequent history.

The Debate over Slavery

The debate over the Constitution was not the only time people debated a critical issue in such a serious fashion. Seventy-one years later, another major problem faced the country: slavery. The cancer of slavery had plagued the nation since its founding.

The compromise between the slave and free states permitted the adoption of the Constitution at the cost of allowing slavery to exist in the South. Essentially codifying the status quo, the Northern states banned slavery while the Southern states permitted it.

While many at the Constitutional Convention expected slavery would die out, that did not happen. Two movements emerged. The abolitionist movement was still new at the time of the convention and would only grow in the coming decades. Attitudes in the South changed as well. Rather than seeing slavery as a moral problem, many began to argue it was a moral good. As a result,

---

3   Ralph Ketcham, *The Anti-Federalist Papers and the Constitutional Convention Debates,* (New York: Signet Classics, 1986), 20

4   Clinton Rossiter, Introduction, *The Federalist Papers,* (New York: New American Library, 1961) xi.

any hope slavery would die out vanished. Slavery kept coming up as a festering wound each time a new state or territory came into the union, lest the North or the South gain a majority.

The issue began to come to a head in 1857 with two diametrically opposed events. One was the Supreme Court's now-infamous pro-slavery Dred Scott decision. As discussed in Chapter Five, the Dred Scott decision represented a severe overreaching of the Court where the Justices led by Chief Justice Taney, writing for the majority, effectively ignored what the Constitution said and reinterpreted it to say what they wanted it to say.

The other significant event in 1857 was the publication of Harriet Beecher Stowe's anti-slavery novel Uncle Tom's Cabin, which was a huge success, giving the abolition movement a considerable boost. The novel sold over 300,000 copies in its first year. Even by today's standards, the sale of 300,000 books would make any author very happy. In 1857, such a huge number was truly phenomenal.[5]

The Lincoln – Douglas Debate

As might be expected, the Dred Scott decision was highly controversial, particularly in Illinois, where in 1858, the new Republican Party, formed around the opposition to slavery just four years earlier, nominated Abraham Lincoln to challenge Stephen Douglas for the U.S. Senate seat. In the campaign, Lincoln and Douglas met for seven public debates, one for each of the seven congressional districts in Illinois, during the late summer and early fall of that year.

These debates were considerably different from the presidential debates we currently see. The format consisted of one speaker speaking for about an hour.[6] Then, the other candidate would

---

5   John William Ward, Afterward *Uncle Tom's Cabin,* (New York: Signet Classics, 1966), 479

6   They would alternate who would go first, with Douglas going first in the first debate, and Lincoln going first in the second.

receive an hour and a half to present their case and make their rebuttal. After that, the first candidate would have half an hour for rebuttal. The debate would last three hours, though the later debates were shorter.[7]

Today, the idea of people going to hear two senate candidates speak on an important issue for three hours seems unthinkable. Yet, thousands attended the debates. Between 15,000 and 20,000 people reportedly attended the second debate in Freeport, even though the town had only a population of 5,000 at the time. They were also transcribed by reporters and, like the Federalist Papers, published in papers of the time, reaching far more than could attend.[8]

Quantity versus Quality?

It was a different time. It was a time of great speakers. People would hear great speakers like we might go to a movie today. And at times, the speeches were just as long. For example, Edward Everett, who spoke at the dedication of Gettysburg just before Lincoln, spoke for two hours.

Today, we do not produce great speakers who can hold an audience's attention for extended periods. Nor if a renowned speaker like Everett somehow entered a time machine and was transported to our time, would he be able to hold an audience's attention. Instead, as John McWhorter, a professor of linguistics at the University of California at Berkeley, summarized it, today we would see him as "too windy, too puffed up." His language would not "even look sincere – language like this smells of snake oil to us."[9]

---

7   An excellent way to experience the debates is through an audio rendition with David Strathairn playing the part of Lincoln, and Richard Dreyfuss taking the role of Douglas. The Lincoln-Douglas Debates, Blackstone Audio, 2009, https://www.audible.com/pd/The-Lincoln-Douglas-Debates-Audiobook/B002V0Q6UK

8   Illinois Historical digitization project, http://www.comportone.com/cpo/comty/il-city/freeport/debate.htm (accessed April 3, 2009).

9   John McWhorter, *Doing Our Own Thing: The Degradation of Language*

Today, we want it short, sweet, and to the point, often just bullet points. But is this an improvement? Does our language matter much as long as we get our point across? The simple answer is yes, it does.

It matters because the point you get across will be determined mainly by your language. It is just a simple fact that someone who listens to an issue intelligently discussed for three hours, as Lincoln and Douglas discussed slavery, will have a much better understanding of the issues and the ramifications of particular solutions than someone whose 'serious analysis' consists of trying to decide if they agree or disagree with a thirty-second sound bite.

Even if we listen to a long 'speech' today, we are still not likely to get the same information as in earlier generations. As McWhorter points out,

> Today, however, it is simply not part of American culture for a person to make a speech putting forth an argument with almost lawyerly care and precision – i.e., rendering an oral version of a use of language only possible when writing exists. Our speeches are mostly symbolic exercises packaging a few large points in short, punchy sentences. State of the Union addresses are today composed in sequences of sentence packets designed to elicit applause like the chest-beating speeches that pro-wrestlers make.[10]

McWhorter is not viewing the past as some golden age of discourse, with a fully informed population listening to intelligent, rational debate. On the contrary, public discourse in the past also had its "sloganeering, shorthand, and sloppiness," as you can find intelligent discussion today. While this is more a difference of degree, "there remains a stark contrast in degree with the past." With today's speeches, "the goal is the gut rather than the head."[11]

---

and Music (New York: Gotham Books, 2003), pg xi.

10   John McWhorter, *Doing Our Own Thing: The Degradation of Language and Music* (New York: Gotham Books, 2003), 71

11   John McWhorter, *Doing Our Own Thing: The Degradation of Language and Music* (New York: Gotham Books, 2003), 70

This difference is essential, for if reason does not govern our decision, emotions will. This distinction is the heart of the fundamental problems with democracy. As Madison warned, "The *passions,* therefore, not the *reason,* of the public would sit in judgment."[12] One of the significant problems with the public's passions is that they are highly susceptible to propaganda.

Propaganda?

Propaganda is a tool of manipulation. Rather than arguing based on cogent and sound reasoning, it attempts to get the point across through artifices, allusions, fallacies, and falsehoods. Adolf Hitler, a master of propaganda, said,

> The art of propaganda lies in understanding the emotional ideas of the great masses and finding, through a psychologically correct form, the way to the attention and thence to the heart of the broad masses. [13]

He went on to say,

> In consequence, all effective propaganda must be limited to a very few points and must harp on these in slogans until the last member of the public understands what you want him to understand by your slogan.[14]

When Michael Moore's film *Fahrenheit 911* came out, there was some dispute about whether the film qualified as propaganda. While it was, the question somewhat missed the more significant point. The question is not so much whether Moore's film qualified as propaganda, but rather what in modern political debate does not! We have become so used to the 30-second television ad and the bumper sticker approach to political debate that propaganda is the norm. The title of Anthony Pratkanis and Elliot Aronson's

---

12   Madison, Federalist No. 49 https://founders.archives.gov/documents/Madison/01-10-02-0270 (accessed August 16, 2023)
13   Adolph Hitler, *Mein Kampf (1924),* Volume One Chapter Six.
14   Adolph Hitler, *Mein Kampf (1924),* Volume One Chapter Six.

book, *The Age of Propaganda,*[15] sums up the current situation. Not only is propaganda commonplace, but often, the arguments drift into passionate pleas aimed directly at people's emotions and prejudice, thereby entering into the realm of demagoguery.

This problem is serious, for without an energetic debate and reasoned consideration of the pros and cons along with the ramifications of any proposed solution, what good is the people's vote? A decision without considering the pros, cons, and ramifications is no better than simply flipping a coin. It may be worse. At least when flipping a coin, you have a fifty percent chance of being correct. Careless reasoning generally leads to bad decisions.

Television

While many factors contribute to this problem, TV and now streaming play a considerable role, a role visible in the first televised debate. On September 26, 1960, John F. Kennedy and Richard Nixon faced off in the first of a series of Presidential debates.

Nixon had been ill. He also had knee trouble, and Kennedy's staff had asked that the two candidates stand throughout the debate.[16] In addition, Kennedy, having come from campaigning in California and who was nicely tanned, spoke with Nixon just before the debate, mentioning he was going to forgo makeup. Nixon decided to skip it as well.[17]

As a result of his recent illness, knee, and lack of makeup, Nixon looked terrible. Afterward, those who saw the debate believed that Kennedy had clearly won. Interestingly, as the first televised debate, many people still heard it on the radio rather than

---

15   Anthony Pratkanis and Elliot Aronson, *The Age of Propaganda,* (New York: Henry Holt, 2001).

16   Paul Johnson, *A History of the American People,* (HarperCollins, 1997), 853.

17   Eagleton Digital Archive of American Politics, 1960: Kennedy-Nixon Debates
http://www.eagleton.rutgers.edu/e-gov/e-politicalarchive-JFK-Nixon.htm (accessed April 3, 2009).

watching it on TV. Since they only listened, they could not see the contrasts in appearance between the candidates. All they could do was evaluate what they said. Those who heard the debate believed that Nixon won.[18]

The focus on the visual is a problem, but television's effect on language is more subtle. One factor is that TV and movies are primarily emotional mediums. While a picture need not evoke an emotional response, it is far easier to do so, and emotions evoked are likely stronger than those found in the printed word.

While there are some exceptions, one reason is that words are primarily an intellectual process in ways images need not be. Before words can evoke emotions, one must first understand the words and their meaning. An exception is swear words whose primary social purpose is to shock, a purpose undermined by over-use. Still, most languages take time to process. The pro-abolition-ist novel *Uncle Tom's Cabin* evokes strong emotions against slavery. Still, one must first take the time to read it and understand the story.

Images are far more immediate. With an image, one can have an emotional reaction almost instantly. Many have pointed to the fact that a multitude of stories and articles can have little impact. Yet, a single picture can start a movement. Since the invention of the camera, numerous examples of iconic photographs have moved people in ways the printed works never could. In this sense, a picture is worth a thousand words.

The power of images is something advertisers have long known, as has Hollywood. One of the changes in more recent films versus those made decades ago is the shortening of the time between edits. A scene with two characters talking that in earlier movies would have been a long single shot, in modern films has a multitude of shots, constantly switching between camera angles and perspectives every few seconds. When there is a long shot, it

---

18   Paul Johnson, *A History of the American People*, (Harper-Collins, 1997), 853.

is because the camera moves, such as when it rotates around the actors.

You can see an example of this by comparing the same story in two films made decades apart. This is what you have with the play Parfumerie by the Hungarian playwright Miklós Lász-ló, as the story has been the basis of several Hollywood movies. In 1940, it became Ernst Lubitsch's *The Shop Around the Corner*, starring Margaret Sullavan and James Stwart. Nora Ephron used it in 1998, making *You've Got Mail* starring Meg Ryan and Tom Hanks.

A romantic comedy, the story centers on a couple who dislike each other in person, but unknowingly are in a pen pal relationship that is getting very serious. While there are some other significant differences, what concerns us here are the more technical aspects of how the movie was shot.

A pivotal scene in each movie is when the pen pals agree to meet, the Café scene. The content is basically the same in both movies, with both versions running a little under 10 minutes. Lubitsch used nineteen shots for his scene, an average of 26.2 seconds per shot. Ephron made essentially the same scene using 133 shots, an average of only 4.4 seconds per shot. Lubitsch's shots were nearly six times longer.[19] In Ephron's version, there is no time to think about what you are seeing, only time to react, and the director is in control.

Perhaps even more critical are the time constraints of television. It is costly, and every second counts. Usually, there is not enough time to develop a coherent argument, even if one wants to.[20] The result is that carefully worded opinions based on precision and accuracy get dropped in favor of broad generalities and

---

19   Nerdwriter1, *Two Ways To Film The Same Scene*, December 24, 2023 YouTube, https://www.youtube.com/watch?v=kmvvA7wudKo
20   Here the increasing popularity of podcasts may be improving things. Podcasts are relatively easier and cheaper to produce and do not have fixed time constraints. Thus, they allow for the development and examination of arguments.

slogans. The slogans that work in one debate are then recycled again and again. Before long, people begin considering these often repeated slogans as general principles of truth.

One common slogan both sides used is "the ends don't justify the means." As with many of these, this claim has some truth. It is possible to reach this conclusion when looking at specific ends and means. Those particular ends do not justify those particular means.

If this were the extent of use, there would not be a problem. However, some increasingly use the slogan as a general rule and an argument against all such justifications. Some state it as the ends can never justify the means. Any attempt to justify an action based on the results is then labeled immoral.

While the ends cannot always justify the means, sometimes they do. To see this, consider the 'means' of cutting a person open with a knife: this would be utterly unjustified if the 'ends' were to get some money. However, it would be completely justified if the 'ends' were to remove a tumor.

The Rich Must Pay

The further problem is that these slogans are often so vague and open to interpretation that they mean very little, if anything. For example, a commonly heard slogan is 'the rich must pay their fair share of taxes.' Okay. Few would disagree with such a vague generality.

Yet, laws enacted and enforced by the government are not vague generalities. They are specific policies. As such, when a politician says that when elected, they will ensure that the rich will pay their fair share, what does this actually mean? What is it that they are pledging to do? The actual meaning of this statement turns on the definition of two words: 'rich' and 'fair.'

So, what does 'rich' mean? Is it a measure of how much money someone has? Is it a measure of how much money someone makes each year? As we saw in Chapter Two, these are different concepts. In addition to these problems, there is the question of the actual dollar amount at which a person is 'rich.' $10 million? $1 million? $500,000? $200,000? $100,000? $50,000? $30,000? Is it anyone making more than I do? Add to this where someone lives.

Given the differences in the cost of living between various sections of the country, where one lives has a significant impact. For example, someone making $45,000 per year might see someone who makes $100,000 per year as 'rich,' yet differences in the cost of living between where they live can affect this significantly.

Many websites have 'Cost of Living' calculators, allowing you to determine the equivalent salary for different areas. While $100,000 may seem 'rich' to someone making $45,000, if the person making $100,000 happens to live in Manhattan, while the person making $45,000 lives in Tulsa, Oklahoma, at the time of the first edition, when adjusted for the difference in cost of living between the two locations, $100,000 in Manhattan is equivalent to only $40,522 in Tulsa.[21] So, the person making $45,000 would have relatively more disposable income.

Politicians' use of language is often so loose that it only worsens things. In an attempt to raise additional funds, in 2004, the Governor of New Jersey pushed for a 'millionaire tax.' At first, one might think this was a tax on those making more than 1 million dollars. Yet, "under the legislation, the tax rate on income earned above $500,000 will rise nearly 41 percent, affecting about 35,000 residents."[22] In short, the governor's millionaire tax raised taxes on those earning less than a million dollars.

So far, we have only looked at the ambiguity in the term "rich." We have not even gotten to what is meant by fair. As we saw in Chapter Two, according to IRS figures, the top 5 percent of

---

21   *Bankrate.com, Cost of Living comparison calculator,* http://www.bank-rate.com/brm/movecalc.asp?a=0&d1=100000&d2=218.75557087294 &d3=88.6445562365025 (accessed April 3, 2009).

22   Joe Donohue, *Governor puts signature on the 'millionaire's tax',* The Star Ledger, June 29, 2004.

taxpayers make 35.3 percent of the income and pay 56.5 percent of the income tax. If this is not fair, which apparently it is not, if the politicians claim they will make it fair, then just how much would be fair? 60 percent? 70 percent? 80 percent? What would be fair?

When a politician says, "The rich should pay their fair share," they have really said nothing. They have said nothing because there is no way to evaluate their proposal until 'rich' and 'fair' are defined. All they have said is that some undefined group should pay some undefined amount.

If you object because you think the rich do not pay their fair share, you have missed the point. The point here is not what the rich should pay but the ambiguity of the discussion. Even if you can give a specific definition of these terms, they remain ambiguous in the public debate. Who's to say the majority would accept your definitions? How can we have a majority agreement on rich and fair if they are never defined?

Yet, one can find such argument-by-ambiguity throughout the political debate. Politicians frequently ask people to vote for what are effectively little more than political blank checks, where the specific details will be filled in later, often in committee rooms, out of sight of most voters who do not pay much attention to the particular facts of the legislation.

Building Blocks

The fundamental building blocks of language are words. When the meaning of words is distorted, intelligent discussion becomes extremely difficult, if not impossible. Confucius taught that,

> If names be not correct, language is not in accordance with the truth of things. If language be not in accordance with the truth of things, affairs cannot be carried on to success.[23]

---

23 Confucius, *The Analects, XIII.3 http://www.wsu.edu:8080/~dee/CHPHIL/ANALECTS.HTM* (accessed April 3, 2009).

A significant result of misusing words is that it leads to either the uncritical acceptance or rejection of policies and ideas. Label a policy patriotic, and you are supposed to accept it. Label a policy partisan, and you will tend to reject it. This is fine if the words are accurately used, but what about when they are not?

Part of the problem is that while some languages use different words for related concepts, English often uses a single word with modifiers. In English, we have the word love and use modifiers to indicate the various types, such as puppy love, romantic love, and brotherly love. This system works fine, except the modifiers are often dropped in the current trend to simplify and shorten speech. Thus, we will say we love ice cream, and we love our spouse. We know the word love is used differently because of the context.

This dependency on context becomes a problem in political speech as words can be misapplied or used with unique meanings to block debate. One example of this is the word partisan. Merriam-Webster defines partisan when used as an adjective,

> feeling, showing, or deriving from strong and sometimes blind adherence to a particular party, faction, cause, or person : exhibiting, characterized by, or resulting from partisanship.[24]

The Cambridge Dictionary defines it as

> strongly supporting a person, principle, or political party, often without considering or judging the matter very carefully:[25]

Note the qualifiers in each definition: "sometimes blind adherence" and "often without considering or judging the matter carefully." To see the problem, suppose a party supports a given policy. Two party members said they support it. Can we label both partisan? What if one supports the policy because the party supports it, while the other has done considerable research and supports it because of this research? Are they still equally partisan?

---

24   Merriam-Webster.com https://www.merriam-webster.com/dictionary/partisan (accessed November 30, 2023)
25   Dictionary.Cambridge.org https://dictionary.cambridge.org/dictionary/english/partisan (accessed November 30, 2023)

If not, does agreeing with a party position automatically make you partisan?

It gets problematic when someone gives specific reasons for supporting a given position. Yet, the reasons are ignored or rejected as partisan. When someone uses labels such as partisan in this fashion, they are blockers – strategies used to deflect and avoid opposing arguments rather than deal with them.[26] They are used to shut down discussions.

Avoiding evidence and difficult counterarguments may be an effective debating tactic, yet it is never rational. It is also counter-productive in building consensus, as dealing with counterarguments can help the various sides reach a consensus on which they can agree.

The other major problem is when people give common words unique or special meanings that are not clarified. Using a common term with a unique definition is perfectly fine as long as it is clear you are doing so. It is particularly problematic when both sides use the same word with different meanings.

We can see an excellent example of this in the debate over the Congressional Budget Office (CBO) report on the effects of the tax cuts discussed earlier in Chapter Two. In an article in The Washington Post entitled *Tax Burden Shifts to the Middle*,[27] Democrats claimed that the tax cuts shifted the tax burden from "the wealthy" to "the middle class." Republicans disagreed, arguing that the tax cuts for the poor and middle class were proportionally more significant than those for the rich, shifting the tax burden to the rich. So, who is correct?

While possibly a surprise, both the Republican and Democrat claims were correct, even though they seemed to contradict each other. The entire matter depends on precisely what you mean by

---

26   see Elgin Hushbeck, *Seeking Truth: How To Move From Partisan Bickering to Building Consensus, Energion Publications 2022, 245-6*
27   Jonathan Weisman, *Tax Burden Shifts to the Middle, Washington Post,* August 13, 2004, p A04 http://www.washingtonpost.com/wp-dyn/articles/A61178-2004Aug12.html (accessed April 3, 2009).

a range of words such as rich, poor, and most importantly, what taxes and tax burden mean. How you define these terms then determines which tables of statistics you look at in the CBO report and what results you get.

In accordance with Democrats' claims, the CBO report[28] showed that the "Share of Total Federal Tax Liabilities" shifted to the middle class when defined as those making between $51,200 and $195,300. The rich, those making above $195,300, paid 65.3 percent of total federal tax revenue in 2001. This percentage dropped to 64.1 percent in 2003. At the same time, the total federal tax burden for the middle class increased from 28.5 to 29.6 percent. So, the Democrats were correct.

Yet, if the Democrats were correct, how can the Republicans also be correct when saying the tax burden shifted in the other direction to the rich? The key is that the figures cited by the Democrats related to the "Total Federal Tax Liabilities." The CBO defined "Total Federal Tax Liabilities" as the combination of all federal taxes, not just the income tax. The significant tax cuts were to income taxes, so Republicans argued that is where we should look to see the effects, not other taxes, such as payroll taxes, that the law did not affect.

So, while the Democrats cited the tables in the CBO report that referred to the 'Total Federal Tax Liabilities', Republicans cited the figures for the 'Income Tax Liabilities.' In that table, those making above $195,300 paid 82.5 percent of the total federal income taxes in 2001, which increased to 83.0 percent in 2003.

In addition, had the tax cuts not become law, the CBO estimated that instead of 83.0 percent, the rich would have only paid 78.7 percent. On the other hand, those defined as middle class would have paid 21.5 percent of total individual income tax liabilities without the tax cuts, yet with the change, they only paid 20.0 percent. So, the Republicans were also correct.

28   CBO, *Effective Federal Tax Rates Under Current Law, 2001 to 2014, August 2004* http://www.cbo.gov/ftpdoc.cfm?index=5746&type=1 (accessed April 3, 2009).

Both were correct, but it is hard to make sense of their competing claims without a detailed analysis of the CBO report. Then there is the further confusion of 'tax liabilities' versus 'share of tax liabilities,' introducing even more complexities to the discussion.

Much of the problem here is one of comparing apples and oranges, and this is where language comes in. Essentially, the tax cuts were income tax cuts. As a result of the cuts, many lower-income earners went from paying taxes to receiving "taxes" through mechanisms such as the earned income tax credit. For example, those making from $34,200 to $51,500 saw their share of total income taxes drop from 0.3 percent of income taxes to -0.2 percent. They went from paying to receiving money.

As a result of the tax cuts, the lowest 40 percent of those filing tax returns in 2003 got more money back than they paid in. For the remaining 60 percent, while the dollar amount they paid was lower, their share of the overall income taxes increased since the tax cuts reduced the number of people paying taxes.

Adding in other federal taxes resulted in the figures cited by the Democrats. Still, these additional taxes are more "payments into the system" to fund programs such as Social Security and Medicare. They are more premiums than income taxes and, therefore, capped – after you have paid the maximum for the year, you do not need to pay more. This "capping of premiums" is what distinguishes Social Security as a retirement program rather than a welfare program.

Yet, this complexity will not fit on a bumper sticker, nor is someone likely to get enough time on a news show to give even a partial explanation. Without the details, how will people ever be able to make an intelligent decision as to which side is telling the truth? Thus, most see "their side" as correct and yet another example of how the "other side" lies.

Political Labels

Before moving on, let me say a few words defending labels. It is common today to hear people complain about political labels. Author and economist Mark Skousen is hardly alone when he argues that we should drop, or at least significantly reduce, the use of political labels for the following reasons,

> (1) Labels are often an inaccurate description of a person's or group's views. (2) Labels often become pejorative terms used in character assassination (3) Labels put people into political boxes and keep them there, preventing individuals from objectively considering alternative opinions and changing their minds.[29]

Skousen's argument has a lot of truth, particularly in the current climate. Labels are often misused. However, the solution is not to eliminate them. Nor could we if we wanted to if for no other reason than ultimately, all words are nothing more than labels. If you eliminate labels, you eliminate words and, thus, all communication.

In Skousen's defense, he and others raising similar complaints are not asking for such a total ban. They focus their criticism on a few political labels, particularly 'Liberal,' 'Conservative,' 'Left,' and 'Right.'

Even if we were only to drop these political labels, that would not solve the problem. The simple fact is that there is a political spectrum. There are specific approaches and ways of thinking about the government shared by people such as Barack Obama, Nancy Pelosi, and many other Democrats. These differ from those of Ronald Reagan, Kevin McCarthy, and most Republicans. There is a political Left and a political Right, with different approaches and views.[30]

---

29   Mark Skousen, "No More Political Labels, Please," *Mskousen.com,* http://www.mskousen.com/Books/Articles/labels.html (accessed April 3, 2009).

30   For a more in-depth discussion of the origin of the political spectrum and the different views of the Left and Right, see Elgin Hushbeck, *Seeking*

If we eliminate terms such as Liberal and Conservative, Left and Right, what will we use to replace them? If nothing, then in what way can we say that Obama and Pelosi share a common approach to government, an approach to government that is different from the one McCarthy and Reagan share? It cannot simply be party affiliation, as at times, there are Democrats who vote more like McCarthy and Reagan and Republicans who vote more like Obama and Pelosi.

In addition, if we ban labels, we will not know how to avoid certain ideologies if we cannot label them. Some ideologies may sound good in theory, but historically, they have been disasters and the source of great evil when put into practice. This problem is pretty much the current situation with the word Fascism.

As Jonah Goldberg pointed out in his book *Liberal Fascism*, "There is no word in the English language that gets thrown around more freely by people who don't know what it means than 'fascism.'"[31] For most people, fascism means Hitler and the holocaust, a danger from the Right. As a result, the label is used as a hyperbolic criticism of Republicans and others on the right side of the political spectrum.

Most people have a completely distorted view of fascism. While Hitler was a fascist, the Nazis were just one form of Fascism. Mussolini, the Italian dictator, is the political founder of Fascism. Yet, Mussolini had Jews in his government, and Italian Fascism showed no significant signs of antisemitism until it fell under the dominance of Hitler's government.

In reality, fascism is a Left-wing movement[32] created by Marxists to solve some problems with Marx's theory. It is another type

Truth: How To Move From Partisan Bickering to Building Consensus, Energion Publications 2022, 106-126 For a somewhat smaller analysis focused on the Constitution, see Elgin Hushbeck, *The United States Constitution: A History,* Energion Publications 2022

31 Jonah Goldberg's book *Liberal Fascism: The Secret History of the American Left, From Mussolini to the Politics of Change.* Forum Books, 200, 2

32 Elgin Hushbeck, *Seeking Truth: How To Move From Partisan Bickering to Building Consensus,* Energion Publications 2022, 106-126

of socialism, like Communism. There are two significant differences between Communism and Fascism. The first is that whereas Communism is a universal movement, with the slogan, 'workers of the world unite,' Fascism is more of a national movement, a national socialism. The term Nazi is a contraction for the German *Nationalsozialismus* or National Socialism. Hitler's party was the National Socialist German Workers Party.

The second key difference is that whereas Communism held that control of business required state ownership, Fascists allowed private ownership, though they still retained state control. Thus, Fascists often saw themselves as the 'middle way' between the free market approach of classical liberalism and the state ownership of communism. Still, their emphasis on state control over liberty put them much closer to communism. While their acceptance of private property might make them seem closer to capitalism, they rejected the concepts of individual freedom and free markets that are key to capitalism in favor of strict state control.

Now, this might be considered just an interesting historical discussion, except many of the same fundamental problems of government that led to these various political movements are still with us today. People can drift into fascist solutions without realizing where such policies have historically led.

Again, label something fascist, and people immediately think you are referring to Hitler and the Holocaust. Yet, some of the programs and policies put forth by people in both parties would have fit, and in some cases are even mirror images, of programs and policies of fascist governments like Italy under Mussolini, even down to the rationales used to justify them.

Because of the distortion of language, people cannot oppose these policies based on the type of government to which they lead, even though historically, we have seen this before. If we adopt No-Labels, how can you warn about the encroachments of fascism if the No Labels movement succeeds and you can't use the word?

The same is true if it is consistently misused. Suppose fascist is little more than a hyperbolic label used to attack political opponents. What will people do if real fascists appear? How can you re-fer to fascism and the dangers it leads to without saying "fascism" or pointing to the risks?[33] The real problem is not the use of labels but their misuse. What is needed is not a movement to No Labels but an insistence on their correct and accurate use.

Two additional factors compound the problems with the mis-use of labels. The first is the sound-bite-driven news coverage that limits serious consideration. In such an environment, dropping labels will not lead to more nuanced information but simply less information. The second is the general lack of critical thinking.

Uncritical Thinking

Examples of uncritical thinking are numerous, some of which we have already seen, such as in any number of slogans used in arguments as if they were general rules when they are nothing of the sort. In fact, as general rules, they don't even make sense. Another example would be the common claim that we should not judge others, often expressed in the question, 'Who are we/you to judge?'[34] Today, one of the worst things you can be is 'judgmental.'

But while a widespread view, does it make sense? In some cases, yes, but as a general rule, it doesn't. If for nothing else, to condemn someone as judgmental is a judgment.

Ultimately, it does not make sense to ban all judgments about people. After all, if someone lies or cheats us, can we not make any judgments about their actions? Should we interact with them precisely the same as someone who has always treated us fairly and

---

33   For examples, see Jonah Goldberg's book *Liberal Fascism: The Secret History of the American Left, From Mussolini to the Politics of Change.* Forum Books, 2009. Goldberg's detailed analysis gives numerous examples, though the book was attacked based on some of the very problems discussed in this chapter.

34   In fact, I have heard some claim that the most quoted verse in the Bible is no longer John 3:16, "For God so loved the world that he gave his one and only Son, that whoever believes in him shall not perish but have eternal life." (NIV), but is now Matthew 7:1 "Do not judge, or you too will be judged."

has been honest? The real issue is not whether we will judge, but whether we will judge correctly.

Formerly, 'to be judgmental' meant judging too harshly, or too much, or that one was overly critical. But these distinctions and nuances have dropped off in the bumper sticker approach to discussion. As a slogan, being non-judgmental has seeped uncritically into the culture with, at times, some bizarre results.

Following the murder of nine people at a Mall in Omaha in 2007, an NBC TV reporter interviewed a friend of the murderer,[35]

> Reporter: "What are you thinking about now, now that you know that [your friend] was involved in the shooting earlier today"
> Friend of Murderer: "I don't think anything less of him, because I know that [he] would never have done anything like this just for the fun of it, it was he wanted to go out in style and that is what he did, he went out in style."

No judgment for the lives taken. No judgment for the family and friends whose lives will never be the same because of the loss of a loved one. No judgment for the wounded or their pain and suffering. Instead, "I don't think anything less of him... he wanted to go out in style."

The word 'intolerance' is closely linked to the term 'judgmental.' Today, being labeled intolerant is terrible, like being judgmental. Yet, we are all intolerant of many things. Not only are we, but more importantly, we should be. Should we be tolerant of murderers or child molesters?

Again, the subtle distinctions are abandoned. Being tolerant is good; intolerance is terrible. As with judgmental, this slogan approach also suffers from the inherent conflict of being very intolerant of those labeled 'intolerant!'

In addition, another subtle change is going on with the word 'tolerate' itself. The concept of toleration meant allowing or per-

---

35   played by Dennis Prager on his show. Dec 6 2007 Third Hour
http://townhall.com/talkradio/show.aspx?radioshowid=3 (accessed April 3, 2009).

mitting something you disagreed or disapproved of. If you did not disagree or dislike, the whole question of toleration does not even enter into the picture. After all, no one has to 'tolerate' the things they like. Yet, increasingly, the label of 'intolerant' is being applied to those who disagree or dislike something, regardless of whether they are willing to tolerate it.

We see this superficial use of slogans throughout the political discourse. A politician who takes an unpopular stand one agrees with is "voting on principles." At the same time, the other side will attack them as "out of touch with the people" or "pandering to special interests." The groups that one likes represent "the voice of the people." Those on the other side are "special interests." Politicians who change to a position a person approves of have "grown." At the same time, those who switch to a view with which one disagrees have been "corrupted by the system."

The fact that people use these terms, phrases, and slogans is not, in and of itself, terrible. The problem is that these slogans have often become so cut off from reality that they have little meaning. For example, when someone says that a politician is "voting on principle" versus "out of touch with the people," it often means nothing other than "I agree with them" or "I disagree with them." They tell you more about the person speaking than the person they are talking about.

In the sound-bite culture of TV, such slogans are sadly inevitable. However, there are two ways to tell if there is a meaningful point behind the slogans or whether they are nothing more than empty rhetoric. The first is to listen to how they justify their view when challenged. If they merely repeat the slogan, sometimes with more force, or at least with a louder voice, or if they defend one slogan with another, you can safely conclude that it is little more than empty rhetoric.

The second and somewhat related test is to see if they give any justification to back up the slogans, particularly in the way of examples. I have made a lot of statements in this book that some might consider slogans. Still, I have also included many examples that show what I mean. It is perfectly acceptable to make a general point, even use a slogan, when using particular examples to support and give meaning to the claim.

Poll Tested, Politician Approved

A further source of confusion occurs when advocates discard commonly used terms in favor of new phrases that have been poll-tested to have the desired effect. These distortions of language play themselves out in a political debate in many ways. With the issues in Chapter Two, tax increases are renamed 'revenue enhancements', and spending becomes 'investing' to lessen the resistance.

The economist Thomas Sowell gives an example of this distortion of language with how politicians distort the word "ask" in defense of a tax increase with the statement, "We are just asking everyone to pay their fair share,"

> But of course governments do not ask, they *tell*. The Internal Revenue Service does not "ask" for contributions. It takes. It can confiscate bank accounts and other assets and it can put people behind bars for not paying. Yet, the word "ask" is used in all sorts of public policy contexts.[36]

Even worse is when advocates take commonly understood terms and give them new and special meanings. These new meanings make it extremely difficult to follow a debate intelligently.

We can see a classic example of this in a debate over Medicare in the mid-1990s. At the time, there was a problem with the rising cost of the program, and some congressmen proposed reforming the program to get the costs under control. Opponents viciously attacked the proposal.

Opponents claimed the plan cut Medicare spending by $270 billion, which "would have made the largest cuts in Medicare's history, increased out-of-pocket costs for seniors."[37] The news media

---

36　Thomas Sowell, *The Vision of the Anointed*, (Basic Books, 1996), 196-7.
37　Senator Byron Dorgan, "Forty Years of Republican Opposition to Medi-

picked up this language, which reported that the "plan would cut $270 billion in Medicare spending over seven years," that it would "slash the Medicare budget," and that it would result in "big cuts in Medicare."[38]

As a result of such language, it is little wonder that the public moved sharply against the plan. A New York Times Poll showed that 67 percent were against these significant "cuts."[39] A *Public Opinion Strategies* survey found similar results, showing that only 38 percent had a favorable view of the plan. Given the number of seniors who depend on Medicare, such results are unsurprising.

The *Public Opinion Strategies* survey also asked about a plan that would increase the yearly spending per each Medicare recipient over the same period from $4,800, the level at the time, to a projected $6,700, nearly a 40 percent increase. This increase represented a growth rate of 6.4 percent per year, twice the projected inflation rate. When *Public Opinion Strategies* asked the same respondents about the increased spending in this plan, 80 percent said this plan increased spending too much.[40]

At first glance, these answers would seem entirely consistent and reasonable. One plan cut the program too much, while the other plan increased the program too much. Based on these polls, the American people wanted a program somewhere in the middle. The problem is they were the same plan.

The public was thoroughly confused to the point that it condemned the same proposal as simultaneously cutting and increasing spending too much. The problem was not with the public

care", *Democratic Policy Committee.*

38   *MediaWatch,* "Reporters Unable to Master 2nd Grade Math, Call Spending Hikes 'Cuts'," November 1995, page one. http://www.mrc.org/mediawatch/1995/watch19951101.asp (accessed April 3, 2009).

39   *MediaWatch, "Reporters Unable to Master 2nd Grade Math, Call Spending Hikes 'Cuts',"* November 1995, page one. http://www.mrc.org/mediawatch/1995/watch19951101.asp (accessed April 3, 2009).

40   Nation Center, Hill Watch: Update on Budgetary Issues on Capitol Hill http://www.nationalcenter.org/WatchIss22.html (accessed April 3, 2009).

but with how the government developed a budget and the special meaning that the word 'cut' has.

When doing your home budget for the next year, let's say you believe you will get a raise at the end of this year. Based on this expected raise, you project that you will increase the amount you spend on entertainment (or any other category) by ten percent the following year. If inflation is only two percent, the other eight percent will be extra money for you to spend in that area.

This plan looks good on paper. However, at the end of the year, your raise ends up smaller than you had hoped. When you reevaluate your budget, you can only afford a six percent increase instead of the ten percent projected. If inflation remains the same at 2 percent, this is still a four percent increase after inflation, so you are still ahead. After all, it is not like you had to cut back on your spending.

In the scenario above, the concepts of *increase* and *cut* are easily understood. Few would call the six percent increase a 'cut.' However, in government, things are not so straightforward. From a government budget perspective, since the increase was going to be ten percent, this is called a four percent cut instead of a six percent increase. This unique terminology is what happened in the Medicare plan discussed above.

Earlier budgets had projected increases in spending for the Medicare program. The size of these increases made some concerned, as many believed the costs were out of control. The plan tried to control the growth in spending before it threatened the program's viability.

Opponents of the change compared the earlier spending projections to the new ones. Since the goal was to control spending, the plan reduced spending. As the government refers to these reductions, they are "cuts."

It probably would not have been an issue if the debate had had that level of detail. Yet, with the slogan-style discussions we now have, this came down to "big cuts in Medicare."[41] The 'fine print' that these cuts were not cuts but simply reductions in the growth rate was lost on most people, particularly those who depend on the program. As a result of this confusion in language, the same people could condemn the plan as simultaneously cutting and increasing spending too much!

The confusion in language causes incoherent opinions like this. It occurs in many areas, from taxes, to abortion, to same-sex marriage. Whether or not the public supports a particular side depends significantly on the terms used and how the media frames the debate.

Thus, for example, both sides in the abortion debate frequently claim the "support of the American People" for their side and cite polls to support them. Neither side's polls are wrong; instead, whether or not one "side" is supported by the majority depends strongly on precisely the question and how pollsters ask it. In reality, neither extreme of the abortion debate has the support of a majority of the American people.

Looking at all the polls, the American people are currently in the middle, wanting abortion legal in some cases, restricted in others, and illegal in others. The earlier the pregnancy, the more people support legal abortion. The later, the more they oppose it. Both a complete ban and total legalization are minority positions.

Exactly where the majority are is unknown because we do not have that discussion. Instead, the choice is artificially one extreme or the other. As such, either side can claim to be with the majority by citing polls that accurately say that most people reject the other side.

As a result of these and many other factors, there is an increasing fragmentation in the discussion. A healthy democracy depends on a healthy debate that includes each side's pros, cons, and ramifications and their proposals. But genuine, honest debates are

---

41   *MediaWatch, "Reporters Unable to Master 2nd Grade Math, Call Spending Hikes 'Cuts',"* November 1995, page one. http://www.mrc.org/mediawatch/1995/watch19951101.asp (accessed April 3, 2009).

impossible when discussion consists primarily of slogans, bumper stickers, and thirty-second TV spots where people do not use similar meanings for words.

Furthermore, with so many outlets for information, groups are increasingly becoming more insular. Democrats talk primarily to Democrats, Republicans to Republicans, and Libertarians to Libertarians. Each group looks to its sources and insulates itself from others, effectively becoming self-reinforcing, feeding on its own rhetoric rather than reality.

This phenomenon affects political parties and the nation as a whole. Genuine national debates are becoming increasingly more difficult as there is no national discussion but rather various groups self-reinforcing their beliefs: Conservatives, Liberals, City, Rural, Secular, and Religious. When those from different groups discuss issues, at least in public forums, it is often little more than a recital of established talking points, with both sides talking past each other rather than actually discussing and debating issues.

As pointed out earlier, democracy is not merely voting. It is a process of debate and deliberation in which voting is simply the final step in making decisions. A valid discussion should include an analysis of the issue, the competing alternatives, and the ramifications of those alternatives.

This debate and discussion cannot occur without clear, consistent, and standard language among all participants. At its most basic, there must be a common language of dialogue and debate. People must know what an advocate means when they use terms like 'cut.'

For a democracy to thrive, both sides must respect the other. In a democracy, the people rule. The people will not all agree but have a say in the outcome. Therefore, another goal of discussion must be to seek a compromise that all, or at least most, can accept. A democracy where the debate aims to defeat the other side will be short-lived.

What Can Be Done

Responsibility for effective communication lies with both sides of the discussion. The political leaders seeking to persuade the public will use whatever is most effective. It ultimately comes down to the issue of who is in charge. Is it the people who control the politicians or the politicians who control the people?

If people continue to settle for clever wording that relies on ambiguity, then that is what they will get. However, if people demand clear, concise, and correct statements of arguments and positions, we can get past the language problems and onto a serious and rational debate of the issues that democracy depends on.

To do this, people will need to seek news outlets that get behind the poll-driven horse race aspects of a debate and delve into the issues, the proposed solutions, and the ramifications of the various proposed solutions.

Here is a question to consider. Why does the other side disagree with you? If the only answer you can give is one that, in some fashion, demonizes them, you do not know enough about the issue. There are pros and cons to everything. There are good and bad people on all sides of an issue. Sure, rejecting the bad people on the other side is easy, but what about the good and sincere people who disagree? If you don't know how they can believe what you reject, perhaps it would be beneficial to find out.

If you do, you may find they are correct, or you will be better equipped to explain why they are wrong. It will likely be some mixture of the two. Still, it will be beneficial and make seeking a compromise easier.

One of the great things about the Internet is the plenty of space to explore subjects deeply. While there are a lot of irrational, emotion-based arguments, mudslinging, and hate, there is also a lot of serious discussion and debate on a whole range of issues. The problem can be finding it.

If a majority of people begin to demand more from political leaders and news organizations, they will respond for no other reasons than to win those people over. Let a few politicians lose because they could not get beyond sound bites and slogans, and you will begin to see politicians becoming more specific. Voting for candidates seeking compromise with the other side rather than their defeat will reduce polarization and build consensus.

Unfortunately, this won't be easy. For it to work will take both sides. It is important to remember that an all-or-nothing approach often leaves you with nothing. It is currently in the politicians' best interest to be vague, for providing people with clarity means that some will not like them. But they want your vote, and if they have to be clear, concise, and specific to get it, then that is what they will be.

AN INFORMED
ELECTORATE?

No nation is permitted to live in ignorance with impunity.
Thomas Jefferson[1]

The best defense of democracy is an informed electorate.
Thomas Jefferson

H IS LIFE, IN MANY WAYS, reflected the poetry for
which he was famous; nobility with a dark side, free
from convention, even a little arrogance, full of life,
always on the move, searching, seeking to be where things were
happening. This attitude brought him to Greece to join their war
for independence. He was not one to do things halfway. Having
his agents in England sell everything he had of any value, he headed for Greece with supplies enough for 1,000 men for two years.
When he arrived and saw the state of the Greek Navy, he spent
even more of his money refurbishing it.[2]

Before he left, he told a friend that he believed he would die
in Greece, but he added that he hoped at least his death would be

---

1   Thomas Jefferson: *Virginia Board of Visitors Minutes, 1821. ME 19:408*
http://etext.virginia.edu/jefferson/quotations/jeff1350.htm (accessed April 3,
2009
2   Will and Ariel Durant, *The Age of Napoleon,* (Simon and Schuster,
1975), 498

in battle, for that would be "a good finish."[3] He would die within the year, but he was not to get his wish. Rather than the noble death storming a battlement he had hoped for, he was caught in a storm while riding. By that evening, he was running a fever. A day later, he could not leave his bed.

A team of doctors treated him, and while he resisted their treatments, eventually, he relented. Still, his condition worsened. Ten days after falling ill, he died. To this day, the Greeks honor the English poet who gave so much, celebrating each April 19th as Byron Day.[4]

Byron did not get his wish to die fighting for a noble cause, but it probably was not the illness he caught while riding that killed him. It was ignorance. The doctors treated him with what they believed to be the best and most advanced medical treatment of the time. They bled him. In fact, according to reports, they drained two pounds of blood out of him.

One of the problems with 'cures' that make things worse is that, as we saw earlier with planning and control when things get worse, the tendency is to try even more of the 'cure.' So, when Byron's condition worsened, the doctors took another two pounds of blood.[5]

Compounding the problem further, it would be several more decades before doctors started to learn what we teach every child: the benefits of washing your hands. The idea of using a sterile knife was even further off. Byron died of ignorance.

There is a tendency to be critical of these early doctors. Today, one does not need to be a medical doctor to know there is a problem with bleeding the sick or using unsterilized knives. From

3   Will and Ariel Durant, *The Age of Napoleon*, (Simon and Schuster, 1975), 498

4   *Evening Post (Nottingham, UK)*, *"Greece Honours Lord Byron's memory,"* Oct 21, 2008, http://www.thisisnottingham.co.uk/bygones/Greece-hon-ours-Lord-Byron-s-memoryarticle-415769-details/article.html (accessed April 3, 2009)

5   Will and Ariel Durant, *The Age of Napoleon*, (Simon and Schuster, 1975), 499

early childhood, everyone learns about the link between germs and sickness.

At the time of Byron's death, it had only been about 150 years since Leeuwenhoek had used the first microscope to observe microscopic life forms. It would be nearly another fifty years until doctors accepted the Germ Theory of disease.

These doctors were only guilty of doing what everyone does: making the best decision they can based on what they know. While there are some notable exceptions, we judge actions based on ignorance differently than actions based on actual knowledge.

Suppose you do something that results in the death of a person without realizing that your action might lead to death. A prosecutor might charge you with manslaughter or not at all, depending on the circumstances. Yet, doing the same thing with the full knowledge that it would kill someone would be murder.

Most agree that it is wrong to hold someone responsible for something they could not know. As we saw in Chapter Six, dealing with the law, this principle has considerably weakened in the search for deep pockets. But the more difficult question is, what about the ignorance of something you should know? Moral issues aside, how can one make good decisions without vital and relevant information?

This problem is critical in a democratic form of government. It is a significant factor in favor of a republic over a direct democracy. In a direct democracy, all citizens would vote on all laws. Not only would this be difficult logistically, but there is the problem of expecting the citizenry to learn all the relevant details about farm policy, international trade, etc., to make informed decisions. For some issues, most people would possess the appropriate knowledge. Still, many, if not most issues, would require particular expertise or study.

One notable change to the system designed by the founding fathers took place in the early part of the twentieth century when Progressives were able to get several states to include more direct forms of democracy, most notably the ability to place proposed laws on the ballot, bypassing, and in some cases, overriding, their elected representatives.

Such ballot measures have a mixed history. As with many subjects we have examined, looking at the problems encountered with propositions is best done with specific examples. Still, these examples risk getting bound up with the issue under consideration in the proposition rather than the problems with the process.

Proposition 71

A prime example of the problems with such ballot measures is Proposition 71, a state constitutional amendment funding stem cell research that passed in California in 2004. This proposition is an excellent example because after it passed and was going into effect, some supporters realized they had not fully understood the proposed law and began to regret what they had done.

The initial problem relates to language and definitions discussed in the last chapter. It surrounds much of the debate on stem cell research. Stem cells in the body can develop into other types of cells, such as nerve cells or the cells that make up the heart or lung. The idea is if we could learn how to control this, it would be possible to replace cells that have been damaged and thereby cure many diseases, conditions, and injuries.

So far, so good, and there is minimal controversy over this, as virtually everyone supports stem cell research. Where controversy emerged is that stem cells exist in people of all ages, which means that stem cells are in a fetus. While there is little controversy over stem cell research on adult stem cells, there is, unsurprisingly, a great deal of controversy over using stem cells from a fetus, as it becomes closely intertwined with the debate over abortion.

A further complication arises when the controversy rages, not over the research but over whether the government will fund the research. Private organizations could do so. Yet, the public debate was often presented as prohibiting fetal stem cell research rather than permitting government funding. Thus, the first problem with Proposition 71 was that, since it dealt with a controversial issue surrounded by significant confusion, there was a great deal of confusion about the proposition.

Given all the controversy over stem cell research, or more precisely, government funding of embryonic stem cell research, this quickly became a referendum on the issue rather than the ballot measure itself. Many who supported embryonic stem cell research voted yes. Those opposed voted no. For many in the middle, this was more of a referendum on stem cell research without understanding the differences between adult versus embryonic. For some, it was just an issue of simple medical research. In the end, the proposition passed with 59 percent of the vote.

You probably think this was a good result if you support embryonic stem cell research. If you oppose it, you probably think it was not. Still, the point here is not stem cell research of any kind or its funding but the proposition process. Most Californians who went to the polls in November 2004 thought they were voting up or down on stem cell research. Yet, they were actually voting on a particular piece of legislation. Few took, or had, the time to read the 11,000-word bill.[6]

Once passed into law, the bill took effect, and as it did, some supporters were shocked to find what they had voted for. Rather than getting new cures, what Californians got was the creation of the California Institute for Regenerative Medicine, a government-created and funded entity with lots of money to give out, little accountability, and exemptions from the ordinary laws dealing with governmental ethics and conflict of interest.[7] The price tag

---

6   *California Institute For Regenerative Medicine, "Text of Proposed Laws, Proposition 71"* https://www.cirm.ca.gov/wp-content/uploads/archive/files/about_cirm/prop71.pdf (accessed December 13, 2023).

7   For example, The provision "Except as provided in this section, the Public Contract Code shall not apply to contracts let by the institute." *California Institute For Regenerative Medicine, "Text of Proposed Laws, Proposition 71"* https://www.cirm.ca.gov/wp-content/uploads/archive/files/about_cirm/prop71.pdf (accessed December 13, 2023).

for all this was $3 billion in a state already facing severe financial troubles that a few years before resulted in the governor's recall.

Nor was it simply the opponents who came to question this. State Senator Deborah Ortiz, a vocal supporter, soon expressed concern and eventually became a leader of a movement trying to fix the bill and bring some accountability and oversight to the new institute.

That turned out to be difficult, however, for along with granting themselves exemptions from standard oversight and ethics laws, the proposition's authors explicitly forbade any changes for three years. After that, lawmakers could change the proposition to "enhance the ability of the institute to further the purposes of the grant and loan programs" with the nearly-impossible margin of 70 percent of the vote.[8]

If the ethical and legislative limitations were not enough, there are additional potential problems with how specific medical science facts were presented and understood. One of the claims frequently made by supporters was that Proposition 71 banned cloning. In the "For Argument" in the state voter's pamphlet, supporters wrote, "71 prohibits cloning to create babies." The proposition stated,

> SEC. 3. No funds authorized for, or made available to, the institute shall be used for research involving human reproductive cloning. [9]

---

8   "The statutory provisions of this measure, except the bond provisions, may be amended to enhance the ability of the institute to further the purposes of the grant and loan programs created by the measure, by a bill introduced and passed no earlier than the third full calendar year following adoption, by 70 percent of the membership of both houses of the Legislature and signed by the Governor, provided that at least 14 days prior to passage in each house, copies of the bill in final form shall be made available by the clerk of each house to the public and news media." *California Institute For Regenerative Medicine, "Text of Proposed Laws, Proposition 71"* https://www.cirm.ca.gov/wp-content/uploads/archive/files/about_cirm/prop71.pdf (accessed December 13, 2023).

9   *California Institute For Regenerative Medicine, "Text of Proposed Laws, Proposition 71"* https://www.cirm.ca.gov/wp-content/uploads/archive/files/

It defined human reproductive cloning as,

> "Human reproductive cloning" means the practice of creating or attempting to create a human being by transferring the nucleus from a human cell into an egg cell from which the nucleus has been removed for the purpose of implanting the resulting product in a uterus to initiate a pregnancy[10]

So, the Pro argument was only partially correct. The bill did not ban cloning. It only said the funds in the proposition could not fund it. The bill also said,

> SEC 5 There is hereby established a right to conduct stem cell research which includes research involving adult stem cells, cord blood stem cells, pluripotent stem cells, and/or progenitor cells. Pluripotent stem cells are cells that are capable of self-renewal, and have broad potential to differentiate into multiple adult cell types. Pluripotent stem cells may be derived from somatic cell nuclear transfer or from surplus products of in vitro fertilization treatments when such products are donated under appropriate informed consent procedures. Progenitor cells are multipotent or precursor cells that are partially differentiated, but retain the ability to divide and give rise to differentiated cells. [11]

Little wonder the average voter in the state did not fully understand what the proposition said or what this newly created constitutional right entailed. Somatic cell nuclear transfer is also known as Therapeutic Cloning. So, while the voters of California believed they were banning cloning, or at least cloning, to create human babies, they were not only allowing it but making a new constitutional right to Therapeutic Cloning. It is unclear how many thought they were banning human cloning but were only

---

about_cirm/prop71.pdf (accessed December 13, 2023).

10   *California Institute For Regenerative Medicine, "Text of Proposed Laws, Proposition 71"* https://www.cirm.ca.gov/wp-content/uploads/archive/files/about_cirm/prop71.pdf (accessed December 13, 2023).

11   *California Institute For Regenerative Medicine, "Text of Proposed Laws, Proposition 71"* https://www.cirm.ca.gov/wp-content/uploads/archive/files/about_cirm/prop71.pdf (accessed December 13, 2023).

not funding human reproductive cloning with this proposition. In 2008, the Legislative Analyst Office said that,

> Proposition 71, enacted by the voters in 2004, amended the State Constitution to establish a right to conduct stem cell research, which could be interpreted to include therapeutic cloning.[12]

But again, this is one of the problems with such direct democracy. The longer the proposition, the more fine print and legalese it contains, the less likely people will fully understand what they vote for. After all, how many average citizens know that "somatic cell nuclear transfer" is just another name for Therapeutic Cloning?

In a normal legislative process, opponents to proposed bills can comment and propose alternative language to eliminate concerns such as whether or not a bill permits or prohibits cloning. But propositions are presented as a 'take it' or 'leave it' situation, frequently with broader social implications.

In logic, there is the fallacy of the complex question, which does not have a 'yes' or 'no' answer because it contains too many parts. The classic example is, 'Have you stopped beating your wife?' Answer 'Yes,' because you don't beat your wife, and you imply that at one time you did. Yet, answer 'No' because you never did, and thus, never needed to stop, and you indicate that you are still beating your wife. One of the big problems with propositions is that they are essentially massive, complex questions to which voters must say yes or no.

For example, consider what would have happened if the people of California had read the bill and, because of concerns about accountability and oversight, the ambiguity about cloning, or simply the cost given the state's fiscal problems, had rejected it. Many would have taken this as a defeat for stem cell research. So, what is a voter who supports stem cell research but opposes this particular bill supposed to do?

---

12   *California Legislative Analyst's Office,* http://www.lao.ca.gov/ballot/2008/080088.aspx (accessed April 3, 2009)

Represent What?

Due to such issues, the Founding Fathers preferred a republic over a direct democracy. In a republic, the citizens vote for representatives, whose job is to become informed on all the relevant details. But this, in and of itself, presents a problem. While it is the job of the duly elected representative to become informed, it is also their job to represent their constituents. Thus, voters are not entirely off the hook, even in a representative government. While they do not need to get down into the minutia of proposed laws, they still need enough knowledge to form an opinion that the representative can represent.

The sad fact is that many have little, if any, knowledge of the issues, and one has only to look at the length of the modern election cycle to see this. Thus, voters fall into one of several groups. To be sure, there are well-informed people across the political spectrum. Since they are well informed and know the issues, their opinions, and the candidates, they usually know who they will support early in the process. The main problem for them is which primary candidate will win the nomination.

As for the voters who are not involved in politics, they fall into several categories. Some blindly vote for their party every election. Again, these are on both sides. That leaves the other groups where campaigns can affect voters.

While there are undoubtedly well-informed and interested people who have difficulty choosing between the candidates, they are rarely, if ever, a large number. Most of the campaign cycle is for the people who are not well-informed and don't have clear positions or need to be convinced to go to the polls. In short, modern campaigns consist mainly of trying to get noticed positively or getting your opponent noticed negatively by people who are not paying attention and where many don't care.

The interested and well-informed tend to cancel themselves out. The result is that the swing vote decides elections. Many swing voters are the least interested and the least informed, except those not interested enough to vote.

The evidence supporting this abounds. The media portrayed the elections in 2008 as a repudiation of Republicans. With President Bush's approval rating being in the 20-30 percent range,[13] there was considerable justification for this conclusion. Yet, at the same time, approval levels for Congress, controlled by the Democrats, was about ten points lower than Bush's – in the teens.[14] If the Democratic Congress had even lower approval ratings, why did the Democrats do so well?

A key reason is that while most people know who the President is,[15] a significant number of voters have no clue about Congress. In a Zogby poll of those who voted for Obama conducted shortly after the 2008 election, less than half, 42.6 percent, even knew that the Democrats controlled Congress, and 36.5 percent believed that the Republicans were in control.[16] In a USA Today/ Gallup Poll conducted just after the election, 28 percent[17] of those asked said they had never heard of Harry Reid, the Senate Majority Leader, while Nancy Pelosi, the Speaker of the House, was better known with only eight percent[18] having never heard of her.

If you don't know a party is in charge, then it is hard to hold them accountable. Then again, for those voters who thought in

---

13   *PollingReport.com, "President Bush – Overall Job Rating in National Polls,"* http://www.pollingreport.com/BushJob.htm (accessed April 3, 2009)

14   *PollingReport.com, "Congress – Job Rating in National Polls,"* http://www. pollingreport.com/CongJob.htm (accessed April 3, 2009)

15   Along these lines, we had a foreign exchange student who was shocked to find that there was a student in her High School history class who did not know who the President was. This occurred in the seventh year of the Bush administration.

16   *Zogby International, "Zobgy America National Poll of Barack Obama Voters 11/13/08 thru 11/15/08"* http://www.zogby.com/news/wf-dfs.pdf (accessed April 3, 2009)

17   USA Today/Gallup Poll. Nov. 7-9, 2008. http://www.pollingreport. com/r.htm (Accessed April 8, 2009)

18   USA Today/Gallup Poll. Nov. 7-9, 2008. http://www.pollingreport. com/r.htm (Accessed April 8, 2009)

2008 the Republicans controlled both the presidency and Congress, it is pretty easy to see why they would want to replace them with Democrats.

Ultimately, like the doctors who bled Byron, people can only make decisions based on what they know or think they know. Few people have the time or the inclination to keep up with all the significant issues, much less all the issues, nor should they. Yet, the poll cited shows that millions of voters do not even keep up with the basics. Their knowledge of events is based solely on what the major media outlets report.

Fair and Balanced?

An ill-informed voter has become increasingly problematic as the legacy media has mostly ceased any pretense of balance or objectivity. While many reporters still profess some neutrality, many studies and reports clearly show that, on the whole, the coverage is far from balanced.

The Pew Research Center's Project for Excellence in Journalism study on the 2008 election coverage[19] is just one of many studies showing the problem. According to the survey, the press coverage of Obama was "somewhat more positive than negative." As for McCain, the press coverage was "heavily unfavorable."

A review of the Press coverage from September 8 to October 16 showed that there were twice as many positive or neutral stories as negative ones for Obama. But for McCain, the situation was nearly reversed. Almost 60 percent of the stories were negative, and only 14 percent were positive. Put another way, Obama had over twice as many positive stories while having half the negative stories compared to McCain.

The situation on three major cable news networks was even worse, with one notable exception. While the coverage on CNN was similar to the rest of the press, MSNBC's coverage tilted even

19   *Pew Research Center, "Winning the Media Campaign", Oct 22, 2008* http://www.journalism.org/node/13307 (accessed April 3, 2009).

more in favor of Obama. On MSNBC, the positive stories about Obama outnumber the negative stories 43 percent to 14 or 3 to 1. In contrast, for McCain, the negative stories far outnumbered everything else, with a whopping 73 percent of the stories being negative. Only one in ten stories on McCain were positive.

The study tried to spin this away by claiming that "winning in politics begat winning coverage."[20] But the actual data does not support that conclusion. If that were the case, the situation should have been reversed in 2004 when Bush won. Yet, a similar study of the 2004 election[21] also done by the Project for Excellence in Journalism found that the coverage of Bush was, like McCain, much more negative than positive, with the stories being 59 percent negative to 14 percent positive. For Kerry, as for Obama, it was somewhat more positive than negative – 34 percent positive to 25 percent negative.

You must go back to the 2000 election before getting any sort of balance. The Project for Excellence in Journalism's review of the 2000 election shows markedly different and much more balanced coverage. In 2000, the coverage of both candidates was significantly more negative than positive, with 56 percent of the stories on Gore being negative, while 49 percent of the stories for Bush were negative[22].

The significant change for Republicans from 2000 to 2004 was that the coverage became more negative, with 10 percent of the stories moving from the positive category to the negative while the percentage of neutral stories remained the same. The Democrats saw their negative stories cut in half, and their positive stories more than doubled, with the remainder going into the neutral category. In short, press coverage for the Republicans got much

---

20   *Pew Research Center, "Winning the Media Campaign", Oct 22, 2008*
http://www.journalism.org/node/13307 (accessed April 3, 2009)
21   *Pew Research Center, "The Debate Effect", Oct 27, 2004*
http://www.journalism.org/node/196 (accessed April 3, 2009)
22   *Pew Research Center, "The Last Lap", Oct 31, 2000*
http://www.journalism.org/node/309 (accessed April 3, 2009)

worse, while coverage for the Democrats got much better in 2004. Coverage since then has continued this shift.

Surprisingly, the conservative channel Fox News was the only network with anything close to balanced coverage. While openly favoring Republicans on their opinion shows, in 2008, Fox News was equally critical in their news stores, with 40 percent being negative for both candidates. As for the positive stories, 25 percent of the stories about Obama fell into this category, compared with a slightly lower 21 percent for McCain.

Newspapers were not much better than their television counterparts. Deborah Howell, the Ombudsman for the Washington Post, summed up her paper's coverage of the 2008 election, writing,

> Readers have been consistently critical of the lack of probing issues coverage and what they saw as a tilt towards Democrat Barack Obama. My surveys, which ended on Election Day, show that they were right on both counts.[23]

Not only were the stories on Obama more positive and those on McCain more negative, but there were more Obama stories, even after both had locked up their party's nominations. This bias reflected the overall trend in media, where 66 percent of stories featured Obama, while 53 percent featured McCain.[24] Obama also was featured in more photos. The imbalance in the number of photos would have been even worse, except that a preliminary analysis in early August had shown "a much wider disparity." The photo editors "made a more conscious effort at balance afterwards."[25]

---

23   Deborah Howell, "An Obama Tilt in the Campaign Coverage", *Washington Post, Nov 9, 2008, B06* http://www.washingtonpost.com/wp-dyn/content/article/2008/11/07/AR2008110702895.html (accessed April 3, 2009)

24   The reason for the number exceeding 100% is that some stories featured both candidates.
Deborah Howell, "An Obama Tilt in the Campaign Coverage", *Washington Post, Nov 9, 2008, B06* http://www.washingtonpost.com/wp-dyn/content/article/2008/11/07/AR2008110702895.html (accessed April 3, 2009)

25   Deborah Howell, "An Obama Tilt in the Campaign Coverage", *Washing-*

In short, Howell summed up the Post's coverage of Obama writing,

> But Obama deserved tougher scrutiny than he got, especially of his undergraduate years, his start in Chicago and his relationship with Antoin "Tony" Rezko, who was convicted this year of influence-peddling in Chicago. The Post did nothing on Obama's acknowledged drug use as a teenager.[26]

Nor was the slanted coverage limited simply to the Presidential candidates. Concerning the coverage of the Vice Presidential candidates, Howell wrote,

> One gaping hole in coverage involved Joe Biden, Obama's running mate. When Gov. Sarah Palin was nominated for vice president, reporters were booking the next flight to Alaska. Some readers thought The Post went over Palin with a fine-tooth comb and neglected Biden. They are right; it was a serious omission.[27]

Again, the point here is not Obama versus McCain but the slanted coverage of these candidates. How can voters make informed decisions when the information sources are slanting the information, and they are misinformed or unaware of the basic facts?

Generally, if most of what you hear about someone is positive, you will have a favorable view of them. If most of what you hear about someone is negative, you will have a negative opinion of them. For the well-informed voter, biased coverage has little, if any, effect. There are so many sources of information that those seeking to be well-informed can find the information they need. But for those whose only knowledge about the candidates is what

ton Post, Nov 9, 2008, B06 http://www.washingtonpost.com/wp-dyn/content/article/2008/11/07/AR2008110702895.html (accessed April 3, 2009)

26   Deborah Howell, "An Obama Tilt in the Campaign Coverage", *Washington Post, Nov 9, 2008, B06* http://www.washingtonpost.com/wp-dyn/content/article/2008/11/07/AR2008110702895.html (accessed April 3, 2009)

27   Deborah Howell, "An Obama Tilt in the Campaign Coverage", *Washington Post, Nov 9, 2008, B06* http://www.washingtonpost.com/wp-dyn/content/article/2008/11/07/AR2008110702895.html (accessed April 3, 2009)

they pick up directly or indirectly from the news, such bias will have a significant effect.

In the 2008 presidential election, most of the reporting about Obama was positive, while most of the reporting about McCain was negative. Thus, we would expect that those voters who formed their opinions based on this coverage would have a favorable view of Obama and a negative view of McCain.

For example, we saw earlier that 42.6 percent of Obama voters did not know the Democrats controlled Congress. If more than one in ten of these voters had switched their vote, had they known, the election would have gone the other way. Again, this is not to argue that Obama's election was illegitimate in some way. It was not. The point is that a lack of information can affect the outcome of elections.

However, the worst part about the press coverage is not even that it tilts in favor of one candidate or the other but that most deals with what some call the horserace— stories about who was ahead or behind, political strategies, etc.—less than a quarter of the coverage dealt with the policies put forth by the candidates. Thus, it was little wonder that many Obama supporters could not say what he would do once elected.

There is the famous adage with computers: "garbage in, garbage out." It refers to the reality that the best computer program cannot produce good results from bad data. When voters get poor-quality information about the candidates and their plans, how can they be expected to make good decisions about whom to support? Voters cannot make objective decisions based on biased information.

Even when they get unbiased information about individual policies, there is the additional problem of how they will evaluate that information. Given the current educational system, many voters have little understanding concerning how our government is structured, much less of the basics of economics, history, or world events. Yet, they are voting on candidates who are supposed to represent their views. To see the problems this creates, one has only to consider the insanity that surrounds gas prices.

Gas Insanity

Einstein is incorrectly said[28] to have defined insanity as doing the same thing repeatedly and expecting a different result. Based on this definition, we are clearly into insanity regarding gas prices. I have been observing this since the 1980s, and I am sure it goes further back. Most summers, prices increase, and people start grumbling about "Big Oil." If prices go up a lot, the politicians get involved, demanding investigations of the oil companies.

The summer turns to fall, demand lessens, prices decline, and people's interest turns to other things. Then, the investigation results come out, clearing the oil companies. Net result? Nothing happens. Then, the following summer, the whole cycle repeats, except that the problem slowly worsens most years. Insanity!

In reality, there are two main problems here. The first is refineries. In 1982, there were 301 operable refineries in the United States.[29] By 2009, the number of refineries was only 150[30], less than half the number. Meanwhile, from 1983 to 2006, average U.S. Total Gasoline Sales by Prime Suppliers went from 287 million to 376 million gallons per day.[31] Unsurprisingly, this increase

28   The earliest clear occurrence of this phrase appears in article about Al-Anon in 1981. By 1990, it was being attributed to Einstein. https://quotein-vestigator.com/2017/03/23/same/ (accessed November 27, 2023)

29   *Energy Information Administration, "Annual U.S. Number of Operable Refineries as of January 1"*
http://tonto.eia.doe.gov/dnav/pet/hist/8_na_8o0_nus_ca.htm (accessed April 3, 2009)

30   *Energy Information Administration, "Annual U.S. Number of Operable Refineries as of January 1"*
http://tonto.eia.doe.gov/dnav/pet/hist/8_na_8o0_nus_ca.htm (accessed April 3, 2009)

31   *Energy Information Administration, "Annual U.S. Total Gasoline All Sales/ Deliveries by Prime Supplier"*
http://tonto.eia.doe.gov/dnav/pet/hist/c100000001A.htm (accessed April 3,

was accompanied by increased utilization rates for the refineries, now about 90 percent.[32] By 2009, we could no longer refine all the gasoline we needed but had to import 250,000 barrels daily, adding additional shipping costs to the price at the pump.

While we increased our consumption by 32 percent, we cut the number of refineries by 50 percent. These changes are why the prices jump whenever a problem occurs at a refinery. There is simply no slack in the system. Doesn't it make more sense to consider building new refineries as a better solution to higher gas prices?

Despite all the claims of gouging, manipulating oil prices, speculators, etc., the real problem is basic economics and supply and demand. Over the last couple of decades, the need for gas has steadily increased while the ability to supply it has fallen. Nor is this because we are running out of oil. Between 1980 and 2008, known oil reserves more than doubled, going from 644 billion barrels to 1,331 billion barrels.[33]

The problem is not that we do not have the oil; the problem has been limits placed on how and where we can get it and the limitation on the number of refineries to process it. Ultimately, the solution is simple. If you want cheaper oil, you can increase the supply, lessen the demand, or find alternatives. Given the importance of oil in the economy, short of an economic downturn, lessening the demand is unlikely. Nearly 40 years of efforts have, at best, only slowed the rate of increase, with the minor success in the United States offset by growth in the rest of the world.

When it comes to alternatives, while some promising technologies could replace oil in some areas, the use of oil and its various products is so widespread that the only real way to reduce

2009)

32 *Energy Information Administration, "Annual U.S. Percentage Utilization of Refinery Operable Capacity"*
http://tonto.eia.doe.gov/dnav/pet/hist/mopueus2a.htm
(accessed April 3, 2009)

33 *Energy Information Administration, "World Proven Crude Oil Reserves,"*
http://www.eia.doe.gov/pub/international/iealf/crudeoilreserves.xls (accessed April 3, 2009)

oil consumption is to reduce the economy. In addition, all the alternatives have problems and cost more than oil.

In fact, rather than a solution to high gas prices, many have argued we need higher gas prices to make alternatives to oil more viable. A more recent example of this argument came from Philip Gordon of the Brookings Institution, who wrote,

> Americans will not make long-term decisions to buy fuel-effi-
> cient automobiles, create distribution networks for alternative
> fuels, or invest in technologies like hydrogen fuel cells, flex-fu-
> el vehicles or wind power unless they know that a future sharp
> fall in oil prices will not undercut them.[34]

The Washington Post's 'On Wheels' columnist Warren Brown had this suggestion in 2008,

> Let's also have a floor under the price of gasoline. Four dol-
> lars a gallon seems to have done the job. It helped consumers
> make more considered judgments of the kinds of cars and
> trucks they buy. And it has also had some tangible effect on
> their driving behavior and fuel-wasting habits on the high-
> way. The bottom line is that consumers need some skin in the
> game.[35]

In short, while alternative fuels have some positive contribu-
tions to make, lower fuel prices are not one of them. If the goal is to reduce fuel prices, increasing supply is the only real solution that permits economic growth. While doable, environmentalists oppose this option. Thus, we continue to repeat the yearly cycle: Insanity.

This problem somewhat came to a head in the summer of 2008, when gas prices rose to over $4.00 a gallon. While there was the yearly finger-pointing at the oil companies, people were so upset that they began to look at things closer. A significant move-

34   Philip H. Gordon, *Winning the Right War*, (Macmillan, 2008), 95
http://books.google.com/books?id=X1aineYRpc4C&pg=PA67&source=gbs_
toc_r&cad=0_0#PPA95,M1 (accessed April 3, 2009)
35   Warren Brown, interviewed on the Diane Rehm Show, *The Future of the
U.S. Car Industry, NPR, October 23, 2008 10:00* http://wamu.org/programs/
dr/08/10/23.php#22451 (accessed April 3, 2009)

ment started to open up some areas where oil is known to exist but are currently off-limits.

During the summer, President Bush rescinded the Executive Order preventing drilling offshore. Support for drilling was so strong that when the Congressional ban came up for renewal that September, there were not enough votes to support it, and it was allowed to expire.

Again, the point is not the issue of oil prices as much as the process. If given the relevant information, voters can decide. They may decide drilling offshore is too risky and protecting the environment is worth $4.00, $5.00, or $6.00 per gallon. They may choose something else, but it will be their decision based on good information. However, the problem for decades has been that voters, angry at high gas prices, focused on false causes. So, nothing changed, and the situation got worse.

Unfortunately, many of the country's problems are much more complicated than the simple supply and demand issue of gas prices. Some try to avoid discussing the complexity by saying they want someone who will "solve the problem." But solve the problem how?

Even if there is agreement on the nature and causes of the problem, there are still a lot of questions, such as whether the solution should be more market-based or government-based. Further, what is a "solution" when the primary issue is one of trade-offs between competing interests, such as in the case of gas prices, where the trade-off is between gas prices and environmental protection? What is "the solution" when some want higher prices to spur reduced consumption and make alternatives to oil more economically viable while others demand lower prices?

The Two-Party System

Others point to the two-party system as the reason for our problems. The founders did not like factions, and many equate these with political parties. Yet the comparison is not one-to-one. In Federalist 10, Madison defined faction as

> a number of citizens, whether amounting to a majority or minority of the whole, who are united and actuated by some common impulse of passion, or of interest, adverse to the rights of other citizens, or to the permanent and aggregate interests of the community.[36]

This definition has two significant parts. First, a faction is a group centered around some passion or interest. This could be a political party, but it could also be the country as a whole. So Madison adds the second part of his definition, that the interest around which the group unites is "adverse to the rights of other citizens, or to the permanent and aggregate interests of the community."

Some would say this still defines a political party, as they always seek what is best for the party, not the people or the country. I believe this latter view is not only inaccurate but harmful. It is incorrect because it is too broad and sweeping. Thus, in the current political makeup of the country, there are not only the two major parties but several smaller ones. Many of these are not putting the party first but often acting contrary to its best interests, for they would rather lose an election than compromise on the principles they believe are best for the country.

Rather than party, perhaps a better term would be special interest group. Still, while a special interest might put their interest ahead of the country, some are formed around an interest they believe is best for the country. Then there is the problem mentioned in Chapters One and Eight: the term is often little more than a pejorative to mean any group one disagrees with.

Probably the best comparison would be with a political machine such as Tammany Hall in New York or the Pendergast machine in St Louis. While these machines fit Madison's definition of faction, they are perhaps too narrow. While political machines

---

36   Madison, Federalist No. 10 https://founders.archives.gov/documents/ Madison/01-10-02-0178 (accessed 9/5/2023)

are factions, not all factions are political machines. Still, the more a political party becomes a machine, the closer it is to faction.

One might think that the best solution is to eliminate factions or political parties. Madison considers this option but sees only two ways: destroy liberty or make everyone the same. As for destroying liberty, he writes

> that it is worse than the disease. Liberty is to faction, what air is to fire, an aliment without which it instantly expires. But it could not be a less folly to abolish liberty, which is essential to political life, because it nourishes faction, than it would be to wish the annihilation of air, which is essential to animal life because it imparts to fire its destructive agency. [37]

That leaves the second. Yet, Madison considers the second,

> is as impracticable, as the first would be unwise. As long as the reason of man continues fallible, and he is at liberty to exercise it, different opinions will be formed. As long as the connection subsists between his reason and his self-love, his opinions and his passions will have a reciprocal influence on each other; and the former will be objects to which the latter will attach themselves. The diversity in the faculties of men from which the rights of property originate, is not less an insuperable obstacle to an uniformity of interests. The protection of these faculties is the first object of government. [38]

In the end, Madison concluded,

> The inference to which we are brought, is, that the causes of faction cannot be removed; and that relief is only to be sought in the means of controlling its effects. [39]

The control that Madison sought was the Constitution, a republic with a division of power and checks and balances. The Constitution divided power between the state and federal governments, with the national divided among the legislative, executive,

---

37 Madison, Federalist No. 10 https://founders.archives.gov/documents/Madison/01-10-02-0178 (accessed 9/5/2023)
38 Madison, Federalist No. 10 https://founders.archives.gov/documents/Madison/01-10-02-0178 (accessed 9/5/2023)
39 Madison, Federalist No. 10 https://founders.archives.gov/documents/Madison/01-10-02-0178 (accessed 9/5/2023)

and judicial branches. The system limited power to force compromise and consensus.

Progressives rejected this in the early twentieth century, seeking a more powerful government that could get things done. As a result, they weakened many of the checks and balances. The founders would not be surprised that, following this weakening, the factional nature of the parties grew.

In any democratic system, political parties are inevitable, and only three options exist. You can have a one-, two-, or multiparty system. While in theory, you could have a three-party system, these seem less stable and quickly become either a two-party or multi-party system.

Few would argue for a one-party system, except, of course, those in the one party. Such systems exist in the United States, as many cities and a few states are effectively one-party systems. Most political machines in the country are centered around such one-party systems, though again, not all one-party systems are machines.

One-party systems are inherently undemocratic. Their biggest problem is the inability to correct, as the voters have little say. You can see this in some large cities with issues such as rising crime or failing infrastructure or schools, yet little, if anything, is done. Why should the party in power change and try something new when they keep winning elections? Thus, the problems continue for decades.

That leaves the choice in a democratic system between two parties or multi-parties. Both have strengths and weaknesses. The United States is effectively a two-party system. There are other parties, but they have little, if any, impact on elections, except perhaps as a spoiler in close elections. Yet, even this is uncertain, as it is not clear how members of that party would have voted or even if they would have voted. Without their party of choice, they may have skipped the election. Thus, the other existing parties give members the illusion of participating in the elections without actually having any effect. They can, and usually are, ignored.

While many in the United States complain about the two-party system, some of this is grounded in a grass-is-always-greener mentality. Neither the two-party nor the multi-party system are without problems. Both are imperfect answers to a core problem in a democratic system. Given the vast range of opinions, how do you make a choice?

In an election for a country's leader, like a President or Prime Minister, there will only be a single winner. So how do you take the diversity of opinion and distill it down to a single result: selecting a particular person to hold the office? You must group people into coalitions until you have two groups: the one large enough to win and the opposition.

The creation of coalitions happens in both systems, with the two-party system doing it before the election. In contrast, the multi-party system does it after. Handling this before the election has, I believe, several advantages. First, it gives individual people more of a say in the outcome. They are free to change at any time until they vote and voting chooses the winner.

In a multi-party system like a parliamentary system, elections are a two-step process; people vote for parties, and after the election, the parties form coalitions to select a winner. While voters may have more choices in the elections, they will have little say in the coalition building afterward. It is possible, for example, for the party they voted for to join the coalition of a candidate they oppose.

Another problem is that smaller parties typically want something in exchange for support. This magnifies their power and results in the winning coalition supporting fringe policies that otherwise would never get majority support. Since the negotiations forming coalitions occur after the vote, voters have little say.

The worst problem in such a multi-party system is the increased chance of failing to reach a conclusion and the resulting instability. While this can happen in a two-party system, it is far less likely than in a multi-party system and its fragmented vote. Two-party systems usually produce a clear winner. Multi-party systems typically don't and require the leading candidate to build a coalition. When the coalition is weak and unstable, so will the government. If no candidate can form a coalition large enough to govern, another election is needed. As I was updating the 3rd edition of this book, Israel had just gone through five elections in four years.

The United States is not free of these problems as they stem from core problems with any democratic system. Both major parties are, in reality, governing coalitions of various groups. The significant difference is that the coalitions form before the election. Since the United States has no real mechanism for creating coalitions after an election, multiple parties would only cause instability and uncertainty. They would not enhance the democratic process but detract from it.

Nor is the two-party system the major problem we face. The founders designed a system to force compromise and discussion. The division of power with its checks and balances ensures no group can dominate the other. To get anything done required working with others to reach a compromise. While far from perfect, this system worked reasonably well until the last several decades.

With the weakening of checks and balances and the growing importance of the federal government in all aspects of life, it is now possible for one group to dominate. Thus, we should not be surprised that the emphasis has changed from building coalitions to defeating opponents. A crucial and significant aspect of these changes is demonizing the other.

Too many see people who disagree as not just wrong but dangerous. They are not people you can work with but must be defeated. As the rhetoric becomes more extreme, it generates a counter-response and, ultimately, a vicious cycle. It no longer matters who started what or when. Discussion becomes impossible; defeating the other is all that matters. This growing cycle of polarization is toxic to democracy and is the real problem, not the two-party system.

What Can Be Done

The solutions here are by far the most difficult and yet the most important. As Jefferson said in the quote that started this chapter, "The best defense of democracy is an informed electorate." Fix this problem, and most other issues in the book would quickly take care of themselves, as an informed electorate would insist on it and give pretty clear direction on how to proceed.

But getting an informed electorate will not be easy. Even if desirable, the Founding Fathers' initial solution is no longer acceptable. They wanted people to have a stake in the outcome, so they had property requirements. Owning property meant you had an investment in the community; you had skin in the game. Yet, even by the early 19th century, this was no longer a good indicator, and states dropped these requirements.

Some thought poll taxes and literacy tests were a better indicator, but states often abused these in the past; they are now correctly unacceptable. The 24th Amendment to the Constitution banned taxes as a condition of voting. Some have suggested that voters should take the same test as those seeking American citizenship; this would require a constitutional amendment.

Thus, we have a quandary. On the one hand, we want everyone to vote, yet on the other, we want all voters informed on the issues. These are conflicting goals, and thus, there are only three possible outcomes. We can stay as we are, such that while there are well-informed and interested voters across the political spectrum, the least informed and the least interested voters are the ones who tip the election one way or the other. In 2000 and 2004, the least informed and interested tipped toward Bush; in 2008 and 2012, they tipped toward Obama. In 2016, they tipped toward Trump, while in 2020, they tipped toward Biden. Where will they go next?

Another option is limiting voting by the least informed and least interested. To some extent, this already happens, as the least interested are not interested enough to even bother to vote—however, the current trend of making voting easier appeals to the least interested.

After all, the highly motivated are already voting. In addition, requiring prior registration, returning to a single day of voting, limiting absentee voters, etc., has other advantages, as it would also lessen the chances and opportunities for voter fraud.

By far, the best way, at least in theory, would be to make it easier for voters to become informed, reducing uninterested and uninformed voters to an insignificant level. While the best, it will also be the hardest. For this to happen, people must take the initiative to research the candidates. They must demand a more substantial discussion of issues, less hype, and fewer slogans.

A huge problem is the bias in the media, which has become increasingly worse since 2000. The growth of streaming and the internet, while increasing access to information, also resulted in more silos. People now tend to get only information that reinforces what they believe. They rarely have to confront any real challenges to what they think. This siloing has dramatically increased the polarization of public opinion.

Democracy requires public discussion, which requires hearing both sides, the pros and cons, and the ramifications of the various options. That rarely happens today, and we see the results around us.

A large part of the problem here is simply self-awareness. While Howell's review of the Washington Post's coverage showed a bias in favor of Obama, she also pointed out how the photo editors had been surprised by the slant in their choice of photographs. When they realized it, they took steps to correct the situation.

While the Pew Research Studies and Howell's postmortems were good, even if a bit defensive, the press needs to develop some internal correcting mechanisms that will help detect bias and, more importantly, catch it in real-time and then fix it quickly, not months later.

Such fixes cannot happen until they admit there is a problem. Perhaps that is why Fox's news coverage did so well in the Pew study. Since they realize they are conservative in their opinion programming, they recognize that they must be more careful in their news coverage. Thus, for the rest of the media, simply admitting they have bias can help them correct the problem.

People now have a lot more choices about where they get their information. They can influence this. If sources get a reputation for fairness and objectivity from both sides, and people from both sides seek them out, other sources will follow suit. Some are trying, but we are not there yet.

Some argue this approach is fundamentally unfair. It blames people rather than those who are in charge. After all, what can an individual voter do? While there is some truth in this objection, in a democratic system, the people have the final say and thus have the ultimate responsibility. We get the leaders we vote for.

Some complain that the candidates put forth by either major party are unacceptable. Yet, these are the candidates that won the primary. At each stage of the process, in a democratic system, it is the people who are supposed to be in charge, and that is where any solution must begin.

Ultimately, the solution will be in the reemergence of the idea that voting is not only a right but a duty one takes seriously and with careful forethought and consideration, where people take the time to understand how their government works, who the candidates are, what the issues are, and then make an informed choice for who will best represent them.

THE LOSS OF
AMERICAN VALUES

*Don't it always seem to go
That you don't know what you've got
Till it's gone.*
                    Joni Mitchell

Charles' scheme was born from a mixture of depression, alcohol, and naïveté. Like many such schemes, the results were nothing like he intended. Instead, the result would radically change the rest of his life, ultimately teaching him the importance of what he had so taken for granted in the country he deserted.

Charles Jenkins grew up in North Carolina during the late 1940s and 50s. As a child, Charles was a troublemaker; he and school "never got along well."[1] He was from a poor but hard-working family, and things only got more challenging when his father died when he was eleven.

When he was fifteen, Jenkins convinced his mother to sign enlistment papers saying he was seventeen, and he enlisted in the North Carolina National Guard. He did not enlist because of a love of his country. The reasons were much simpler from a young man's perspective. On Mondays, he would often see members of

---

1   Charles Robert Jenkins with Jim Frederick, *The Reluctant Communist,* (University of California Press, Berkeley), 2008, 9

the Guard after their weekly drills, and "the girls went crazy over them."[2]

Charles liked his time in the Guard, the weekly practice, a couple of weekends here and there, and the two weeks in the summer. While the training was sometimes challenging, he always felt he had accomplished something. Charles particularly liked being one of the guys in uniform that the girls went crazy for. After three years in the Guard, he had worked up to corporal and was trying for sergeant when he decided on a bigger step. He joined the U.S. Army.

His first few years in the military went fine, and he eventually became a sergeant. Then, in 1964, he was sent for a second tour of duty in South Korea. There, he led men on "hunter-killer teams." These patrols were during the day rather than at night, and Charles was concerned he could come under hostile fire from North Korea.

These patrols differed from impressing girls with his uniform at the local skating rink. Even worse were rumors that the Army might redeploy his unit to the new and growing conflict in Vietnam. Charles had had enough; he just wanted to return home to North Carolina. Instead, he was stuck in a foreign country, risking his life.

As 1964 drew to a close, Charles was depressed and drinking heavily. He kept thinking about going home, and before long, his desire became an obsession. He just wanted out, and he began cooking up a plan that he thought, as crazy as it was, would get him home.

At the time, Charles's plan seemed pretty straightforward. He would cross the DMZ and let the North Koreans capture him. Once in their custody, he would ask them to hand him over to the Russians. The Russians could then arrange for him to be sent back to the United States in a diplomatic exchange.

---

2   Charles Robert Jenkins with Jim Frederick, *The Reluctant Communist*, (University of California Press, Berkeley), 2008, 10

Once back in the U.S., Charles figured the Army would charge him with desertion. They would court-martial him and discharge him from the army. But he did not care much about that. That would be a small price to pay to return home.

Eventually, his desire, depression, and ten beers convinced Charles his plan would work. So, early on January 5, 1965, Sergeant Charles Robert Jenkins crossed the DMZ to become one of the few who have ever voluntarily entered the nightmare that is North Korea.

Not long after he sobered up, Charles realized his mistake, as many of his interrogations included brutal beatings. Charles was not handed over to the Russians as he planned. Instead, the North Koreans kept him as a propaganda trophy.

While as a propaganda trophy, Charles had it better than most North Koreans; if he stepped out of line, punishment quickly followed. Still, compared to the freedom he had known and yet had so taken for granted, he was in "literally a giant, demented prison; once someone goes there, they almost never, ever get out." It would be forty years before Charles would be allowed to leave.

Charles Jenkins had always taken for granted what it meant to be an American. He failed to appreciate just how unique America is as a country in the history of the world. When he was finally allowed to leave after forty years in North Korea, he was amazed by so much of what many Americans don't think twice about.

He surrendered himself to the U.S. Military and, as he expected, was charged and put on trial. To his surprise, the military not only provided him with a defense lawyer, it was free of charge! Eventually, he was convicted and sentenced to 30 days of confinement, yet the court suspended even that. He had suffered enough in North Korea. When he returned to the U.S. to visit his mother, things as commonplace as Walmart, with its size and selection, overwhelmed him.

Ultimately, Charles's actual error was that he failed to appreciate what America was or what it meant to be an American. He had no idea what he was giving up when he walked across the DMZ early that January morning in 1965.

While they will not betray their country, many Americans have a similar ambivalence about their nation. Oh, they love their country, but what they love is unclear. When asked why they love America, some say it is the physical country, the mountains, the national parks, the countryside, or the cities. Some say it is the people; others say freedom, the Constitution, or even the Bill of Rights. While there is some truth in all these answers, they do not get to the core of what is unique and special about this country, what has inspired people worldwide to come and live here.

Sadly, one of the most common answers I get to the question, "What is America," especially among those from younger generations, is simply a puzzled look. A Gallup poll in 2022, found that only 38% of respondents said they were extremely proud to be Americans. The result was the lowest Gallup ever recorded, down from about 70 percent in 2003.[3] Since Gallup began asking the question, 55 percent have said yes on average. Now, it is increasingly common to hear people proudly claim they are citizens of the world and even to look down on such questions as fostering a primitive and dangerous nationalism.

Finally, there is a growing number who do not like the country. As one website claimed, note the use of 'we' and 'us,'

> The United States of America today is the most barbaric nation on earth. No other nation can compete with us for the crimes we committed and continue to commit against the innocent people of this world.[4]

Yet, if America is so bad, what is it about this country that inspires people worldwide to come here and has done so since its founding?

---

3   Megan Brenan, *Record-Low 38% Extremely Proud to Be American, Gallup, June 29, 2022,* https://news.gallup.com/poll/394202/record-low-extremely-proud-american.aspx (accessed August 23, 2023)

4   *World Prout Assembly,* "The Crimes of America" http://www.worldproutassembly.org/archives/2005/11/the_crimes_of_a.html (accessed April 3, 2009).

At least until very recently, there was a general agreement about what was special and unique about America. This agreement centered around three principles or ideas. It was so common that all three are on every dollar bill. Dennis Prager has called them the American Trinity: Liberty, In God We Trust, and E Pluribus Unum.

Still, in the last few decades, a growing number have attacked one or all of these values, particularly in education. In their place, they push for new and competing values. This change is one of the reasons for the indifference of so many young people. The distinctiveness of America is not taught, so they don't know.

Liberty

Liberty has been an essential American value from before the beginning of the country. The American Revolution was solidly grounded in Liberty. The Declaration of Independence is a logical argument for independence. Its central premise is we have self-evident and unalienable rights to "life, liberty, and the pursuit of happiness."

Supporters of the American Revolution erected Liberty Poles and flew Liberty flags. They would join the Sons of Liberty, which in Boston would meet at the Liberty Tree in the Commons. This emphasis on liberty inspired other towns to designate their own liberty trees as rallying points for those seeking liberty from British rule.

Patrick Henry summed up much of the sentiment of the time when he famously said, "I know not what course others may take; but as for me, give me liberty or give me death!" And so the Constitution gives one of the stated reasons for establishing the country, to "secure the Blessings of Liberty."

The importance of Liberty, while central, was not fully realized. Slavery existed, but so did a new and emerging abolitionist movement. This failure would plague the country until a civil war ended slavery. Even then, the brief expansion of liberty only flowered until reconstruction ended and was replaced by Jim Crow. Even then, the aspiration for liberty remained.

In the early 1960s, the Declaration's promise that all men are created equal remained unfulfilled. In 1963, at the March on Washington, Dr. Martin Luther King Jr. delivered one of the most historic speeches in American history, his *I Have a Dream* speech. On the step of the Lincoln Memorial, King began by pointing out that Lincoln signed the Emancipation Proclamation 100 years earlier, "But one hundred years later, the Negro still is not free;" He went on,

> When the architects of our republic wrote the magnificent words of the Constitution and the Declaration of Independence, they were signing a promissory note to which every American was to fall heir. This note was the promise that all men, yes, black men as well as white men, would be guaranteed the unalienable rights of life, Liberty, and the pursuit of happiness.

This central role of liberty remains today, and, at times, some still mention it when asked about America's distinctiveness. Still, for many, while present, liberty no longer plays the critical and dominant role it once did. Much of the talk of liberty today is little more than empty words, stripped of all real meaning. Something one is supposed to say before moving to what they really mean.

In place of liberty, a new value is coming to dominance in America: equality. As a result, the government, which the Constitution says was established to "secure the Blessings of Liberty," is now more aimed at ensuring equality, with the government pushing for equality not just before the law and in civil rights but in employment, transportation, credit, and any number of other areas.

In one sense, there is nothing wrong with this change, and many don't see a problem. Equality is good; we should and would have equality in a perfect world. But once again, we do not live in an ideal world. Equality comes at a cost, and the price is liberty.

While liberty and equality are noble and reasonable goals, they are mutually exclusive, particularly regarding government.

The more the government pushes for one, the less you will have of the other. If the government tries for liberty, the result will be less equality. The more the government pushes for equality, the less liberty there will be.

Many find the idea that liberty and equality are mutually exclusive so new that it is difficult to accept. Some even attempt to deny it. So, to demonstrate this, let's take one aspect of equality, financial equality, and consider the following thought experiment.

Suppose the government decided it wanted complete economic equality. To achieve this, they take all the country's wealth and divide it equally among everyone. Granted, there would be all sorts of practical issues that would prevent this from happening. However, the nice thing about thought experiments is that we can ignore such problems to focus on the critical issue. The key point is that everyone will be equal in terms of wealth.

Would everyone still be equal if we jump to some point in the future, a week, a month, or a year? No. Some people would take their wealth and would spend it. Some would gamble and lose; some would win. Some would invest their money. But ultimately, people would make various choices that would affect their wealth. In short, equality, once established, would quickly fade away. The more time passed, the more inequality would grow.

The only way to maintain equality would be for the government to limit people's choices. Gambling has winners and losers and, thus, would introduce inequality by its very nature. Therefore, if the government wants to maintain equality, it cannot allow people to gamble. In fact, if the government wants to maintain equality, it cannot allow people to make any choice that might lead to inequality. In short, the more equality the government seeks, the less liberty it can allow.

We can mitigate the inherent conflict between liberty and equality by distinguishing between opportunity and outcome. The government should ensure equality in opportunity, as this does not limit liberty. Returning to the gambling example, they must ensure the game is fair.

The Problems of Equality

While promoting equal opportunity instead of results helps, in the end, real-world considerations still leave equality and liberty in conflict, though granted not as much as with equality of outcome. This conflict stems from five fundamental problems when it comes to equality.

The first is that we are not all the same. We are individuals, and all of us have different strengths and weaknesses. We all have the things we are good at and the things we struggle with. With practice and diligence, you can do a great many things.

Still, these can only take one so far. No matter how much I practice and train, I will never have an equal opportunity to win in the Olympics or play professional sports. I can become a good golfer but will never win a Masters trophy. As the saying goes, you cannot put in what God left out.

Then, there is the problem of our background and circumstances. Some may have the natural ability to win an Olympic medal or play professional sports. Still, their background and circumstances are such that they never had the opportunity to play. As a result, their talent went unnoticed and undeveloped.

There is also the issue of desire, such as in the movie *Center Stage*, a story where one of the characters had the talent to be the best ballerina, and yet not the desire. As she put it, she did not want to spend "a life of wishing that I'd found something I really loved instead of something I just happened to do well."[5]

Some see success as a matter of luck, of having the talent or opportunity. Others see it as a matter of effort and doing the hard work. Success is a mixture of talent, opportunity, desire, and effort. These are not and cannot be the same for all.

---

5   SugarPlumJade, *Center Stage – Part 10,* YouTube, https://www.youtube.com/watch?v=-5nvARS2bus

The first two are largely out of an individual's control. We do not control our genetic makeup or the environments in which we are raised. Some in the early 20th century tried to control genetic makeup through the now rightly discredited science of Eugenics. Still, Society can and should take steps to improve opportunity, universal education being the most notable example.

The second two, desire and effort, are largely under the control of the individual, and these are often more important. Without luck and opportunity, you might not reach the pinnacle of a profession, but you will still do all right if you put in the effort. Yet, even with luck and opportunity, without effort you will never succeed. This brings us to the third problem.

The third problem has to do with time and our choices. We all make numerous choices daily, and we don't all make the same ones. Many decisions over time have a cumulative effect on who we are and our circumstances. When should equality be applied? How can equality exist with people who made other choices?

Suppose there are two applicants for a job where one chooses to spend their high school years studying hard to get good grades. In contrast, the second decided to do the minimum required so they had more free time to play video games. Should they be considered equally qualified candidates?

These three problems with equality are then magnified and exacerbated by the fourth problem: How can a government address all of these issues? Government is a clumsy and awkward tool and functions best when it can make broad, sweeping rules it can apply to everyone.

For example, the law says you stop at red lights and go on green for safety reasons. Still, every driver has experienced times when the law does not make sense, for example, when stopped at a red light at 2:00 in the morning. There is not another car in sight, yet you sit there, waiting, because that is the law.

You also know it would be your luck that as soon as you went through the red light, a police car would appear and catch you.

The critical point is that while the law exists for safety reasons, safety has nothing to do with why you sit at a red light at 2:00 A.M.

There are few laws that the government should apply universally. Thus, there are exceptions written into the law. 'The speed limit in a school zone shall be 25 mph, except on weekends.' Still, the more exceptions, the more complicated the law becomes and the harder it is to follow and administer. Just consider the Federal Tax code as described by former U.S. Representative J.C. Watts,

> Most of the folks who work for the IRS are good people just trying to do their job, but they are caught in a bad, overextended tax system. At 3,458 pages, twice the length of the Bible, it's impossible for the average taxpayer to know, understand, and accurately apply its provisions. The length is twice that of the Bible! Even tax experts cannot do so reliably.[6]

Even if it could develop a clear vision of equality, the government is ill-suited to make the sorts of carefully tailored laws and regulations considering all the relevant issues. Government is, at best, a blunt club, where a surgeon's scalpel is required.

In addition, there is the paradox that the level of government best suited to enforce equality is the local level closest to the people. Yet, by its very nature, equality requires a single set of rules applied to all. In short, mandating equality requires that the most distant form of government try to do what it is least capable of doing. It is a prescription for failure.

Thus, we come to the final problem, which is that for government to do anything requires limits on liberty. Laws and regulations are, by their very nature, limits on freedom. Laws that attempt to enforce some vision of equality are no different. As is the case with so many areas of government, failure to achieve the desired goal results in even more laws and regulations and, thus, even further restrictions on freedom. The more the government pursues equality, the less liberty people will have.

---

6   *Trygve's digital diary,* *"How Long is It? (The United States tax code)"* http://www.trygve.com/taxcode.html (accessed April 3, 2009).

To be clear, the tension between liberty and equality is not an either-or question where one must choose perfect liberty or equality. Too little liberty or too much inequality are real problems. Instead, there are two points here. First, liberty and equality conflict where increasing one limits the other. Second, the country focused on liberty from our founding until relatively recently.

Some inequality is so repugnant that the loss of freedom resulting from the government's action to limit it is acceptable, racial inequality being the most obvious example. But even in such a clear-cut case, the problems of ensuring equality quickly became apparent. Thus, the country has struggled to define the line between affirmative action and a quota for decades.

The American Revolution was born out of a desire for liberty, and this has been a defining principle of America. Shortly after the American Revolution, another revolution emphasized equality instead of Liberty, the French Revolution. While it started by proclaiming Liberty, Equality, and Fraternity, it quickly focused on Equality; everyone had a single title: 'Citizen.' Its emphasis on equality was one of the reasons for the vastly different outcome in the Reign of Terror followed by a dictatorship.

We can see a small indication of the problems in store for democracy in the growing limits on free speech in much of Europe and Canada, where equality remains the dominant value over liberty. In 2008, columnist and author Mark Steyn found himself on trial for his book, *America Alone*, arguing that radical Islam threatens the West. When Maclean's magazine published an excerpt from the book, the Canadian Islamic Congress filed a complaint with the British Columbia Human Rights Commission. Steyn found himself in a serious trial for the words he had written.

Such attempts to limit speech are a natural outgrowth of equality laws. By their very nature, such laws seek to protect people from discrimination by limiting things that support inequality. Thus, the complaint against Steyn was that he "discriminates against Muslims on the basis of their religion. It exposes Muslims to hatred and contempt due to their religion."[7] Steyn supporters were outraged and believed that the Canadian Islamic Congress was simply using the law to try and suppress anything critical of Islam, even anything critical of Islamic terrorism.

A poll done by Rasmussen in 2008 revealed that the danger is not restricted simply to Europe and Canada, for support for free speech had only a slim majority of 53 percent if that speech can be labeled "hate speech." Of course, precisely what is and is not hate speech varies widely, as the French actress and animal rights activist Brigitte Bardot discovered in 2008 when a French Court fined her for being critical of how sheep were slaughtered during an Islamic feast. The court considered her remarks to be "inciting hatred."[8]

Since the first edition, attempts to limit speech have grown into what some label cancel culture, yet has also created a backlash and an emerging free speech movement, creating various views among the public. According to a Pew Research Center poll in 2021,

> About two-thirds of U.S. adults (65%) say that "people being too easily offended" is a major problem in the country today, while a slimmer majority – 53% – say that "people saying offensive things to others" is a major problem.[9]

The American Revolution was born out of a desire for liberty, and this has been a defining principle of America for most of its history. If America is to remain faithful to the values that made so many people want to come here, liberty must once again become a dominant value.

---

7   Neil MacDonald, "Free speech, eh? Why is Canada prosecuting Mark Steyn?" *CBC News, June 13, 2008.* http://www.cbc.ca/world/story/|2008/ 06/13/f-rfa-macdonald.html (accessed April 3, 2009)

8   L.A. Unleashed, "French Court convicts Brigitte Bardot over animal-related remarks", *LA Times, June 4, 2008,* http://latimesblogs.latimes.com/unleashed/2008/06/french-court-co.html (accessed April 3, 2009)

9   J. Baxter Oliphant, "For many Americans, views of offensive speech aren't necessarily clear-cut." Pewresearch.org, December 14, 2021, https:// www.pewresearch.org/short-reads/2021/12/14/for-many-americans-views-of-offensive-speech-arent-necessarily-clear-cut/ (accessed December 5, 2023)

In God We Trust

Perhaps the most overtly challenged of the American Trinity is 'In God We Trust.' This first began appearing on coins during the Civil War. It served as one of two de facto mottoes for the country until Congress made its status official in 1956.

In Chapter Four, I discussed the importance of religion and its role in the country's founding, how that resulted in the original understanding of the First Amendment, and how, in recent years, that understanding changed in favor of the separation of church and state. As a result of this change to the Constitution, much debate and confusion has ensued over whether or not America is a Christian nation.

I did not address earlier why the Founding Fathers saw religion as necessary. The Founding Fathers understood that society needs some structure and control. This structure and control is what we generally call civilization as opposed to anarchy and barbarism. The Founders believed that religion played a vital role in providing this structure.

As Steven Waldman, author of *Founding Faith: Providence Politics and the Birth of Religious Freedom in America*, summarized the views of the Founding Fathers,

> They did want to encourage Religion. All the founders believed that the republic was not going to work unless you have a religiously vibrant society.[10]

The founders' view is well summed up in the Northwest Ordinance passed by the Congress of the Confederation the same year as the Constitution. Among its provisions were,

---

10   Christopher Quinn, "Author digs into founding father's view on religion, govt." Atlanta Journal-Constitution, 5/30/08, http://www.ajc.com/news/content/living/stories/2008/05/30/waldman_steven_religion.html (accessed April 3, 2009)

Religion, morality and knowledge being necessary to good government and the happiness of mankind, schools and the means of education shall forever be encouraged.[11]

Alexis de Tocqueville in *Democracy in America,* a book based on his study of the new government, noted the critical role religion plays in America as opposed to his country,

Upon my arrival in the United States, the religious aspect of the country was the first thing that struck my attention; and the longer I stayed there, the more did I perceive the great political consequences resulting from this state of things, to which I was unaccustomed. In France I had almost always seen the spirit of religion and the spirit of freedom pursuing courses diametrically opposed to each other; but in America I found that they were intimately united, and that they reigned in common over the same country.[12]

de Tocqueville also noted that,

The Americans combine the notions of Christianity and of liberty so intimately in their minds, that it is impossible to make them conceive the one without the other; and with them this conviction does not spring from that barren traditionary faith which seems to vegetate in the soul rather than to live.[13]

However, all this does not mean that the Founding Fathers wanted the government to be Christian. The history of Europe clearly showed the danger of intermixing religion and government too closely. As de Tocqueville also noted,

Religion in America takes no direct part in the government of society, but nevertheless it must be regarded as the foremost

---

11   Northwest Ordinance, Article 3, Archiving Early America http://www. earlyamerica.com/earlyamerica/milestones/ordinance/text.html (accessed April 3, 2009)

12   Alexis de Tocqueville, *Democracy in America, pg 332,* http://books.google.com/books?id=vPEtAAAAIAAJ&printsec=titlepage&-source=gbs_summary_r&cad=0#PPA332,M1 (accessed April 3, 2009)

13   Alexis de Tocqueville, Democracy in America, pg 329, http://books.google.com/books?id=vPEtAAAAIAAJ&printsec=titlepage&-source=gbs_summary_r&cad=0#PPA332,M1 (accessed April 3, 2009)

of the political institutions of that country; for if it does not impart a taste for freedom, it facilitates the use of free institutions.

Religion in America serves three essential functions in regards to democracy. The first is that it provided the intellectual foundation for the country, as stated by the Declaration of Independence. Remove the Declaration's claim that our rights come from our creator, and you have the question: Where do they come from?

Second, the more religion controls social conduct, the less government needs to control it. If religion does less, the only recourse is for the government to do more, which is precisely what we have seen with the explosion in the size of the government.

Finally, while it was true that the Founding Fathers feared establishing an official religion that would then use its favored position to limit and oppress other religions, they also stressed that the government would become too strong and oppressive. In short, they worried about anything that could restrict liberty.

In this light, the historical tensions that have always existed between religion and government would serve as an additional check on the government. It is not by accident that those seeking the most limits on religion often seek the most significant expansion of government.

This view of an America where religion is essential, strong, acknowledged, and yet was not established struck de Tocqueville. He saw an America where religion was an essential factor. Yet, people were free to choose any religion or even no religion.

Using their newly minted understanding of the First Amendment, courts started changing this view in the 1960s as they became increasingly hostile to any expression of religion. As pointed out earlier, the thoughts of many intellectual elites had changed from that of the Founding Fathers. Where religion was so important, it had to be protected, became one where religion was so dangerous, the government needed protection from religion.

Supporters of this new view, using their position of power, particularly in the courts, have pushed for a new view of America, an idea where secularism is the established belief system, and anything that conflicts with that belief system needs to be limited and suppressed, a view where, rather than important and robust, religion is weak and ignored.

Thus, the courts have limited public expressions of religion over the last few decades. The Bible and prayer in public schools were the first to go. But it has even reached the point where American history texts change to limit or remove the country's religious roots. Some now describe the Pilgrims as simply "people who take long trips" instead of a religious group. The first Thanksgiving was a celebration of the harvest that gave thanks to the Native Americans instead of to God.[14]

The ultimate symbolic expression of this drive to transform America into a completely secular state would be removing "In God We Trust" from our money and "One Nation Under God" from the pledge. While lawsuits have been filed to attempt this last change, they have failed.[15] With the new originalist majority, they are unlikely to win unless the courts change again.

E Pluribus Unum

The third part of the American Trinity, *E Pluribus Unum,* was the other de facto motto of the United States. It first began to appear on coins in 1795. It also appears on the Great Seal of the United States, created by Benjamin Franklin, John Adams, and Thomas Jefferson.[16]

---

14   Paul Vitz, *Censorship: Evidence of Bias in our Children's Textbooks* (Ann Arbor, MI, Servant Books, 1986), 18-19. In my college classes, I have sometimes asked students about this, and have found in my informal surveys that half of the students I had in Southern California were taught this new secular view.

15   AP, *Atheist challenges 'In God We Trust,' Nov 18, 2005,* http://www.msnbc.msn.com/id/10103424/ (accessed April 3, 2009)

16   United States Department of State, *The Great Seal of the United States, Sept 1996,* http://www.state.gov/www/publications/great_seal.pdf (accessed April 3, 2009).

Sadly, many today do not know the Latin words for "Out of many, One." Initially, the motto referred to the thirteen colonies becoming one nation. Still, as the new nation grew, it soon took on a broader meaning, representing that America is a nation of immigrants comprising people of many different backgrounds coming together to form a single unified country.

Nor was this an uncommon view at the time. Hector St. John de Crevecoeur, in his *Letters from an American Farmer* written in 1782, addressed the question of "What is an American?"[17] Even at this early date, when the new immigrants were primarily from Europe, the idea of many into one was strong.

Though his definition of an American was obviously limited to the immigrants of the time, it remained a reasonably accurate view, only needing revision to add the immigrants from other countries and regions of the world as they came. As such, it deserves quoting at some length.

> In this great American asylum, the poor of Europe have by some means met together, and in consequence of various causes...
>
> Formerly they were not numbered in any civil lists of their country, except in those of the poor; here they rank as citizens...
>
> I could point out to you a family whose grandfather was an Englishman, whose wife was Dutch, whose son married a French woman, and whose present four sons have now four wives of different nations. He is an American, who, leaving behind him all his ancient prejudices and manners, receives new ones from the new mode of life he has embraced, the new government he obeys, and the new rank he holds. He becomes an American by being received in the broad lap of our great Alma Mater. Here individuals of all nations are melted into a new race of men, whose labours and posterity will one day cause great changes in the world. Americans are the western pilgrims, who are carrying along with them that great mass of arts, sciences, vigour, and industry which

17 Hector St. John de Crevecoeur, Letters from an American Farmer, Project Gutenberg Literary Archive Foundation, http://www.gutenberg.org/dirs/etext03/lttaf10.txt (accessed April 3, 2009)

began long since in the east; they will finish the great circle. The Americans were once scattered all over Europe; here they are incorporated into one of the finest systems of population which has ever appeared, and which will hereafter become distinct by the power of the different climates they inhabit. The American ought therefore to love this country much better than that wherein either he or his forefathers were born. Here the rewards of his industry follow with equal steps the progress of his labour; his labour is founded on the basis of nature, SELF-INTEREST: can it want a stronger allurement? Wives and children, who before in vain demanded of him a morsel of bread, now, fat and frolicsome, gladly help their father to clear those fields whence exuberant crops are to arise to feed and to clothe them all; without any part being claimed, either by a despotic prince, a rich abbot, or a mighty lord. Here religion demands but little of him; a small voluntary salary to the minister, and gratitude to God; can he refuse these? The American is a new man, who acts upon new principles; he must therefore entertain new ideas, and form new opinions. From involuntary idleness, servile dependence, penury, and useless labour, he has passed to toils of a very different nature, rewarded by ample subsistence.–This is an American.

This view of many "melted into" one America remained strong and was eventually to be symbolized in a gift from France 100 years later. Initially created as a symbol of another American value, the placement of Liberty Enlightening the World, or as it is more commonly called the Statue of Liberty, in New York Harbor, gave it additional meaning, particularly with the inscription inside that included the lines,

> "Keep ancient lands, your storied pomp!" cries she
> With silent lips. "Give me your tired, your poor,
> Your huddled masses yearning to breathe free,
> The wretched refuse of your teeming shore.
> Send these, the homeless, tempest-tossed to me,
> I lift my lamp beside the golden door!"[18]

---

18   Emma Lazarus, *The New Colossus, http://www.nps.gov/archive/stli/ newcolossus/index.html* (accessed April 3, 2009)

Eventually, the idea came to be summed up in the term "The Melting Pot," coming from a popular play in 1912 by Israel Zangwill. Like the Statue of Liberty, Zangwill's play combined two of the three American values. Zangwill believed "God was using America as 'a crucible' to melt the 'fifty' barbarian tribes of Europe into a metal from which He can cast Americans."[19]

More recent critics have severely attacked the concept of the Melting Pot. Mark Penn, author of the book *Microtrends,* said,

> But most importantly, let's get over the melting pot myth. The truth is we're more like a Tower of Babel, doing remarkably well at communicating given the fact that U.S. residents today speak over 300 languages.[20]

It is true that over our history, not all groups have been warmly accepted into the pot, and some groups have faced outright hostility. But there is a vast difference between failing to achieve a goal and not having one in the first place. America has yet to reach its goal of a melting pot, but that does not mean that America did not have that goal. Many groups were resisted when they arrived, yet the country accepted them over time.

However, the real point here is not immigration. In *E Pluribus Unum,* immigration is the *E Pluribus* part. What is most threatened today is the *Unum,* the one. What is this 'One' that the immigrant should become? Just as Equality is replacing Liberty and secularism is replacing In God We Trust, starting in the 1980s, an opposing value started replacing *E Pluribus Unum:* multiculturalism.[21] Rather than the many becoming one, the many remain the many.

19   Ben Wattenberg, *The First Measured Century,* PBS, *http://www.pbs.org/ fmc/timeline/emeltpot.htm* (accessed April 3, 2009).

20   Mark Penn, Microtrends, as cited by Jim Geraghty, *The Campaign Spot, National Review Online, Oct 15, 2007*
http://campaignspot.nationalreview.com/post/?q=ZmQzYjMxMjZjOTEw-ZDIwMDgyNjczYjJiZjVhM2Y1NWU= (accessed April 3, 2009)

21   Gregory Jay, *What is Multiculturalism?,* University of Wisconsin- Milwaukee http://www.uwm.edu/~gjay/Multicult/whatismc.pdf (accessed April 3, 2009)

Drawing on the change from liberty to equality, the initial motives for multiculturalism came from recognizing that much of the traditional curriculum was 'Eurocentric' or, in more derisive terms, based on 'dead white men.' The conventional curriculum ignored the voices of women and people of color, so people began pushing for their inclusion into the process to bring about more equality.

Exploring the richness and diversity of all peoples and cultures would be wonderful. Few have any objection to this. The problem comes from two facts. First, there is a limited amount of time in the school day, and thus, there is not enough time to teach everything. Second, it is simply a historical fact that the history and culture of America have been primarily shaped and influenced by 'dead white men' in the traditional curriculum.

So, the first victim of multiculturalism is the truth. In their attempt to bring equality to the school curriculum, they must exaggerate the influence of people and groups that, however excellent and interesting, had little impact on America while downplaying those who had the most. It may not be fair, but it is what happened.

This problem is further compounded by another somewhat unrelated educational trend: the move more and more toward the visual. The result is that textbooks are filled with more charts, pictures, maps, and graphs, leaving less and less room for text. The remaining text is increasingly devoted to supporting the multicultural mandates imposed by many states.

Even worse, in an attempt to provide a more "balanced" view, the treatment of other cultures tends to be more positive. Lest we get an overly positive picture of the U.S., much of the remaining space is devoted to the problems and crimes of those dead white guys.

Recently, this change has generated a lot of controversy under the headings Diversity, Equity, and Inclusion (DE&I) and Critical Race Theory (CRT). Yet the roots go back decades. We can see this trend in a review of High School history textbooks done in 1989 that showed that the most space any textbook gave Lincoln was a mere six paragraphs.[22]

Often, the standards the textbooks must meet are the real problem. These are determined more by goals such as multiculturalism than the subject area itself. Thus, the initial National History Standards developed for the National Endowment for the Humanities by UCLA's National Center for History in the Schools, published in 1994, had the following questionable features:

- "George Washington makes only a fleeting appearance and is never described as our first president."[23]
- McCarthy has 19 references, the Ku Klux Klan 17, while Ulysses S. Grant has 1. People like Robert E. Lee, Alexander Graham Bell, Thomas Edison, Albert Einstein, Jonas Salk, and the Wright brothers get zero.[24]
- The treatment of Aztec culture stresses their architecture, skills, labor systems, and agriculture, with no mention of their human sacrifice.
- As a part of U.S. history, "students are encouraged to 'analyze the achievements and grandeur of Mansa Musa's court, and the social customs and wealth of the kingdom of Mali.'"[25]

---

22   Julie Johnson, "Teacher Union Faults History Books", Special to the New York Times, Sept 14, 1989.
http://query.nytimes.com/gst/fullpage.html?res=950DE1D9163DF937A2575AC0A96F948260&sec=&spon=&pagewanted=all (accessed April 3, 2009)
23   Lynne Cheney, *The End of History, Wall Street Journal*, Oct 20, 1994
http://www-personal.umich.edu/~mlassite/discussions261/cheney.html (accessed April 3, 2009)
24   Lynne Cheney, *The End of History, Wall Street Journal*, Oct 20, 1994
http://www-personal.umich.edu/~mlassite/discussions261/cheney.html (accessed April 3, 2009)
25   Lynne Cheney, *The End of History, Wall Street Journal*, Oct 20, 1994
http://www-personal.umich.edu/~mlassite/discussions261/cheney.html (accessed April 3, 2009)

As summarized by Diane Ravitch and Arthur Schlesinger, Jr.,

> We too were not satisfied with the standards. Each of us, in different settings, criticized them for their failure to balance *pluribus* and *unum* and to place the nation's democratic ideals at the center of its history.[26]

When commissioned, Lynne Cheney was chairman of the National Endowment for the Humanities, later becoming one of the study's greatest critics. Addressing the question of what went wrong, she cited one member of the National Council for History Standards who pointed to

> the forces of political correctness. According to this person, who wishes not to be named, those who were "pursuing the revisionist agenda" no longer bothered to conceal their "great hatred for traditional history."[27]

As a result of the uproar that accompanied the release of the Standards, the UCLA Center revised them. As Diane Ravitch and Arthur Schlesinger, Jr., wrote of the newly revised standards,

> Out went references to the grandeur of Mansa Musa and the fabled wealth of Mali; out went numerous references to the Ku Klux Klan; out went the excessive focus on Senator Joseph McCarthy. Out indeed went references to obscure people whose main credential seemed to be that they were not dead white males. The Constitution and the Bill of Rights are now the subject of a major standard, and America's developing democratic tradition.[28]

Yet, while suffering a setback, the forces behind the original standards did not go away. The pattern is clear. Push the new view until it generates controversy. If you lose, retreat a little, but once

26   Diane Ravitch and Arthur Schlesinger, Jr., *The New, Improved History Standards, Wall Street Journal, April 3, 1996.* http://www.edexcellence.net/ detail/news.cfm?news_id=75 (accessed April 3, 2009)

27   Lynne Cheney, *The End of History, Wall Street Journal, Oct 20, 1994* http://www-personal.umich.edu/~mlassite/discussions261/cheney.html (accessed April 3, 2009)

28   Diane Ravitch and Arthur Schlesinger, Jr., *The New, Improved History Standards, Wall Street Journal, April 3, 1996.* http://www.edexcellence.net/ detail/news.cfm?news_id=75 (accessed April 3, 2009)

the controversy subsides, push forward again. Thus, Multiculturalism still dominates academic circles and continues to shape and influence history textbooks. While the revised standards did deal with most of the objections, as Lynn Vincent, writing a couple of years after the release of the revised standards, noted,

> the "revision" turned out to be the academic equivalent of hiding the dirty pictures until mommy and daddy left the room. After removing much of the content critics found offensive, NCHS re-released the same material in a two-volume guide for teachers called *Bring History Alive*.[29]

Supporters of the new curriculum often distort the critics to the point of lying, claiming that they don't want students exposed to anything bad and instead want a "sugar-coated history." Thus, Gary Nash wrote defending the National History Standard,

> For the Cheney-led cohort, children who learn about the Ku Klux Klan and McCarthyism will not learn to love their country. It will embarrass and make cynics of them.[30]

This criticism ignores Cheney's praise for "Lessons From History" in the same article, which "is honest about the failings of the U.S."[31] The critics of the new view of American history do not want a sugar-coated view. As Bill Bennett summarized at the beginning of his two-volume history of America, one of the reasons he wrote the book was

> to tell the truth, get the facts out, correct the record, and put forward a reasoned, balanced presentation of the American

29   Lynn Vincent, *Whose Standards? Rejected revisionist history standards are finding their way through the back door of American education, World Magazine (Nov. 20, 1999)* http://www-personal.umich.edu/~mlassite/discussions261/vincent.html (accessed April 3, 2009)

30   Gary Nash, *Reflections on the National History Standards, National Forum (Summer 1997)* http://www-personal.umich.edu/~mlassite/discussions261/nash.html (accessed April 3, 2009)

31   Lynne Cheney, *The End of History, Wall Street Journal, Oct 20, 1994* http://www-personal.umich.edu/~mlassite/discussions261/cheney.html (accessed April 3, 2009)

Story. In this work, I will not try to cover up great wrongs. Injustices need sunlight – always, as Justice Brandeis said, the best disinfectant. I will try to paint America as Oliver Cromwell asked to be painted: warts and all. But I will not follow the fashion of some today who see America as nothing *but warts.*[32]

Ultimately, nothing reveals the effect of the new view of history better than the students themselves. Guidelines, curriculum, and textbooks are good, but what do students learn? Michael Barone summed up the situation,

> They learn that America had slavery and treated women unequally and that colonists and settlers behaved in beastly ways toward "Native Americans." They learn that military units were racially segregated in World War II and Japanese Americans interned. They end up not knowing whether the Civil War came before or after the American Revolution or who attacked Pearl Harbor.[33][272]

In a survey of teenagers about World War II, two-thirds knew about the Japanese Internment camps. At the same time, "only one-third could name even one World War II general, and about half could name a World War II battle."[34]

Nor is this just an issue of students who don't do well. One student interviewed received a B in history, yet when asked about World War II, she did not know what year it ended, could not name any general or battle, and did not even know who the Pres-

---

32   William J. Bennett, *America: The Last Best Hope, Volume 1, (New York: Nelson Current, 2006)*, xv
also *The Hill, July 13, 2006 William Bennett's history as moral reckoning,* http://thehill.com/bookshelf/william-bennetts-history-as-moral-reckoning-2006-07-13.html (accessed April 3, 2009)
33   Michael Barone, *Land of the Free, Claremont Institute, Fall 2007* http://www.claremont.org/publications/crb/id.1476/article_detail.asp (accessed April 3, 2009)
34   Jay Matthews, *A Battle on the WWII Knowledge Front, Washington Post,* May 28, 2004, B01 http://www.washingtonpost.com/ac2/wp-dyn/A61803-2004May27 (accessed April 3, 2009)

ident was during the war. Some answers: 1945; Eisenhower, Midway, Roosevelt.

However, she did remember details about the Japanese internment camps, for as she said, "We talked a lot about those concentration camps."[35] However, they evidently did not talk enough about them that she would know the difference between a concentration camp and an internment camp.[36]

What Can Be Done

The reason for all the conflict is simply that if American democracy is to survive, people will have to know what it is they are preserving. The current struggle is between two groups. On the one side are those who defend the traditional view of America, one based on the three values outlined here: liberty, in God We Trust, and *e pluribus unum*. On the other are those defending a new view of America centered around equality, secularism, and multiculturalism.

For America to survive, there must be a consensus on something. As Lincoln said when announcing his run for Senate, referencing the words of Jesus, "a house divided against itself cannot stand." America cannot be all things to all people if for no other reason than something that can mean anything, ultimately means nothing.

On a more practical note, democracy takes a lot of effort to maintain. Democracy could be termed a high-maintenance form of government. Many Americans have given, and continue to give, their lives defending this country. For people to put forth

---

35   Jay Matthews, *A Battle on the WWII Knowledge Front, Washington Post, May 28, 2004, B01* http://www.washingtonpost.com/ac2/wp-dyn/A61803-2004May27 (accessed April 3, 2009)

36   For those who claim there was no difference, consider this: How many people in Manzanar would willingly have accepted a transfer to a Nazi or Soviet concentration camp, seeing no difference? On the other hand, how many in a Nazi or Soviet concentration camp would have refused to go to Manzanar, seeing no difference?

the effort and sacrifice required to preserve and defend democracy, they must know what they are working and sacrificing for.

Another group consists of the apathetic. This group does not care enough one way or the other. If measured in terms of voter turnout, this group is the largest of all, for on average, only a little over half of those of voting age vote in a presidential year and a little over a third in non-presidential federal elections for the House and Senate.[37] The turnout is often lower for elections that are strictly state and local.

The best thing to happen would be a serious national discussion on what America is. What are the values that guide us? Will it continue to be Liberty? Or should we change to Equality? Will our motto continue to be "In God We Trust," or will secularism become the official government view? Will *E Pluribus Unum* be a guiding principle, or will multiculturalism become the new goal? Perhaps it will be some combination of the above or something new. However, it needs to be something.

Frankly, I think the debate would probably reach a consensus pretty quickly. However, it came out, at least there would be a clear view of what it means to be an American, and the Pluribus will once again be Unum. In that way, as Abraham Lincoln said in the Gettysburg Address,

> this nation, under God, shall have a new birth of freedom – and that government of the people, by the people, for the people, shall not perish from the earth.

---

37   infoplease.com, "National Voter Turnout in Federal Elections: 1960-2008" http://www.infoplease.com/ipa/A0781453.html (accessed April 3, 2009).

THE NEVER ENDING STRUGGLE

Give me Liberty, or give me Death

Patrick Henry

Patrick Henry was determined to stop the recently proposed Constitution. In his mind, it gave far too much power to the federal government and undermined the states, risking the liberty so recently won in the revolution. Worse still, it had no protection for individual rights.

Henry lost his first battle when Virginia became the tenth state to ratify the new Constitution by a vote of 89 to 79. Since the Constitution had gone into effect when New Hampshire had ratified it four days earlier, there was no way to stop the new government from forming.

Nevertheless, Henry – a brilliant orator and political leader – was not about to give up. Liberty was too essential. Henry could still derail the new government before it could take root by getting the new Congress to call for a second constitutional convention. This convention could make all the changes he believed were needed.

Those like James Madison, who had been at the first constitutional convention during the long, hot summer in 1787, abhorred the idea. They knew how difficult it had been to draft the first constitution, how hard-fought the debates, and how tenuous the compromises needed to get a majority. Even then, some of the delegates at the convention just left and never returned. Some who remained refused to sign the newly minted constitution.

With the hard-fought battles for ratification still fresh on everyone's mind, the delegates to any second constitutional convention would almost certainly have careful instructions on a whole range of issues, making compromise virtually impossible. A second convention would fail and only undermine the new constitution's authority just as it was going into effect.

Still, Henry was determined to get a second convention, and he had a two-part plan. First, he was going to use the concerns expressed by many about the new constitution, particularly its lack of protection for individual rights, to build support for a second convention in the upcoming elections for the new Congress.

There was a danger with this approach. In addition to calling for a new convention, Congress also had the power to propose amendments directly. Henry feared that if this happened, the amendments could deflate the desire for a second convention without making all the changes Henry and other anti-federalists believed were needed.[1]

The danger, however, seemed remote. Many of the strongest supporters of the new constitution rejected the need for any amendments, including even amendments securing individual rights. To them, amendments were unnecessary and possibly even dangerous. Madison, in a letter to Thomas Jefferson,

> offered up four reasons why he had "not viewed it in an important light": Rights not given up were reserved to the people; an

---

1   Richard E. Labunski, *James Madison and the struggle for the Bill of Rights*, Pg 236
http://books.google.com/books?id=JvmZbFMxCHsC&dq=James+Madison:+and+the+struggle+for+the+bill+of+rights&printsec=frontcover&source=bl&ots=dI81iA8ArY&sig=vZtu2c0ZXmACk4IILEhHmFLx-l2o&hl=en&ei=Q__dSpjPO8vAlAeM_oWoAw&sa=X&oi=book_result&ct=result&resnum=8&ved=0CCEQ6AEwBw#v=snippet&q=individual%20Rights&f=false

amendment on religious freedom and other subjects could be either too broad or too narrow and not offer sufficient protection to those rights; state governments would be "jealous" of the powers granted to the new federal government and would thus provide a check on its power "which had not existed" before; and a bill of rights might not be effective.[2]

Madison makes four points here. First, he believed the Constitution inherently left all rights with the people, except those powers expressly granted to the government, so there was no need for a list to restrict the federal government. The government could not do anything not explicitly granted by the Constitution.

Second, any list was bound to be incomplete. Rights would be left off. If the Constitution contained such a list, it would only be a matter of time before the only rights protected were those on the list. As such, a Bill of Rights would be counterproductive.

Third, since, in his view, the Constitution created a government of enumerated power, the power to do everything else remained with the people and their state governments. Madison believed that state governments would be very reluctant to relinquish this power and would jealously guard against any encroachment by the federal government.

Finally, suppose the government did not respect the limits imposed by the Constitution. Why would a bill of rights be any more effective?

Looking back, Madison's arguments have some merit, as rights today are generally limited to those specified in the Bill of Rights. However, the Supreme Court has added a few. Madison tried to address this concern with the last two amendments.

---

2   Richard E. Labunski, *James Madison and the struggle for the Bill of Rights,* Pg 236

http://books.google.com/books?id=JvmZbFMxCHsC&dq=James+Madison:+and+the+struggle+for+the+bill+of+rights&printsec=frontcover&source=bl&ots=dI81iA8ArY&sig=vZtu2c0ZXmACk4IILEhHmFLx-l2o&hl=en&ei=Q__dSpjPO8vAlAeM_oWoAw&sa=X&oi=book_result&ct=result&resnum=8&ved=0CCEQ6AEwBw#v=snippet&q=individual%20Rights&f=false

Amendment 9 - Other Rights Kept by the People
The enumeration in the Constitution of certain rights shall
not be construed to deny or disparage others retained by the
people.

Amendment 10 - Undelegated Powers Kept by the States and
the People
The powers not delegated to the United States by the Constitution, nor prohibited by it to the states, are reserved to the
states respectively, or to the people.

Where Madison was incorrect was in the ability of the states
to limit the federal government's powers to only those listed in the
Constitution. For example, today, the commerce clause provides
no significant limits and is sometimes called dormant. Even when
limits remain, the federal government has frequently found ways
around them.

For example, Congress does not have the power to set a national age limit for alcohol. That remains a state issue. Still, it used
its spending power to withhold highway funds from any state with
a drinking age below 21. At that point, all fifty states bowed to the
federal wishes rather than jealously guarding their power. Money
speaks, and the Federal Government has the money.

Still, this was all in the future. As Henry saw things, a new
convention was possible as long as supporters of the new Constitution maintained their resistance to any amendments. However,
to do any of this, Henry needed to be successful in the second part
of his plan: ensuring the elections of anti-federalist candidates to
the newly created Senate and House of Representatives. Above all,
Henry wanted to keep his nemesis, James Madison, out of Congress in all this.

The first round went to Henry. In the new Constitution, state
legislatures[3] chose Senators. Using his power in the General Assembly, which he dominated, Henry secured the appointment of

---

3   This was changed by the 17th amendment, which calls for Senators to
be elected by the people. It was ratified in 1913.

two solidly Anti-Federalist Senators. The House of Representatives was not so easy, as the people voted for representatives.

Still, Henry used his power to block Madison. Voting for representatives required congressional districts. Before "gerrymander" entered the lexicon, Henry created a district just for Madison from counties known as anti-federalist strongholds. To ensure that Madison did not try to run in another district, he pushed through a residency requirement to keep Madison in the district Henry had explicitly created to ensure his loss.

Still not content, Henry ensured Madison's election to the still-existing Continental Congress, knowing that it would mean Madison would have to be out of the state in the crucial time leading up to the elections for the new Congress.

Even then, Henry was not done. He passed a law preventing the new federal government from using state officials. This law meant the new federal government would need to hire people, which would cost more money. More money meant higher taxes, turning people against the new government. Finally, Henry recruited a stellar candidate to oppose Madison, James Monroe, who would later become America's fifth President. Henry got everything he wanted, his plan was coming together, and Madison's defeat seemed assured.

Yet, getting everything you want is not always a good thing. Henry had overplayed his hand. The shy and soft-spoken Madison despised campaigning. In the previous election, Madison was elected a delegate to the Richmond convention to consider ratification of the new Constitution. Still, he had only returned home to campaign the day before the election.

Because of Henry's efforts, friends and supporters were concerned. One day would not be enough, so they strongly and repeatedly wrote to Madison, warning him about Henry's plans and encouraging him to return home early to campaign. Madison eventually relented and came home five weeks before the election.

More importantly, Madison had a change of mind. Seeing the growing opposition, he feared the new Congress might actually call a second convention. Madison dropped his opposition to a Bill of Rights and favored adding one to the Constitution.

He campaigned on adding a bill of rights, which won over enough people to win the election. True to his word, once in Congress, he not only submitted but strenuously fought for and won passage of a series of amendments that Congress submitted to the states, which came to be called the Bill of Rights.[4]

Federalism Develops

Looking back some two hundred and thirty years later, the anti-federalists' concerns remain valid. While some of their concerns were unwarranted, others have come to pass. While so far, they were incorrect that the presidency would become a monarchy, it is more powerful. In 1973, historian Arthur Schlesinger Jr. wrote about this concern in *The Imperial Presidency*, warning,

> When the constitutional balance is upset in favor of presidential power and at the expense of presidential accountability, the presidency can be said to become imperial.[5]

Schlesinger saw this mainly as an issue of the Cold War and foreign policy. Still, the federal government's power in domestic affairs has also grown. The anti-federalists were correct that the new government would come to dominate the states.

They were also correct that the power of direct taxation would threaten the people's liberty. In fact, reading over the arguments made by anti-federalists such as Henry and then looking at where

---

4   Twelve amendments were proposed by Congress and submitted to the states. Only amendments 3-12 were ratified by the states to become the Bill of Rights. One of the other two became the 27th. See Elgin Hushbeck, *The United States Constitution: A History*, Energion Publications 2022

5   Arthur M. Schlesinger Jr., *The Imperial Presidency*, Mariner Books; Reprint edition, 2004

we are today, it is clear that, in many respects, the anti-federalists understated the problems.

On the other hand, as we have seen in chapters four and five, rather than the Constitution as written and ratified, much of this stems from changes to the Constitution and, more importantly, new understandings of the Constitution that have effectively rendered it and the Bill of Rights a vague outline to be filled in by the current majority of justices on the Supreme Court.

The Progressive Movement, starting in the early nineteenth century, openly rejected the country's founding principles.[6] Rather than a limited federal government constrained by checks and balances, they wanted a powerful government to get things done. Woodrow Wilson objected to the notion of checks and balances because the government was more like a living thing than a machine,

> No living thing can have its organs offset against each other, as checks, and live. On the contrary, its life is dependent upon their quick cooperation, their ready response to the commands of instinct or intelligence, their amicable community of purpose. Government is not a body of blind forces; it is a body of men... Their cooperation is indispensable, their warfare fatal. There can be no successful government without the intimate, instinctive coordination of the organs of life and action.[7]

As a result of these new views, we have significantly changed how our government works. Yet, however understated the threat to liberty from a robust federal government may have been, never has the threat been so significant as in the last twenty years.

With the housing bubble's collapse, the market turmoil, and the government's response, budget deficits that would have been

---

6   For a more detailed discussion of the many differences between the founders and Progressives and how the government has changed as a result, see: Elgin Hushbeck, *The United States Constitution: A History,* Energion Publications 2022

7   Woodrow Wilson, *Constitutional Government in the United States,* (New York: Columbia University Press, 1908), p 56-7

unimaginable a year or two earlier suddenly became the norm; many wondered what happened. This explosion of spending happened again with COVID-19.

The critical problem with the housing bubble and COVID-19 is that, at the time, few understood what was happening, and the issue was quickly politicized. In short, there was more finger-pointing than analysis. That both of these problems were significant issues during presidential election years only made things worse. Leaders did not know what to do except throw money at the problem, and throw they did.

As I updated this third edition, several unanswered questions remain surrounding COVID-19, and it remains a somewhat politicized issue. However, enough time has passed to better understand the housing bubble's origin and consequences.

The Housing Bubble

While complex topics can be challenging to discuss, the big-picture view of what happened with the Housing bubble is reasonably uncomplicated. If you have read this far, it will not be surprising that the roots of the housing bubble were significantly driven by government policies and actions, resulting from some of the issues discussed in earlier chapters.

These policies and actions have particular supporters and opponents; still, rather than Republicans and Democrats, a better way to view the participants in the housing bubble is between those who see solutions in government action and those who see government action as a last resort.

There is also the issue of actions leading to a problem and steps taken to mitigate a problem. Here, the conflict is often between short-term effects and long-term. Short-term concerns usually get the majority of the attention. Compounding this issue, long-term concerns are generally more abstract, even theoretical. Often, the attitude is: We will deal with that if and when the need arises. Still, as we will see shortly, attempts to deal with an immediate problem can lead to even more significant issues in the long term.

While both Republicans and Democrats were behind the policies, programs, and institutions leading to the housing bubble, it was not an equal distribution. It is simply a matter of the historical record that it was primarily Democrats who started and promoted the policies that led to the bubble and, near the end, blocked efforts at reform, allowing the problem to grow larger until the bubble burst, with the resulting financial turmoil.

Generally, a president has more power and influence during their first year in office than during the last few months of their eighth. This lack of authority was particularly true given that in the last two years of Bush's presidency, the Democrats controlled the Congress. So, nothing could happen without their approval.

In Obama's first year, Democrats held such strong majorities that they could pass any bill without Republican support. This majority was unusual. Republicans last had such control in 1923. From FDR to the 1960s, it was common for Democrats. Still, this happened last during Jimmy Carter's presidency in the 1970s.[8]

Thus, while the problems may not have started under President Obama, and we will see that the roots of the current troubles go back decades, Democrats, including then-Senator Obama, played a crucial role in the closing years of the Bush presidency.

In the earlier years of Bush's presidency, minority Democrats still held enough seats that under Senate rules, they could block any piece of legislation if they held together, which is how they blocked efforts at reform. When Obama became president, they played the dominant role as Republicans did not have the votes to stop anything until the election of Scott Brown to the Senate in early 2010. Still, as we will see, the fault was truly bi-partisan at a critical moment.

---

8   United States Senate, *Party Division in the Senate 1789-Present* http://www.senate.gov/pagelayout/history/one_item_and_teasers/partydiv. htm (accessed April 3, 2009)

So, what happened? First, we can dispense with the simplistic and mostly partisan attempts to blame Bush or Obama merely because the former was the president when this started or the latter was the president during some of the worst problems. Who happens to be the president at a given time is not an explanation for economic events. For a president to be responsible, there would have to be specific policies or actions on their part leading or directly contributing to the problems.

Because of this, I do not blame President Clinton for the recession that resulted from the collapse of the earlier Internet bubble, even though he was President from the formation of the bubble to when it popped. Presidents can affect the economy, but they cannot control it. When bubbles happen, they are often essentially, though not wholly, outside government control.

The reasons for economic bubbles are unique to the individual bubbles and may or may not involve the government. While theoretically, one could argue that the government was responsible for the Internet bubble because it created the Internet in the 1960s, I think that would be a stretch.

The Internet bubble occurred when markets confronted a significant new technology that everyone believed would be important. Yet few, if any, knew what to do with it. People invested expecting substantial returns. Before long, expectations exceeded reality, a virtual bubble definition, and one began. When reality did finally set in, the bubble collapsed. Clinton was president throughout this time, but he was hardly responsible for it.

The housing bubble had completely different roots going back long before Bush became president. The foundations for the housing bubble were in place when Bush started his presidency, waiting merely for something to trigger it. Ironically, as we shall see shortly, the collapse of the Internet bubble triggered the housing bubble. In the end, Bush was no more the cause of the housing bubble than Clinton was the cause of the Internet bubble. That does not absolve the government.

The roots of the bubble go back decades and stem from the issues discussed in this book, the desire for government planning, and the move to equality instead of liberty. Like so many government programs, it started with what seemed to be such good intentions.

Affordable Housing?

In the late 1970s, many thought it would be good for low-income families to purchase a home. At the time, and for many reasons, people were leaving cities for the suburbs. As cities deteriorated, it became increasingly difficult for middle and lower-income people to get loans for properties in these areas.

Both President Carter and the Congress of the time tended to see solutions in government. So, in 1977, they passed the Community Redevelopment Act, or CRA, to solve the problem. Under CRA, all banks insured by the FDIC, which is pretty much all banks, are evaluated and thereby encouraged,

> to help meet the credit needs of the local communities in which they are chartered consistent with the safe and sound operation of such institutions.[9]

Of course, the keywords here are "safe and sound." It is important to note at this point that the purpose of a bank is to make money, and one of their primary means is by loaning it out. Therefore, the banks already had a strong self-interest, a financial one, to make as many loans as they safely can, for the more safe loans they have, the more money they make.

If a bank failed to meet these new government expectations for "safe and sound," regulators could pressure the bank to conform. Presidents Reagan and the first Bush did not prioritize the CRA, so not much happened.

This policy changed when Clinton, another solutions-in-government guy, became president, and he began a significant push

9   Title VIII, Sec 802.(b) http://www.fdic.gov/regulations/laws/rules/6500-2515.html#6500hcda1977 (accessed Aug 7, 2009)

to use the CRA. The change became apparent when the Federal Reserve blocked Shawmut National's attempt to purchase another bank in 1993 because the bank did not meet these new expectations. The Fed's Board of Governors was not persuaded of the bank's compliance with the CRA despite loosening its lending requirements, allowing more "flexible income criteria" and smaller down payments as low as 2.5 percent.[10]

In a New York Times article on the rejection, a banking consultant said, "It clearly means they're taking a tougher attitude. We're going to see a great deal more of this type of pressure from banking authorities."[11] The "tougher attitude" involved pushing banks to make loans previously considered too risky. A banking analyst said, "The Fed is sending a strong signal to the banking industry that they're going to be looking at banks' lending practices, clearly Shawmut is being made a little bit of scapegoat." The bottom line was: make riskier loans or else.

To make matters worse, the Federal Reserve was not the only agency stepping up its scrutiny of banks because of the CRA. "The Justice Department, the Department of Housing and Urban Development, and banking regulators all promised to step up efforts."[12]

As a side note, this is one of the problems with so much government regulation. The CRA passed in 1977, but it was 15 years later when regulators really began to crack down. It would be an-

10   Steven Greenhouse, *Fed Stops Bank Merger; Cites Lending Concerns New Your Times, Nov 17, 1993* http://www.nytimes.com/1993/11/17/business/fed-stops-bank-merger-cites-lending-concerns.html (accessed May 12, 2010)
11   Steven Greenhouse, *Fed Stops Bank Merger; Cites Lending Concerns New Your Times, Nov 17, 1993* http://www.nytimes.com/1993/11/17/business/fed-stops-bank-merger-cites-lending-concerns.html (accessed May 12, 2010)
12   John Carney, *Sorry, Folks, The CRA Really Did Require Crap Lending Standards, The Business Insider, Clusterstock, Jun 23, 2009,* http://www.businessinsider.com/sorry-folks-the-cra-really-did-require-crap-lending-standards-2009-6 (accessed May 12, 2010)

other 15 years before the full effect became apparent. When the problems occurred, how many people remembered the 1977 law or the 1993 beginning of the crackdown? All they see is the problem. Thus, there is a fundamental disconnect between the passage of legislation and its adverse effects.

As I pointed out in chapter three, the failure of government planning and control typically results in not abandoning the effort but its redoubling. This result is what happened here as well. In 1995, the government issued new regulations, that is, more controls, requiring banks to show that they actually made a certain number of loans in the groups formerly considered high risk. To achieve this, the CRA's "safe and sound" in the new regulation effectively became "innovative or flexible."[13]

Still, the law did not have the desired effect even with the stepped-up enforcement. One problem was that mortgage rates remained high, at least by more recent standards. These high rates meant payments were still too high for many in the high-risk group. In addition, while down payments were being forced lower, they still required people to come up with significant amounts of cash.

On top of all this, there was still the factor of risk. Qualifying for a loan is the bank's way of reducing the risk that the borrower will default. While the federal government was pushing banks to weaken those standards, thereby increasing the risks, the banks would still suffer from any loss at the end of the day.

Fannie and Freddie

The Federal National Mortgage Association, aka Fannie Mae, is one of the legacies of FDR's New Deal and was created to help local banks make home loans by creating a secondary mortgage market. In simple terms, the US government borrowed money at

---

13   Directory, Department of the Treasury, To the Chief Executive Officer of the Saving Association Addressed, May 16, 1995 http://files.ots.treas. gov/25039.pdf (accessed May 12, 2010)

a very low rate, which it used to provide home loans at a rate lower than would otherwise be available. In the 1960s, the government privatized Fannie Mae, at least somewhat. Since Fannie Mae held a virtual monopoly, the government created the Federal Home Mortgage Corporation, a.k.a. Freddie Mac, to provide some competition.

While Fannie and Freddie are technically private corporations, they are still government-sponsored enterprises and, as such, not completely private. Their links to the federal government still allowed them to borrow at very favorable rates, as many assumed that since the federal government sponsored them, it still backed them.

In addition, they received special treatment and exemptions from the laws. For example, while both were Fortune 500 companies, they were the only two allowed to hide any financial difficulties from the public.[14]

With their ties to government, it is unsurprising that the Boards of Directors of Fannie and Freddie had so many people involved in politics they were "a political organization that happened to be in the mortgage business."[15] These organizations maintained their position by hiring "well-placed politicos for big salaries."[16] As a result, they became, as the Wall Street Journal called them, "a relentless and untouchable political force."[17]

---

14   Rob Alford, *What are the Origins of Freddie Mac and Fannie Mae? History News Network, Dec 9, 03* http://hnn.us/articles/1849.html (accessed May 12, 2010)

15   Peter Overby, *How Fannie, Freddie Became Kings of the Hill, NPR, July 15, 2008* http://www.npr.org/templates/story/story.php?storyId=92540620 (accessed May 12, 2010

16   Peter Overby, *How Fannie, Freddie Became Kings of the Hill, NPR, July 15, 2008* http://www.npr.org/templates/story/story.php?storyId=92540620 (accessed May 12, 2010

17   Paul Gigot, *The Fannie Mae Gang, Wall Street Journal, July 23, 2008*, pg A17, http://online.wsj.com/article/SB121677050160675397.html (accessed May 12, 2010)

In the early 1990s, Fannie and Freddie joined the push for affordable housing. In response, they began changing the standards for the loans they underwrite to reflect the CRA regulations' more "innovative or flexible" criteria. By 2001, they were underwriting loans with no down payment at all.

As the Clinton administration was ending, several administration officials landed jobs at Fannie Mae.[18] Franklin Raines, the director of the Office of Management and Budget during the Clinton administration, became Fannie Mae's chairman and chief executive officer, for which he was paid $90 million in six years.[19] Jamie Gorelick, a deputy Attorney General under Clinton, landed a job as vice chairman and was paid over $26 million.[20]

Republicans were involved as well, but Democrats held the key positions. More importantly, they protected their own when people started asking questions about Freddie and Fannie. They also blocked efforts at reform that might have avoided, or at least lessened, the problems of the housing collapse.

The enlistment of Fannie and Freddie solved the risk issue, or so it seemed. Banks and other lenders were free to follow the new "innovative or flexible" lending practices demanded by the CRA with the loans purchased by Fannie and Freddie. Fannie and Freddie, and thereby the Federal Government, would bear the risk, not the banks making the loans.

In case this was not enough of an incentive for the banks, Freddie and Fannie went even further. They required that a certain percentage of the loans they purchased be from groups targeted by the CRA. In short, if you wanted to be in the home loan business

---

18   Jack Shafer, *Fannie Mae and the Vast Bipartisan Conspiracy. Slate*, Sept 16, *2008*, http://www.slate.com/id/2200160/   (accessed May 12, 2010)
19   Bruce Feirstien, *100 To Blame, Vanity Fair*, *Sept 16, 2009*
http://www.vanityfair.com/online/politics/2009/09/100-to-blame-goldman-sachs-goody-bags-and-more.html (accessed May 12, 2010)
20   Bruce Feirstien, *100 To Blame, Vanity Fair*, *Sept 16, 2009*
http://www.vanityfair.com/online/politics/2009/09/100-to-blame-goldman-sachs-goody-bags-and-more.html (accessed May 12, 2010)

from the 1990s forward, you pretty much had to make these risky loans. By the time the party was coming to an end in 2007,

> Fannie and Freddie were required to show that 55 percent of their mortgage purchases were LMI (Low-and Moderate-Income) loans and, within that goal, 38 percent of all purchases were to come from underserved areas (usually inner cities) and 25 percent were to be loans to low-income and very-low-income borrowers.[21]

Still, that was in the future. By the turn of the century, the foundations for the bubble were in place, and all that remained was for something to trigger it. The trigger was the collapse of the Internet bubble. In addition to destroying a great deal of wealth, this collapse had two critical side effects that launched the housing bubble.

First, the Internet bubble collapse left the people who still had some money looking for someplace they could put it. Second, in response to the recession that followed the collapse, the Federal Reserve Board lowered interest rates to historically low levels.

Thus, there were all these new ways to borrow money for a house, many with no down payment, historically low interest rates, and many people looking for someplace to put their money. People began to move their money into the housing market.

With more buyers than sellers, prices rose quickly, making the housing market look even better and causing even more people to enter. At the same time, people set up businesses to effectively lend out Fannie's and Freddie's money. It was a classic bubble.

The story gets very complex at this point, particularly with all the financial instruments developed to fund the growing bubble. Many point to these financial instruments as the real problem. There, indeed, was the greed and questionable practices typical of a bubble. Yet these explain the growth of a bubble, not its origin.

---

21   Peter J. Wallison, *The True Origins of This Financial Crisis, The American Spectator, Feb 2009,* http://spectator.org/archives/2009/02/06/the-true-origins-of-this-finan/ (accessed May 12, 2010)

What is central here is that most of this would not have existed had there not been a housing bubble in the first place.[22] They were a result of the bubble, not its cause. The housing bubble came from the government's attempt to influence the housing market to provide more affordable housing in disadvantaged areas by pushing lenders to make what had formally been considered risky loans. Banks and Financial institutions responded to this pressure by creating new and innovative ways to borrow, leading to a bubble.

Warning Flags

As in most things, there are some good guys and some villains, with plenty of finger-pointing and enough blame to go around, though not as equally as some would have you believe. A few were trying to raise warning flags. The Wall Street Journal had long warned of problems at Freddie and Fannie. In early 2002, after detailing the growing risk, they wrote,

> We aren't trying to scare readers here, and perhaps all of these concerns will come to nothing… Then again, unlike Enron, where only shareholders got taken to the cleaners, in the case of Fannie and Freddie taxpayers will take any bath. Maybe this time Congress should hold hearings before things go wrong.[23]

---

22   Many people point to some of the effects of the bubble as the real cause of the problem. This is, for the most part, merely another manifestation of the failure of planning being found in the lack of planning, as can be seen in the resulting calls for even more regulations, i.e., controls.
John Carney initially opposed the idea that the CRA was at the heart of the problem but changes his mind after reviewing the evidence. He compiled a summary of the charges made by those defending the CRA.
John Carney, *Here's How The Community Reinvestment Act Led To The Housing Bubble's Lax Lending, The Business Insider, Clusterstock, Jun 27, 2009,* http://www.businessinsider.com/the-cra-debate-a-users-guide-2009-6 (accessed May 12, 2010)
23   *Fannie Mae Enron?, Wall Street Journal, Review & Outlook, Feb 20, 2002,* http://online.wsj.com/article/SB1014169323358510560.html (accessed May 12, 2010)

After three months in office, President Bush warned that Freddie and Fannie were "a potential problem."[24] Throughout his Presidency, while supporting the goals of affordable housing, he and those in his administration frequently pointed to potential and actual problems at these companies and called for reform.

In 2003, the Bush administration recommended what the New York Times called "the most significant regulatory overhaul in the housing finance industry since the savings and loan crisis a decade ago."[25] Democrats blocked these efforts at reform and portrayed them as an attack on the CRA's goal of affordable housing. Representative Barney Frank echoed the concern of many Democrats, saying,

> These two entities -- Fannie Mae and Freddie Mac -- are not facing any kind of financial crisis... The more people exaggerate these problems, the more pressure there is on these companies, the less we will see in terms of affordable housing.[26]

Still, the warnings continued. Following the disclosure of "a series of questionable accounting practices that led to an overstatement of its earnings and an understatement of its risk,"[27] 2005-2006 saw a second significant effort to avoid the growing problems at Freddie and Fannie before they got out of hand. An editorial in

---

24   Jim Hoft, *Bush Called for Reform of Fannie Mae & Freddie Mac 17 Times in 2008 Alone… Dems Ignored Warnings, First Things, Sept 21, 2008,* http:// gatewaypundit.firstthings.com/2008/09/bush-called-for-reform-of-fannie-mae-freddie-mac-17-times-in-2008-alone-dems-ignored-warnings/ (accessed May 12, 2010)

25   Stephen Labaton, *New Agency Proposed to Oversee Freddie Mac and Fannie Mae, New York Times, Sept 11, 2003,* http://www.nytimes. com/2003/09/11/business/new-agency-proposed-to-oversee-freddie-mac-and-fannie-mae.html?sec=&spon=&pagewanted=print (accessed May 12, 2010)

26   Stephen Labaton, *New Agency Proposed to Oversee Freddie Mac and Fannie Mae, New York Times, Sept 11, 2003,* http://www.nytimes. com/2003/09/11/business/new-agency-proposed-to-oversee-freddie-mac-and-fannie-mae.html?sec=&spon=&pagewanted=print (accessed May 12, 2010)

27   Ronald D. Utt, *Time to Reform Fannie Mae and Freddie Mac, The Heritage Foundation, June 20, 2005* http://www.heritage.org/Research/GovernmentReform/bg1861.cfm (accessed May 12, 2010)

the Wall Street Journal later described it, "In light of the current financial crisis, this bill was probably the most important piece of financial regulation before Congress in 2005 and 2006."[28]

The bill passed the House, but only after adding yet another program to push affordable housing.[29] From there, it went to the Senate. It passed out of committee on a party-line vote, with Republicans supporting the bill. Given the narrow margins in the Senate, Democrats kept the bill from coming to a vote on the floor.[30] When the Democrats won back control of Congress in 2006, any hope of reform vanished, and by then, the bubble was beginning to burst.

In 2003, the Housing bubble was still relatively small. At that time, less than eight percent of Fannie's and Freddie's loans fell into the high-risk categories.[31] By 2005, 14 percent of the Freddie and Fannie business involved risky loans, which grew to a third by 2008. Yet, even with this considerable growth, they still "missed government-mandated affordable housing goals in 2007."[32] The sad fact is that the very areas the CRA was supposed to help have been some of the hardest hit due to the bubble's collapse.

---

28   Charles W. Calomiris and Peter J. Wallison, *Blame Fannie Mae and Congress for the Credit Mess, Wall Street Journal*, Sept 23, 2008, A29 http://online. wsj.com/article/SB122212948811465427.html (accessed May 12, 2010)
29   *Fannie Mae's House, Wall Street Journal, Review and Outlook, Oct 25, 2005, p A20*, http://online.wsj.com/article/SB113020760654078447.html (accessed May 12, 2010)
30   Charles W. Calomiris and Peter J. Wallison, *Blame Fannie Mae and Congress for the Credit Mess, Wall Street Journal*, Sept 23, 2008, A29 http://online. wsj.com/article/SB122212948811465427.html (accessed May 12, 2010)
31   Charles W. Calomiris and Peter J. Wallison, *Blame Fannie Mae and Congress for the Credit Mess, Wall Street Journal*, Sept 23, 2008, A29 http://online. wsj.com/article/SB122212948811465427.html (accessed May 12, 2010)
32   Zachary A. Goldfarb, *Affordable-Housing Goals Scaled Back, Washington Post, Sept 24, 2008.* http://www.washingtonpost.com/wp-dyn/content/article/2008/09/23/AR2008092301718.html (accessed May 12, 2010)

Pop!

By the end of 2005, housing prices peaked and began to decline. Throughout 2006, the inventory of unsold homes increased. By 2007, housing prices were falling rapidly. The bubble had burst, even though Fannie and Freddie were still pushing risky loans.

As economic problems spread, politicians predictably began pointing fingers and promising help. For the most part, this was all just a typical aftermath of a financial bubble, not all that much different from the bubbles that had preceded it. But things were not the same as in past economic downturns. There were two significant differences.

The first was the innovations that affected how Freddie and Fannie raised the money to fund their loans. In simple terms, Freddie and Fannie bought home loans, bundled them up, and resold them as mortgage-backed securities, which sold quite well because of the bubble.

Compounding the problem, it was unclear whether the federal government backed these securities since it had established Freddie and Fannie. As an article written in 2003 put it,

> In the event that there was some sort of financial collapse within either of these companies, U.S. taxpayers could be held responsible for hundreds of billions of dollars in outstanding debts.[33]

The net result was that Fannie and Freddie were selling these securities. Investors were not examining them as closely as they otherwise might have because of the special exemptions given to Fannie and Freddie in the reporting laws and because many believed that the U.S. Government backed them in any event. How were these to be rated, given the ambiguity?

Most did not worry about this during the good times; such is the nature of a bubble. Because of the bundling of loans, when the

---

33   Rob Alford, *What are the Origins of Freddie Mac and Fannie Mae? History News Network, Dec 9, 03* http://hnn.us/articles/1849.html (accessed May 12, 2010)

bubble burst, and housing prices fell, it was hard to tell what these securities were worth. How many high-risk loans did any given bundle have? With all the uncertainty, few, if any, were willing to purchase them, bringing us to the second difference.

Mark To Market

The second significant difference was an accounting principle called Mark to Market or MTM (aka Fair Value Accounting). Mark to Market is simply an accounting rule that says the value of something should be set at its current value if you sold it. This principle seems like a common sense rule and normally causes few problems in a stable market. However, it has a particularly nasty danger that manifests itself in declining markets.

To understand the danger, suppose you have a long-term asset, such as a stock or factory, producing income for you. Then there is a recession. Even with the recession, your asset is still producing revenue similar to what it has been, so you might think there is no problem, and at least not much has changed for you.

However, with MTM, even though you are not planning to sell the asset and it is still producing income, its value is what it would be if you were trying to sell it. Thus, on paper, you could suddenly "lose" a lot of money even though, in reality, little has changed.

For an individual, this is bad enough; for a corporation, this can be very serious, as it affects the company's bottom line, making it appear like it is suddenly losing a lot of money. This situation is doubly worse for financial institutions that are required to maintain a minimum level of readily accessible assets.

If counted as part of the minimum asset requirements, their sudden devaluation could put the institution in trouble. Yet, the appearance of losing money makes it extremely difficult to raise additional capital to replace them. As these paper losses begin to ripple throughout the economy, they have a cascading effect, driving losses ever higher and higher.

MTM was in effect during the Great Depression, and economist Milton Friedman cited this as a critical factor in why the depression lasted so long. FDR evidently also came to believe this, for he finally suspended it in 1938.[34] But, like a monster in some bad horror movie, MTM was not completely dead.

One thing that is clear in history is that economies go up and down. While the government plays an important role and can help this, their propensity to harm is much greater than their ability to help. Yet, this does not stop politicians, particularly those who tend to see solutions in government action, from attempting to score a few points by claiming to "fix" the problems that caused whatever is behind the then-current financial crisis.

A case in point would be the aftermath of the Internet bubble. It is much easier to hide financial problems during good times than bad. Because of this, following any economic downturn, particularly a bubble, there will be a shake out of those who had played fast and loose when things were looking up. The Internet bubble was no different, and following the collapse, many asked questions about what failed companies had been worth. In addition, many called to "fix" things.

As a result, the U.S. Financial Accounting Standards Board issued Rule 157, which basically reinstated MTM starting on Nov 15, 2007. After that date, when a company started its fiscal year, it had to start using MTM. It could not have happened at a worse time.

The problem was that although most homeowners were still paying their mortgages and not in trouble, nobody purchased mortgage-backed securities because of the housing market's collapse. Under the old accounting rules, a mortgage back security with 97 percent of its borrowers still making payments may have been rated very close to its face value. Because of short-term

---

34   Brian S. Wesbury and Robert Stein, *Why Mark-To-Market Accounting Rules Must Die, Forbes.com, Feb 24, 2009.* http://www.forbes.com/2009/02/23/mark-to-market-opinions-columnists_recovery_stimulus.html (accessed May 12, 2010)

market conditions, the companies holding those securities had to record them on their books as essentially worthless. The net result was tens of billions of dollars in losses, not actual dollar losses, but losses on paper simply because of a change in the accounting rules.[35]

As in the 1930s, this started a ripple effect throughout 2008 as more and more companies began their fiscal year and fell under the new regulations, thereby having to report huge losses. What had been a problem with mortgages became a problem for mortgage-backed securities and those institutions that held them, particularly for the institutions that depended on them. As a GAO report summarized it,

> Some institutions found themselves so exposed that they were threatened with failure—and some failed—because they were unable to raise the necessary capital as the value of their portfolios declined. Other institutions, ranging from government-sponsored enterprises such as Fannie Mae and Freddie Mac to Wall Street firms, were left holding "toxic" mortgages that became increasingly difficult to value, were illiquid, and potentially had little worth.[36]

Again, this was of little worth in the short term. Since many of these institutions were financial institutions, a side effect of MTM was that doubts spread about the financial system as a whole, and, as the GAO reported, investors

> became reluctant to buy securities backed by many types of assets. Because of uncertainty about the financial condition and solvency of financial entities, the prices banks charged each other for funds rose dramatically, and interbank lending effectively came to a halt. The resulting credit crunch made the financing on which businesses and individuals depend in-

---

35   Matt Hudgins, FASB 157:Warning Light or Smoking Gun, National Real Estate Investor, Oct 7, 2008, http://nreionline.com/finance/news/FASB_ Warning_light_smoking_gun_1007/ (accessed May 12, 2010)

36   *GAO-09-161 Trouble Asset Relief Program,* http://www.gao.gov/new. items/d09161.pdf (accessed May 12, 2010)

creasingly difficult to obtain as cash-strapped banks held onto their assets.[37]

In short, MTM took what had been a severe problem and threatened to make it a catastrophe by putting the entire economic system into a tailspin. By September 2008, something had to be done. While some were calling for the repeal of MTM,[38] those in government rarely looked for such solutions. Instead, they looked to see how the government could do more, how the government could 'fix' things.

If these assets were poisoning the system, the solution was to get them out. So, as Treasury Secretary Henry Paulson put it, "The federal government must implement a program to remove these illiquid assets that are weighing down our financial institutions and threatening our economy."[39] Thus, the Troubled Asset Relief Program.

TARP

The Troubled Asset Relief Program, or TARP, was truly a bi-partisan effort. President Bush, who has always been somewhat of a solutions-in-government guy, obviously supported the program as his Treasury Secretary backed it. Both presidential candidates, Obama and McCain, and solutions-in-government supporters likewise endorsed the bill. The final vote in the Senate had

37   *GAO-09-161 Trouble Asset Relief Program,* http://www.gao.gov/new. items/d09161.pdf (accessed May 12, 2010)

38   For example, see John Berlau, *Maybe the Banks Are Just Counting Wrong. Wall Street Journal, Sept 20, 2008, pg A15* http://online.wsj.com/article/ SB122186515562158671.html?mod=djemEditorialPage   (accessed May 12, 2010)

And

William M. Issac, *How to Save the Financial System. Wall Street Journal, Sept 19, 2008, pg A23* http://online.wsj.com/article/SB122178603685354943. html?mod=djemEditorialPage   (accessed May 12, 2010)

39   *Statement by Secretary Henry M. Paulson, Jr. on Comprehensive Approach to Market Developments, Sept 19, 2008, hp-1149* http://www.ustreas.gov/press/ releases/hp1149.htm   (accessed May 12, 2010)

39 Democrats and 34 Republicans voting in favor of the $700 billion bill. At the same time, 172 Democrats supported it in the House, along with 91 Republicans.

While TARP started as an attempt to buy toxic assets, freeing up credit markets to begin lending again, it quickly morphed into an effort to prop up banks by purchasing stock. It then went on to "prop up automotive giants General Motors Corp and Chrysler and bailout American International Group."[40] Not too surprisingly, since it did not address the problem of the MTM accounting rule, it did not have the desired effect. Rather than increasing their lending,

> Ten of the 13 big beneficiaries of the Treasury Department's Troubled Asset Relief Program, or TARP, saw their outstanding loan balances decline by a total of about $46 billion, or 1.4%, between the third and fourth quarters of 2008.[41]

Three months later, support for the bailout had cooled considerably. With little time left in his presidency, Bush deferred to Obama, by then the President-elect, the decision on what to do with the remaining $350 billion left in the TARP program. At Obama's behest, the Senate approved releasing the second half of the funds in a vote called "a decisive and hard-fought victory for President-elect Barack Obama."[42]

Failure begets Failure

I wrote in the introduction to this book, purely as a hypothetical,

---

40   UPI, TARP sets sights on original purpose, Sept 29, 2009 http://www.upi.com/Business_News/2009/09/29/TARP-sets-sights-on-original-purpose/UPI-83891254240102/ (accessed May 12, 2010)

41   David Enrich, *Lending Drops at Big U.S. Banks, Wall Street Journal, Jan 26, 2009,* http://online.wsj.com/article/SB123293041915314113.html?mod=djemalertNEWS (accessed May 12, 2010)

42   Jonathan Karl, *Obama Wins $350B Senate TARP Vote, ABC News, Jan 15, 2009.* http://abcnews.go.com/Politics/Economy/story?id=6654133&page=1&page=1 (accessed May 12, 2010)

The apparent problem may be a severe economic slowdown, with the voters demanding more government intervention to fix it. Yet, suppose government intervention caused the problem in the first place. In that case, more government intervention will only exacerbate the situation, leading to more demands for more intervention.

In the chapter on planning and control, I wrote that the failure of government planning typically results in even more government planning. This result pretty much summarizes the financial problems of the housing bubble. The government attempts to fix a problem but instead causes new problems, which it then tries to resolve, causing even more problems.

The government wanted more equality in home ownership. Hence, it attempted to control how financial institutions made home mortgages to achieve that goal. Supporters accused those warning about problems of being against equality.[43] The result was the housing bubble. The attempts to 'fix' the previous Internet bubble with MTM further exacerbated the economic downturn, risking the collapse of the credit markets.

In response to the resulting credit crunch, the government passed TARP, authorizing up to $700 billion to fix that problem. When that didn't work, and the economy continued declining, they passed a $787 billion stimulus bill along with an omnibus

43   Nancy Pelosi, Barney Frank, and Democrats are Clueless on Freddie Mac Fannie Mae and the financial credit crisis. http://www.youtube.com/watch?v=hxMInSfanqg (accessed May 12, 2010)
Explosive Video, Fannie Mae CEO calling Obama and the Dems the "Family" and "Conscience" of Fannie Mae
http://www.youtube.com/watch?v=usvG-s_Ssb0&NR=1 (accessed May 12, 2010)
Shocking Video Unearthed Democrats in their own words Covering up the Fannie Mae, Freddie Mac Scam that caused our Economic Crisis http://www.youtube.com/watch?v=_MGT_cSi7Rs&annotation_id=annotation_443797&feature=iv (accessed May 12, 2010) Who is Responsible? (Meltdown): Fannie Mae - Freddie Mac - Wall Street - Bill Clinton - George Bush?
http://www.youtube.com/watch?v=RYz1rbB5V1s (accessed May 12, 2010)

spending bill in a further attempt to spur growth. When that didn't work, politicians began discussing a second TARP or another stimulus bill.

Meanwhile, though somewhat quietly, it would seem that eventually, some did wake up to the problem of MTM accounting. In March 2009, the Financial Accounting Standard Board announced[44] that it was moving away from MTM and did so the following month.[45]

The market reaction to this change was evident. As shown in Figure 11.1,[46] before the shift to Mark-To-Market, the Stock market was pretty level throughout most of 2007. Once MTM began phasing in starting Nov 15, 2007, the stock market began its decline, bottoming out almost to the day of the FSAB announcement of MTM's forthcoming end. One can only speculate what would have happened if the government had repealed MTM in September 2008 instead of passing TARP, or better yet, it had never taken effect in the first place.

The Aftermath

Unfortunately, by April 2009 and the repeal of MTM, the housing bubble, its collapse, and the attempts to fix it had already caused much of the damage. Not only were billions of dollars lost, but the federal government deficit soared to a record 1.41 trillion dollars.

To put this in perspective, this was more than the government's total spending each year, as recently as 1993, and was nearly ten times the budget deficit in 2007 (162 billion). Over the next ten years, the administration predicted adding about $9 trillion to

44   Frank Ahrens, *FASB Head: Mark-to-Market Relaxation Within Three Weeks, The Ticker, The Washington Post, March 12, 2009.*
45   Kara Scannell, *FASB Eases Mark-to-Market Rules, Wall Street Journal, April 2, 2009* http://online.wsj.com/article/SB123867739560682309.html (accessed May 12, 2010)
46   Chart based on data from Yahoo Finance http://finance.yahoo.com

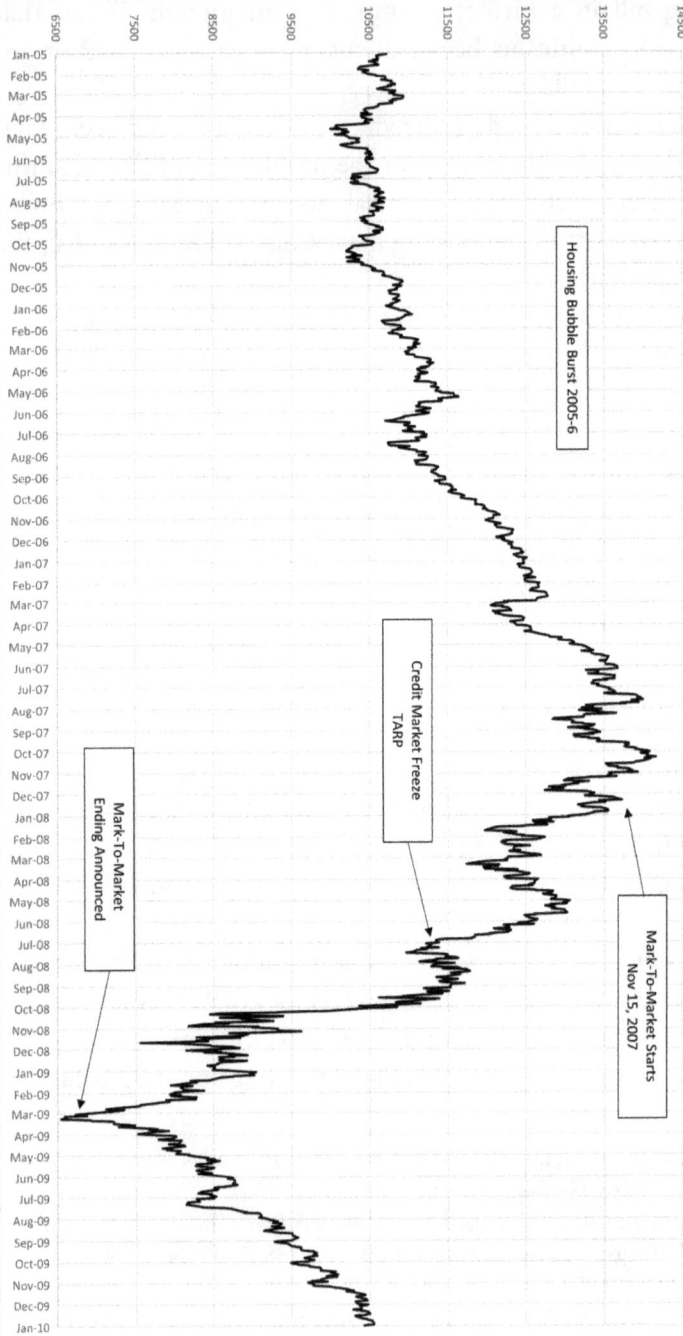

The Dow and Mark-To-Market
Figure 11.1

Housing Bubble Burst 2005-6

Credit Market Freeze
TARP

Mark-To-Market Starts
Nov 15, 2007

Mark-To-Market
Ending Announced

the national debt.[47] Even if their estimates were correct, the lowest deficit would still be higher than before 2009. As it turned out, from 2010 to 2019, the Federal government added $10.8 trillion to the debt, $1.8 trillion higher than predicted, with the lowest yearly deficit occurring in 2015 with $442 billion, nearly three times the recent low in 2007.

The consistent pattern we saw in Chapter Two repeated, and the deficit began to climb. In 2019, the year before COVID-19, it had reached $918 billion. With the pandemic, it soared again to a previously unimaginable high. 2020 saw a budget deficit of $3.1 trillion, which dropped to $2.8 trillion in 2021. As the pandemic ended, it dropped down to 1.3 trillion in 2022. The Congressional Budget Office's current projections increase yearly until 2033, when it will reach $2.8 trillion again. By that time, the federal debt will exceed $50 trillion.

These numbers are truly staggering and beyond any real comprehension. Even though beyond comprehension, the threat they pose is nevertheless very real. A 2010 study by Charles K Rowley, the Duncan Black Professor of Economics at George Mason University, and Nathanael Smith of The Locke Institute concluded that,

> The prognosis is catastrophic if projected government policies are not cut back. According to the White House's own estimates, the federal budget deficit in 2009 will be $1.6 trillion, approximately 11.2pc of the overall economy, the highest on record since the end of the Second World War. In 2019, the national debt will represent 76.5pc of the US national economy, the highest proportion since just after the Second World War. In such circumstances, the international reserve status of the US dollar will not survive. As it fades, so interest rates on government securities will rise and the real burden of servicing the debt will increase. In such circumstances, the US economy will teeter on the edge of a black hole.[48]

47   Jeff Mason, *CBO: 2009 Deficit Down, 10-year up by $2 Trillion,* *Reuters, Aug 24, 2009* http://www.dollarsandsense.org/blog/2009/08/cbo-2009-deficit-down-10-year-up-by-2.html (accessed May 12, 2010)
48   Charles K Rowley, *Adam Smith would not be optimistic in today's economic*

The situation since 2010 has only gotten worse. By 2019, rather than the predicted 76.5%, it was over 100%, while 2023 ended at 121.68%.[49] In the end, these dollars must come from somewhere. As pointed out in Chapter Two, the government can only get money in three places. The first is higher taxes. Yet, to cover such deficits, the increase would be staggering. It would undoubtedly stifle any economic growth, resulting in lower revenues than expected while further driving up the demand for government services.

Another would be to cut spending. However, the history of the last 100 years shows that such cuts would be tough. In addition, rather than cutting spending, spending is increasing even faster. While many in both parties were critical of the spending increase under Bush, "Obama is not the anti-Bush. He is Bush on steroids."[50] Neither Trump nor Biden were any better in terms of the deficit. Even if you remove all of the cost of TARP and the Stimulus, Obama still increased spending in virtually every area of government, plus trying to expand government into whole new areas—the same with Presidents Trump and Biden.

The only remaining place to get money is through inflation. Inflation results when the amount of money increases faster than goods and services. In short, if the federal government inflates the money supply either by borrowing or printing more quickly than the economy grows, the dollars will be worth less, and prices will increase.

The government can print the money it needs, paying off the debt in dollars that are not worth as much. Reduce the value of the dollar by half, and it is the same as paying off half the debt.

world, Telegraph.co.uk. Sept, 6, 2009, http://www.telegraph.co.uk/finance/comment/6146873/Adam-Smith-would-not-be-optimistic-in-todays-economic-world.html (accessed May 12, 2010)

49   Macrotrends, *Debt to GDP Ratio Historical Chart, https://www.macrotrends.net/1381/debt-to-gdp-ratio-historical-chart (Accessed March 7, 2024)*

50   Kevin Hassett, *Obama Spending Shocks in Scale, Builds Upon Bush, Bloomberg.com, March 2, 2009* http://www.bloomberg.com/apps/news?pid=20601039&sid=aYgo3fufKIbI (accessed May 12, 2010)

While this might work out for the government's debt, inflation is difficult to live through and wreaks havoc on the economy. It is the classic, short-term gain, long-term pain. Still, it seems that this is the course the government is taking. The period following the housing bubble collapse saw "the greatest printing of money in our nation's history. Never before has the federal money supply been increased so much so fast."[51] At least until COVID-19.

During the last months of the Bush administration and the beginning months of the Obama administration, the Fed increased the money supply ten times more than the next most significant increase over the last 50 years. The economist Arthur B. Laffer wrote that the recent increase "is so far outside the realm of our prior experiential base that historical comparisons are rendered difficult if not meaningless."[52] Before the housing bubble collapsed, the currency-in-circulation – paper bills and coins – comprised 95 percent of the money supply; by June 2009, it had fallen below 50 percent.

While difficult, perhaps the closest historical comparison would be the policies of the 1970s. But as Laffer points out,

> It's difficult to estimate the magnitude of the inflationary and interest-rate consequences of the Fed's actions because, frankly, we haven't ever seen anything like this in the U.S. To date what's happened is potentially far more inflationary than were the monetary policies of the 1970s, when the prime interest rate peaked at 21.5% and inflation peaked in the low double digits. Gold prices went from $35 per ounce to $850 per ounce, and the dollar collapsed on the foreign exchanges. It wasn't a pretty picture.[53]

---

51   Tom Cambell, *Obama presiding over huge inflation risk, The San Francisco Chronicle, April 27, 2009, A 11.* http://www.sfgate.com/cgi-bin/article.cgi?f=/c/a/2009/04/27/EDTC175INR.DTL   (accessed May 12, 2010)

52   Arthur Laffer, *Get Ready for Inflation and Higher Interest Rates, The Wall Street Journal, June 11, 2009, A15,* http://online.wsj.com/article/SB124458888993599879.html (accessed May 12, 2010)

53   Arthur Laffer, *Get Ready for Inflation and Higher Interest Rates, The Wall Street Journal, June 11, 2009, A15,* http://online.wsj.com/article/SB124458888993599879.html (accessed May 12, 2010)

As Laffer pointed out, these increases took the country into uncharted territory. We were driving towards a cliff in the dark. While we risked igniting inflation, no one could say when it would occur. The government got away with massive spending increases, at least in terms of inflation following the housing bubble. Ten years later, when COVID-19 hit, sparking another round of even larger spending increases, the government was not as lucky. Inflation became a significant problem.

Democratic Obstacles

So far, I have focused on the actions taken in response to the economic downturn following the housing bubble. However, President Obama's agenda was far broader than fixing the financial problems. Shortly after the election, Rahm Emanuel, Obama's close advisor and soon to become his Chief of Staff, said, "Never let a serious crisis go to waste. What I mean by that is it's an opportunity to do things you couldn't do before."[54]

Before long, it became clear to many that Obama was taking these words to heart and was using the financial crisis as an excuse to push through sweeping changes that would fundamentally alter the country. After all, that was his goal. Just before his election, he said, "We are five days away from fundamentally transforming the United States of America."[55]

When the Wall Street Journal reviewed the stimulus bill, which Obama said contained "dramatic investments to revive our flagging economy," they found that only 12 percent could "plau-

---

54   *A 40-Year Wish List, Wall Street Journal, Jan 28, 2009, pg A14*
http://online.wsj.com/article_email/SB1233104665514522309-lMyQjAxM-DI5MzIzNzEyMDc0Wj.html (accessed May 12, 2010)
55   Victor David Hanson, *Obama: Transforming America, Real Clear Politics, Oct 1, 2013.*
https://www.realclearpolitics.com/articles/2013/10/01/obama_transforming_america_120170.html (accessed September 18, 2023)

sibly be considered a growth stimulus."[56] They called it instead a 40-year wish list.

A detailed breakdown of the bill by the Washington Post supports this analysis. A third of the spending supposed to stimulate the economy would not even come for years.[57] One has to wonder how dollars spent in 2018 will help to stimulate the economy in 2009.

President Obama's attempts at change in healthcare and Global Warming were even broader. However, as 2009 faded into 2010, it became clear that Obama had lost the democratic fight over both policies.

The Obama administration sought to impose a Cap-and-Trade system to limit carbon emissions in climate change. Cap-and-trade is a plan essentially aimed at preventing Global Warming by taxing carbon to make it costly, assigning everyone a set of carbon credits to limit carbon use, and then letting those who use less carbon than allotted sell their credits to those who use more.

Supporters estimate the cost of Cap and Trade to be between $50 and $300 billion per year.[58] People would see this tax in higher prices, particularly in higher energy costs, as the whole purpose of the tax is to force people to use less energy and, thus, less carbon.

A 2010 study by the Belfer Center for Science and International Affairs at Harvard's Kennedy School concluded that reducing carbon emissions was "harder than it looks" and that gas prices might need to rise above $7.00 per gallon to achieve the proposed

56   *A 40-Year Wish List, Wall Street Journal, Jan 28, 2009, pg A14*
http://online.wsj.com/article_email/SB123310466514522309-lMyQjAxM-DI5MzIzNzEyMDc0Wj.html (accessed May 12, 2010)
57   Karen Yourish, Laura Stanton, *Taking Apart the $819 billion Stimulus Package, Washington Post, Feb 1, 2009*
http://www.washingtonpost.com/wp-dyn/content/graphic/2009/02/01/GR2009020100154.html
58   Center For American Progress, *Cap and Trade 101, Jan 16, 2008.* http://www.americanprogress.org/issues/2008/01/capandtrade101.html (accessed May 12, 2010)

carbon reductions.[59] With the economy already in economic trouble, even Obama's Democratic allies were in no mood to impose the massive new carbon taxes.

In addition to these higher costs, there would also be indirect costs. We are creating greenhouse gases because of industrialization, which is the very thing that has improved our quality of life. No one questions that Cap and Trade will cost jobs, particularly in those sectors of the economy that produce the most greenhouse gases.

The National Association of Manufacturers and the American Council for Capital Formation released a study that stated that the job losses from Cap-and-Trade would be between 1.8 million and 2.4 million jobs by 2030.[60] On the other hand, supporters question whether the number of jobs lost will be that large and counter that Cap-and-Trade will create more "green jobs" than those lost while preserving the planet.[61]

Douglas Elmendorf, director of the CBO, stated in testimony before Congress that while the impact on jobs would be significant in some areas, the job loss would be small overall. Yet, as one report on Elmendorf's testimony noted,

> "One of the great uncertainties of the cost of reducing carbon emissions is how readily the economy can move," [Elmen-

---

59   W. Ross Morrow, Henry Lee, Kelly Sims Gallagher, and Gustavo Collantes, *Reducing the U.S. Transportation Sector's Oil Consumption and Greenhouse Gas Emissions, Belfer Center for Science and International Affairs, Harvard Kennedy School, March 2010,*
http://belfercenter.ksg.harvard.edu/publication/19973/reducing_the_us_
transportation_sectors_oil_consumption_and_greenhouse_gas_emissions.
html (accessed May 12, 2010)

60   *United States Economic Impact of Waxman-Markey Bill, H.R. 2454 Proposed Legislation to Reduce Greenhouse Gas Emissions.* http://www.ifca.com/
show_file.php?DID=295 (accessed May 12, 2010)

61   *House Passes Historic Waxman-Markey Clean Energy Bill, House Committee On Energy and Commerce. Jun 28, 2009* http://energycommerce.house.gov/
index.php?option=com_content&view=article&id=1697:house-passes-his-
toric-waxman-markey-clean-energy-bill&catid=155:statements&Itemid=55
(accessed May 12, 2010)

dorf] said, noting that the CBO is to a large degree "guessing the rate." Elmendorf added, "I used the word guess deliberately."[62]

These claims are not equally balanced. The effects of increased prices and taxes are well-known and established. What is unknown is the speed of the switch and, more importantly, whether it can be done quickly and smoothly enough to offset the known problems. Cap-and-trade will cost jobs, but if you make the correct "guesses," these problems go away, at least if the guesses are correct.

A further problem was that Europe already imposed a similar system. Europe's experience was that the Belfer report was correct when it said it was more complicated than it looked. Rather than cut emissions as planned, emissions actually increased 1.9 percent. In short, European proponents tried to reduce the cost to reduce the negative impact of Cap and Trade and get it passed. These changes resulted in a system that did not work but cost €24.9 billion in 2006 alone.[63]

Based on Europe's example, it is very likely that any Cap-and-Trade system will have to cost a lot more and, thus, do far more damage than its supporters suggested to be effective. With the economy struggling and people losing their jobs, Congress had no desire to pass Cap-and-Trade.

In Nov 2009, 160 MB of emails and documents from East Anglia University's Climate Research Unit, a leading supporter of the theory of human-caused global warming, were posted to several skeptical websites in an incident quickly labeled Climategate.[64]

---

62   Kent Garber, *CBO Director: Cap and Trade Impact on Employment 'Small'*

63   Martin Livermore, *Cap and Trade Doesn't Work, Wall Street Journal Europe, June 25, 2009* http://online.wsj.com/article/SB124587942001349765. html (accessed May 12, 2010)

64   Leo Hickman and James Randerson, *Climate skeptics claim leaked emails are evidence of collusion among scientists, guardian.co.uk, Nov 20, 2009,* http://www.guardian.co.uk/environment/2009/nov/20/climate-sceptics-hackers-leaked-emails (accessed May 12, 2010)

The emails and documents called into question both the data and the methodology behind the claims of Global Warming. Soon, the questions spread beyond East Anglia, casting doubt on Global Warming research worldwide.[65] This scandal drove yet another nail into the coffin of Obama's effort to push Cap-and-Trade. Without man-made global warming, there is no reason for Cap-and-Trade and the damage it would cause.

Obama's signature issue was healthcare reform. Surprisingly, Obama, though he frequently talked about "his plan" and even criticized people for distorting "his plan," never actually submitted a bill. Instead, he left it up to Congress to write their own.

The debate over health care reform raged throughout Obama's first year. Supporters kept setting deadlines for passing a bill and missing them as opposition mounted. When members of Congress returned to work after their summer break, healthcare reform seemed dead. The people had spoken and spoken clearly in town halls held around the country. The vast majority said no.

Rather than leading the country to seek a consensus that a majority could agree on, Obama decided to try and push the bill through. Predictably, this caused public opposition to the bill to rise even more. In November, House Speaker Nancy Pelosi finally got the House to pass its version of health care reform by a narrow margin with only Democrat votes. Thus, the battle moved to the Senate.

The plan was to have the Senate pass a version and then have the actual work take place in the conference of the House and Senate. After considerable effort, and on Christmas Eve, in a rush to get out of town, Senate Democrats were able to cobble together a bill that all Democrat Senators could vote yes on.

While most were unhappy with the bill, they were not that concerned because they believed that this bill would never become

---

65   Marc Sheppard, *Climategate: CRU Was But the Tip of the Iceberg, American Thinker, Jan 22, 2010,*
http://www.americanthinker.com/2010/01/climategate_cru_was_but_the_ti.html (accessed May 12, 2010)

law. Instead, it was an opening bid in the upcoming conference with the House. The conference committee will write the final bill. Meanwhile, the public was growing increasingly incensed at being ignored.

Then the unthinkable happened. Opposition to the plan grew so strong that in late January, Republican Scott Brown leveraged opposition to the bill to win a special election for Ted Kennedy's former senate seat. With the resulting loss of their filibuster-proof majority in the Senate, Obama's plans of forcing the bill through seemed doomed.

Democratic Breakdown

Yet, Obama's pass-the-bill-at-all-cost attitude would not let him surrender to the people's will, even when expressed in an election. Thwarted on Cap-and-Trade, Healthcare Reform, and a range of other measures by the democratic process, Obama, like Tiberius Gracchus,[66] began to look for different ways to push his agenda, As the New York Times reported in early February,

> With much of his legislative agenda stalled in Congress, President Obama and his team are preparing an array of actions using his executive power to advance energy, environmental, fiscal and other domestic policy priorities.[67]

If the rules get in the way, change them. Thus, healthcare came back yet again. Over the following two months, Obama, Reid, and Pelosi worked on several ways to push a bill through and make it seem like they were still following the rules and, in some cases, even the Constitution.[68]

---

66 Roman Tribune who broke the rules to push through his agenda, see chapter 1.

67 Peter Baker, *Obama Making Plans to Use Executive Power, New York Times, Feb 13, 2010*, A13, http://www.nytimes.com/2010/02/13/us/politics/13obama.html?ref=us (accessed May 12, 2010)

68 Peter Ferrar, *Turning America Into a Banana Republic, The American Spectator, March 17, 2010*. http://spectator.org/archives/2010/03/17/turning-america-into-a-banana/print (accessed May 12, 2010)

Yet, in the end, the process was summed up best by Democrat Alcee Hasting when he said, "When the deal goes down, all this talk about rules, we make them up as we go along."[69] Healthcare reform was passed not as an exercise of the democratic process but as an example of raw political power imposed against the clearly expressed will of the people. Worse, the methods used became precedents for future Congresses and Presidents.

The ink had hardly dried before the grandiose claims made by the bill supporters began to ring hollow. In a speech a few days before pushing through the bill, President Obama claimed that employers "would see premiums fall by as much as 3000%, which means they could give you a raise."[70] The White House press spokesman later corrected the 3000 percent to $3000.

Either way, the reality was vastly different once the bill became law and people could read it. Rather than saving money, as they began to dig into the provisions, businesses found that their actual costs would be higher.

Under the financial laws, publicly traded companies must report such losses to investors. As a result of the bill, Caterpillar announced a $100 million charge. Deere, who makes farm equipment, $150 million, and AT&T reported a $1 billion charge.[71] Rather than having savings for employee raises, these companies looked to cut spending to make up for higher healthcare costs.

At the other end of the business spectrum, owners of tanning salons had a new 10 percent tax. These usually are small operations

69   Thomas Lifson, *Rules: 'We make 'em up as we go along' American Thinker,* *March 21, 2010,* http://www.americanthinker.com/blog/2010/03/rules_we_ make_em_up_as_we_go_a.html   (accessed May 12, 2010)

70   *Remarks by the President on Health Care in Strongville, Ohio, March 15,* *2010, Office of the Press Secretary, The White House,* http://www.whitehouse. gov/the-press-office/remarks-president-health-care-reform-strongsville-ohio (accessed May 12, 2010)

71   Sinead Carew, Lisa Richwine, and Karen Wutkowski, *AT&T sees $1* *billion healthcare related charge, Reuters, March 26, 2009*

already struggling in a tight economy, so the new tax threatened many with closing, putting thousands of jobs at risk.[72]

Having forced through healthcare reform, Obama turned to the rest of his agenda. Given all the problems with Cap-and-Trade, even the new Congressional rules did not help much. So Obama sought to go around Congress and simply impose much of his agenda through Environmental Protection Agency regulations and Executive Orders.[73]

The massive expansion of Government was everywhere. Buried in the health care reform bill was a complete government takeover of the student loan program.[74] Under Obama, the government took control of GM and Chrysler. While Obama said he was not interested in the day-to-day operations, the administration did remove the CEO[75] and set salaries.[76] Virtually everywhere you look, the government was seeking more and more control over almost every aspect of people's lives.

Along these lines, Obama appointed over 32 "czars" to oversee areas like Afghanistan, Aids, Cars, Green jobs, and executive pay.[77] While presidents since Franklin Roosevelt have used Czars,

---

72   Blake Ellis, *Tanning salons burned by health care bill,* *CNNMoney.com,* *March 24, 2010.* http://money.cnn.com/2010/03/24/news/economy/tanning_tax/ (accessed May 12, 2010)

73   Peter Baker, *Obama Making Plans to Use Executive Power,* New York *Times, Feb 13, 2010, A13,* http://www.nytimes.com/2010/02/13/us/politics/13obama.html?ref=us (accessed May 12, 2010)

74   AnnaMaria Andriotis, *Health-Care Reform and Your Student Loans,* *SmartMoney, March 24, 2010,* http://www.smartmoney.com/personal-finance/college-planning/the-health-care-bill-and-your-student-loans/ (accessed May 12, 2010)

75   AP, *Obama fires GM's CEO, Chicago Sun-Times, March 29, 2009* http://www.suntimes.com/business/1501561,w-obama-gm-wagoner032909.article (accessed May 12, 2010)

76   Stephen Gandel, *Wall Street, Meet Ken Feinberg, the Pay Czar, Time, Nov 2, 2009,* http://www.time.com/time/business/article/0,8599,1933078,00.html (accessed May 12, 2010)

77   Glenn Beck, *List of Obama's Czars, Aug 21, 2009 http://www.glennbeck.com/content/articles/article/198/29391/* (accessed May 12, 2010)

the concern was with the number of czars, the wide range of areas they oversee, and the scope of their power. This concern led Senator Liebermann to hold hearings,[78] for czars are essentially people appointed by the President without oversight from Congress to be in charge of various aspects of the country and our lives.

All this costs money, and the federal budget reflects the scale of the changes. Throughout the Bush years, Democrats constantly complained about the deficits. The last budget deficit before Democrats won back control of Congress in 2006, and thus control over the budget, was $160 billion.

As discussed earlier, with all the turmoil resulting from the Housing Bubble, the budget jumped to a previously unimaginable $1.41 trillion. Without the stimulus and TARP, the 2010 budget should reflect a return to normal. Yet rather than going down, Obama's 2010 budget increased the deficit even more, to $1.3 trillion, nearly ten times more than the 2007 deficit.

John Dingell, the longest-serving member in the history of the House of Representatives, was asked why, given all the statements about the need to pass the bill so quickly, most of it did not take effect until 2014. He answered,

> ...it takes a long time to do the necessary administrative steps that have to be taken to put the legislation together to control the people.[79]

Whether or not that was what he intended to say, that is what the health care bill ultimately does, for that is what all government legislation does; it controls what people can do; it limits people's

---

78   Eric Zimmermann, *Lieberman to hold czars hearing*, *The Hill*, Oct 19, *2009*, http://thehill.com/blogs/blog-briefing-room/news/63657-lieberman-to-hold-czars-hearing (accessed May 12, 2010)

79   Andrea Simoncic, *Audio clip of Rep Dingell indicates Health care legislation aims to "control the people"*, *St Louis Conservative Examiner*, *March 25, 2010*. http://www.examiner.com/x-27580-St-Louis-Conservative-Examiner-y2010m3d25-Audio-clip-of-Rep-Dingell-indicates-health-care-legislation-aims-to-control-the-people (accessed May 12, 2010)

freedom. It is why the founding fathers wanted limited government in the first place.

Worst of all, to achieve this dream, Obama and the Democrats were willing to disregard the people's will, the rules, and sometimes even the Constitution to get what they wanted, thereby setting precedents that future presidents and Congress in both parties would use. Still, not all of his efforts were successful.

Any government action has the potential for disagreement and, thus, opposition. Most of these disputes are political questions about the best course of action. Some fall into questions of legality. Does an action conflict with existing law or the Constitution? When this happens, the issue ends up in the courts. This conflict is a normal part of the process and is unavoidable. Life is complex, and it is not always clear if a particular action is permissible.

Given the complexity, the actions of some presidents are bound to be rejected by the courts later. Such rejection is probably a desirable outcome. In theory, a president whose acts the courts always upheld would be good. Yet, it would also suggest that the president was too cautious and not taking needed and permissible actions that were legal out of fear a court might rule against them.

One measure of how cautious a president is, is their record before the courts. The higher the win rate, the more cautious the President. We have already seen this with FDR's early record before the courts. When he became President, because of the Depression, FDR tried many things to turn the economy around. Many of these were later ruled unconstitutional.

Returning to Obama, like FDR, opponents challenged many of his actions, resulting in a poor record before the Supreme Court, which occurred before the changes in justices under Trump. While Obama did have some big wins, such as upholding his Healthcare bill, as one analyst put it, "the Obama administration, by historical standards, has done exceedingly poorly before the Supreme Court."[80]

By the last year of this presidency, Obama had only won 45 percent of his cases before the courts. Put into perspective, George W. Bush won 60 percent, Clinton 63 percent, George H. W. Bush 70 percent, and Reagan 75%. In his last term alone, Obama lost ten cases before the court without a single justice, even the ones he put on the court, voting in his favor. [81]

Rising Populism

As with Patrick Henry and his attempt to stop Madison and the Constitution, things are not static. Henry's attempt resulted in a backlash that allowed Madison to win his election to the House of Representatives and increased the federalists in the Virginia Assembly. When the Bill of Rights came before them for ratification, Henry no longer had the power to stop it. Early on, Henry had gotten everything he wanted, but in the backlash, he lost what he really sought. With the ratification of the Bill of Rights, the chances for a second constitutional convention quickly faded.

The problems in the final years of the Bush administration, combined with Obama's attempt to change America, also brought about a reaction. Many people were troubled by what they saw happening. They may not have understood the details of the problems, but they realized something was seriously wrong. They did not believe that politicians in either party were listening to them. Their frustration grew, initially over the spending resulting from TARP, passed under Bush, and then the stimulus, passed under Obama.

80   Ilya Shapiro, Obama Has Lost in the Supreme Court More Than Any Modern President, The Federalist, July 6' 2016, https://www.cato.org/commentary/obama-has-lost-supreme-court-more-any-modern-president (accessed December 8, 2023)

81   Ilya Shapiro, Obama Has Lost in the Supreme Court More Than Any Modern President, The Federalist, July 6, 2016, https://www.cato.org/commentary/obama-has-lost-supreme-court-more-any-modern-president (accessed December 8, 2023)

On February 19ᵗʰ, 2009, Rick Santelli, a financial reporter for CNBC, was doing a spot from the floor of the Chicago Futures Exchange. He was complaining about all the government spending. He ended by saying, "I'll tell you what, if you read our founding fathers, people like Benjamin Franklin and Jefferson,... What we're doing in this country now is making them roll over in their graves."[82]

Afterward, he didn't see it as all that different from many other spots he had done in his career. For him, it "probably wasn't even in my top 5."[83] Yet, that is not how people across America saw it. Later that day, it appeared on YouTube with the heading "Rant of the Year."[84]

In the middle of the spot, amongst the traders cheering on the floor, Santelli said, "We're thinking of having a Chicago Tea Party in July. All you capitalists that want to show up to Lake Michigan, I'm gonna start organizing."[85] The Tea Party movement was born.

While often portrayed by critics as artificial and "Astroturf"[86] or vilely disparaged with sexual references, tea parties were a loose connection of people coming together to express a general frustration with the government. Most of this frustration centers around TARP, the stimulus bill, and the calls for even more spending and a further expansion of Government. While a few tried to catch up

---

82   This can be found in many places, YouTube, Rick Santelli and the "Rant of the Year" http://www.youtube.com/watch?v=bEZB4taSEoA a transcript is at, Freedom Eden, http://freedomeden.blogspot.com/2009/02/rick-santelli-tea-party.html (accessed May 12, 2010)

83   Rick Santelli, *I Want to Set the Record Straight, CNBC.com March 2, 2009,* http://www.cnbc.com/id/29471026 (accessed May 12, 2010

84   YouTube, *Rick Santelli and the "Rant of the Year"* http://www.youtube.com/watch?v=bEZB4taSEoA (accessed May 12, 2010)

85   This can be found in many places, YouTube, *Rick Santelli and the "Rant of the Year"* http://www.youtube.com/watch?v=bEZB4taSEoA a transcript is at, Freedom Eden, http://freedomeden.blogspot.com/2009/02/rick-santelli-tea-party.html (accessed May 12, 2010)

86   For example, Frank Rich, *Tea Parties Forever, New York Times, April 13, 2009, A21,* http://www.nytimes.com/2009/04/13/opinion/13krugman.html (accessed May 12, 2010)

to claim leadership of the movement, there was no leader, and it was indeed grassroots.

Meg Ellefson, organizer of the Tea Party in Wausau, Wisconsin, tells a typical story. She had not been active in politics, and at least until then, she did not follow the news very closely. Even when she began to get concerned and followed the news, she remained relatively distant from politics. Then, the economy slipped into recession, followed by TARP, the stimulus, and a range of new government programs.

When Ellefson saw the Santelli spot on YouTube, like so many others, it struck a chord. As Ellefson described it,

> he was so passionate... he just inspired something in me when he called for a tea party on the shores of Lake Michigan and all these traders in the background were just cheering him on. I saw that a number of times and I kept thinking to myself, that's a really good idea.[87]

Looking around, she found that many people were anxious to be heard. Many were not even waiting for July, the time Santelli suggested. Given the focus on government spending, April 15th, Tax Day, seemed not only a logical date but a closer one. While a big protest was planned in Madison, the state capital, and a few other Wisconsin cities on that date, those were still too far away, given her schedule.

Although new to her community and having never done anything like this, Ellefson, the mother of two boys who describes herself as "just a regular mom," decided she had to do something.

> I could no longer sit and just let things happen without my involvement... What is going on in our country is going to affect my children and their future. [88]

So, she started calling some friends, and as word of mouth spread, the Wausau Tea Party began to take shape. A local bar owner donated the stage and sound system and offered to provide a band. Another person offered to print the flyers. As the needs

---

87   Interview with Meg Ellefson, conducted 11/17/2009
88   Interview with Meg Ellefson, conducted 11/17/2009

arose, people "came out of the woodwork" to fill those needs. As she put it,

> The success of the Wausau Tea Party is really due in great part to the amazing volunteers. The only way you could make this work is to have people who are genuinely concerned about the cause and have their hearts in it. [89]

Rather than an artificial movement directed from above, the tea parties were about as genuine a grassroots movement as possible, probably explaining some of the harsh reactions of those in the usual circles of power. Ellefson said,

> There were millions of people who assembled at various tea parties all over the country. They just decided that 'I'm tired of the people in elected office. They don't represent me. We send them letters, we make phone calls and they aren't abiding by the will of the people.'[90]

Notice that Ellefson said she was tired "of the *people* in elected office." Many at the Tea Parties were angry at both parties. This anger is what made them so dangerous to those in the regular circles of power. While the Democrats then held the Presidency and solid majorities in both chambers of Congress and, thus, saw the brunt of the criticism, the Tea Parties were not automatically in the Republican camp. One did not have to look hard among Tea Party members to find criticism of Bush and the Republicans.

The tea parties sprang up, not out of partisan concerns but from frustration with how things were going. They were outside the control of the ruling elite. Ellefson's response to the question of what sparked the Tea Party is an excellent summary of the movement,

> If you could boil it down, I would have to say, freedom. So many of the issues have to do with freedom, our economy, our country's great capitalistic history, our national security is tied to freedom. Even social issues are tied to freedom. The government's grand plan is to control us as much as they can. That is not the America of our forefathers. That is not the

89 Interview with Meg Ellefson, conducted 11/17/2009
90 Interview with Meg Ellefson, conducted 11/17/2009

> America that I grew up in, and that is not the America I want
> my children to grow up in... It is about our freedom and our
> liberty, our ability to make decisions about our lives... Our
> liberties are being taken from us. [91]

What would Ellefson like to see come from the movement?

> I just want people to get involved and quit yelling at the TV
> and complaining amongst themselves, or believing that com-
> placency is an option, because it's not anymore...[92]

Whether the members of the Tea Party were right or wrong,
they were citizens who were upset by what they saw happening and
felt both parties were ignoring them. Nor was this general feeling
limited to the Tea Party. While they may disagree with the Tea Party's financial concerns, many others had similar views in other areas.

Making things worse is the growing polarization among the
public. When Obama became the first Black President, even many
on the losing side celebrated, believing his election marked the
beginning of a new era. Unfortunately, they were wrong. By the
end of his presidency, race relations had gotten worse.[93]

Even this was a source of controversy. Some believed this division was real; America was more racist. Others claimed it was
artificial, created or at least exaggerated for political advantage, or
used by the media to get ratings. Others claim America has always
been racist; we are just paying more attention. As with most areas of life, reality is complex, and there is truth in many of these
claims.

There certainly are racists in America. Whether the number is
increasing is unclear, but they are more visible for various reasons.
The internet allows them to connect, organize, and get noticed.
Given the current state of the media, racial stories get ratings and,
thus, a lot of coverage. We can see this when some stories initially

---

91   Interview with Meg Ellefson, conducted 11/17/2009

92   Interview with Meg Ellefson, conducted 11/17/2009

93   Jennifer Agiesta, *Most say race relations worsened under Obama, poll finds,*
CNN, https://www.cnn.com/2016/10/05/politics/obama-race-relations-poll/
index.html (accessed Sept 16, 2023)

get a lot of airtime until the racial element disappears, at which point they disappear.

Some see the charge of racism as an easy way to disparage an opponent. We can see this with the Tea Party, whose concerns were primarily financial but were frequently labeled racist. Such tactics are not only wrong; they are short-sighted. You might realize a short-term political victory but at a higher long-term cost.

The Tea Party did not completely disappear. They did what all successful movements do: they integrated into one of the two parties. Initially, the Tea Party was dissatisfied with both. Democrats got the focus, but only because they were in power then. Still, many Democrats attacked the Tea Party as racist. It may have worked to discredit them in the short run, but in the long run, it drove them to the Republicans.

They were not exactly welcome with open arms by more establishment Republicans. However, they impacted and changed the Republican party, creating tension within the party, still seen among the presidential candidates in 2024. They were one of the factors that led to Trump's nomination in 2016. Again, some opponents labeled Trump and his supporters racist, but this time, they did not even get the short-term victory, as Trump won.

False charges of racism distort and corrupt the political discourse in myriad ways. Not least, as a result, many ignored what drove people to vote for Trump. Following Trump's election, Zalena Zito and Brad Todd went to areas that had traditionally been Democratic strongholds yet voted for Trump in 2016—places like Ashtabula County, Ohio.

> Ashtabula County had given its votes to John Kerry, Al Gore, Bill Clinton, and Michael Dukakis. It gave Barack Obama a 55 percent majority share of its vote twice – before turning 180 degrees to prefer Trump over Hillary Clinton by a margin of 57 percent to 38 percent, a 31-point swing from one election to the next. [94]

---

94   Salena Zito, Brad Tood, *The Great Revolt*, Crown Publishing Group, 2018, p 3

Zito and Todd had a simple question: Why? Then they listened. Like all successful candidates, they found that Trump built a coalition of voters. Zito and Todd found what many had missed. As they wrote, for the analysts to see it, they "would have to visit places they had stopped visiting and listen to people they had stopped listening to."[95] Whatever you think of his politics, Trump listened to these people who believed no one in either party cared about them. He spoke for them, and they supported him.

Nor was it a single reason or issue. After listening to hundreds of voters, they identified seven archetypes. They described them in their book by profiling individual voters who represent each archetype.

> The specific voters who exemplified these seven archetypes of the Trump coalition and are profiled here were discovered in ten pivotal counties in the five Great Lakes states that tipped the electoral college to Donald Trump: Pennsylvania, Ohio, Michigan, Wisconsin, and Iowa. All ten of these counties had been in President Barack Obama's column in 2012, and most of them gave Trump a larger margin than any other Republican in this era.[96]

Thus, while labeling Trump supporters as racist or disparaging them in other ways may have the short-term benefit of winning the next election, long-term it is very harmful to the country. While Trump's coalition included some who feel left behind and that the system no longer listens to them, it hardly represented all those disaffected by politics. While not successful, you can see a similar reaction to the candidacy of Bernie Sanders in 2020.

Attacking people is unlikely to win their support and will likely generate a similar response. The most significant problem facing the country today is the increasing polarization. There are only two ways to settle disputes: Discussion and compromise or

---

95   Salena Zito, Brad Tood, *The Great Revolt,* Crown Publishing Group, 2018, p 5
96   Salena Zito, Brad Tood, *The Great Revolt,* Crown Publishing Group, 2018, p 17-18

power and force. We will either talk and listen to each other, trying to find a compromise, or we will try to defeat our opponents.

Going Forward

In the conflict with England, rather than listening to the colonists and seeking a compromise to each side's legitimate concerns, the King and Parliament doubled down on their demands and resorted to force. At first, the founding fathers sought compromise, but when the king rejected it, they declared Independence.

Hard-fought debates and numerous compromises marked the Constitutional Convention. It almost failed several times. Nobody got everything they wanted; everyone gave up something. Yet the delegates, or at least most of them, kept talking. The result was the Constitution. Even then, discussion and compromises continued, resulting in the Bill of Rights.

In 2017, Hillary Clinton was interviewed on the Hugh Hewitt radio show. Hewitt asked her about racism in America.

> Hewitt: I don't think there are 100,000 in any given state. I don't think there are a half million in the United States. Do you disagree with me? Do you think there are more than a half million, you know, honest-to-God white nationalists running around the United States?
> Clinton: Probably not, no. But I think there are people who are unfortunately kind of reverting back to rather virulent attitudes about race in part because I think that it's become "politically acceptable," no longer politically correct to try to overcome our own feelings that often block us from seeing each other as fellow human beings. So no, the hardcore people, I agree with you, I don't think that is a very large number. Unfortunately, their views, which used to be quite beyond the mainstream, you know, have a much broader audience now, because you know, of being online and having outlets and media presence that can promote those attitudes.[97]

---

97 Duane Patterson, *Hillary Rodham Clinton on "What Happened"*, November 22, 2017, *HughHewitt*, https://hughhewitt.com/hillary-rodham-clinton-happened

What makes this exchange significant is that while Clinton is a Democrat, Hewitt is very much a Republican and one who voted for Trump. Politically, they are opponents, yet they could have a long and substantive discussion. Near the end of the interview, Hewitt said,

> Hewitt: My very last question, Madame Secretary, thanks for the time. Again, I urge everyone to read *What Happened*...
> Clinton: Well you know, Hugh, I'm really enjoying this. I can go for a few more minutes, if you want to. [98]

So, the interview lasted a few more minutes. While few, if any, changed their mind, this interview informed people far more than the gotcha questions and mudslinging that makes up so much of what passes for journalism today. A journalist who is pursuing an agenda is not pursuing a story. Most journalism today is agenda journalism.

Ultimately, it comes down to the question: do you believe in the democratic form of government and thus trust the people working through the Constitutional system to make choices? This question is difficult; everyone likes democracy when they win, but what about when you lose? Which is more important, our democratic system or winning?

Ellefson was right. America is at a turning point. For too many on both sides, winning is all that matters. Discussion is increasingly difficult, making matters worse. Too many demonize anyone who disagrees, so people are afraid even to discuss issues. Yet, without dialogue and listening, you cannot have a democratic system. The real threats to our system of government are those who suppress discussions, particularly by demonizing those who disagree.

The decisions made over the next few years will set the country's course for the rest of the century. They could even determine its continued existence as the world's leading Superpower and pos-

---

98   Duane Patterson, *Hillary Rodham Clinton on "What Happened"*, *November 22,2017*, *HughHewitt,* https://hughhewitt.com/hillary-rodham-clinton-happened

sibly as a single nation. All countries before us eventually failed. How long will America last, and what will we be? Will America continue as it has since its founding, a country where the freedom and responsibility of the individual to control their own life is the dominant factor, where the individual is more important than the government? Or will it be transformed into a country where the government and what it will or will not do for you is the dominant factor, where the government is more important than the individual? Will it be a country where citizens must always look to the government, which controls virtually every aspect of their lives? These are just some of the questions before us.

At the end of the Constitutional Convention, a woman reportedly asked Benjamin Franklin what kind of government the convention had proposed. He answered, "A Republic, if you can keep it."[99] The question is still before us today. Can we keep it? Do we want to?

---

99   Cited in The American Historical Review, vol. 11, 1906, p. 618, http://www.bartleby.com/73/1593.html (accessed May 12, 2010)

QUESTIONS FOR AN INFORMED VOTER

The following is a series of questions we can ask about government programs, laws, court rulings, politicians, news sources, etc. Not all questions will make sense in all situations, nor will all questions result in a clear yes or no answer. Often, there will be trade-offs. However, an informed decision requires a clear understanding of the trade-off involved. Hopefully, these will provide a good starting framework for evaluating changes in light of the issues raised in this book.

Government and Laws

1. Will it result in a bigger or smaller government?

2. What will it cost, now and in the future?

3. Is it based on centralized planning and control or individual choice and competition?

4. Will it solve the problem?

5. How many other programs do the same thing? Why aren't they enough?

6. Will it build dependency on the government or promote freedom and independence?

7. Does this need to be done by the government?

8. Can it be done at a lower level of government?

9. Is the law clearly stated so judges can rule and the bureaucracies enforce it?

10. Does the law encourage 'citizen' (vigilante) lawsuits?

Courts

11. Is a court ruling based on the law and Constitution or something else, penumbras, evolving standards, foreign law, etc.?

12. Is a court ruling in line with what the law says as historically understood, or is it introducing or discovering something new?

13. Is there a clear link between a judgment and culpability in civil suits?

Voting

14. Do voting laws make fraud easier or harder?

15. In redistricting, do the lines favor representation and choice for the voters or safety for the politicians?

16. Do campaign laws make it easier for ordinary people, or do they further insulate and protect the politicians?

Information and Elections

17. Is a politician speaking clearly and precisely about what they plan to do? Is there anything behind the slogans?

18. What do the words and phrases they use mean?

19. Is the politician using special terminology or unique meanings to reach their desired conclusion?

20. Does what politicians say make sense, or does it just sound good?

21. For any given government action, what are the pros? What are the cons? What are the ramifications?

22. Are the sources of information objective? Do they present both sides equally and fairly?

23. Do the sources of information cover the issues or just the horse-race?

American Values

24. What are American values?

25. Is a new law consistent with the core American values?

www.ingramcontent.com/pod-product-compliance
Lightning Source LLC
Chambersburg PA
CBHW020237290326
41929CB00044B/84